Conjuring the Buddha

Columbia University Press
Publishers Since 1893
New York   Chichester, West Sussex
cup.columbia.edu

Library of Congress Cataloging-in-Publication Data
Names: Dalton, Jacob Paul, author.
Title: Conjuring the Buddha : ritual manuals in early Tantric Buddhism / Jacob P. Dalton.
Description: New York : Columbia University Press, 2023. | Includes bibliographical references and index.
Identifiers: LCCN 2022019223 (print) | LCCN 2022019224 (ebook) | ISBN 9780231205825 (hardback) | ISBN 9780231205832 (trade paperback) | ISBN 9780231556187 (ebook)
Subjects: LCSH: Tantric Buddhism—Rituals—History. | Tantric Buddhism—History. | Tantric Buddhism—Handbooks, manuals, etc.
Classification: LCC BQ8920.4 .D35 2023 (print) | LCC BQ8920.4 (ebook) | DDC 294.3/925—dc23/eng/20220622
LC record available at https://lccn.loc.gov/2022019223
LC ebook record available at https://lccn.loc.gov/2022019224

CONJURING THE BUDDHA

Ritual Manuals in Early Tantric Buddhism

JACOB P. DALTON

COLUMBIA UNIVERSITY PRESS *NEW YORK*

Preface

The present study first took root in the three years from 2002 to 2005, when I was fortunate enough to be hired under an Arts and Humanities Research Council (AHRC) grant to catalogue the tantric Tibetan manuscripts from Dunhuang that are preserved in the Stein collection at the British Library. Fresh out of my doctoral program, with no knowledge of Dunhuang or even much of tantric ritual, I soon recognized the significance of the manuscripts to which I suddenly had free access. Young and excitable, I fired off three articles littered with mistakes. Only over the next couple of years did I begin to understand just how woefully underprepared I was to do these ancient treasures proper justice. I stopped publishing on them and began the long process of educating myself in tantric studies. This book is the result: my attempt to understand the tantric manuscripts from Dunhuang within the larger context of early tantric ritual development in India.

Over the past fifteen years, my re-education benefited tremendously from my contacts with numerous excellent scholars. At Yale University, I learned more than I can express from both Phyllis Granoff and Koichi Shinohara, with whom I cotaught seminars and enthusiastically exchanged ideas. Around this time, I also began an ongoing and ever-enlightening series of conversations with Ronald Davidson, who taught just down the road at Fairfield University. Even since leaving Yale, he and Marko Geslani have continued to teach me about Indian ritual. At Hamburg University, meeting Harunaga Isaacson and attending his seminar was a bolt of lightning, as I discovered that most of what I hoped someday to learn was already known by this remarkable reader of Sanskrit texts. At UC Berkeley, my colleagues Robert Sharf and Alex von Rospatt have been the most generous and exacting conversation colleagues anyone could hope for. Berkeley's Center for Buddhist Studies has also hosted countless visiting scholars from whom I have learned a great deal. But perhaps most of all, I must recognize the brilliant PhD students I have had the privilege to teach and learn from. In my seminars at Berkeley, we have read many of the manuals translated herein, and my understanding of them has been transformed by the innumerable insights offered by my students. The excellent PhD thesis of Catherine Dalton (no relation) was particularly important. Beyond Buddhist studies, at Berkeley I have also learned about literary theory, the art of close reading, and much more from my dear friends, Alan Tansman and Paula Varsano, in the Department of East Asian Languages and Cultures. I also thank all the colleagues from whom I have learned about tantric ritual: David Germano, Kurt Keutzer, David Gray, Shaman Hatley, Péter Szántó, Kukuya Ryūta, and Yael Bentor; on the Dunhuang side of my work, Sam van Schaik, Amanda Goodman, Brandon Dotson, and Nathan Hill have been particularly invigorating conversation partners. All these excellent scholars and many others besides have made the past fifteen years a true pleasure.

Despite all I have learned in these years, I have surely made mistakes now buried in these pages. These are my fault alone. Tantric studies is still in its infancy, and perhaps I should have waited still more years before publishing this rather ambitious study. The inevitable gaps in my research reflect the limits of not just the idiosyncratic Dunhuang archive but also my own experiences, personal interests, and intellectual shortcomings. In the end, this book is just a snapshot of an ongoing process of learning that I hope will continue for many years.

This project has also benefited from an NEH Fellowship, a Guggenheim Fellowship, and from UC Berkeley, a Mellon Project Grant and a Townsend Center Associate Professor Fellowship. I thank all these organizations for their generous support.

Conjuring the Buddha

Introduction

THE RISE OF the tantras changed the face of religious practice across Asia, bringing elaborate new rites that revolved around and flowed forth from the tantric ritualist, a highly creative subject brimming with imaginary worlds. Scholars now largely agree that the first tantras (or *āgamas*, their equivalent on the Śaiva side) were composed in India in the seventh century. From there they spread, reshaping religious traditions from Sri Lanka to Japan, Mongolia to Indonesia. The tantras introduced ritual technologies foremost, though the extent of their influence is hard to delimit. They offered new myths, cosmologies, deities, and rhetorical strategies of rulership, secrecy, and transgression, but all these elements were grounded in the complex rituals that formed the core of tantric religiosity. The Buddhist tantras were thus cast as the ritual counterparts to the generally earlier canonical sutras, the scriptures said to record Śākyamuni Buddha's own, more doctrinal teachings.[1] Like the sutras, the tantras claimed the high status of being "the word of the Buddha" (*buddhavacana*), yet they did not travel alone; they were accompanied by a coterie of related texts. Occasionally the most influential tantras might warrant scholarly commentaries (many did not), but nearly all tantras traveled through Asia within an ever-shifting circle of ritual manuals—*sādhanas* for accomplishing ritual transformations, but also assorted liturgical works, *kalpas* for constructing the ritual spaces, *vidhis* for granting initiations or making offerings, and so on. This genre of locally produced manuals served as the primary point of contact between the tantric subject and their ritual tradition. And it was this same genre, as the present study argues, that facilitated a shift in early tantric practice from externally focused image worship to the bodily interior, unprecedented involvements in ritual subjectivity, and the intimate imaginings that came to characterize tantric Buddhism.

To this day, ritual manuals are one of the most read forms of Buddhist literature. In Tibet, every monk, nun, or layperson with a regular meditation practice has their own *sādhana* (literally "means of accomplishment") on how to perform their daily rites, carefully wrapped in cloth and tucked into their robes or placed on the altar at home. Often personalized with handwritten notes, interlinear additions, and favorite prayers, these well-worn texts are reflections of their owners' idiosyncratic lives, their travels, teachers, and individual tastes. They are, in this sense, ephemeral evidence of the changing nature of religious practice: the literature of lived Buddhism. And upon their owners' deaths, they likewise expire, disposed of and quickly forgotten. The manuals of a few great teachers may be bequeathed to their closest disciples, but the vast majority of Buddhist ritual manuals simply disappear. This is quite unlike the tantras, the sutras, and the other great books kept in the Tibetan canon—the words of the Buddha and other eminent Indian authorities that are carved into woodblocks, reprinted, and distributed throughout Inner Asia. The histories and the fates of these two classes of religious literature—common ritual manuals and the (relatively) timeless canons—differ dramatically. Whereas the tantras have been preserved in carefully edited collections, their countless ritual manuals have been largely lost to the sands of time.[2]

Despite their evanescent nature, ritual manuals constitute a remarkably innovative form of tantric literature. Indeed, this study argues, their extraordinary mutability and extracanonical status are precisely what make them so creative. Ritual manuals were, and to a lesser degree remain,[3] a particularly creative source of innovation thanks to their extraordinary flexibility. They can be composed or altered by anyone claiming the necessary qualifications. They can declare allegiance to any given canonical tantra and easily be updated to include the very latest ritual techniques. The Buddhist tradition and modern scholars alike commonly assume that tantras come first and the associated ritual manuals follow, as extractions from or ritual distillations of the material in the canonical tantras. Accordingly, the tantras are regularly presented as the original teachings, accounts of the mythic first performances of primordial rites upon which all later manuals should be based. Historically, however, precisely the opposite seems sometimes to have been the case, at least during the crucial first few centuries of tantric ritual development, from the seventh to the eleventh centuries, after which Indian Buddhists largely stopped writing new tantras.) Ritual manuals provided the principal literary space for early tantric creativity, and the tantras were written and rewritten to encapsulate and canonize these innovations. In this way, the ritual manuals that burgeoned across India (and all of Asia) from the sixth century on were crucial to the development of tantric Buddhism, and they remain our best hope for tracing that evolution. They reveal, in this sense, the invisible hands behind the tantras.

Fortunately, a number of early tantric ritual manuals have been preserved among the ancient manuscripts discovered near Dunhuang, on the old Silk Road. This study takes a comprehensive look at these tantric manuscripts, most of which are preserved in Tibetan and date from the ninth and tenth centuries, to see what these unique documents can tell us about the changing nature of early tantric practice in India. In terms of content, it is highly significant that only three tantras are to be found in the Dunhuang collection; the rest of the tantric manuscripts consist almost entirely of ritual manuals.[4] The tantras may be what Buddhists have preserved in their modern canons, but historically they are not what most actually read. The collection is thus extraordinary not only for its age but also for the kinds of texts it contains: the ephemeral writings of living Buddhists, extracanonical works normally deemed not worth saving. Through these ancient manuscripts, we may draw closer to lived religion to discern not just what but often how early Buddhists actually read. We may glimpse ritual practice *between* the canonical tantras, tantric Buddhism in the process of evolving.

While ritual manuals reflect local interests and the idiosyncrasies of their owners' lives, they do so along somewhat predictable lines. Ritual manuals allowed complex rituals already shaped by unknown authors to move across Asia in highly adaptable forms, bringing new methods for addressing local (and even individual) concerns. They represented in this regard a technology that allowed but also limited creativity. They not only facilitated the localization of Buddhist ritual but also, perhaps more significantly, introduced and determined new languages in which to express the local. As paradoxical as it may sound, the rise of ritual manuals enabled the spread of the local, not just in the sense of specific local practices becoming translocal but in the sense of the very possibility for local concerns to be articulated along specific Buddhist lines itself becoming translocal. A given ritual innovation may be specific to a locale and reflect local concerns, but the same *kinds* of innovations, obeying similar guidelines and making similar moves, may be seen elsewhere. The ritual manuals from Dunhuang therefore reflect local interests, but according to patterns seen across Asia.

This study reads the Tibetan ritual manuals from Dunhuang for insights into the development of early tantric Buddhist ritual in India. This is a delicate task, as the Indic and local concerns expressed in these texts are so intricately interwoven, but well worth attempting, given how rare such a cache of early tantric manuals is. It requires disaggregating what is specific to Dunhuang from what is unique to early Tibet, and all that from what is Indian. Elsewhere I have considered what the tantric manuscripts from Dunhuang (particularly those myths and rituals relating to demon taming) reveal about Tibetan history.[5] Here I investigate what these manuscripts reveal about India. Inevitably, this requires identifying and comprehending non-Indic elements, if only to exclude them more accurately, but my focus remains Indian tantric Buddhism.

This aim determined which manuscripts were selected. After chapter 1, each chapter focuses on one particular manual. Chapters 3 and 4 examine *sādhanas* chosen for being likely translations of Indic originals. Chapters 2 and 5 take manuals (an initiation manual and a *sādhana*) that are probably Tibetan compositions but nonetheless reveal significant aspects of tantric ritual development in India. While this study offers certain insights into the nature of tantric practice in Tibet, and even at Dunhuang, it considers them more for what they show about larger processes of ritual localization, how Buddhist ritual manuals functioned more generally to enable novel transformations of Indic practice.

This book therefore strives to strike a fine balance between detailed treatments of local ritual innovations and the conditions that produced them and considerations of more global innovations, or patterns of innovations, made possible by the genre. This may seem a problematic project, perhaps even an impossibly contradictory one, but such is the nature of ritual manuals; such is the problematic of the genre that this study seeks to explore.

Early Tantric Buddhism

How one understands the origins of tantric religion depends to a large degree on how one defines the concept. Tantra comes into being when certain characteristics coalesce, certain features that compose one's own *a priori* definition. In this sense, any history of the origins of tantra involves circular reasoning. If we define tantra as primarily about initiation or transgressive behavior, we might see it already in the liberative initiatory cults of the fourth-to-sixth-century Śaiva Atimarga. If we define it in terms of imaginative identification with the deity or "the royal metaphor," we might see it in the Buddhist Yoga tantras of the late seventh century. If we define it as all about tantric sexual fluids, we might see it in the *yoginī*-focused materials of the eighth to tenth centuries. And so on.[6] The resulting ambiguities have enabled Asian and Western authors alike to project all sorts of fanciful ideas onto the concept, both romantic and derogatory. Some scholars have even suggested that "tantrism" or tantric Buddhism is "largely a product of nineteenth-century Orientalist" imaginings.[7] Such claims are contradicted by the long history of the term "tantra" in Indian religious discourse, though warnings against unfounded projections are certainly well taken.

Rather than depend on the circular reasoning of definition-based narratives and other modern scholarly conceptions, we might do better by turning to the texts themselves. There is ample evidence that already by the seventh century, some Buddhists, at least, were recognizing something new was afoot. Perhaps best known is the report of Wuxing (630–674), a Chinese pilgrim who sent several important tantric texts back to China but never made it home himself. Among his dispatches he includes the observation: "Recently there is a new doctrine of mantra that is held in great honor throughout the country."[8] Arriving toward the end of Wuxing's visit, another Chinese pilgrim, Yixing (684–727), similarly reports on the existence of a mythic hundred-thousand-verse *Vidyādharapiṭaka*, the remains of which formed a smaller collection "not yet available in China." This abbreviated collection, he recounts, which offered rituals of spells and *mudrās* to be performed before mandalas, had been criticized by earlier logicians such as Dignāga. Nonetheless, he concludes, "I have touched on the main points of these new teachings here, in order to make them known."[9] Such references, especially when they promote an independent *piṭaka* ("basket") to be listed alongside the (near-)canonical Buddhist *tripiṭaka*, would seem to reflect a perceived need among some seventh-century Buddhists for a new category of *buddhavacana* ("word of the Buddha") to encapsulate these novel teachings.[10] And it was perhaps this same perceived need that motivated the composition of the first "tantric" sutras, often essentially just collections of ritual manuals, also around the early seventh century.

Indian Buddhists may have perceived the proliferation of spell-based ritual texts as something new, but they did not write "tantras" per se until the mid-eighth century. This fact is easily overlooked, as they soon began to apply the label "tantra" retroactively to some of the earlier ritually focused "sutras" that had been composed from the early seventh century on.[11] Such a move is typical with emerging new genres. Michel de Certeau observes the same trend in the rise of a new form of "mystic" writing in seventeenth-century Europe: "A corpus can be considered the effect of this relation between a name (which symbolizes circumscription) and rules (which specify a mode of production), even if, as is often the case, the name is used to add different or earlier productions to the constellation of texts it isolates."[12] We may thus distinguish the initial period of the seventh century, when the burgeoning ritual manuals started to be collected and reframed as *buddhavacana*, with the Buddha in clearly specified narrative settings offering detailed instruction on complex ritual practice, from the later period of "tantras" proper. Although at least some of the rules that guided the production of the earliest "tantras" were in place by the early seventh century, the name came later. Precisely which of the earlier works should be considered tantras, despite their not originally carrying that title, continued to be a matter of some disagreement over the centuries that followed (discussed further in chapter 1).

Much the same may be said of tantric Śaivism, which likewise seems to have taken shape in the early seventh century.[13] Why did such a marked shift occur across religious traditions and at the same time? Whatever their differences, Davidson and Sanderson, writing on tantric Buddhism and Śaivism respectively, both point to a mix of interrelated socioeconomic changes that accompanied the gradual collapse of the Gupta dynasty. The spread of new regional dynasties brought a period of deurbanization combined with a proliferation of new urban centers. At the religious level, this was accompanied by the bestowal of land grants to brahmins in rural areas and the concomitant multiplication of temples that supported new settlements and agrarian expansion. Both scholars further agree that the result was a shift in religious priorities toward greater ritual engagement with kingship. Tantric priests oversaw the king's initiation, which they modeled on earlier royal coronation ceremonies; maintained his health and spiritual purity; and supported him in battle with apotropaic and malevolent rites. And they were rewarded handsomely for their services, in gold, land, temples, and political influence.[14] Taken together, the contributions of Davidson and Sanderson, published in 2002 and 2009, respectively, have moved forward our understanding of the socioeconomic causes behind the rise of tantric ritual.[15] Both highlight the influence of societal forces, political ideology, and the power of the "royal metaphor." Their shared conclusions may to some extent be tied to the kinds of sources they employed. Relying heavily on canonical sources as well as archaeological and epigraphic evidence,[16] they focused primarily on the remains left by those rich and powerful enough to afford such grand projects.

The present study in no way contradicts these valuable findings, but its close readings of ritual manuals offer something different. These were texts that could be produced by anyone and in great numbers, anywhere and anytime, only to die off and disappear soon afterward. Using an evolutionary model, we might describe ritual manuals as the DNA of early tantric Buddhism, the quickly mutating substance that shaped the larger canonical tradition. The various species that finally emerged in the form of tantras and the fossilized archaeological remains tell some of the story, but by looking to ritual manuals such as those preserved at Dunhuang we can recover a different perspective on the early evolution of tantric ritual.

The Tantric Manuscripts from Dunhuang

This book's own conclusions are therefore just as predetermined by its sources, limited by the fragmentary and (not entirely) arbitrary character of what was left behind in Cave 17 at Dunhuang. Yet it does tell another story that may be less "important," more local and idiosyncratic, but is nonetheless significant, perhaps even precisely in its unimportance. One step closer to "lived religion," these manuscripts represent a genre so fundamental as to be taken for granted; often assumed and overlooked, it underlay the canonical writings of great scholars.

The Dunhuang manuscripts thus provide a rare window onto the early history of tantric Buddhism, reflecting a crucial period of Indian creativity. Precisely which period is a matter of possible confusion. Until recently, it was commonly assumed that the bulk of the Tibetan manuscripts date from the Tibetan occupation of Dunhuang between 786 and 848 C.E., the height of the Pugyel dynasty, when Tibetans controlled Dunhuang and much of Central Asia.[17] However, closer examination reveals that much of the collection actually dates from the tenth century, particularly the tantric materials.[18]

Despite their mostly tenth-century dates, the Dunhuang tantric manuscripts reflect a significantly earlier stage in the development of Buddhism in India. The kinds of rituals represented and texts quoted correspond to the state of Indian tantric ritual in the second half of the eighth century. So, for example, no mention is made of the later two initiations (the wisdom-gnosis and fourth initiations), nor of the early ninth-century Jñānapāda and the somewhat later Ārya school writings associated with the *Guhyasamāja-tantra*.[19] Nor is there any mention of the *Cakrasaṃvara* and *Hevajra* tantras, the two principal "Yoginī" tantras that date from the ninth and tenth century, respectively. Some of the innovations reflected in the manuscripts—specific to either Tibet or the Buddhists of Dunhuang—may date from the ninth and tenth centuries, but for most intents and purposes, these tenth-century tantric manuscripts from Dunhuang reflect a late eighth-century period of Indian ritual development.[20]

Why not a moment closer to their own tenth-century dates? There seems to have been an interruption in the transmission of Buddhism from India to Tibet. Sure enough, traditional Tibetan historians describe precisely such a break beginning around 842 C.E., when the Pugyel dynasty and imperial support for Buddhist monasteries and official translation efforts collapsed. Still, this doesn't explain why the manuscripts reflect an even earlier break of around 800 C.E. Lacking further evidence, we may attribute the remaining difference of roughly forty years to a somewhat to-be-expected time lag between when tantric texts began to circulate in India and when they would actually arrive and be translated in Tibet. In any case, the Dunhuang documents generally seem to reflect a point in the development of Indian tantric ritual right around the mid-to-late eighth century.[21]

But what of their relationship to Tibet? That the tantric manuscripts reflect imperial-period translation efforts of the late eighth and early ninth centuries already suggests that central Tibet was their main source. This is to say not that the texts necessarily originated in central Tibet (though many likely did) but that even when composed in Dunhuang, they were informed and inspired by the Tibetan translations of the imperial period. It is certain that close religious ties between Tibet and Dunhuang were maintained throughout the imperial period. Dunhuang was a significant religious center for the Tibetan court, as evidenced by records of large-scale court-sponsored sutra-copying projects, the recent discovery of at least one *Prajñāpāramitā* sutra copied in ninth-century Dunhuang in the Drepung library near Lhasa, the key roles played in the later Tibetan Buddhist imagination by at least two highly educated Chinese monks from Dunhuang (Heshang Moheyan and Facheng), and so on.[22]

It may seem odd that the Dunhuang manuscripts relating to the transgressive practices of Mahāyoga also stemmed from imperial-period Tibet. The Pugyel court, after all, explicitly prohibited the circulation and study of such texts. The early ninth-century *Grammar in Two Volumes* (*Sgra sbyor bam po gnyis pa*), a guide for early Tibetan translators, states that "the mantra-tantras and the words of the mantras are not to be collected nor translated," and the *Pangtangma* (*'Phang thang ma*), a ninth-century imperial-period catalogue of Tibetan translations, closes by stating that the "inner" tantras (apparently meaning the Mahāyoga tantras, as the Yoga tantras are included in the same catalogue) were "put into a separate list" that perhaps not surprisingly did not survive.[23] Nonetheless, this indicates that such works were translated and did make their way into imperial libraries. A further glimpse of the situation is gained from a colophon appended to an early ninth-century Tibetan composition on Mahāyoga practice, the *Questions and Answers of Vajrasattva* (*Rdo rje sems dpa'i zhus lan*) by Nyen Pelyang (Gnyan Dpal dbyangs), several copies of which were found at Dunhuang: "Regarding [this work's] purpose, it was taught for Nanam Dongkhyu and for the minds of future generations of yogins, with the aim of clarifying any unclear, doubtful, or difficult points."[24] We get a picture of not only the imperial court but also a small circle of tantric practitioners, perhaps closely affiliated aristocratic clans, having access to and interest in Mahāyoga rituals, with elite monks writing lengthy explanations for them.

In any case, following the collapse of the Pugyel empire and imperially sponsored monastic institutions in central Tibet, Mahāyoga texts spread throughout Tibet. By the end of the tenth century, Mahāyoga was so popular that, as King Lha Lama Yeshe Ö attempted to regain control of western Tibet, it once again became a target. Mahāyoga had become too widespread to proscribe completely, but it could be regulated. Yeshe Ö's widely distributed edicts proclaimed that only "in accordance with the [proper] methods, and with the pure ritual procedures, should he lead [a few qualified disciples] into the mandala in precise accordance with how it is explained, bestow [upon them] the vows (*samaya*) for the three doors of mantra, and so on. They must work through the vehicles step by step and practice the genuine scriptures of mantra as foremost."[25] A tantric teacher should be appointed with care and must abide by certain rules, never teaching for personal gain or favoring his own family. Should he ever explain a tantra incorrectly, he should be punished: "His texts must be confiscated, and he should be ordered to pronounce three times, 'Henceforth I must not act like that.' If there is no improvement [in his behavior], then the words 'This is one who has disrespected the words of the Conqueror' should be written onto his forehead, and he should be banished elsewhere."[26] Tantric teachers often worked beyond the manageable confines of monastic institutions. They therefore represented a potential threat to Yeshe Ö's larger project of re-establishing the rule of law and centralized religious and political authority. The Dunhuang manuscripts offer a snapshot of the kinds of texts he found so objectionable.

Who Wrote Them?

This raises the difficult question of who penned and read the manuscripts used in this study. Precious few are signed. The *dhāraṇī*-based materials occasionally are, as are some Yogatantra items. Thus, IOL Tib J 351 is a collection of short works relating to the bodhisattva Avalokiteśvara that was "penned by the Bhikṣu Dorje."[27] IOL Tib J 790 (probably a ninth-century manuscript) has both a *dhāraṇī* and the end of an apparently Yogatantra ritual manual, penned by a monk from Tsang province in central Tibet.[28] Another Yogatantra work, the *Tattvasaṃgrahasādhana* in Pelliot tibétain 792 that is the focus of chapter 3, was written as a gift (*sku yon*) for the monk Bande Jangchup Yang.[29] Among manuscripts dating from the tenth century, however, the names reflect a wider range of cultural origins. IOL Tib J 463 contains two *dhāraṇi* sutras and says it was "translated and edited, then practiced as a daily commitment, and cleaned up and copied by the Uyghur Bhikṣu Rinchen Dzak."[30] Pelliot tibétain 103, which contains several short liturgical texts (the *Devatāsūtra* and several praises), includes a couple of scribal names. The manuscript's first and last works were penned by one Bak Bhiṣu Rinchen Lama; Bak ('Bag) was a common Kuchean name and even the name of the Kuchean royal family.[31] In the more specifically Mahāyoga manuscripts, however, the names dry up. A rare case is the above-cited copy of Nyen Pelyang's *Questions and Answers of Vajrasattva*, which ends with the line, "Penned by Fushi (副使) Meng Huaiyu (孟壞玉)," Fushi being a Chinese title for the third highest ranking official in a district.[32] Here then is a layman with an interest in Mahāyoga. However, this text is not a ritual manual but a treatise on the theory behind Mahāyoga practice. Similar is an extensive and annotated commentary on the Mahāyoga tantra, the *Lasso of Means* (*Thabs kyi zhags pa*), preserved in IOL Tib J 321, by another apparently Chinese scribe: "Penned by Bo'u ko of Ganzhou."[33] Among the Mahāyoga ritual manuals themselves, not one has yet been definitively linked to a name, which may well be because such works were personally held manuals that did not circulate much beyond their owner and were copied not for merit nor even for study, but for daily use.

The few tantric manuscripts that can be attributed to specific scribes, particularly those from the tenth century, therefore paint a remarkably multicultural picture. Buddhists from a wide array of Silk Road cultures—Uyghurs, Kucheans, Khotanese, and Chinese—seem to have practiced tantric Buddhism around Dunhuang, and when they did so, they wrote in Tibetan.[34] This also implies that Tibetan Buddhism, and particularly Tibetan tantric Buddhism, was a remarkably distinct tradition around tenth-century Dunhuang. Buddhists from an array of cultural backgrounds were interested in tantric Buddhism, but to further their interests in this area they had to step into a distinctly Tibetan Buddhist milieu shaped by the translation efforts of the earlier imperial period.

Apart from scribal colophons, we have some evidence of monastic participation in Mahāyoga practice in manuscripts describing the tantric feast

(Skt. *gaṇacakra*; Tib. *tshogs 'khor*). Pelliot tibétain 321 provides a particularly lengthy manual for such a feast, to be performed by a group of "dharma brethren" (*mched* or sometimes *mched lcam dral*), presumably headed by the patron (*yon bdag*) and all together led by a tantric ritual master (*vajrācārya*) who is sometimes referred to as the "vajra king" (*rdo rje rgyal po*).[35] "Dharma brethren" is a vague term that could include monastic or lay participants, bound together only by their shared tantric vow (*samaya*). At one point, however, as they offer a final confession before receiving the sacramental fivefold ambrosia (*pañcāmṛta*), they recite: "Because our strength from pleasing those of the past has diminished, we are obscured by not attending all the *poṣadha*."[36] That the participants might have neglected their *poṣadha*, the bimonthly confession ceremony required of Buddhist monks, suggests that at least some were monastic. Perhaps relevant too are some notes on monastic rules found appended to a lengthy collection of works on performing another tantric feast.[37] Despite the closure of monasteries in central Tibet, traditional histories agree that Tibetan monasticism continued to thrive along the Gansu corridor and in the vicinity of Dunhuang.

Finally, the famous art of Dunhuang depicts performed tantric rites. Particularly useful is a crude ink drawing on paper of a wrathful mandala surrounded by four gate guardians (fig. Int.1). Before the mandala sits a monk, robed and with head shaven, alongside an apparently ill patron, lying beneath a blanket. Next to the monk are some ritual implements—a vajra and bell, an incense censer, two small offering stands, and an effigy of the demon personifying the illness violently staked to the ground. Tantric demon-taming rites, then, appear to have been within the purview of monks.

Given the scribal names, ritual content, and artistic renderings of tantric practice at Dunhuang, we may conclude that monks were the primary creators and readers of the manuscripts, with lay Buddhists acting as patrons and interested parties, and perhaps sometimes as ritual participants. Of course, what being a monk meant in tenth-century Dunhuang is less than clear. To what extent did the Tibetan Buddhist monks of Dunhuang maintain celibacy? Did they sleep in monasteries or their homes? Such questions are beyond the scope of this study and so must remain unanswered. As we have seen, community practice was part of tantric Buddhism at Dunhuang, most clearly in the form of the tantric feast.[38] The Mahāyoga *sādhana* discussed in chapter 4, however, opens by recommending performing the ritual "in an extremely solitary place," which the Dunhuang version of the text

FIGURE INT.1 Exorcistic ritual being performed before a wrathful mandala
Source: National Museum-New Delhi Collection, Acc. no.: Ch.00379.

extends to: "In a solitary place, a pleasure grove with flowering branches that is surrounded by mountains."[39] An emphasis on isolated practice is common in Dunhuang *sādhanas* generally, and it is possible that the advice given in these manuscripts was more of an ideal than a rule. Certainly today, *sādhanas* are performed in a variety of settings, from monastic cells to group retreats. Nonetheless, the *sādhanas* examined here seem to have been relatively private and personal affairs.

Form and Content

How the Dunhuang manuscripts were used is reflected not only in their contents but also in their material formats.[40] Positioned on the Silk Road, Dunhuang sat at a crossroads of multiple cultures, and the varied book formats found in the collection embody those encounters. Buddhism is a religion not of the book but of books. When one speaks of it traveling across Asia, one often refers to the movement of books. Buddhist teachers, statues, paintings, and ritual objects also journeyed along the Silk Road, but books were the primary focus for most foreign pilgrims to India and Buddhist missionaries going abroad, at least according to many later accounts. As thousands of scriptures, commentaries, histories, ritual manuals, and more were hauled across deserts and oceans, their larger bibliographic traditions accompanied them. These volumes were surrounded and suffused by Buddhism's rich book culture, explained and embodied by the monks escorting them. As this culture entered new regions, it transformed and was transformed by those environments, as the horizontally elongated, loose-leaf *potis* (Skt. *pustaka*) of India became the *rotuli* of China and palm leaves became paper.

Potis, concertinas, codices, and both vertical and horizontal scrolls are all seen regularly among the Tibetan manuscripts, along with several less-common formats such as single sheets and fragments. A complex array, these formats functioned within a web of cultural and religious connotations about which some general observations may be made. There are broad correlations between format and content in the Tibetan manuscripts:

1. *Poti*: "canonical" sutras and commentaries
2. Concertina: "semicanonical" liturgies and treatises

3. Codex: ritual manuals and personal notes
4. Scroll: vertical histories, letters, tantric ritual manuals; horizontal imperially sponsored, professionally scribed texts

The *poti* is the most common format (fig. Int.2). Inspired by Indian palm-leaf manuscripts, these can even have holes drilled through the pages through which, in India, strings were run to hold the loose leaves together. At Dunhuang, the strings do not appear to have been used (nor in later Tibet), but the holes were retained for their symbolic and decorative function, marking the manuscript as a sacred scripture containing the *buddhadharma*. Given the holy pedigree of this highly symbolic format, we may not be surprised that a large-sized *poti* style was used for some of the professionally scribed sutras ordered by the Tibetan court to be copied for merit-making purposes. Otherwise, the *poti*-style manuscripts often contain translations of Buddhist sutras and important commentaries of the sort that would later be included in the Tibetan canons, as well as prayers written for the purpose of making merit. They also contain many tantric *sādhanas*, especially those based in some way on Indic originals, perhaps reflecting the high status that some had attained. It appears that Tibetans living around Dunhuang in the ninth and tenth centuries were well aware of the symbolic significance of this format and deployed it accordingly.[41]

The concertina, or leporello, format (fig. Int.3) may be seen as one step removed from the *poti* in that it retains the same vertically elongated pages, but its folios are no longer unbound. In this sense it represents a kind of synthesis of the Indian *poti* and the Chinese scroll formats; folded, it looks like a *poti*, but unfolded, it reads like a scroll, with the text extending straight down the recto, followed by the verso, of the entire manuscript. That the concertina was understood to be related to the *poti* is apparent from the string

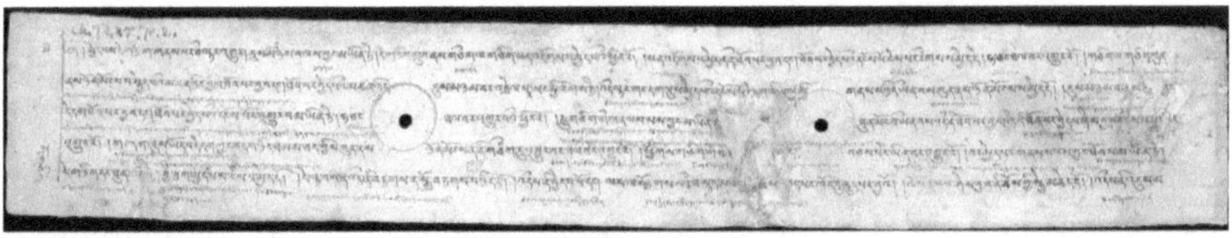

FIGURE INT.2 Example of the *poti* format
Source: IOL Tib J 177, Courtesy of the British Library

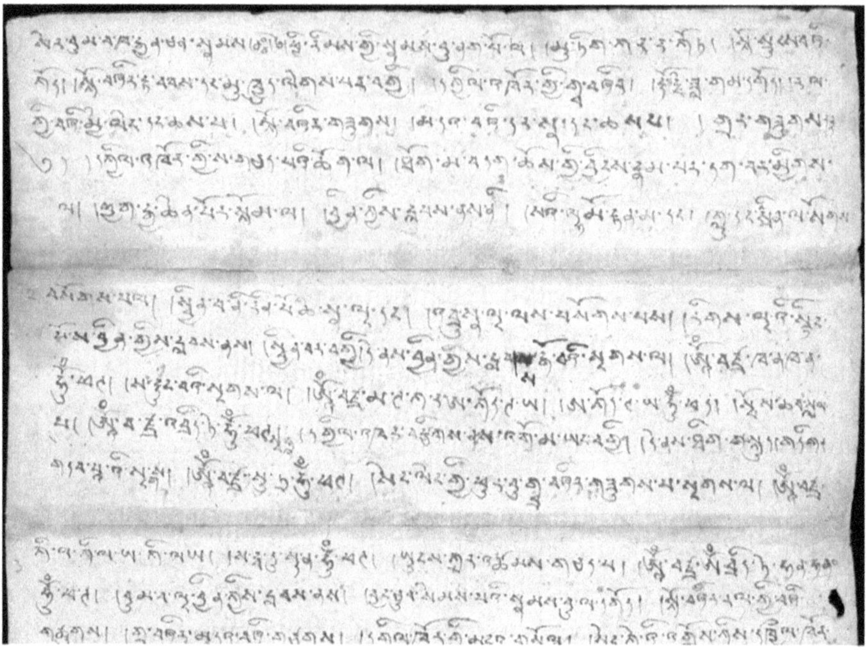

FIGURE INT.3 Example of the concertina format
Source: IOL Tib J 384, Courtesy of the British Library

holes that still occasionally appear, though less regularly and typically only singly, whereas *potis* exhibit cases of both single and double string holes, with the latter spaced roughly one-third and two-thirds of the way along the sheet. The concertina thus retained something of the *poti*'s sacred character while offering a far more practical format whose pages could not become so easily disordered. Compared to the *poti*, the concertinas contain more varied kinds of writings—still some translated sutras, but often more liturgical works. Some were intended for leading group practices, like the tantric feast manual (contained in Pelliot tibétain 36/IOL Tib J 419/Pelliot tibétain 42) and the Chan "initiation manuscript" (Pelliot tibétain 116). Similarly, there are numerous *dhāraṇīsaṃgraha*, liturgical collections of *dhāraṇī* sūtras and spells. Such works lie on the boundaries between *buddhavacana* and ritual manuals, just as we might expect from this intermediate format that is part *poti*, part scroll, and in some sense too, part codex.

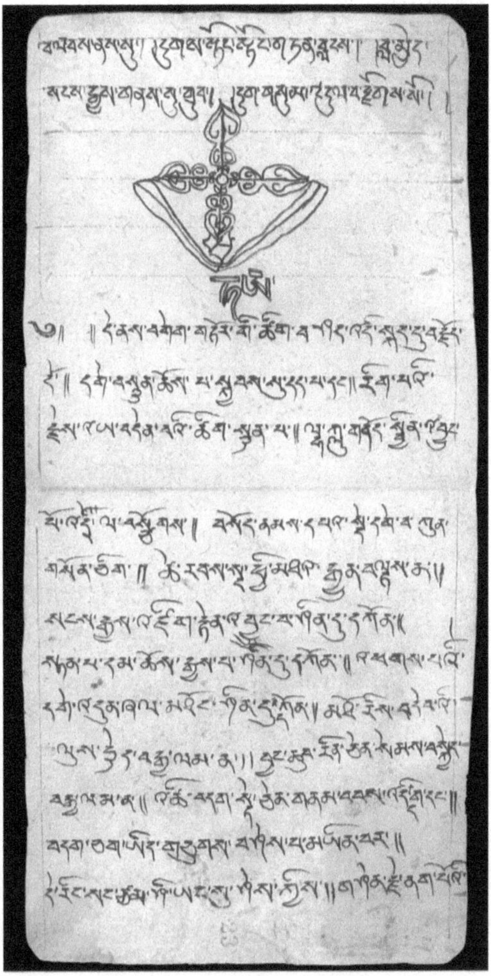

FIGURE INT.4 Example of the codex format
Source: IOL Tib J 420, Courtesy of the British Library

The codices are booklets generally bound along the left side but occasionally along the top, as in IOL Tib J 420 (fig. Int.4), and here we find ourselves more fully in the world of liturgies and ritual manuals. These are almost all tantric or *dhāraṇī* based. Many contain liturgical collections of *dhāraṇī* sutras, sutra extracts, and prayers; others may have medical rites (as in IOL Tib J 401, apparently owned by one Bhikṣu Prajñāprabhā) or funerary rituals (as in Pelliot tibétain 37). One (IOL Tib J 437/Pelliot tibétain 324) contains two Mahāyoga rites—a fivefold ambrosia offering and a generation-stage visualization practice.[42] Whatever their religious origins, the codices are often idiosyncratic in content, their owners having cobbled them together for their own individual ritual purposes, sometimes with personal notes appended. The vast majority of codices from Dunhuang date from the tenth century, and other scholars have ascribed the format to Western influence.[43]

Finally, the scrolls are of two sorts—the vertical and the horizontal. The vertical scrolls (fig. Int.5) contain a wide variety of texts, often tantric treatises and ritual manuals, but also letters and official documents, perhaps most famously the *Old Tibetan Annals* and the *Tibetan Chronicle*. Manuscripts in this format often show some Chinese cultural influence; many are written on the verso of Chinese scrolls (the *Annals* and the *Chronicles* being two good examples), sometimes in a messy, probably non-native hand (as in Or.8210/S.95), while others include interlinear notations in Chinese (as in IOL Tib J 612) (fig. Int.6). The well-known Tibetan-Chinese glossary and phrasebook (Or.8210/S.1000 and S.2736) is likewise copied on the verso of a Chinese scroll.[44] There are Tibetan scrolls containing tantric treatises that are well copied onto clean vertical scrolls with no easily discernible Chinese influence (such as Pelliot tibétain 283, IOL Tib J 454, and Pelliot tibétain 849), though this does not preclude the possibility of such influence.[45]

The horizontal scrolls are something different again (fig. 7). Most are professionally scribed sutras copied for the purpose of merit production. Many date from the ninth century, when the Tibetan empire was at the height of its power and in a position to sponsor copies from the scriptoriums of Dunhuang. Horizontal scrolls would have allowed professionals working in Tibetan to continue the Chinese scribal practices, as they unfurl horizontally, like Chinese scrolls. (And Dunhuang-based scribes working under the Tibetan empire tended to be culturally Chinese.) Scrolls also were an almost

FIGURE INT.5 Example of the vertical scroll format
Source: IOL Tib J 750, Courtesy of the British Library

FIGURE INT.6 Vertical scroll format with interlinear Chinese notes
Source: IOL Tib J 612, Courtesy of the British Library

infinitely expandable format, as additional pages can always easily be added, and they would have been easier to produce than *potis*, as they required less cutting of large sheets into individual folios. Taken together, these characteristics help to explain why the horizontal scroll might have been selected as a format of convenience for large-scale imperially sponsored copying projects.

Many of the above observations hold true only in general terms. It is significant that certain patterns of correlation between form and content are discernible, but multiple exceptions may also be found. Ritual manuals, moreoever, appear in all formats, reflecting a spectrum of contents, from

FIGURE INT.7 Example of the horizontal scroll format
Source: Schøyen ms. 2100, Courtesy of The Schøyen Collection, Oslo and London

scrappy codices written for portable performances to holy ceremonies meant to carry their readers into awakening. The four manuscripts that constitute the focus of chapters 2 to 5 (and many others related to them) all contain ritual manuals written on *poti*-style paper. An initiation manual and three *sādhanas*, their formats suggest they were highly valued by their owners. This may not be entirely coincidental; all four have been selected for being significant works that can shed light on tantric ritual in India. Two are probable translations from Sanskrit, and all are fully intact, well organized, stand-alone (i.e., not sharing their manuscripts with other works) manuals, well penned and carefully composed. Marked by their physical *poti* formats as sacred and authoritative, they offer intimate encounters with the divine.

The Poetry of Ritual Manuals

Ritual manuals constitute a genre of Buddhist writing defined by certain formal and stylistic features. Most obviously, they tend to instruct their readers in the imperative tense: clear the ground, sprinkle flowers, recite the spell, and so on. Of course, Mahāyāna sutras often speak in the imperative too, as when buddhas or bodhisattvas instruct their assembled followers to copy the sutra, build shrines around it, worship it, and so on, but there the directives are spoken by an awakened being and embedded within the larger narrative setting of the sutra. Such instructions are one step removed from the reader, meant to be emulated but still not immediately addressing them. The reader may imagine being within the sutra's narrative setting, but in doing so, they leave their immediate physical environment to enter the past or parallel worlds of the sutras. In contrast, ritual manuals speak directly to the present reader, less inviting them in than reaching out, instructing them directly. These are entirely human oriented, writings of our world.

Early ritual manuals were often embedded within *dhāraṇī* sutras and thus put into the mouths of buddhas. "As for the ritual procedures . . . ," the Buddha might say, then launch into his instructions. "Whoever does this will acquire every good fortune," he might even add. As chapter 1 observes, such early *vidhis* were often added after the sutra had already been circulating, sometimes even just appended to the sutra's end. In such cases, the tone of the instructions is ambivalent, suspended somewhere between *buddhavacana* and human authorship. As ritual manuals came into their own as a stand-alone genre, however, the human took over. These were compositions by people and for people.

With the seventh century and the emergence of tantric manuals came a further stylistic development. The earliest manuals focused on simple instructions, typically (though not always) written in prose, regarding the preparation of the ritual space, making offerings, and reciting the spell. Now, the manuals eventually classed as Yogatantra began to introduce moments of poetic language, sometimes in verse, using metaphor and other literary devices to signal a shift in the proceedings and produce specific effects in the reader. Again, the Mahāyāna sutras also exhibit such tendencies. Whereas early Buddhist sutras are generally written in prose, the Mahāyāna sutras more regularly incorporate verse passages, sometimes even repeating in parallel the prose.[46] Mahāyāna readers were aware of the change; witness the complaints of Māra disguised as a conservative *śramaṇa* in the *Aṣṭasāhasrikā*: "What you have heard just now, that is not the word of the Buddha. It is poetry, the work of poets. But what I here teach to you, that is the teaching of the Buddha, that is the word of the Buddha."[47] For some early Buddhists, it seems, poetry was not the language of the buddhas. Over time, however, poetic expression and "inspired eloquence" (*pratibhāna*) more generally increasingly became "a source of authentic dharma."[48] Still later, however, and most significantly within the genre of ritual manuals, such poetic communications of awakening were ritualized. Through metaphor, simile, rhythm, rhyme, and more, utilizing multiple senses in concert, sometimes even accompanied with dance and song, ritual manuals from the seventh century on led readers through a series of rites that culminated in a taste of awakening.

The present study culminates in its fifth chapter's analysis of a stunningly creative Mahāyoga *sadhana* written in verse and meant to instigate in the reader immediate experiences of emptiness, light, movement, and completeness. In some sense, the preceding chapters tell the story of how the language of Buddhist ritual manuals got to that point. To understand the stylistic shifts witnessed within the genre, one must apply not only the philological and historical lenses typical of Buddhist Studies but also a more literary lens—being sensitive to changes in meter but also to the subtle differences between direct instruction and the often-indirect workings of poetic imagery. When a manual is no longer just telling its reader what to do but explaining how to do it, something has shifted. I suggest that such changes in register are significant, that the use of poetic language is intentional, to mark key moments in the proceedings and even to shape the reader's aesthetic experience. That a movement toward the evocation of affective experience developed within the very human genre of ritual manuals is surely no coincidence. How precisely this shift unfolds is a primary focus of this study. It is significant for our understanding of tantric practice that the frequency and the sophistication of the poetics witnessed increases with each chapter.

With the advent of the so-called Yogatantras, Buddhist ritual underwent a revolution of its own. Ritual manuals of the sixth century focused on an image of a Buddha who was distant in both space and time. Set before the worshipper upon an altar (i.e., a mandala), with offerings carefully arranged around him, the Buddha represented a remote state of awakening that one could only dream of attaining aeons hence. Until then, the good Buddhist could only hope that he might condescend to bestow his blessings. But in the seventh century, the ritualist ascended that altar to become the Buddha himself. Seated at the center of the mandala, the ritual subject now received offerings and radiated blessings, already a fully awakened being. From this awakened perspective, there was no difference between the divine and the human, pure and impure. All that had been excluded from monastic Buddhism, whether desire or aversion, sex or violence, was now allowed in. These remarkable changes were accompanied by similarly radical shifts at the societal level, as other scholars, such as Davidson and Sanderson, have observed. At the level of ritual, however, the focus shifted from the altar in front to the body's interior. Consecration was no longer just a bathing of the body's exterior but an internal purification through the entry (*āveśa*) of gnosis into the heart. The ritualist's subtlest breath became the coursing of that gnosis, the felt energy of awakening that could be manipulated at will. As complex mandalas were mapped onto the body, the invisible interior became the secret, parallel plane on which the "real" ritual unfolded. The subject's imagination became the root of all phenomena; the entire universe emanated out of their awakened mind.[49]

Of course, Buddhists themselves voice suspicion of the fleeting and potentially even dangerous nature of subjective experience. They regularly caution against attachment to experiences that arise as signs of meditative progress; all such things are merely the results of one's deluded karma, unreal, and therefore not to be engaged with.[50] Yet when we turn to tantric Buddhism, we find a markedly different approach. Even as some passages warn against attachment to beauty or pleasure, ritualized dancing, singing, feasting, and even sexual longing are all being performed as Buddhist practices. Occasionally such pleasures are framed as offerings, in which case one might argue that they are merely about outward performance and not truly felt.[51] But the tantras take sensory pleasure further, suggesting a more interior approach to such ostensibly worldly experiences. Thus, the *Sarvabuddhasamāyoga* claims that performing each of the nine moods (Skt. *rasa*; Tib. *nyams*) of Indian aesthetics opens the ritual actor to possession (*āveśa*) by a particular buddha:

> Gently joining your palms, and with song, cymbals, and dance,
>
> With eroticism, heroism, compassion, laughter, ferocity, terror,
> Disgust, surprise, and tranquility: with the *mudrās* of these affects, the aims are accomplished.
>
> By being endowed with the affects of eroticism, etc. and performing the dances with the various *mudrās*,
> One unites with the *mudrā* that is the nature of all, whereby all the [states of] possession (*āveśa*) are accomplished.

Eroticism is Vajrasattva, heroism the hero Tathāgata,
Compassion is Vajradhara, laughter the supreme Lokeśvara,

Ferocity is Vajrasūrya, terror Vajrarudra,
Disgust is Śākyamuni Buddha, wonder Āralli,

And peace is always the Buddha, as it pacifies all suffering.[52]

The ritualized expression of each poetic mood can thus bring one into union with the corresponding buddha. *Āveśa* (here, "possession"), as chapter 3 of this study confirms, is central to the practice of tantric Buddhism. Indeed, one of the most significant themes of this book is that of *āveśa* and how it functioned as a transmission of awakening in not only the Yoga tantras but also the early Mahāyoga tantras. From the time of the Yoga tantras (seventh century) on, to act as and be possessed by the deity is key. Through *āveśa*, the deity is interiorized. As the buddhas take possession, their gnosis enters the practitioner's heart, merging with his mind and causing an instantaneous taste of awakening. Outward performance, then, can lead to inward transformation.

Perhaps so, one might respond, but surely the resulting transformation, the "taste" of awakening, is no mere aesthetic experience. Many Indian and Tibetan Buddhists might likewise balk at the idea of awakening being treated in this way. For just this reason, some tantric authors were careful to add that the nine moods are deployed by the buddhas only as expedient means, adventitious adornments for converting the deluded but not Buddhism's central point. Thus, the ninth-century *Gathering of Intentions Sutra* refers to the nine dances that express the nine moods as "childish practices to which [the buddha] adapts."[53] It seems that, contra the *Sarvabuddhasamāyoga* passage above, some early tantric Buddhists saw the moods as somehow extrinsic to Buddhism proper, adopted by buddhas only as skillful means.

The *Sarvabuddhasamāyoga* passage, then, may represent a more open-minded approach to the nine *rasas*, and it gives particular privilege to the ninth mood of peace (*śānta*): "And peace is always the Buddha, as it pacifies all suffering." Indian aesthetics commonly considers peace to be the religious mood, "the emotion of emotionlessness," and the mood seems to have been added to the originally eightfold list of *rasas* only around the eighth century.[54] The *Sarvabuddhsamāyoga* dates to the mid-eighth, as indicated by its appearance in the writings of Amoghavajra, whose summary of the work explicitly recognizes the significance of the nine moods appearing there.[55] The above-cited passage, then, is evidence that some tantric Buddhists were remarkably early adopters of this new religious mood and quick to identify it with the Buddha. As Indian writers on aesthetics, with their ninth mood, moved into the religious sphere, so were religious authors moving into the realm of aesthetics.

In the Dunhuang manuscripts too (probably representing a view typical of late eighth-century India), tantric Buddhists recognized the affective experience of peace as identical with the ultimate. A Dunhuang *Guhyagarbha*-based *sādhana* instructs its reader: "One clearly cultivates that there comes oneself as the Bhagavan Buddhaheruka, endowed with the nine dances of great blazing in the moods of erotic, heroic, terrifying, as well as laughing, disgusted, surprised, compassionate, ferocious, and the ultimately tranquil, [that are danced] without wavering from the reality body, terrifying like the time of the universe's destruction."[56]

The eighth century was a moment, then, when the lines between Indian aesthetics and religious insight were blurring, when poetry and poetics were shaping tantric practice. All this was happening in the background as tantric ritual manuals began to use poetic language to mark key moments in the proceedings and to induce certain experiences, of consecration, union with the deity, dissolution, and so on.[57]

In reading the ritual manuals from Dunhuang, I have attempted to tread a fine line, to follow each through its intricate maze of ritual twists and turns while remaining open to the possibility of unexpected moments of poetry, when time slows, space opens, and a different kind of experience is suggested. Anyone who has wandered the *galis* of Banaras, encountering their sights, smells, and sounds one after another, then suddenly emerged onto the *ghats*, where the floodplains of the Ganges fall away into the shimmering distance, and stopped for a moment in surprise before turning back into the fray, will have some idea of what I mean. These texts are not reducible to their poetic moments; nor can they be understood apart from them. Michel de Certeau writes of reading "mystic" texts of sixteenth- and seventeenth-century Europe:

> If we envision the procedures of this mystic writing, if we "interpret" that writing (in the musical sense) as a different mode of utterance, we are treating it as

> a past apart from us, rather than pretending that we are in the same place it is. Such an approach [of treating it as a past] involves an attempt to repeat its movements ourselves, to follow, though at a distance, in the footsteps of its workings; it means refusing to equate this thing, which transformed graphs into hieroglyphs as it passed, with an object of knowledge. We must remain within a certain experience of writing, and observe a modesty that is respectful of distances. These guidelines, adopted in the textual suburbs, soon teach the way to get lost (even if it is only the way to lose a form of knowledge); following them may lead us, by the sound of its streets, to the city transformed into sea. A genre of literature would thus have revealed a part of what constructs it: the power to induce a departure.[58]

In the pages that follow, I hope to apply de Certeau's approach, to follow these manuals while respecting their radical otherness, not reducing them to mere objects of knowledge.

ONE

Ritual Manuals and the Spread of the Local

TODAY, MOST TIBETAN Buddhist households will own a small collection of ritual manuals and likely read from them every day. The pages of such a collection probably contain a highly idiosyncratic hodgepodge of prayers and other short liturgical works, perhaps a *sādhana*, often with small notes jotted here and there in the margins—an assembly of writings that reflects its owner's individual interests and life experiences. Despite the ubiquity of such collections, however, this genre is not well studied. Scholars generally prefer important canonical works—the sutras, tantras, and other works ascribed to the Buddha, or influential commentaries by well-known Buddhist authors of the past. Yet much can be learned from locally produced ritual manuals. In fact, their insignificance is precisely what can make them so valuable. Functioning as they do outside the canon, they constitute a highly flexible genre that is remarkably open to innovation. Contemporary Buddhist teachers regularly compose new manuals for their disciples, and those disciples then make them their own by combining them with other short works, writing in the margins, and so on. Much can be learned about how the tradition constantly remakes itself, forever being reshaped to fit the specificities of Buddhists' lives. In the topsy-turvy world of ritual manuals, where the unimportant is all the more significant, one may glimpse local innovations and individual interests, changes outside the canon and often beneath the gaze of large institutions.

A scholarly study of such a local and all-too-human genre must therefore attend to the idiosyncrasies of each manuscript while also remaining alert to larger patterns that may emerge. A paradoxical approach must be followed in investigating this genre of specificities that is nonetheless so ubiquitous. The innovations facilitated by ritual manuals may be specific to a place or even a person, yet they are *of a kind*, typical of the genre. They follow discernible patterns that can be traced. As in genetic evolution, some of these local mutations may be successful; they may spread elsewhere or even become enshrined in new canonical sutras or tantras. Others enjoy a more limited success before dying off or perhaps existing in some out-of-the-way pocket of Buddhist practice. Still others simply die off with their authors, forgotten forever. Yet the mechanics of these mutations are governed by laws that may change over time but are discernible nonetheless. In this sense, with the rise of ritual manuals, the local spread everywhere.

This chapter further argues that ritual manuals have not always played such a significant role in Buddhist practice. Evidence suggests that they began to gain influence only in the second half of the fifth century. The genre's adoption within orthodox circles and its fast-spreading popularity across Asia changed the face of Buddhism forever. Today it is hard to imagine a Buddhism without ritual manuals, much less one without the countless changes they have wrought, yet before the fifth century, there is little evidence of their existence. The proliferation of ritual manuals in the late fifth and sixth centuries is of considerable significance for the history of Buddhism, for little more than a hundred years later, the first tantras began to appear. Ritual manuals helped make tantric Buddhism possible.

Such are the dramatic changes examined here, with reference to the precious trove of documents discovered a century ago near Dunhuang, for in these long-lost manuscripts we have a time capsule of lived religion.[1] The Dunhuang collection is extraordinary not only for its age but also for the kinds of texts it contains. Setting aside the professionally scribed sutras (and of course the nonreligious items), these are the ephemeral writings of living Buddhists, extracanonical works generally deemed not worth saving. Through these ancient manuscripts, we may discern what and *how* early Buddhists actually read. We may glimpse ritual practice between the canonical sutras and tantras, Buddhist practice in the process of evolving.

Dhāraṇī Sutras

Though extracanonical by nature, ritual manuals often moved across Asia alongside the canonical *dhāraṇī* sutras,[2] a subgenre of Mahāyāna sutras that focus on particular *dhāraṇī* spells. How exactly to distinguish them from ordinary Mahāyāna sutras is a vexing issue. Buddhists themselves have often been confused about which were which. Thus, the Tibetan canon has a distinct section called the "*Dhāraṇī* Collection" (Tib. *gzungs 'dus*; Skt. *dhāraṇīsaṃgraha*), yet the ordinary "Sutra Section" (*mdo sde*) includes many works that bear the title of *dhāraṇī* and are indistinguishable from *dhāraṇī* sutras in terms of content; sometimes copies of the same sutra appear in both sections. The dividing line is vague at best. Meanwhile, in East Asia, Chinese, Korean, and Japanese Buddhists often have viewed most *dhāraṇī* sutras in the same light as the tantras, labeling them "esoteric" (Ch. *mijiao*; Jap. *mikkyō*).[3]

That classification has given rise to an ongoing debate among Buddhologists, especially those working with Chinese sources, over the role that *dhāraṇī* sutras may have played in the rise of the Buddhist tantras. In his 1996 book, *Mantras et mandarins*, Michel Strickmann coined the term "proto-tantric" to describe the literature and practices of Buddhist *dhāraṇī*.[4] Since Strickmann first made his suggestion, the term "proto-tantric" has been adopted by some and, particularly in more recent years, rejected by others. The skeptics have pointed to the teleology implicit in the term, warning that it leads to anachronistic assumptions about how early authors and readers of *dhāraṇīs* understood their sutras.[5] With such critiques in mind, we should remind ourselves that early readers of *dhāraṇī* sutras, at least before the emergence of the tantras in the seventh and eighth centuries, did not see their texts as representing a self-conscious tradition apart from other forms of Mahāyāna. The *dhāraṇī* sutras should therefore be taken as merely Mahāyāna sutras and distinct from the generally (though not always) later tantras.

This said, the *dhāraṇī* sutras do—very generally speaking—have a discernibly different character from other Mahāyāna sutras,[6] in large part due to the *dhāraṇī* spells that lie at the heart of the genre. Similar to mantras, which are common to all three of India's major religions (Buddhism, Hinduism, and Jainism), *dhāraṇī* spells are unique to Mahāyāna Buddhism. Typically (but not always) absent from early Mahāyāna sutras, they had become almost ubiquitous by the Gupta period.[7] What is more, such *dhāraṇī* spells often function within wider ritual environments that also distinguish the spells and their sutras from other, non-*dhāraṇī*-based Mahāyāna sutras.[8] These were scriptures read less for their deep philosophical insights than for the meritorious ritual of reading's own sake.[9] How they were used was often more important than the significance of their contents. In these senses, *dhāraṇī* sutras constitute a genre of Buddhist scripture distinct from other Mahāyāna sutras.

Given that the uses of *dhāraṇīs* are of such historical significance, the manuscript cultures surrounding them can be particularly illuminating. *Dhāraṇī* spells were typically recited within ritual performances, the traces of which may be discerned in not only their attendant ritual manuals but also the formal features of the very manuscripts in which the spells were penned. By considering the practices of writing, reading, and performing *dhāraṇīs*, we can better understand this intriguing genre of Buddhist literature. And what better place to explore Buddhist manuscript culture than the Dunhuang archive? Before turning to ritual manuals proper, I begin with some observations on what the Tibetan Dunhuang manuscripts can tell us more generally about how *dhāraṇīs* were used, and what their uses can tell us about the place of *dhāraṇīs* in the historical development of Buddhist ritual practice.

Dhāraṇī Liturgies[10]

The ritual power of *dhāraṇī* may be said to lie partly in the ambiguity of the term. The word "*dhāraṇī*" can refer either to a whole sutra or to the spell contained in that sutra. Mahāyāna sutras in general regularly exhort their readers to copy, recite, worship, and propagate the sutras themselves, and these same kinds of self-promotion are found throughout the *dhāraṇī* sutras, but it is often unclear whether the entire *dhāraṇī* sutra is intended or just the spell.

One might assume the spell is intended, as the spell *holds* (the term's Sanskrit root, *dhṛ*, means "to hold") the power of the entire sutra, and indeed such a reading is sometimes understood. As Matsunaga observes, "the hope of averting misfortune through the recitation of an entire *Mahāyāna-sūtra* came to be fulfilled in the recitation of a single *dhāraṇī*."[11] That said, it is equally clear that the injunctions to copy or recite a *dhāraṇī* can also refer to the entire sutra, and sometimes the two possibilities even may be made explicit. The *Jayavatī-nāma-dhāraṇī*, for example, seems to instruct the reader to "copy the letters (*yi ge*) [of the spell] or copy the volume (*glegs bam*)."[12]

Both kinds of copying, of spells and sutras, were practiced at Dunhuang. Pelliot tibétain 72 and 73 (fig. 1.1) are two examples of *dhāraṇī* spells that have been copied for merit. Their similarity indicates that they may have been penned by the same hand, apparently an ethnically Chinese scribe (*sku yon pa*) named Zhen Ten Kong (Zhen brtan kong) who lived in Dunhuang.[13] Each manuscript contains two spells, the *Uṣṇīṣavijayā-dhāraṇī* and the *Mahāpratisarāvidyārājñī*, and the merit associated with both manuscripts is dedicated to local ministers with Tibetanized names, the first to Minister Dodra (Blon Mdo sgra) and the second to Minister Pelzang (Blon Dpal bzang).

On the other hand, we also have entire *dhāraṇī* sutras that were copied for merit. IOL Tib J 463 (fig. 1.2) is a concertina-style manuscript containing two works—the Chinese apocryphal *Eight Illuminations Sutra* (Tib. *Snang brgyad mdo*; Ch. *Ba yang jing*) and the common *Aparamitāyur-nāma-mahāyāna-sūtra*.[14] These were penned by the Uyghur monk Druhu Rinchen, and in a colophon, he dedicates the merit from copying both sutras to his parents.[15]

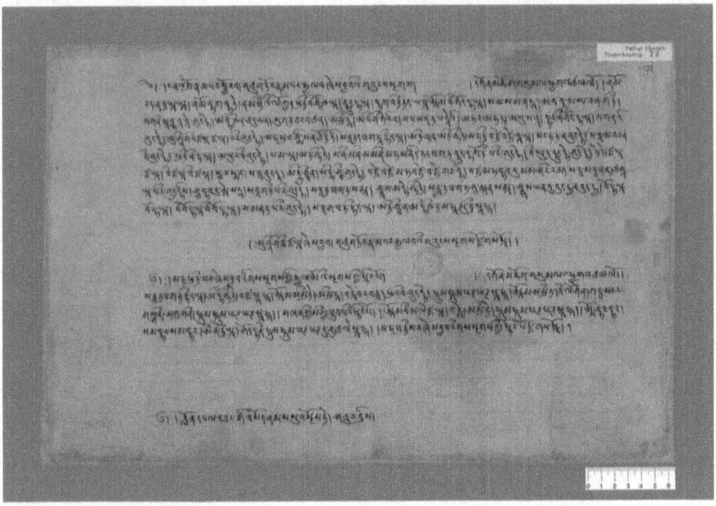

FIGURE 1.1 Two *dhāraṇī* spells copied for merit-making purposes
Source: Pelliot tibétain 72, Courtesy of the Bibliothèque Nationale

FIGURE 1.2 *Dhāraṇī* sutra copied for merit-making purposes
Source: IOL Tib J 463, Courtesy of the British Library

We can conclude that when Buddhists at Dunhuang read the injunction to "copy this *dhāraṇī*," they took it variously to mean either just the spell or the entire sutra.

Though the copying of sutras for merit-making purposes was already central to early Mahāyāna Buddhism, the *dhāraṇī* sutras therefore added a further element into the mix: the spell. Early on, the spells were subservient to their sutras, but as they rose in importance, they gradually separated from their parent sutras, and soon entire spell books—stand-alone lists of *dhāraṇī* spells extracted for ease of use—began to circulate. IOL Tib J 363 is just such a case; its spells are all from the *Uṣṇīṣasitātapatre-aparājitā-nāma-dhāraṇī* and listed in the same order in which they appear in that sutra. Such spell books may have been copied less for merit-making purposes than for liturgical use.

This brings us to a second kind of *dhāraṇī*-based manuscript found among the Dunhuang manuscripts, a second way that both the spells and the larger sutras were used in practice. The collecting of *dhāraṇī* for liturgical purposes correlates particularly closely with the many collections of *dhāraṇīs*, both sutras and spells. Often the precise contents reflect their owner's idiosyncratic purposes, but some circulated as standard sets, the best-known example being the *Pañcarakṣā*, a more or less fixed collection of five *dhāraṇī* sutras.[16] Collections of extracted spells only also circulated, like IOL Tib J 312, a *poti*-style book that includes mantras and *dhāraṇīs* for all sorts of curative, apotropaic, and mnemic purposes. Then there are mixed collections such as IOL Tib J 311 (fig. 1.3), containing both sutras and extracted spells. This manuscript opens with the line, "extracted for recitation, that is, as a daily commitment,"[17] and it closes to a similar effect: "This is the daily commitment of Venerable Sherap Pel."[18] Here we see that sutras and spells could be collected as liturgical texts, functioning in a daily practice.

Another way to engage with liturgical collections may have been for the reader to dip in to read specific parts. Pelliot tibétain 49 contains another collection of both sutras and extracted spells, with one item including both "the mantra and the ritual procedures extracted for ritual use."[19] Such procedures likely would seem not to have been extracted for daily recitation but for occasional use. Similarly, collections of multiple spells only such as IOL Tib J 312 may have been intended for selective use, with the reader reciting a particular spell depending on their circumstances. Liturgical collections of entire *dhāraṇī* sutras, called *dhāraṇīsaṃgraha*, suggest a vaguely similar use. The reader might first read some prayers that open the entire collection, then cut to the appropriate sutra, then jump to the closing prayers. When found in this form, the *dhāraṇīsaṃgraha* manuscripts generally lack

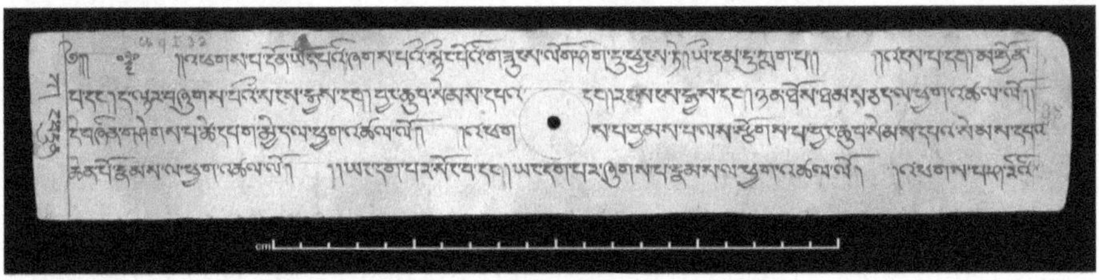

FIGURE 1.3 Mix of *dhāraṇī* sutras and spells
Source: IOL Tib J 311, Courtesy of the British Library

the merit dedications seen at the end of some of the individual *dhāraṇī* sutras. This makes some sense, as they were penned more for ritual use than for generating merit.

A standard format for the *dhāraṇīsaṃgraha* is discernible in a number of Dunhuang manuscripts, collections that begin with an invitation to the mundane gods and spirits, then provide the *dhāraṇīs* themselves, and finally close with a series of praises and prayers.[20] The full significance of this basic triadic structure becomes apparent when one sees that it also shapes the *dhāraṇī* section (itself called the *dhāraṇīsaṃgraha*) of the later Tibetan canons.[21] There too, the same invitation prayer (Q. 470–471) comes first, followed by all the *dhāraṇī* sutras, then a closing series of praises and prayers (Q. 710–729).[22] These clear parallels suggest that early *dhāraṇī* liturgical collections of the sort found in Dunhuang likely served as formal models for the later canons.

The invitation prayer that sometimes opens the collections was clearly popular, as a number of recensions appear in both the Dunhuang manuscripts and the later canons. The Dunhuang versions bear the title *An Invitation to the Great Gods and Nāgas* (*Lha klu chen po rnams spyan drang ba*), or sometimes just the *Rgyud gsum pa*, which I will not hazard to translate. As the title suggests, the invitations are directed to the mundane gods and spirits of the Indian pantheon, from Indra to the seven mothers (Skt. *saptamātaraḥ*), to come and observe the recitations of the *dhāraṇī* that will follow. Thus, the closing line of the prayer reads, "Listen all [of you] to these words of the profound conqueror."[23]

After the mundane gods had been invited, the *dhāraṇī* would be recited. This liturgical order is made explicit in one version of the *Invitation* prayer, Pelliot tibétain 25, where immediately following the final line commanding those summoned to listen, some additional instructions are given: "At this point," it says, "one reads the sutra, . . . those verses that were spoken [by the Buddha]."[24] The formal *dhāraṇī* collections were not simply canonical anthologies. They functioned as liturgies, compiled for recitation in a prescribed ritual order.

Further information on how these *dhāraṇī* collections were read can be gleaned from a detailed and unique commentary on the *Invitation* prayer that is also found among the Stein manuscripts in London. IOL Tib J 711 situates the *Invitation* within a familiar tantric narrative: in Vaiśālī there was once a prince who accomplished seven *samādhis* over the course of seven days.[25]

Having gained all the accomplishments (*siddhis*), he prostrated to the supreme nondual Buddha and caused all the gods and demons of the universe to tremble in fear. Now a wrathful *heruka* buddha, the prince rained down blazing vajras on the demons and bound them all to serve the Buddhist teachings. This is a full-blown tantric commentary on a prayer more commonly associated with the ritual recitation of *dhāraṇī* sutras. The myth of the mundane gods' subjugation implies that by reciting the *Invitation* prayer, the early Tibetan understood him- or herself to be calling upon the mundane gods and spirits to witness his or her recitations of the *dhāraṇī*. The summoned gods were then bound to serve the reciter thanks to their earlier subjugation by this mythic Vaiśālī prince.[26]

Given the readings of the *Invitation* seen in IOL Tib J 711, it would seem that the ritualized recitation of *dhāraṇīs* was a practice into which early Tibetans interpolated their tantric interests. The story of a *heruka* buddha taming the demon Rudra is the tantric myth par excellence; it is used to explain the power of the *dhāraṇīs* over the gods and demons of the mundane (*laukika*) world. Tantric myth is used to explain *dhāraṇī* ritual. As seen in this manuscript, some early Tibetans, at least, understood their liturgical *dhāraṇī* collections within a tantric mythological context. The extraordinary flexibility of liturgies, like ritual manuals, facilitated this creativity. In such extracanonical writings, authors were free to insert new elements, engage in intersectarian borrowing, and blur the lines between sutra and tantra.

A similar mixing of tantra with *dhāraṇī* sutra is seen in another liturgical format—the *tridaṇḍaka*. IOL Tib J 466 is a scroll that reads horizontally, which suggests a possibly early date (fig. 1.4). Its format makes it unlike the generally later scrolls that read vertically and often contain tantric or historical texts, and like the horizontal professionally scribed copies of the *Aparimitāyurnāma-mahāyāna-sūtra* written for merit in such great numbers in ninth-century Dunhuang.[27] There is no Chinese on the verso, suggesting again that this collection may date to the ninth century, when Tibetans had greater access to paper scrolls.[28]

In terms of content, IOL Tib J 466 includes a copy of the *Invitation to the Great Gods and Nāgas* as well as the *Uṣṇīṣavijayā dhāraṇī* spell, extracted from the sutra, and several other liturgical and *dhāraṇī*-related works. But for present purposes, most significant is the third item in the manuscript, the so-called *Rgyud chags gsum pa*, also known elsewhere as the *Rgyun chags gsum pa* and in Sanskrit as the *Tridaṇḍaka*. The *tridaṇḍaka*, possibly the "three

FIGURE 1.4 *Tridaṇḍaka* liturgy
Source: IOL Tib J 466, Courtesy of the British Library

sticks," is a three-part liturgical sequence that was well known in India. It is referred to multiple times in the *Mūlasarvāstivāda Vinaya* and appears to have been used in a variety of ritual contexts, from funerary rites to *caitya* (sacred site) worship to offering rites performed for a tree spirit before cutting down its tree.[29] In his late seventh-century *Record of the Buddhist Religion*, the Chinese master Yixing (635–713) attributes at least one version of a *tridaṇḍaka* to no less a personage than Aśvaghoṣa and describes its threefold structure as consisting of ten verses exalting the three jewels, followed by an unidentified work of *buddhavacana* ("the word of the Buddha") that is to be recited, and finally ten more lines of closing prayers and dedications.[30] Precisely which work is meant to be recited as the central text appears to be flexible. As Gregory Schopen has observed, Taishō 801 represents a version of the *tridaṇḍaka* that centers on a short sutra on impermanence, perhaps making it well suited for a funerary context.

IOL Tib J 466 is another version, compiled in Dunhuang or early Tibet, possibly (given the format of the manuscript) even dating from the late Tibetan imperial period of the first half of the ninth century. The three parts of this Tibetan *tridaṇḍaka* follow an order very similar to that described by Yixing. There are, however, some significant differences. The first part does indeed contain a series of praises to the three jewels, but here it follows the structure of the "seven-limbed worship," or *saptapūjā* (a.k.a. *anuttarapūjā*), a popular liturgical scheme seen already in some early (perhaps second century CE) Mahāyāna sutras, typically consisting of paying homage, confession, rejoicing in the merits of others, requesting to teach, asking the buddhas to remain in the world, stating the aspiration to awakening, and merit transfer. Also unusual is how this first *daṇḍaka* culminates in a recitation of the *Pūjāmegha-dhāraṇī*, thereby affecting the offerings promised in the preceding prayers. This first part is then followed by the central text to be recited, again just as Yixing describes, and the manuscript ends with a final section of closing prayers and dedications. Notably, each part begins with an instruction on how it should be recited: the first and last parts without a melody and the middle one accompanied by a melody (*dbyangs dang sbyar ba*) marking it as the sacred and well-spoken (*subhāṣita*) word of the Buddha.[31]

This second of the three parts, which in Yixing's description is open to ritual interpretation, consists of a long series of praises offered to an assortment of deities, teachers, and Buddhist patrons of the past, as well as "the teachers of our own Tibet" and even "the great king Tri Songdetsen," described as a "magically emanated lord . . . who has mastered the royal methods of fortune (*phywa*) and [rules] the kingdom with the sword of the sky gods."[32] This early Tibetan king is placed alongside some of the best-known Indian Buddhist kings, including Aśoka, Kaniṣka, and Harṣa Śīlāditya. Clearly the text was written, or at least supplemented significantly, within a Tibetan milieu.

Finally, this central text includes tantric deities in its praises. From the wrathful buddhas Trailokyavijaya and Yamāntaka to the female deities Māmakī and Mahāmāyūrī, "all the deities of the secret mandala" are named and venerated. To these are also added the local gods of Tibet. In this regard, this *Tridaṇḍaka* liturgy is similar to the commentary on the *Invitation* prayers examined above. In both, tantric elements are read into well-known and generally nontantric Indian ritual procedures. In both, liturgical manuals provide a space in which *dhāraṇī*s can be put into conversation with tantras. Liturgical works of this sort are extracanonical and for just this reason open to local innovations. Though closely linked to more canonical works that would have been closed to such changes, in early Tibet they provided a forum for new liturgical and ritual forms to be tested and kept or discarded. With this insight in mind, we may turn to a related genre of Buddhist texts that also seems to have enabled creative innovations among Buddhists of the sixth to tenth centuries and beyond: ritual manuals.

Dhāraṇī-Based Ritual Manuals

Distinct from what I am calling liturgies, which consist of *dhāraṇīsaṃgraha*, *tridaṇḍaka*, the seven-limbed *saptapūjā*, and other forms, are ritual manuals proper—Buddhist texts known as *vidhi*, *kalpa*, and the like that often were appended to or circulated alongside the *dhāraṇī* sutras. As we shall see, the line between liturgy and ritual manual is sometimes less than clear, as when ritual instructions are added to liturgies (e.g., the offering instructions found at the end of IOL Tib J 711, the commentary on the *Invitation* prayer) or conversely, when liturgies are embedded within ritual manuals (the seven-limbed worship appears regularly). IOL Tib J 687 represents a particularly unclear case—a three-folio sampling of teachings drawn from "sutra, *vinaya*, and commentarial treatises" (*mdo sde dang 'dul ba dang bstan bcos rnams las btus*) that was created for reading to householders and termed a *vidhi*.[33] Nonetheless, the liturgy-ritual manual distinction remains helpful. While both genres share much in terms of their uses, adaptability, and extracanonical status, ritual manuals, with their focus on carefully arranged ritual spaces and bodily activities, had a particularly strong impact on the development of Buddhist ritual practice.

A *dhāraṇī* sutra typically consists of two parts—the spell and the narrative that establishes both the setting (*nidāna*) and the various benefits that may be derived from the spell. In addition, some *dhāraṇī* sutras include a third part, a ritual section describing the rites associated with that particular spell. The ritual section is often marked off from the rest of the text in some way. In the *Amoghapāśahṛdaya-dhāraṇī*, the final title in the Dunhuang manuscript makes it explicit that the *vidhi* is an addendum of sorts (fig. 1.5): "So ends the *Ārya Avalokiteśvara Amoghapāśa Heart [Mantra]*, together with its *vidhi*." In the *Mahāpratisarā-vidyārājñī* (fig. 1.6), the *vidhi* is located in the middle of the text, but it closes with its own "the end" (*rdzogs so*), after which the text picks up again. Such awkward arrangements are even still preserved in some of the canonical *dhāraṇī* sutras. The *Mahāśītavana-sūtra* as represented in today's Peking canon, for example, includes a short *vidhi* tacked on at the end of the text, following the final praises and a small gap in the writing (fig. 1.7).

As we consider the awkward formats of the *vidhi* sections in so many *dhāraṇī* sutras, a pattern begins to emerge. Ritual manuals were often composed later, at some point after the early sutras had already been circulating, sutras that initially consisted of just the spell couched within a narrative

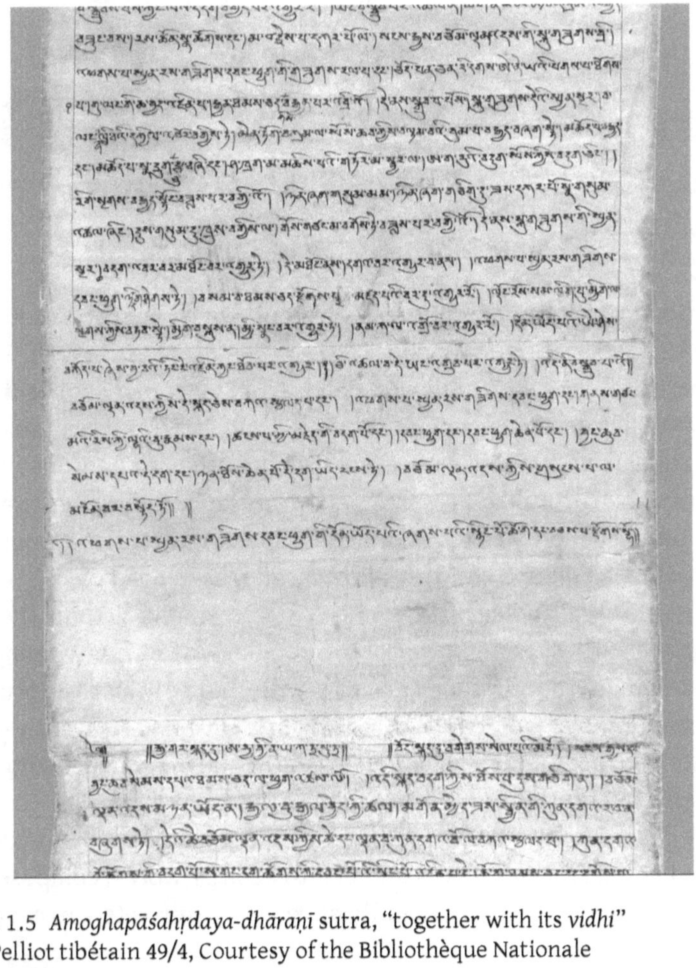

FIGURE 1.5 *Amoghapāśahṛdaya-dhāraṇī* sutra, "together with its *vidhi*"
Source: Pelliot tibétain 49/4, Courtesy of the Bibliothèque Nationale

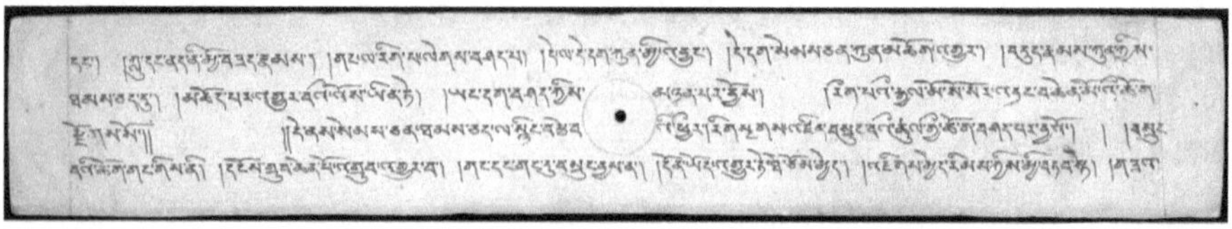

FIGURE 1.6 *Mahāpratisarā-vidyārājñī vidhi* in the middle of the sutra
Source: IOL Tib J 388, Courtesy of the British Library

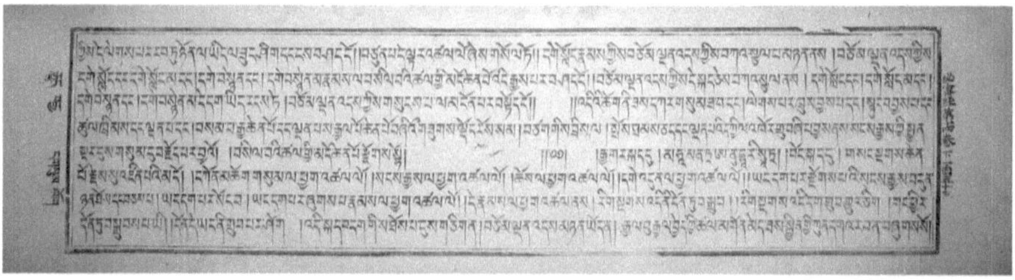

FIGURE 1.7 Final folio of the *Mahāśītavana-sūtra*
Source: Q. 180, Courtesy of the Buddhist Digital Archive

setting. Sometimes the manuals traveled outside their sutras; sometimes they were added to the sutras later.

The pattern may be discerned most clearly by comparing the different Chinese translations of a given sutra across time. Whereas Tibetans tended simply to update or replace their earlier translations with new ones, Chinese Buddhists were careful to preserve each translation, with the result that today's Chinese canon often includes multiple translations of a single sutra. By comparing these, one can track how a sutra developed over a period of centuries, and time and again, the same pattern emerges. Thus, the Taishō canon's three earliest translations of the popular *Mahāmāyūrīvidyārājñī* lack the ritual manual that first appears only with the early sixth-century Chinese translation by *Sanghabhara.[34] Similarly, Divākara's seventh-century translation of the Cundī *dhāraṇī* lacks the ritual manuals found in the eighth-century translations of Vajrabodhi and Amoghavajra.[35]

Some *dhāraṇī* sutras were composed from scratch with already well-integrated ritual sections, but these tend to be later works, composed after the sixth century.[36] And occasionally an entirely separate sutra was even written to present, in a more canonical format, the ritual procedures for a spell already presented in another *dhāraṇī* sutra. Gregory Schopen has observed that the *Samantamukha-praveśa* and the **Sarvaprajñā-dhāraṇīs* both deal with the same *dhāraṇī* spell, but the former is "almost entirely made up of narrative and lacks the detailed descriptions of the necessary ritual procedures. It does not have a *vidhi* section. What appears to be the *vidhi* section, however, is found in the *Śes pas thams cad* [=**Sarvaprajñā*], which—not surprisingly—contains very little narrative."[37] Schopen goes on to argue—on the basis of a scribal error in the copying of the spell—that the ritual text was probably written after the narrative *Samantamukha-praveśa*, probably between the sixth and ninth centuries.[38] Here, then, are two sutras sharing the same spell—the earlier one with just the spell embedded within a narrative, the later supplying the ritual section.

Despite such examples, the general trend was toward distinct ritual manuals that circulated outside of the sutra inspiring them. The significance of the difference between *dhāraṇī* sutras with and without ritual manuals is borne out in early Tibetan writings. The *Pangtangma* is a mid-ninth-century Tibetan catalogue of Buddhist translations that were circulating in Tibet at the time. It includes two lists of *dhāraṇī* sutras: those with *vidhi* attached and those without; some thirteen *dhāraṇī* sutras with ritual sections are listed.[39] Early Tibetan translators themselves, then, distinguished the *vidhi*-bearing sutras; they too recognized ritual manuals as addenda that changed the very nature of these works.

If Tibetan and Chinese cataloguers sometimes treated *vidhi* as an independent form of writing, there is some question how early medieval Indians saw the situation. In India, both *vidhi* and *kalpa* are commonly used in a somewhat broader sense, often better translated as "ritual procedure."[40] In such cases, a *vidhi* may not be a stand-alone text or even a clearly defined section of a larger work, but simply a set of practices for a particular purpose. This is noteworthy, as these two senses of the term—as procedure and as text—were not clearly distinguished in India. Nonetheless, the present study claims that the process by which such "procedures" beginning to circulate as independent texts was highly significant for the history of Buddhist ritual and should be recognized.[41]

The earliest *dhāraṇī* ritual manuals of the late fifth and sixth centuries revolve primarily around image worship.[42] Before then, *dhāraṇī* sutras recommended that their spells be recited within fairly simple circumstances. With relatively little attention paid to arranging a ritual space (it might be recommended that one sit in a sacred site marked by a stupa or a quiet spot), the spells were recited until the desired signs appeared. They might be recited over cords to be tied to the body, over waters to be sprinkled for protection, and so on, but as stand-alone *vidhis* are introduced, the reader is instructed to arrange a complex altar, termed a mandala. A Chinese rendition of such an altar is seen in a small drawing in the upper right-hand margin of a ninth-century Dunhuang painting on silk of Bhaiṣajyaguru's paradise (fig. 1.8).

Early *dhāraṇī*-style mandalas could be formed on raised platforms or directly on the ground, on a cleared piece of earth smeared with mud or cow dung (which is considered a cleansing substance and is used to this day to create clean, smooth floors in India).[43] Thus the *Jayavatī-nāma-mahāvidyārāja-dhāraṇī* directs the officiant simply to "spread a *maṇḍala* with cow dung,"[44] while the *Mahāvairocanābhisaṃbodhi* confirms that such altars were laid out on the ground: "Having firmly trodden down the site, the Master should smear it with cow dung that has not fallen to the ground mixed with cow

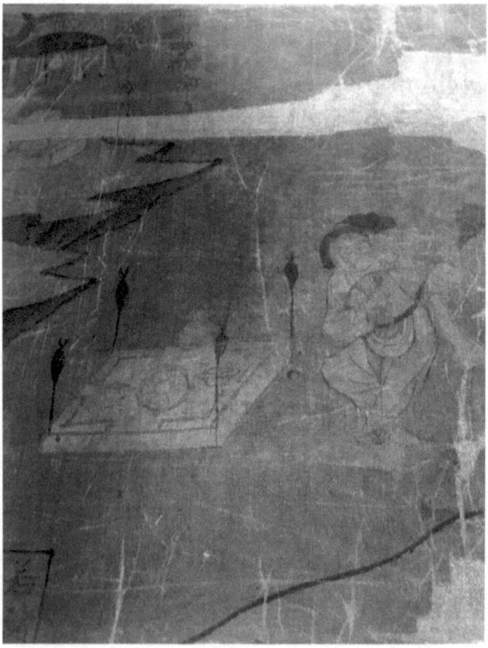

FIGURE 1.8 Image of a mandala altar from a Bhaiṣajyaguru painting
Source: BM 1919,0101,0.36, Courtesy of the British Museum

urine."[45] Other texts, however, recommend raised platforms for image worship. The Dunhuang Cave 427, which dates to the Sui (581–618 C.E.), includes a permanently installed small platform (a little over two feet square) in front of the central image that likely was used for precisely this purpose. While not of great interest to art historians, it is significant for the student of early ritual. Such archaeological evidence highlights the popular role of altar platforms of the sort seen in some *dhāraṇī* ritual manuals during the Sui or Tang.

At the center of the altar, a statue is usually placed or a painting is hung on the wall. This image constitutes the focus for the ritual performance. The *vidhi* section appended to the *Amoghapāśahṛdaya-dhāraṇī* provides a good example:

> Regarding the *vidhi*: A painter who has observed the eight precepts should paint an image of the Bhagavan Buddha, on cloth, with [paints] of various colors and a pure white. Paint the form of noble Avalokiteśvara, with long hair and ribbons, wearing an antelope skin and holding the accoutrements of Paśupati, and adorned with all the ornaments. Then, in front of that image, the practitioner should make a mandala of cow dung. He scatters flowers and places eight vases filled with perfumed water. Prepare the eight offerings, the sixty-four necessities, and the offering cakes free of flesh and blood. Fumigate with an incense of agarwood and perform the recitations of the knowledge mantra 8,000 times. The recitations should be performed by one who, for either one day or three days, has eaten the three kinds of white foods and bathed at the three daily times and who is wearing clean clothes. Then, before the image, gaze intensely. As one becomes joyful from that gazing, noble Avalokiteśvara himself comes and fulfills all wishes. If one recites the mantra over realgar or malachite, then rubs it on one's eyes, one will become invisible and fly through the sky. One will also attain the *samādhi* of the array of effective gnosis. Whatever one seeks to obtain will be attained.[46]

While many elements remain the same as in earlier *dhāraṇī* recitation practices, they are now performed before an image, in a carefully arranged ritual space. Buddha images had been part of the stone monuments of Buddhism since around the first century of the common era, but carefully scripted rites for the worship of images in temporary settings like this seem to have been something new. As *dhāraṇī vidhis* and the attendant creation and use of private images spread, fixed iconographies for specific deities began to be defined. "As the rituals came to focus on images," writes Shinohara, "the iconography of the deities would have become standardized, necessitating detailed instructions for painting them. The ritual specialists who performed the ceremony also, at least in theory, painted the images, but as the iconography became increasingly complex, the instruction may also have been directed to professional artists."[47] Such specificities, of iconography and ritual forms alike, were best transmitted in writing. Ritual manuals and complex image worship were in this sense like the proverbial chicken and egg; each required the other.

Precious few stand-alone *dhāraṇi* ritual manuals are to be found among the Tibetan Dunhuang manuscripts. We are left with those attached to sutras. Apparently by the ninth and tenth centuries, Tibetans preferred tantric ritual manuals. One rare example of a *dhāraṇī* manual is IOL Tib J 325/1236, titled "A Manual for the Four Activities of Uṣṇīṣasitātapatra" (*Gtsug tor gdugs dkar po las bzhi pa'i cho ga*), but even it shows the influence of tantric methods, from *mudrā* to *nyāsa*, *samaya*, and visualization.

The imposition of later, properly tantric elements onto *dhāraṇī*-based rituals is part of why Tibetans and modern scholars alike have been confused about the status of *dhāraṇī* sutras vis-à-vis tantric Buddhism. On their surface, they are largely indistinguishable from Mahāyāna sutras, but the fluidity of their ritual manuals made it easy for tantric elements to flow in. Amoghavajra, writing in the mid-eighth century, regularly read the Yoga tantra system of the *Sarvatathāgata-tattvasaṃgraha* into the *dhāraṇīs* for which he composed new manuals, explicitly distinguishing between his "Yoga system" and "the original teaching" of the *dhāraṇīs*.[48] But such a move was not unique to Amoghavajra. We have already seen how Tibetans similarly wrote tantric elements into both the *tridaṇḍaka* liturgy and the *Rgyud gsum pa* invitation prayer, and Indians themselves blurred the lines. The Padmasambhava-attributed commentary to the *Vajravidāraṇa-dhāraṇī*, for example, assumes an assortment of Yoga and Mahāyoga techniques, claiming that Śākyamuni pronounced the spell at Bodhgāya while in the form of Vajrapāṇi/Vajravidāraṇa at the center of a mandala, and so on.[49] Ritual manuals thus enabled authors to update the *dhāraṇī* sutras with the latest trends in ritual practice, even if those new rites may have been foreign in multiple ways to the original intent behind the sutras.

Dating the Spread of Buddhist Ritual Manuals

All this leads to a further question: When did these Buddhist manuals begin to spread in a significant way? Rituals were, of course, a part of Buddhism right from the beginning, the monastic ordination rites being a prominent example. The principal source for those, however, seems to have been the canonical *Vinaya*, not distinct manuals. Contemporary Theravada ordinations use *kammavaca* manuals, which consist of passages from the *Vinaya*, especially from the *Mahāvagga* volume where the most detailed descriptions of the ceremony are found, but there is little evidence of *kammavaca* in early Buddhism.[50] Another place to look for early ritual manuals might be in connection with the seven-limbed worship, mentioned above, but as Dan Stevenson, in tracing the roots of this liturgical sequence, has remarked, "the Indian sources are noticeably thin in liturgical content (rarely do we find what could be considered a full description of liturgical procedure)."[51]

The lack of ritual manuals in early Buddhism may be tied in part to how monks viewed their role in wider Indian society. Theirs was an ascetic order, and apart from funerals, their involvements in life-cycle rituals were limited. Even lay Indians who considered themselves Buddhists turned to other ritual specialists for their birth, puberty, and marriage rites. While some monks were obligated to attend such ceremonies, to maintain their relations with their lay patrons, they did so merely as guests and not as officiants. Thus, as Gombrich observes, "we find the *Vinaya* almost devoid of liturgy but full of prescriptions for table manners."[52] In short, while scattered ritual notes may have played a limited and now largely undetectable role in early Buddhist circles, the sudden and dramatic proliferation of increasingly elaborate manuals began only later.

To determine when this spread began, one may look once more to the Chinese canon, with its carefully dated translations. A survey of the collection indicates that ritual manuals first started to appear around the middle of the fifth century. Michel Strickmann has noted the anomalously early ritual techniques referenced in the Chinese apocryphal *Consecration Sutra* (*Guanding jing*), which dates from the second half of the fifth century, and a few ritual manuals from the same period may also be found.[53] A ritual section appears at the end of the *Dhāraṇī for Great Benefit*, supposedly translated by Tanyao in

462 C.E.[54] *Sanghabhara's above-cited translation of the *Mahāmāyūrī*, which includes an appended manual, dates to the early sixth century.[55]

Ritual manuals gained popularity through the next decades, and by the middle of the sixth century, Buddhist *vidhis* (mostly preserved now in the Chinese canon) were proliferating rapidly throughout India. Despite the possible existence of earlier notes in connection with ordination rites, the seven-limbed worship, or other simple procedures, this sudden expansion in the late fifth and sixth centuries was unprecedented. It is possible that certain kinds of Buddhist ritual manuals did circulate prior to the fifth-century *dhāraṇī* manuals but were not preserved. If true, this would be significant, for it would still indicate that the fifth and sixth centuries were when ritual manuals started to be preserved and entered the mainstream, orthodox Buddhist sphere. From this perspective, even though the *dhāraṇī* manuals were local and extracanonical, they were not entirely "unimportant." They represent a moment when Buddhist ritual procedures were becoming both complex and significant enough to be put into writing.

In any case, never before had such a number of manuals played such a central role in orthodox Buddhist practice. And compared to the earlier seven-limbed worship, the rites described in the manuals were far more complex and of a completely different order. No longer mere liturgies, the early *dhāraṇī* ritual manuals ordered their readers to arrange increasingly elaborate ritual spaces and perform carefully choreographed rites within them: prepare the ritual ground, construct an altar, hang banners, scatter flowers, sprinkle waters, and worship a central image while reciting the appropriate spells.[56]

Before long, these basic ritual forms were being varied according to the practitioner's desired results: practiced one way for curing disease, another for turning back curses, and so forth. And from these kinds of variable rites, it was a short step to the full-blown rituals the early tantras.

Ritual Manuals and Early Tantric Buddhism

The earliest Buddhist ritual manuals we know of circulated alongside *dhāraṇī* sutras, starting in the second half of the fifth century and dramatically proliferating through the sixth and into the seventh centuries. These *dhāraṇī*-based manuals provided an extracanonical, and thus highly malleable, literary space for Buddhists to adopt, adapt, and develop new ritual techniques. Their growth in the sixth century is of great significance for the history of tantric Buddhism, for within a hundred years of this date the first tantras began to appear. By the early seventh century, the first retroactively labeled "Kriyā tantras" were emerging in India, and by around 650 the seminal *Mahāvairocanābhisaṃbodhi* was in circulation.[57] The authors of these initial tantras looked for precedents not only to the sutras but also to the now ubiquitous genre of Buddhist ritual manuals. The eighth-century scholar Buddhagupta provides one of the earliest significant Indian discussions of the tantras as a whole. Having differentiated the Kriyā tantras from the slightly later Yoga tantras, he distinguishes two subclasses within the typically earlier Kriyā category: the "general tantras that are compilations of ritual manuals" (*spyi'i cho ga bsdus pa'i rgyud*) and the "distinct tantras" (*bye brag gi rgyud*).[58] Under the former type he lists the classic Kriyā sources such as the *Susiddhikara*, the *Subāhuparipṛcchā*, and the *Kalpalaghu*, all essentially compilations of ritual manuals.[59] Many of the earliest Kriyā tantras were simply collections, and in this sense, ritual manuals served as a kind of generic bridge between the earlier *dhāraṇī*s and the later tantras.[60]

Much ink has been spilled on the inherent difficulties of identifying the rise of tantric Buddhism with the advent of any one ritual practice, be it visualization, chanting mantras, or whatever.[61] Scholars observe that the accumulation of such supposedly "tantric" ritual techniques was really an extremely gradual process over many centuries. Yet only with the sixth century did the rapid proliferation of ritual manuals as a distinct genre begin. This new body of literature facilitated more complex ritual sequences, but it also required a new place in the Buddhist systems of canonical classification, and so were born the tantras. Here we should remember that tantras were texts, and their literary forbears were the ritual manuals.[62] In this sense, *dhāraṇī*s may not have been "proto-tantric," but ritual manuals were.[63]

In his 2002 book, *Indian Esoteric Buddhism*, Ronald Davidson traces the general outlines of the political sea changes in early medieval India. Building on the work of earlier Indian historians, he argues that the political fragmentation and socioeconomic regionalism of the period forced Buddhists to adopt new ritual strategies that mirrored the political models at work in the surrounding society. The tantric mandala replicated the organization of the Indian state, with the king at the center surrounded by his ministers and vassals. Ritual manuals played a necessary role in the Buddhist developments of Davidson's model as well; they were needed, for example, to conduct the complex new coronation-style initiation ceremonies. In this sense, shifting focus to ritual manuals does not contradict Davidson's model. Rather, the new manuals can be seen as just another part of the wider ritual changes he so ably describes.

But there is more. For Davidson, "It is only in the second half of the seventh century that the definitive esoteric system emerges,"[64] two centuries, in other words, after the ritual manuals began to spread. Again, a focus on ritual manuals adds another perspective and some further nuance. "Definitive" tantric Buddhism did not appear until the seventh century. However, when Davidson describes his "definitive esoteric system" in terms of a royal metaphor, he limits his narrative to no earlier than the second half of the seventh century. For only when the Yoga tantras began to appear did the royal rites and imagery really take center stage. Ritual manuals started to spread well before then, and these earlier *dhāraṇī*-based materials and some of the so-called Kriyā tantras exhibit far less interest in the kinds of politically inspired rites that Davidson emphasizes. Instead, the earliest Buddhist manuals are concerned more with image worship, preparing the ritual space, and bodily purification, all for the purpose of blessing buildings, curing diseases, and so on. Another explanation is required for the appearance of these "proto-tantras," the early ritual manuals that were so widespread already a century or more before the first Yoga tantras.

With a focus on ritual manuals, the emergence of esoteric Buddhism becomes more affair than Davidson describes. The rise of his esoteric Buddhism is "precipitous," a surprisingly sudden phenomenon "effected in decades, not centuries."[65] Because of his focus on tantric ideology, Davidson concludes that "In the course of a few decades in the mid-seventh century, the most effective strategies for Buddhist support had come unraveled." Such a sudden socioeconomic shift seems improbable. Indeed, Davidson himself traces the causes for this shift to the fall of the Gupta empire, an event that occurred much earlier, in the late fifth and early sixth centuries. The rise of India's early medieval feudalism, as he himself emphasizes, began well before the mid-seventh century, having roots already in the Gupta period.[66] We would do better, then, to understand the appearance of the Buddhist tantras as the culmination of a longer and more gradual process. By highlighting the role of ritual manuals, a more nuanced story is revealed, unfolding over a period of two hundred years, from the mid-fifth to the mid-seventh centuries.

The genre of *dhāraṇī* ritual manuals thus offers an invaluable window onto the development of early tantric Buddhist ritual techniques. Through these texts we can catch a glimpse of a formative period when Buddhist ritual was in full flux. The long-lost manuals from Dunhuang attest to the powerful influence of local innovation and individual practice upon the development of the Tibetan Buddhist tradition. Only the *dhāraṇī*-based ritual manuals and liturgical collections, thanks to their fluid and individualizable character, could allow for the innumerable creative mutations that were necessary for the tantras to evolve.

TWO

From *Dhāraṇī* to Tantra

The Sarvadurgatipariśodhana

WITH THE RISE of the tantras in the seventh and eighth centuries, Buddhist ritual became thoroughly entwined with new mythic narratives. As tantric practitioners began to identify with specific buddhas, they sought to emulate those buddhas' mythic activities. Just as Śākyamuni generated himself as Mahāvairocana atop Mount Meru, so did the *sādhaka* (i.e., the practitioner); just as Trailokyavijaya tamed the demon Maheśvara, so did the *vajrācārya*. A devotee's introduction to this mythic world occurred with his initiation into the mandala of a particular ritual system. Through *abhiṣeka* (initiation), the disciple was led into the imaginative world of tantric myth.

This chapter examines a manual for the performance of initiation. The manual opens with a mythic narrative, a story probably meant to be read aloud to those gathered, that at once explains the Buddha's original performance of the rites and brought the assembled into a shared mythic time and space, infusing the proceedings with sacred significance beyond the mundane present. It is recommended that the reader turn to the translation that follows this chapter and read at least the opening myth of the god named Vimalaprabha, who dies and is saved.

Narrative Continuities Between the *Uṣṇīṣavijayā-dhāraṇī* and the *Sarvadurgatipariśodhana*

The myth forms the framing narrative of the *Sarvadurgatipariśodhana-tantra* (*Purification of All Negative Rebirths Tantra*), as told at the beginning of a Dunhuang manual now divided across two shelf marks at the British Library. Together, IOL Tib J 712 and IOL Tib J 439 form a single original manuscript of sixteen folios, containing an initiation manual for the *Sarvadurgatipariśodhana* mandala (fig. 2.1). The manuscript is nearly complete; likely only a single folio is missing from the end, interrupting some appended ritual notes on the mantras needed for various specific acts, such as constructing the altar, laying the chalk lines, and so on.[1] The main text itself is intact. The manuscript could have been penned in the ninth or the tenth century (probably the latter), but in either case, the rites described likely reflect a somewhat earlier period of Indian ritual development, around the eighth century.[2] The text itself is probably a Tibetan composition, though some passages may be copied from other manuals traceable to Tibetan translations of Indic works. The text lacks any title (a further indication of its Tibetan origin), but it belongs to the subgenre of mandala ritual manuals (Tib. *dkyil chog*; Skt. *maṇḍalavidhi*) or perhaps initiation ritual manuals (Tib. *dbang chog*; Skt. *abhiṣekavidhi*), for constructing mandalas and initiating others into them. The proceedings therefore constitute a group performance, to be officiated by a ritual master (Tib. *slob dpon*; Skt *ācārya*). Tantric initiation into a given mandala is normally required before the initiate can perform daily rites, but this manual also emphasizes the initiation's more immediate purificatory and liberative aspects. As we shall see, this is partly because of its dual purpose as a funerary rite.

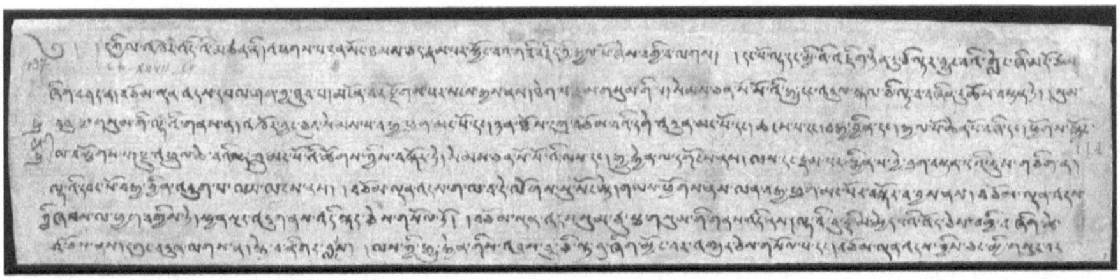

FIGURE 2.1 Sarvadurgatipariśodhana initiation manual
Source: IOL Tib J 439, Courtesy of the British Library

The narrative is largely faithful to that which opens the early translation of the *Sarvadurgatipariśodhana-tantra* itself. There too, Śakra, Lord of Trāyastriṃśa heaven, questions the Buddha about the *devaputra* (son of a god) Vimalamaṇiprabha (instead of our manuscript's Vimalaprabha), who has died and passed out of the god realm, leaving his companions alarmed and wondering about the fate of their compatriot, and about the workings of karma and rebirth more generally. As in the Dunhuang telling, the Buddha responds by teaching the rites for the *Sarvadurgati* mandala. The backstory about the unfortunate *devaputra*'s past life as a patricidal prince likewise appears in the tantra, but elsewhere, not in the opening *nidāna* but in the second chapter; the details are largely the same. In weaving together the two accounts, of Vimalamaṇiprahba's death and rebirth and his activities in his previous life, into one, this narrative is unique. It does change some details, altering names and adding specifics of dialogue to breathe life into the story, but in a skillful and, if the tantra is taken as the yardstick, generally accurate way.

That said, there are a few anomalous elements. First is the Buddha's emission and contraction of light rays from his topknot (*uṣṇīṣa*) to divine Vimalamaṇiprabha's future rebirths, which does not appear in the tantra. Second, and of even more interest, are the results of this divination. In the root tantra, in responding to Śakra's question about the *devaputra*'s karmic fate, the Buddha describes thousands of years he will spend in the hells, as animals and hungry ghosts, and as humans plagued by ignorance and disease. "From one to the next, he will continually experience suffering," the tantra's Buddha concludes.[3] In our Dunhuang account, the Buddha's topknot divination reveals a similar list of rebirths, but following the future existences as hungry ghosts and animals it adds a further, more specific list of animal rebirths, as "a dog, a pig, an antelope, a monkey, a crow, a cat, a snake, and so on." This is oddly redundant, given that the unfortunate soul will only just have escaped from the animal realm.

The insertion of the passage here may be explained by reference to another work: the *Uṣṇīṣavijayā-dhāraṇī*. The *Uṣṇīṣavijayā* (Conquering Topknot) is a *dhāraṇī* sutra that enjoyed considerable popularity across Asia in the seventh and eighth centuries.[4] Like the *Sarvadurgatipariśodhana*, it opens with a narrative about the death of a *devaputra* and Śakra's request to the Buddha to save him. In the *dhāraṇī*, the *devaputra* (there named Supratiṣṭhita) is visited by a voice that tells him he will die in seven days. He will then, the voice continues, suffer seven states of rebirth before being further reborn in the hells for hundreds of lifetimes, interrupted only occasionally by rebirths as a human suffering from poverty and blindness. Supratiṣṭha hastens to Śakra, the chief of the gods, and asks him what to do. Now it is Śakra who enters a prophetic state and announces that the *devaputra*'s first seven rebirths will be as a pig, a dog, a jackal, a monkey, a snake, a vulture, and a crow. Seeing this, Śakra turns to the Buddha, worships him with circumambulations and prostrations, as in the narrative above, and asks him to intervene. It is therefore possible that the author of the Dunhuang narrative was reading this element from the *Uṣṇīṣavijayā* into the *Sarvadurgatipariśodhana*'s story about Vimalamaṇiprabha.

A similar case of narrative interpolation occurs at the end of the narrative. After Vimalamaṇiprabha is freed from his negative rebirths and reestablished in heaven, he cries out in praise, "Ah the Buddha! Ah the dharma! Ah the *saṇgha*!"[5] Again, this line—or one like it—appears not in the tantra but only in the sutra, at precisely the same point, when Supratiṣṭha is freed from his own negative births and proclaims, "Ah the Buddha! Ah the dharma! Ah the appearance in the world of such a *dhāraṇī*!"[6] The last phrase would have been inappropriate in the tantra, so *dhāraṇī* may have been changed to the obvious choice of the *saṇgha*. We may conclude that the author of our Dunhuang narrative was familiar with the *Uṣṇīṣavijayā* and in his synthetic rendering understood the stories of the sutra and the tantra as overlapping.

There is another possibility, that still other sutras and other narratives stood between the *Uṣṇīṣavijayā-dhāraṇī* and our manuscript's retelling. There seems to have been quite a tangle of intertextuality surrounding the story. Renditions of the *devaputra* narrative, sharing many of the same basic elements, are seen in numerous Tibetan writings of the period, as well as in several Indian texts. Both the tantra and especially the *dhāraṇī* sutra appear to have been regularly used and reworked, existing in multiple and variant versions, and still other *dhāraṇī* sutras included more tellings. The *Samantamukha-praveśaraśmi-vimaloṣṇīṣa* (henceforth just *Vimaloṣṇīṣa*), for example, opens with the story of another *devaputra*, this time named *Vimalamaṇigarbha (Nor bu'i snying po dri ma med pa), who learns he will die in seven days. He goes to Śakra, who sends him to the Buddha for the teaching on how to save him. The Buddha sends forth light rays from his *uṣṇīṣa*, illuminating the entire universe, then retracts them, whereupon they circle him three times before disappearing into his mouth. He then tells the hapless god of his future rebirths, one of which is as a large fish that is eaten by seven kinds of animals: a poisonous snake, a crow, a weasel, a dog, a leopard, a bear, and a jackal. Here, then, may be a source for our own narrative's Buddha using similar light rays to divine the *devaputra*'s future rebirths, though the *Vimaloṣṇīṣa* says nothing about the significance of where the rays re-enter the Buddha's body. Finally, upon being saved, the *Vimaloṣṇīṣa*'s *devaputra* exclaims, "Ah the Buddha! Ah the *vidyā mantra*! Ah the dharma!"[7] Once more, we see familiar elements at work, and it is difficult to tell which of the two works—the *Uṣṇīṣavijayā* or the *Vimaloṣṇīṣa*—was more influential upon the Dunhuang author.

Early Tibetan Buddhists too retold the story in a variety of ways. IOL Tib J 384 contains another *Sarvadurgati* initiation manual that includes a rendition of the narrative, though shorter and less well formed (fig. 2.2). The main protagonist remains Vimalamaṇiprabha, but other characters, especially in the backstory about the patricidal prince, have different names. (The tantra itself provides names only for the prince and the hermit; only its hermit's name, Needless Love [Dgos pa myed par byams pa], matches our own manuscript's telling.) IOL Tib J 384 also includes a list of six (not seven) animal realms, though the animals are different and now represent the rebirths that will be suffered by the patricidal prince immediately upon his death, rather than by the *devaputra* following his.[8]

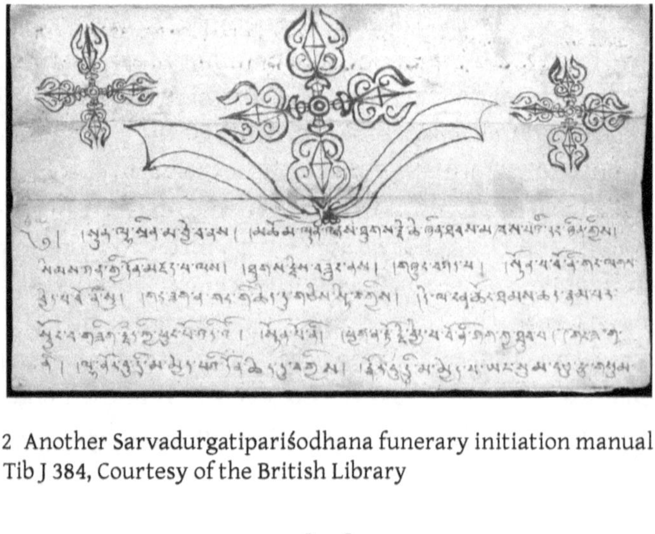

FIGURE 2.2 Another Sarvadurgatipariśodhana funerary initiation manual
Source: IOL Tib J 384, Courtesy of the British Library

But perhaps the most unusual Tibetan retelling of the story appears in the much-discussed *Story of the Cycle of Birth and Death* (*Skye shi'i lo rgyus*). This was a popular text among early Tibetan Buddhists; no fewer than eight copies appear among the Dunhuang manuscripts.[9] The work's stated purpose is to replace the pre-Buddhist funerary practices of the Bon with Buddhist rites. It offers a narrative history in which the king of gods, King of Blazing Light ('Od bar rgyal), suddenly dies, leaving his son Rinchen (Jewel) to mourn him. Rinchen goes to the god (*'phrul chen*) Dutara, who, playing a role parallel to that of Śakra, teaches Rinchen the law of karma and rebirth but explains that he cannot remedy the situation himself. He therefore sends Rinchen on a pilgrimage, loosely based on that of Sudhana in the *Gaṇḍavyūhasūtra*. Following the god's instructions, Rinchen visits twenty-five different teachers, finally reaching Śākyamuni, who teaches him the rites for the *Uṣṇīṣavijayā dhāraṇī*, which closely match those in the sutra with that name.

Yoshirō Imaeda argues that the *Story*'s opening narrative was based in part upon the *Sarvadurgatipariśodhana*. He points to the similarities of the names of the king (King of Blazing Light) and the prince (Jewel) to that of Vimalamaṇiprabha (Stainless Jewel Light).[10] While this argument is not entirely airtight, it is true that the king of gods does actually die, rather than simply being warned of his approaching death as in the *Uṣṇīṣavijayā-dhāraṇī*. In this regard, at least, the narrative resembles that of the *Sarvadurgatipariśodhana*.[11] Imaeda also notes that the *Story* was sometimes transmitted alongside another work, the *Teaching on the Path to the Land of the Gods* (*Lha yul du lam bstan pa*). This text too focuses on replacing the pre-Buddhist funerary rites with Buddhist versions, and it offers the mantra of the *Sarvadurgatipariśodhana* as its foremost formula for guaranteeing rebirth as a god.[12] The connections between the *Story* and this work have, however, been questioned. At the end of the day, it is clear that the *Story of the Cycle of Birth and Death* is based on the *Uṣṇīṣavijayā*; its reliance on the *Sarvadurgatipariśodhana* is considerably less sure.

Ritual Continuities Between the *Uṣṇīṣavijayā-dhāraṇī* and the *Sarvadurgatipariśodhana*

In fact, the *Uṣṇīṣavijayā-dhāraṇī* and the *Sarvadurgatipariśodhana* are linked in ways beyond just their opening narratives. A close relationship is indicated already by the *dhāraṇī*'s full title in the Tibetan canon—the *Sarvadurgatipariśodhana-uṣṇīṣavijayā-dhāraṇī*, or the *Dhāraṇī of the Conquering Uṣṇīṣa That Purifies All Negative Rebirths.*[13] Ronald Davidson, in his work on early tantric sources in Chinese, has identified *uṣṇīṣa*-focused materials that survive in over a dozen texts dating from the seventh century. Taken together, they represent "arguably the earliest surviving integrated system of Buddhist tantric practice, one that did not continue intact but was eclipsed by more popular systems from the eighth century forward. Yet for almost a hundred years, it was perhaps the best represented of tantric Buddhist ritual traditions."[14] Both the *Uṣṇīṣavijayā-dhāraṇī* and the *Sarvadurgatipariśodhana*—and for that matter, the *Vimaloṣṇīṣa-dhāraṇī*—are products of this same line of ritual development.[15]

Several ritual connections between the *Uṣṇīṣavijayā-dhāraṇī* and the *Sarvadurgatipariśodhana-tantra* are also suggested by the ritual manuals surrounding the *dhāraṇī*. Within the Dunhuang archive, we see the influence of these manuals in a relatively well-known Chinese altar diagram for the recitation of the *Uṣṇīṣavijayā-dhāraṇī* (fig. 2.3).[16] Around the central buddha statue, which sits in the middle of the altar, are arranged the expected flowers and incense as well as votive oil lamps and containers of water. On the lotus seats in each corner are also arranged four ancillary buddhas. Immediately before the altar (at the bottom of the diagram) sits the ritual master, with an incense burner behind him.

Unfortunately, no ritual manual precisely matching the diagram has been identified among the Dunhuang manuscripts—a further sign of the diversity of the ritual manuals surrounding the *Uṣṇīṣavijayā*. The *dhāraṇī* itself includes a *vidhi* section that the Buddha teaches in response to a request from the Four Great Kings (*rgyal po chen po bzhi*).[17] Initially, the Buddha instructs them to bathe, put on new clothes, uphold the precepts, and recite the spell 1,008 times on the fifteenth day of the lunar month. Following an explanation of the benefits that might result, the Buddha continues with some further instructions on what to do for a person who has died: "Recite the spell twenty-one times over some clean white mustard seeds, then scatter them over their bones. Then, through the power of this spell, they will be delivered from negative rebirths, be they rebirths in hell, rebirth as an animal, in the realm of Yāma, as a hungry ghost, or whichever evil realm that was otherwise suitable. And having been delivered from those [realms], they will

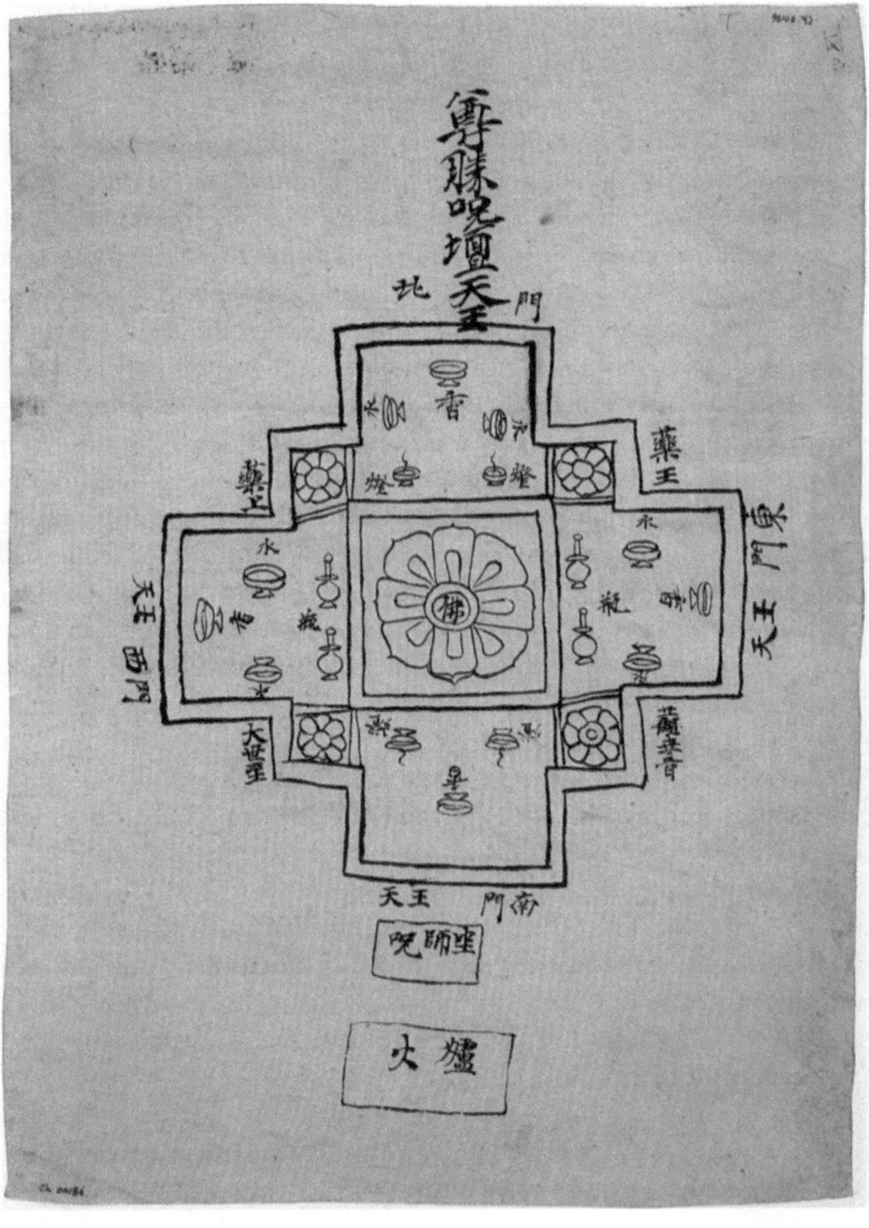

FIGURE 2.3 Chinese Uṣṇīṣavijayā altar diagram
Source: Stein painting 174, BM no. 1919,0101,0.174, Courtesy of the British Museum

be born as a god."[18] At this point, the altar rite is introduced, here translated from the Tibetan Dunhuang version. This is the same ritual with which Imaeda's *Story of the Cycle of Life and Death* culminates:

> To focus one's attention on this *dhāraṇī*, one should make a square altar platform (*maṇḍala*). Worship and make offerings to it with many different kinds of flowers and many different kinds of incense. Kneeling with right knee on the ground, focus intently on all the *tathāgatas*. With one's hands for this *mudrā*: join the palms and, bending the two index fingers from the top, wrap them under the two thumbs, then snap the fingers. Then at that time, recite the *dhāraṇī* 108 times. As soon as that is recited, *tathāgatas* as numerous as the grains in sixty-eight hundreds of thousands of hundreds of millions of Ganges rivers are respectfully paid reverence, and all the *tathāgatas* are worshipped with great offerings. Words then emerge from those [*tathāgatas*]: "Excellent! Sentient beings should know this one to be a child who is born from all the *tathāgatas*!" One becomes endowed with unobscured gnosis and attains being ornamented with a mind of *bodhicitta*. Lord of gods, if one performs the ritual procedures (*vidhi*) for accomplishing this *dhāraṇī* and the methods regarding the correct materials, sentient beings will be delivered from all rebirths (*rgyud*) in the hells and so on, and thenceforth will be liberated from those and be long-lived.[19]

This is informative, but the procedure's altar still lacks the offering lamps and waters, not to mention the surrounding deities, depicted in the Chinese diagram.

An altar with vaguely similar offerings appears in a second *Uṣṇīṣavijayā-dhāraṇī* in the Tibetan canon. Titled the *Sarvatathāgatoṣṇīṣavijayā-nāma-dhāraṇī-kalpasaṃhitā* (*Dhāraṇī of Uṣṇīṣavijayā of All the Tathāgatas, Together with the Ritual Manual*),[20] the work centers on the same *Uṣṇīṣavijayā dhāraṇī* spell, but (as the title suggests) contains a more elaborate ritual manual section that begins as follows:

> With cow dung that is [gathered] without it hitting the ground, make a square maṇḍala and scatter it with white flowers. Place oil lamps with melted butter in the four corners. Make an incense of aloe and fir. Adorn with flowers vessels filled with water that has been similarly perfumed. In the center, place a *stūpa* or a statue containing the heart *dhāraṇī*. While touching it with one's left hand and holding a rosary in one's right, recite the *dhāraṇī* twenty-one times at the three

> times of each day. Then, if one drinks the offering waters in three sips from cupped hands, one will have no illness, one's life will be long, one's enemies will fade, one's intellect will be sharp and speech noble. If one sprinkles those waters around a barn or stables or around a royal palace, there need be no fear of thieves, snakes, spirits, or demons, and there will be no afflictions from illness. If one sprinkles them over someone's head, that person will be cured of any illness. In that way, for whomever and wherever this greatly beneficial *dhāraṇī* for endless life is applied, there will be great peace. If it is recited twenty-one times over a tooth stick, then, when the stick is used, there will be no illness, one will be sharp-witted and have a long life.[21]

The general correspondences between this passage and the Dunhuang diagram provide some idea of how the Dunhuang artist might have intended his drawing to be used, with the consecration of waters playing a particularly important role. A ritual manual resembling the one embedded in this Tibetan *Dhāraṇī-kalpasaṃhitā* sutra, though with additional buddhas located in the corners of the altar, appears have been known to the Chinese Buddhists around Dunhuang. Indeed, it seems that an array of manuals circulated around the main *Uṣṇīṣavijayā-dhāraṇī* sutra from quite early on. Eventually some came to be formulated as independent sutras, as in our anomalous *Dhāraṇī-kalpasaṃhitā*, found in today's *Bka' 'gyur*, but most remained simple manuals.[22]

We still have no precise textual match for the altar as it is depicted in the Dunhuang diagram. The Tibetan "*kalpasaṃhitā*" *dhāraṇī* sutra does not mention the four surrounding deities in the corners of the altar. The Chinese canon includes several additional *Uṣṇīṣavijayā* ritual manuals that place ancillary deities on the altar, but not the same ones. The *Uṣṇīṣavijayā* manual attributed to Amoghavajra (T. 972), the tantric master of Tang China, even describes an altar in a three-by-three arrangement of nine squares, but in place of the offerings and buddhas that surround the central image it has the well-known set of eight bodhisattvas.[23]

In terms of ritual activities, Amoghavajra describes rites that are drawn more from the influential system of the *Vajroṣṇīṣa*, the so-called "root tantra" of the class of Yoga tantras. Amoghavajra thus read his favored tantric techniques back into the *Uṣṇīṣavijayā dhāraṇī*. He makes this explicit when, in the context of determining the proper time for the performance, he writes,

> As for fixing the time, [it may be performed] either twice a day, namely at dawn and dusk, or three times, in which case one adds noon, or four sessions as in the Yoga system, in which case one adds midnight. If one is staying with the original teaching of the *Vijayā Dhāraṇī* and reciting on the fifteenth day of the waxing moon [i.e., of the first half of the month] in order to remove the karmic hindrances, increase merit, and prolong life, then it is important to recite 1,000 times.[24]

The Yoga system Amoghavajra refers to here is certainly that of the *Vajroṣṇīṣa*, also known as the *Sarvatathāgata-tattvasaṃgraha*, in which the four sessions (morning, noon, evening, and midnight) are central.[25]

Still another Chinese canonical manual for the recitation of the *Uṣṇīṣavijayā-dhāraṇī* is attributed to the Indian master Śubhākarasiṃha, active in China in the early eighth century, just a few decades before Amoghavajra. The writings of Śubhākarasiṃha provide many valuable insights into the early formation of tantric Buddhism. Like Amoghavajra, Śubhākarasiṃha read later tantric developments into his *Uṣṇīṣavijayā* manual, but unlike Amoghavajra's, his are allied less with the *Sarvadurgatipariśodhana* than with the *Mahāvairocanābhisaṃbodhi*.[26] This makes some sense, as Śubhākarasiṃha collaborated with the Chinese translator Yixing to translate and compose an extensive commentary on it.[27] Thus, where Amoghavajra surrounds the central buddha with the eight great bodhisattvas of the *Vajroṣṇīṣa*, Śubhākarasiṃha recommends a set of eight *uṣṇīṣa* buddhas, with Vairocana at the center, Uṣṇīṣavijayā or Vikīraṇoṣṇīṣa to the east, Vijayoṣṇīṣa to the south, Tejorāśyuṣṇīṣa to the west, Sitātapatra to the north, and then in the intermediate directions, Mahoṣṇīṣa in the southeast, Anantasvaraghoṣa in the southwest, Abhyudgatoṣṇīṣa in the northwest, and Jayoṣṇīṣa in the northeast.[28] This same set of buddhas appears in the *Mahāvairocana-abhisaṃbodhi*, in chapter 2, which describes the mandala for that system.[29] Here again, an author reads tantric elements back into a *dhāraṇī* ritual manual. And once again, ritual manuals provided a space for the blurring of the lines between *dhāraṇī* sutra and tantra.

The existence of an *Uṣṇīṣavijayā* mandala with Vairocana at the center, surrounded by eight *uṣṇīṣa* buddhas, gains significance when we turn to the *Sarvadurgatipariśodhana* mandala described in both the Dunhuang initiation manual and the tantra itself. In the main mandala described in the tantra's second chapter, Śākyamuni is at the center, surrounded by eight *uṣṇīṣa* buddhas. Their precise identities vary slightly between this canonical mandala and that of Śubhākarasiṃha's *Uṣṇīṣavijayā* manual, but six of them overlap, and it is evident that they are the same basic group. There is also the difference in the central deities—Vairocana in Śubhākarasiṃha's manual and Śākyamuni in the tantra—though the tantra's first chapter describes another mandala with Sarvavid-Vairocana at its center (but without the eight *uṣṇīṣa* buddhas), and among the Dunhuang manuscripts are numerous drawings of the *Sarvadurgatipariśodhana* mandala with Vairocana at the center, surrounded by the eight *uṣṇīṣa* buddhas. All this is to say that the differences between the mandalas in Śubhākarasiṃha's manual and in the tantra all fall within a familiar range of variation.

We are left with a striking possibility: that the *Uṣṇīṣavijayā-dhāraṇī* and the *Sarvadurgatipariśodhana-tantra* are related in more ways than one, and that the developmental bridges linking them are, in part, the multiple ritual manuals that grew up around the *dhāraṇī*, most clearly represented by Śubhākarasiṃha's early eighth-century manual.[30] Given that both works were products of the early *uṣṇīṣa* buddha tradition identified by Davidson and shared similar framing narratives and ritual aims, that Śubhākarasiṃha's *Uṣṇīṣavijayā* manual describes a mandala that is remarkably close to the one in the tantra, and that Tibetans and possibly Indians too saw the narrative and ritual elements as interchangeable, we may surmise that the tantra emerged out of a ritual matrix defined in part by the *Uṣṇīṣavijayā-dhāraṇī*. The narrative with which the Dunhuang initiation manual opens stands as a reflection of this historical relationship.

The Narrative and the Ritual

The story of Vimalaprabha comprises the first of seven topics (*don bdun*) that form a kind of introduction to the work's initiation rite. Following the narrative setting (*gleng gzhi*), the remaining six topics are (2) the necessary ritual materials; (3) the propitiation rite (Tib. *bsnyen pa*; Skt. *sevā*); (4) the etymology of "mandala" and *dkyil 'khor* (i.e., the Tibetan translation of "mandala");[31] (5) the preparatory rites (*sta gon*); (6) the generation of *bodhicitta*; and (7) the benefits (*phan yon*) of performing the rite. The second topic, preparing the materials, starts with an unidentified citation (or perhaps just an "it is said") explaining that in constructing the original mandala platform, the Four Great Kings gathered the five kinds of jewels—gold dust, silver dust, and so on.[32] But for patrons of lesser means, clean earth and powdered stones are sufficient for attaining the *siddhis*, if they perform the visualizations and dedications purely. At this point, the manual moves from the mythic events of the past to the preliminary rites with the words, "As for practicing in the present, . . ."[33] Going forward, the rites are presented in the third person, to be performed by a "master" (*slob dpon*) or "mantra expert" (*sngags mkhan*) on behalf of his patron (Tib. *yon bdag*; Skt. *yajamāna*). After addressing the next four topics, the narrative reaches the final one:

> Now the seventh topic, explaining the benefits (*phan pa*): In accordance with what has been discussed above, the *devaputra* Vimalaprabha, having been freed from his negative rebirths, took the body of a god in the heavens of blissful rebirth and remained in a blissful state of mind. In the same way, through the compassion and blessings of all the noble ones, the current patron too, wherever he may be residing, in the realms of negative rebirths or wherever, will have his mind purified today. Therefore, through the patron's preparing the materials, the compassion of all the noble ones, and the master's intention, [the patron] will be led into the mandala, granted the initiations, and cleansed, whereby, without any doubt whatsoever, the *siddhis* will be attained for [rebirth] in the heavens of blissful rebirth. These are the benefits.[34]

As the manual transitions from its introductory discussions of the mythic narrative and the instructions for the presiding ritual master, it draws an explicit parallel between the Buddha's original acts in the mythic past and the master's present rites for the patron. The world of tantric myth thus breathes life into the present performance.

The practice of reciting a narrative to illustrate the benefits of a ritual to follow has been discussed by several scholars of early Tibetan religion.[35] Pre-Buddhist Tibetan ritual often unfolded within the narrative space of the *smrang*, *rabs*, or *lo rgyus*. In his recent study of both pre-Buddhist and Buddhist funerary rituals from Dunhuang, Brandon Dotson describes these "antecedent tales," to be recited before or during the rituals, "as mimetic templates for ritual practice, in which present-day priests and patients are invited to identify with their heroic, mythical antecedents."[36] Thus, he concludes, "The tale closes with a formula that relates it to the present as an antecedent for success. In its simplest form, this statement of relevance declares, 'what was beneficial in ancient times shall be beneficial now; what was successful in ancient times shall be successful now.'"[37]

Given such formulas, the influence of Tibetan tastes may have shaped the explanation of the seventh topic. Indeed, the very subject of benefits (*phan yon*) may be a partial echo of the Tibetan word used in Dotson's pre-Buddhist formula, *phan pa*, "beneficial." Just as Vimalaprabha was saved, our manual's statement reads, "through the compassion and blessings of all the noble ones, the current patron too, wherever he may be residing, in the realms of negative rebirths or wherever, will have his mind purified today." (It is possible that the "patron," i.e., the initiate, is dead, as discussed below.) This passage closes the seven-part introduction and thus marks a transition to the proceedings proper, playing a role not unlike the line, "what was beneficial in ancient times shall be beneficial now."

This said, the framing of Buddhist ritual as a reenactment of events that took place during the Buddha's lifetime (or in the buddhafields of other buddhas) is not unique to Tibet. With tantric Buddhism and the practitioner's imagined union with the deity, such reenactments came to play an especially important role in Buddhist ritual. The eighth-century Buddhagupta, writing on the *Mahāvairocanābhisaṃbodhi-tantra*, explains, "The Bhagavan Vairocana is to be viewed as like the accomplishing practitioner. . . . This also indicates to future disciples that they should make themselves appear in the body image of their own deity."[38] Discussions of the benefits (Skt. *anuśaṃsa*) of hearing the dharma, meditating, and performing rites have also long been part of Indian Buddhism, often in connection to the framing narratives (*nidāna*) that open so many sutras and tantras.[39] Practitioners mimicking the Buddha's actions described in canonical narratives was therefore already a well-established part of Buddhism in India.

One aspect of indigenous Tibetan antecedent tales that is less commonly seen in tantric Indian charter myths is their ritualized retelling for each rite performed.[40] In this regard too, however, our manual may be a particularly close match. It is quite possible that the Vimalaprabha narrative was meant to be recounted to the patron or any others who might have gathered for the performance. Certainly, the narrative's presence at the opening of the manual would have framed the ritual master's sense of the proceedings, but another *Sarvadurgati* funerary text from Dunhuang suggests more. IOL Tib J 384 also opens with its own version of the Vimalamaṇiprabha myth. There, after preparing the mandala, the ritual master is instructed, "take a seat, hold in one's hand the wooden splint and explain the story of the mandala."[41] Our own Vimalaprabha narrative may have functioned in a similar way. Such retellings may already have been part of the Indic *Sarvadurgati* tradition as a way to include and inform the family of the deceased who had gathered for the funeral.[42] In the Indic context, however, the retelling was probably not held to be quite so necessary to the ritual's efficacy as in indigenous Tibet. Our own narrative may therefore be suspended somewhere between Tibetan pre-Buddhist and Indian Buddhist interests.[43]

The Shifting Language of Ritual Manuals

One last aspect of the narrative is worth dwelling on briefly: its grammar. Given that it tells the story of the Buddha's original performance of the ritual, the myth is written in the past tense. Upon hearing the Buddha describe Vimalaprabha's sufferings, the assembled gods "fainted and fell unconscious" (*'khams te/ brgyal ba gyur*); after discussing his father's wealth with his entourage, the prince "killed" (*bkrongs*) his father.[44] Proceeding to the remaining six topics, the text keeps some portions in the past tense, where it refers to how certain rites were performed in the mythic past, but for the most part, the performance for the patron is described in the imperative or the future tense. Thus, for the preliminary propitiation (Tib. *bsnyen pa*; Skt. *sevā*), the deities "will be invited" (*spyan drang*), and the oath-bound ones "will be offered worship and cakes" (*mchod gtor dbul*).[45] When the future tense is used, it may be understood to have a slight imperative sense, as in, "it will need to be done." Following the seven topics, however, in describing the mandala, the author returns to the past tense. Mahoṣṇīṣa-tejorāśi "held" (*bsnams*) a sun in his hand; Jayoṣṇīṣa "erected" (*btsugs*) the victory banner of power; the emblem of Pratibhānakūṭa "arose" (*byung*) as though in a finger snap, because all actions "were" spontaneously accomplished (*grub*).[46] It seems that this mandala still partakes of the mythic past. Only with the fourteenth folio (out of sixteen) does the narrative finally reach the initiation proper, a point marked by a paragraph break and, significantly, a shift back to a more concerted imperative/future tense.

For our own manual, then, the Buddha's mythic original performance is in the past and his reader's later performances are in the imperative/future. The use of the imperative is typical of ritual manuals, a characteristic style generally distinct from canonical sutras and tantras, which, being reportage on the Buddha's teaching, are typically written in the past tense. Hence the standard opening to most sutras, "Thus have I heard at one time," as a disciple testifies to what he heard while in the presence of the Buddha. With ritual manuals came an increased use of the present and the imperative, direct address to the reader.

The *Uṣṇīṣavijayā-dhāraṇī* provides a fairly typical and an informative case, dating from the mid-seventh century and an example of a *dhāraṇī* sutra with its *vidhi* woven into its narrative fabric. The Four Great Kings raise the subject of the ritual, circumambulating the Buddha and requesting that he teach it in detail. Initially, the Buddha explains the procedures in conditional sentences, along with the benefits that will result: "if one does this, then that will occur."[47] When he comes to the construction of the altar and the ritual proper, however, the Buddha switches to the imperative: "the *dhāraṇī* should be held in mind" (Skt. *susmārayitavyaḥ*; Tib. *dran bar bya*) and "the *dhāraṇī* should be recited" (Skt. *japtavyaṃ*; Tib. *bklag par bya*, or *slos shig* in the Dunhuang).

The Buddha instructing his disciples in the imperative is common in the earlier sutras, but such instructions, like those just referenced in the *Uṣṇīṣavijayā*, are couched in the third-person limited perspective of the sutra as a whole. They are all reportage of the Buddha telling his interlocutors what they should do. The implication may be that we are meant to follow suit, but it is left to the reader to imagine themself into the story. What makes the genre of free-standing ritual manuals different is their use of the imperative (or the present tense in an instructional mode, as observed in the initiation instructions from the Dunhuang manual, i.e., "one performs this" or "one recites that") without this perspective. These are the words of a human teacher speaking directly to the reader.

For the same reason, *dhāraṇī*-based ritual manuals rarely include sentences in the first person. Their instructions focus almost exclusively on what the reader should do with his body and the physical space around the mandala-altar. Speaking is generally limited to the recitations of the spell. In a sense, it constitutes a first-person address by the reader to the deity; some spells even include semantically coherent first-person statements embedded within them. In the middle of the *Mahāpratisarāvidyārājñī-dhāraṇī* spell, for example, there appears the prayer, "Destroy! Destroy all my misdeeds, Glorious One. Protect me! Protect me with all beings everywhere at all times from all dangers and troubles."[48] But such spells were generally left untranslated in Tibetan or Chinese translations of *dhāraṇī* sutras. The contents were not really the point; a spell's power lies largely in the sounds themselves. This said, Tibetan translations of *dhāraṇīs* do appear occasionally in the Dunhuang manuscripts (even then, Buddhists were curious about such matters), and the educated Indian practitioner surely had some sense of the meaning.[49] Part of what marks the spell as different from its surrounding manual (or sutra), then, is precisely its first-person voice. Comprehensible or not, the spell marks the moment in the ritual when the practitioner makes their voice heard.

First-person praises and prayers have long been part of Buddhist practice. Besides spells, they appear to have entered *dhāraṇī*-based practice texts as ritual framing elements, especially in liturgical collections of the kind examined in chapter 1. As already observed, the *dhāraṇīsaṃgraha* often open with invitations to the gods and spirits, then close with prayers and praises. Similar too are the first and last elements of the *tridaṇḍaka*, though we have little to no evidence of *dhāraṇīs* being embedded in this liturgical format before the time of the Tibetan Dunhuang manuscripts. Within early *dhāraṇī*-based ritual manuals (*vidhi* and *kalpa*), however, first-person prayers are largely absent. All this changed with the advent of the tantras and their manuals. Tantric *sādhanas*, initiation *vidhis*, and other kinds of manuals intersperse second- or third-person instructions of the sort seen in earlier *dhāraṇī* manuals with all sorts of first-person prayers, praises, exclamations, and so on, to be read by either the ritual master or the patron/initiate.

In the *Sarvadurgati* initiation manual, the entire procedure assumes the ritual master's preliminary performance of the rites of propitiation and accomplishment (Tib. *bsnyen bsgrub*; Skt. *sevā-sādhana*). Thus, the part about topic 5 says: "Without stopping, until the activities and the *siddhis* [are accomplished], he maintains the intention and compassion, whereby the deities, because of their previous resolutions and compassion, will bestow the blessings and enact myriad kindnesses for the benefit of the patron."[50] (No mention is made of the master's identification with the deity; we shall return to this issue below.) Though some ritual instruction for the propitiation is provided in topic 3, it is possible our manual assumes the presence of an ancillary manual for the performance of these rites, which possibly included additional first-person elements.

In our own manual's instructions on initiating the patron, first-person prayers are offered for the patron to recite. The master does speak, but his words are addressed to the initiate, as in: "'*Cela*! Generate *bodhicitta*.' Then, holding a jeweled ritual dagger in his hands, he commands them to join their hands and pronounce the following [after him]."[51] The words that follow, like all first-person pronouncements in this manual, are therefore to be spoken by the initiate, perhaps repeating after the master:

All phenomena are naturally pure,
so I too am naturally pure.[52]
Through the gathering of all the oceans of conquerors,
may I be united with the treasury body![53]

Oṃ asame trisame mahāsamaye hūṃ![54]
The mandala is taught to be a wheel.
That itself is taught to be the *samaya*.[55]
The deities who have entered the mandala:
may they consecrate me.
When the jewels, flowers, and so forth
have established the principal family,
I have no doubt that attainment will come.[56]

Here, the patron prays for the buddhas to empower the proceedings, to accept them into their heart, and to ensure that the flower they toss into the mandala immediately after this prayer lands appropriately and reveals the true nature of their karmic connections. It is a personal plea by a devotee to his deities. It is also entirely in seven-syllable verse, broken only by the mantra, and as such is unusual within this manual, the vast majority of which is written in prose. The verse also contains two sets of lines that appear in other works (see notes 53 and 55 above). Its significance is thus marked in multiple ways.

Our manual's only other lines in verse are pronounced by the ritual master at the culminating moment, as he grants the initiations of the eight auspicious symbols, each of which represents one of the eight *uṣṇīṣa* buddhas surrounding Śākyamuni at the center of the mythic mandala of the past.[57] The initiations are enacted by handing the patron a series of symbolic items: (1) white mustard seeds; (2) a mirror; (3) *dūrvā* grass; (4) *bilva* fruits; (5) bezoar; (6) yogurt; (7) a conch shell; and (8) vermillion powder.[58] As he bestows each item, the master recites a verse of nine-syllable lines emphasizing its symbolic significance:

> This white mustard seed is the great supreme vajra family.
> By means of this great gnosis of equanimity, free of concepts,
> here may there be supreme auspiciousness.
>
> . . .
> The conch proclaims all the teachings.
> By realizing the significance of the music of all the melodious teachings,
> here may there be supreme auspiciousness.
>
> Red vermillion is the nature of power.
> By gaining mastery over all life force,
> here may there be supreme auspiciousness.[59]

Through poetic utterances, with each verse ending in the same rhythmic refrain, the master evokes in the patron a sense of the ritual moment's import, pointing to what is unfolding at another level beyond that of the senses. With each verse, he uses metaphor to link the object (here the white mustard seed is not so much representing the gnosis of the vajra family as it is continuous with it) first with the nature of its transformative power and second with what shall be gained in the immediacy of the act.[60] As when the patron throws the flower, a change in register to poetic verse is deployed to mark the significance of the event.[61]

Aside from the spell, these kinds of meaningful utterances are almost entirely absent from the *dhāraṇī* manuals. Where those earlier manuals offered straightforward instruction, tantric initiation involved moments when the linguistic register changed, poetic utterance framed the solemnity of the occasion, and the initiate's experience was carefully manipulated. In such ways, tantrism brought changes to the burgeoning genre of Buddhist ritual manuals.

Bodies, Dead or Alive

One point remains unclear: When the patron is dead, does the ritual master recite their prayers on their behalf or simply drop them as irrelevant? The opening sentence of the final section on initiation explains: "now one will lead the patron into the mandala, be they alive or dead, and perform the initiations and ablutions."[62] And later, when the patron actually enters the mandala, "If [the patron] is alive, they will enter through the east. If they are dead, they will enter through the west."[63] That they may be dead is further confirmed by the root tantra itself: "If the dead body is entered into the mandala and initiated, even if they have been born a hell being, they will immediately be delivered and reborn into the family of the gods."[64] The Dunhuang initiation manual, then, doubled as a funerary manual.

Early Tibetan Buddhists, in works such as the *Story of the Cycle of Birth and Death* and the *Lha yul du lam bstan pa*, looked to both the *Uṣṇīṣavijayā-dhāraṇī* and the *Sarvadurgatipariśodhana* for replacements for the pre-Buddhist funerary rites, which often involved blood sacrifice. The "Account of the Food Provisioning [for the Dead]" (*Zas gtad kyi lo rgyus*), which is appended to the *Testament of Wa* (*Dba' bzhed*) and (at least in the received version) may date from the eleventh or twelfth century, does too. There, following a fight between the Bon priests of the Tibetan court and the newly arrived Buddhists over how to perform the funerary rites for Tri Songdetsen, we read: "Thenceforth, funerals were performed on the basis of the mandala of the All-Seeing [Vairocana] and the nine-deity mandala of the *uṣṇīṣa* [-buddhas] as it appears in the *Sarvadurgatipariśodhana*."[65] Just above this passage, it is also stated that the funeral rites for King Tri Songdetsen were performed using the *Lha'i bu dri ma med pa'i mdo*. A note adds just, "the *Gtsug tor dri med kyi gzungs*." Wangdu and Diemberger read the note as adding a second source, but it is more likely an explanation of the otherwise obscure title: *Vimalamaṇigarbha-sūtra*.[66] In other words, the only work named here is the *Vimaloṣṇīṣa-dhāraṇī*, which has as its protagonist Vimalamaṇigarbha (discussed above). Taken together, all this suggests that a large and complex circle of *uṣṇīṣa* buddha funerary rites constituted a primary point of contact, and conflict, between Buddhism and Bon in early Tibet. Perhaps in the Dunhuang manual we may glimpse the kinds of *Sarvadurgati* rites performed by these Buddhist reformers.[67]

In fact, All-Seeing (Sarvavid) Vairocana, the central deity of the mandala mentioned in the *Testament of Wa*, appears to have been primary to the Buddhist identity of the Tibetan imperial court. Later histories describe the layout of Samye, Tibet's first monastery, the top floor of which centered around an image of All-Seeing Vairocana.[68] And the imperial Karchung (Skar chung) temple is said to have been consecrated in the early ninth century during the reign of Tri Relpachen before another All-Seeing Vairocana mandala.[69] Imperial-period catalogues of translated Buddhist scriptures reflect an interest in tantras focusing on Vairocana, the *Sarvadurgatipariśodhana* among them.[70] Turning to the art historical record, Heller and Kapstein have highlighted the repeated appearance of All-Seeing Vairocana statues in imperial-period temples—at least three in eastern Tibet as well as a particularly significant one in Anxi Yulin Cave 25 and possibly another in Dunhuang Cave 14.[71]

Tying all this evidence together are several *Sarvadurgatipariśodhana* amulets found among the Dunhuang manuscripts. Pelliot tibétain 389 (fig. 2.4) is a well-studied drawing of the mandala with All-Seeing Vairocana in the now-familiar form, surrounded in the inner circle by the syllables of the "root mantra" (*mūlavidyā*) of the *Sarvadurgatipariśodhana*.[72] Just beyond this sit the eight *uṣṇīṣa* buddhas, each with his name and heart mantra inscribed above his head. Together, they compose the nine-deity mandala described by the *Testament of Wa* and other sources that stood at the heart of the Tibetan court's Buddhist funerary rites. Beyond these nine are a further four offering goddesses at the corners, each accompanied by her mantra, then again the sixteen bodhisattvas, each named accordingly. Finally there are the four gate guardians, with names and mantras added, at the outer level.

But this is not just a drawing of a thirty-three-deity *Sarvadurgatipariśodhana* mandala. It is surrounded by three additional chunks of text, positioned above, below, and around its exterior. Each paragraph calls upon still further deities to protect an unnamed patron (*yon gyi bdag po*).[73] Repeatedly, each prayer refers to the patron, who was presumably also the owner of the mandala, for the manuscript as a whole almost certainly served as an amulet. This is indicated by the fold lines that suggest the whole page was once folded into a smaller square and carried around; points of deterioration appear where the corners of the folded amulet would have been. Syllables are inscribed at the heart of each image, apparently to consecrate them as live deities. This, then, was a ritually active document.[74]

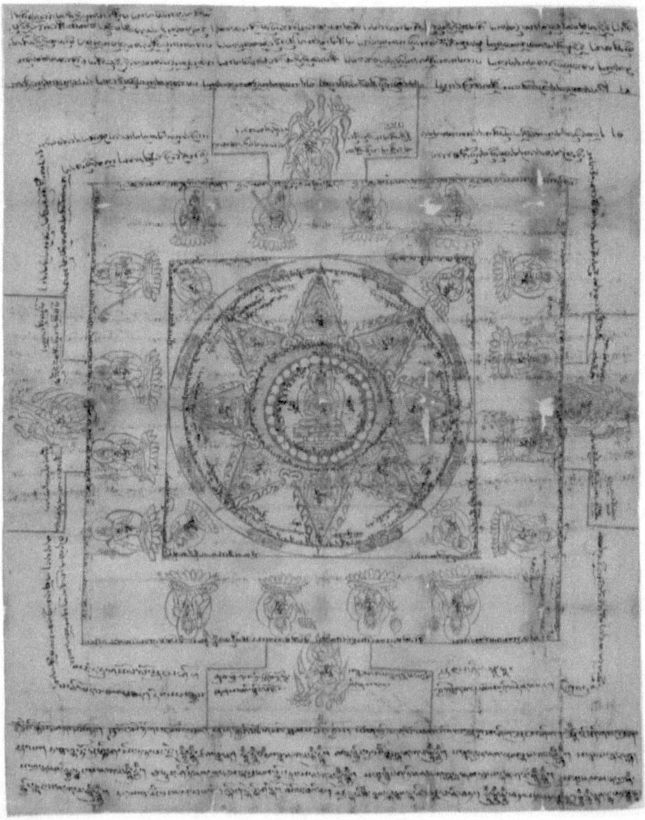

FIGURE 2.4 Sarvadurgatipariśodhana mandala amulet
Source: Pelliot tibétain 389, Courtesy of the Bibliothèque Nationale

In fact, several other *Sarvadurgati* mandala-amulets remarkably similar in appearance were found among the Chinese documents from Dunhuang. Or.8210/S.6348 and Pelliot chinois 4519 (figs. 2.5 and 2.6) are both nearly identical to Pelliot tibétain 389, though with an additional line of directional guardians and auspicious symbols around the outside. These mandalas, which also probably served as protective amulets, are also surrounded by copious writings, this time in Chinese, most of which have been identified as various *dhāraṇīs*.[75] Here again, then, the protections of the central image are supplemented by additional apotropaic text.[76]

Evidence from the Dunhuang manuscripts thus suggests a connection between the *Sarvadurgatipariśodhana* and the imperial-period forms

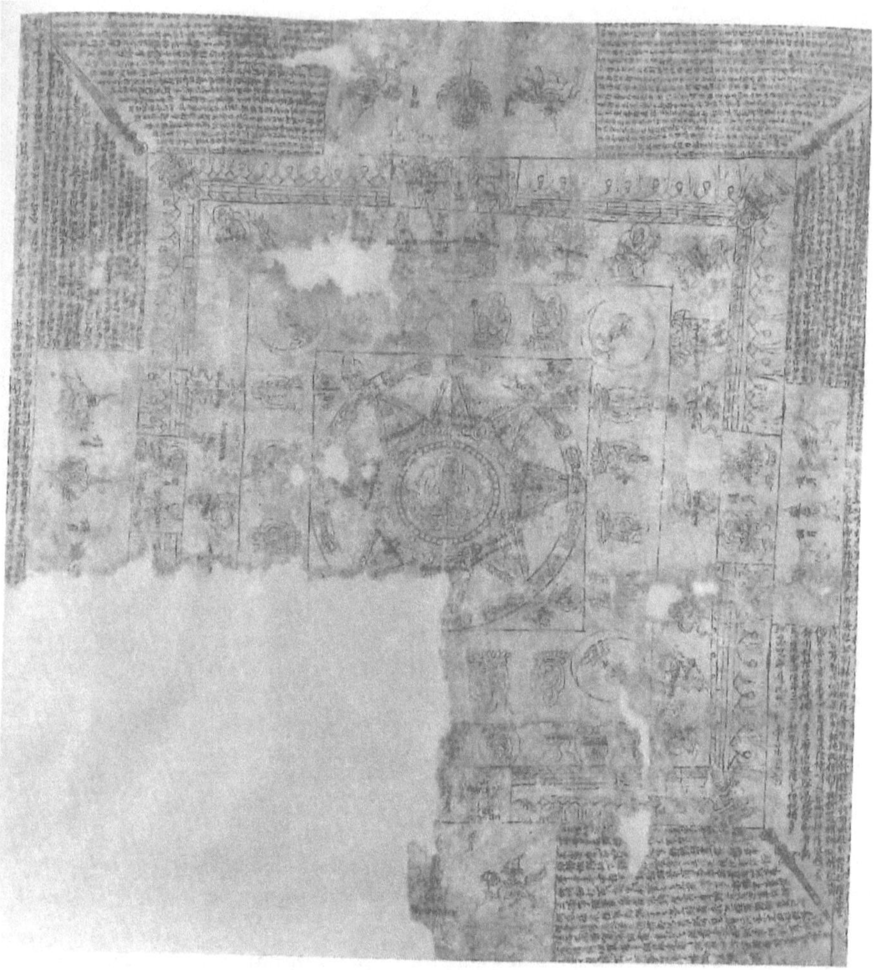

FIGURE 2.5 Sarvadurgatipariśodhana mandala amulet
Source: Or. 8210/S. 6348, Courtesy of the British Library

of All-Seeing Vairocana. Taken together, the three amulets tie the *Sarvadurgatipariśodhana* mandala to the very form of All-Seeing Vairocana seen in early Tibetan temples. (And our own initiation manual further ties all this to imperial funerary practice.) All the (rather copious and varied) Dunhuang ritual materials surrounding the *Sarvadurgatipariśodhana* are written or drawn for the benefit of a patron. We have no *sādhanas* intended for the purpose of one's own awakening (*svārtha*). Given the evidence from Dunhuang,

FIGURE 2.6 Sarvadurgatipariśodhana mandala amulet
Source: Pelliot chinois 4519, Courtesy of the Bibliothèque Nationale

the *Sarvadurgatipariśodhana* lent itself well to rites for the welfare of others (*parārtha*). Whether this is a reflection of early Tibetan interests, as identified above, or of how the tantra functioned in India too remains a question, but it seems that early Tibetans, at least, saw the *Sarvadurgatipariśodhana* in a different light from other Yoga tantra systems such as the *Sarvatathāgata-tattvasaṃgraha*.

Paralleling rites for others and oneself are two distinct ways of engaging with the physical (or imagined) space of the mandala. One may be led into it by a teacher or take possession of it oneself. Being an initiation manual, our text is an example of the former, while *sādhana*-style manuals correspond to the latter (as explored further in chapter 3). In later centuries, the former often incorporates the latter, delegating the ritual master's generation of himself as the deity to *sādhanas* and other texts. Initiations are the most common kind of ritual to involve leading another into the mandala, sometimes literally with the initiate entering and sitting within the space of a mandala. IOL Tib J 579, another *Sarvadurgati* initiation manual from Dunhuang, specifies the use of such a secondary mandala in which the initiate sits, facing the main mandala, to receive the actual initiations.[77] Such an "initiation mandala," usually a simpler space than the main mandala, is seen in several early tantric works of the seventh century, including the *Mahāvairocanābhisaṃbodhi*, where jars of prepared waters (like those described in our own manual) are arranged for sprinkling.[78] As Buddhagupta's commentary explains, such mandalas were constructed so that the initiatory waters would not damage the main mandala.[79] Despite such practical concerns, it is clear that the secondary mandala functioned as a ritual equivalent to the main mandala.

The rise of the mandala for initiation was complicated somewhat by earlier ordination rites of both the monastic and the bodhisattva precept varieties, both of which took place within bounded spaces of their own, called *sīmābandha* or *sīmāmaṇḍala*. Seventh- and eighth-century Chinese authors writing on the bodhisattva precepts even describe ordination platforms that in certain respects resemble mandalas, perhaps reflecting a conflation of the two kinds of ritual spaces.[80] As seen in chapter 1, the rites typically in *dhāraṇī* ritual manuals describe worshipping an image or *stūpa* that sits at the center of a mandala altar. Such altars functioned quite apart from the *sīmābandha/simāmaṇḍala* used for ordinations, perhaps foremost in that they centered on images toward which worship was directed.[81] What made the advent of tantric practice remarkable from the perspective of the earlier *dhāraṇī* manuals and image worship is that the initiate—the patron in the Dunhuang manual—*enters into the space of the altar*, in effect merging *sīmābanda* and mandala.

In this sense, early tantric ritual opened the mandala to new uses. No longer just for *pūjā*, it became a sacred space in which initiation and related purificatory rites could be performed. This shift was not entirely without precedent. The *Mahāpratisarāvidyārājñī-dhāraṇī* directs the officiant to place an ill person in the mandala and recite the spell twenty-one times over them, and similar instructions appear in the ritual manual ending the Dunhuang *Candanāṅga-dhāraṇī*.[82] Such practices seem to parallel the *Sarvadurgati*'s funerary initiations, though it is unclear whether either of these *dhāraṇī* manuals predates the tantra.[83] Which came first, placing an ill person in a mandala for healing purposes or leading a healthy person in for initiation, remains an open question. In any case, our *Sarvadurgati* initiation manual seems to reflect a moment when the separate developmental lines of image worship and ordination, qua initiation, merged. It would not be long before full-fledged union of worshipped and worshipper would become central to tantric practice.

The Dunhuang manual makes no direct mention of the initiation effecting a transformation of the patron into a buddha. Entry into the mandala and the first initiations is described as follows:

> Then, revealing the four doors, remove the mandala blindfold.[84] Then the master who has left the eastern door and arrived at the western side, to the place where the patron sits,[85] having consecrated the patron, will order them to hold the vajra [again]. If [the patron] is alive, they will enter through the east. If they are dead, they will enter through the west. [Both master and patron] arrive at the center of the mandala, [16r] and the master will hold in his hands the central vase. Four great meditators [i.e., assistants] in the four directions will hold the vases of the four directions. Then, from those four directions, they pronounce [the mantras] (*'dzab*) and recite (*bzlas*) the heart [mantra], and the initiations will be granted. As for the sequence of initiations, one will grant initiation by means of the substances that appear in the scripture: (i) vase; (ii) rosary; (iii) head cloth (*cod pan*); (iv) wheel, and so forth. The ablutions will be performed.[86]

The initiate's union with the deity could be implied in the items he is given to hold, symbols of buddhas, but this is not clearly stated. The manual's ritual forms may reflect a transitional moment, for tantric initiation appears to have predated the visualized transformation of the initiate into the deity, if only by a few decades around the middle of the seventh century. The initiation rite described in Atikūṭa's *Dhāraṇīsaṃgraha*, for example, "is the first document that brings together the essential ingredients: a candidate is consecrated with the *abhiṣeka* ceremony into a mandala (a) using *homa* ceremonies, mantra, and *mudrās*; (b) employing forms of Buddhist meditation;

and (c) enjoining the individuals to secrecy following the ceremony."[87] Missing from this list is visualized union with the deity. Shinohara highlights this lacuna in his own analyses of the initiation rites in both Atikūṭa's *Dhāraṇīsaṃgraha* (compiled in China in 654 C.E.) and the *Guhya-tantra* (likely also a seventh-century composition): "The account of the maṇḍala ceremony in the *Guhya Tantra* follows the outline of the All-Gathering Maṇḍala Ceremony [in Atikūṭa's writings] fairly closely and does not involve visualization."[88]

Shinohara juxtaposes these two seventh-century works first with the *Mah āvairocanābhisaṃbodhi* (which dates from around the mid-seventh century) and then with Yixing's (683–727) commentary on the same, which he completed in the last years of his life. Although visualization is absent from Atikūṭa and the *Guhya-tantra*, some "elements appear in the brief account [of the initiation rite] in the [*Mahāvairocana*] Sūtra, but visualization becomes a major emphasis in the *Commentary*, where its application is carefully worked out."[89] Shinohara does not identify precisely which elements appear in the *Mahāvairocana* itself, but union with the deity may be observed at three points. First, the ritual master imagines himself as Vairocana at the center of a mandala in order to take possession of the site at the beginning of the proceedings. He then further consecrates (Tib. *byin gyis brlabs*; Skt. *adhiṣṭhāna*) himself as Vajrasattva before drawing the mandala. Finally, with a *mudrā*, he consecrates the initiate as Vajrasattva during the preliminary purification at the gate before they toss the flower and enter the mandala.[90] All of these "elements" are ritually significant, and it seems safe to say that imagined union with the deity was already part of tantric initiation by the mid-seventh century. At the same time, there is no mention of the actual moment of initiation effecting a union of the initiate with the buddha.[91] Writing in the mid-eighth century, when tantric Buddhism and deity union were better established, Buddhagupta even remarks on this absence: "When the disciple is to be initiated, though it is not actually mentioned here, they should be transformed into the body of Vajrasattva. Since its does not say [the disciple] is transformed into the body of any other [buddha], they should be transformed, or initiated, into the body of Vajrasattva."[92] It is possible that the consecration of the initiate as Vajrasattva before entering was considered enough of a transformation for the authors of the *Mahāvairocana* not to bother repeating it. But even so, they apparently did not understand initiation to be about union with the deity in quite the same way Buddhagupta did. Becoming the deity was part of the proceedings, but only to worship the deity; it was not yet the central moment it would be in later decades. Buddhagupta's eighth-century commentary thus reflects the gradual emergence of visualized union with the deity within the initiation scenario.

The Dunhuang manual may represent a moment when initiation still did not create buddhas. The ritual master and the patron may have been reenacting the Buddha and Vimalaprabha's mythic performance but not completely identifying with those figures. Before long, however, union with the deity would become key to tantric initiation and to the initiate's subsequent meditation practice. The tantric Buddhist not only ascended the altar but also took up residence there as the buddha. This new "god's eye view" is the subject of the next chapter.

Conclusions

Through analysis of the initiation manual found in IOL Tib J 439/712, this chapter has suggested that early Tibetans, and probably Indians too, saw the *Sarvadurgatipariśodhana* as a tantric elaboration of a tangled circle of texts that included the *Uṣṇīṣavijayā-dhāraṇī* and the *Vimaloṣṇīṣa-dhāraṇī*. The intertextualities between these works follow both mythological and ritual continuities. The manual's rendering of the tantra's framing narrative includes elements from the *dhāraṇīs*' own narratives and thus is part of a wider early Tibetan tendency to draw on all three works for their funerary myths and rituals. Chapter 1 identified ritual manuals as an exceedingly prolific extracanonical genre that emerged in connection with *dhāraṇī* sutras in the late fifth and sixth centuries. These *dhāraṇī* manuals provided the literary space where local ritual experimentation met translocal development, so that by the seventh century they were being gathered into the first fully fledged tantras. The ritual manuals surrounding the *Uṣṇīṣavijayā* reflect the kinds of innovations in altar design that could have fed into the *Sarvadurgatipariśodhana* mandala, thereby suggesting how a *dhāraṇī* might have developed into a tantra.

In Tibet, the *Sarvadurgatipariśodhana* tradition continued to be highly malleable. The relevant Dunhuang manuscripts show a constant reworking of its rituals, mostly for funerary purposes but also in creating amulets. These materials shed light on an organic tradition that was ever on the move, ever being updated for new interests. These are the writings of a lived and very human ritual tradition.

While this may be particularly true for the *Sarvadurgatipariśodhana*, it is typical of ritual manuals. The sutras open a gap between their framing narratives and their doctrines, between the past tense of the Buddha and the present tense of the dharma, inviting readers to step in and inhabit the imaginary world of legendary teachings; ritual manuals turn the tables, entering into the world of the reader. Sutras tell what happened in the past; manuals tell what should happen in the present. If the sutras (and Mahāyāna sutras still more) focus on distant worlds, *dhāraṇī* manuals draw readers to the immediate vicinity, to their bodily actions within a material ritual space. With the rise of tantric manuals, however, the imaginary worlds of the buddhas returned and began to suffuse the genre of ritual manuals, pervading the human with the divine. The Buddha's perspective and his first-person voice returned, but now the mythic and the human had been merged.

Appendix

A Sarvadurgatipariśodhana *Initiation Manual*

TRANSLATION OF IOL TIB J 439 AND IOL TIB J 712

The name of this mandala is the Ārya-sarvadurgatipariśodhana-tejorāja.

First, a brief explanation of the narrative setting, or how [this *Sarvadurgatipariśodhana* mandala] arose in the world of gods and humans: The blessed and noble Śākyamuni, having attained manifest complete buddhahood, taught the dharma by means of the three vehicles in accordance with the causes and pedagogical needs of individual beings. In the Trāyastriṃśa heaven, he was surrounded by an assembly of many great miraculous gods and *nāgas*, including a retinue of many hundreds of bodhisattvas, numerous *saṇghas* of *śrāvakas* and *arhats*, Brahmā, Śakra, the Four Great Kings, and the directional guardians. Having considered the karma and the causes and conditions specific to each sentient being, he taught in detail on karma and its ripenings. At that time, Śakra, the chief of the gods, rose from his seat and came before the Bhagavan. He circumambulated clockwise many hundreds of times, then prostrated at the feet of the Bhagavan. Sitting down before him, he spoke these words: "Bhagavan, seven days have passed since the *devaputra* named Vimalaprabha passed away from this Trāyastriṃśa heaven. Where has he taken rebirth? Through the causes and conditions of his karma, what kind of results will he experience?"

The Bhagavan, without saying anything, [1v] smiled and sat there. From the top of his head came fifty million light rays, light rays called "displaying everywhere the varieties of all the buddhas," pervading all the buddhafields of the ten directions, whereupon they disappeared into the soles of his feet. Why was that? Those light rays comprehend the karmic causes and conditions of all sentient beings, so that, when a prophecy of rebirth as a god is indicated, the light rays disappear into the top of [the Buddha's] head. If a prophecy of rebirth as a human is indicated, they disappear into his tongue. If a prophecy of rebirth as a hungry ghost is indicated, they disappear into his heart. If a prophecy of rebirth as an animal is indicated, they disappear into his navel. If a prophecy of rebirth as a hell being is indicated, they disappear into the soles of his feet. The light rays having regathered in this [latter] way, [the Buddha] spoke these words to the chief of the gods, Indra: "The *devaputra* Vimalaprabha, having passed from this heaven, was born as a hell being in the great Avīci hell. There he will experience sufferings for many hundreds of years. Having passed from that life, he will come to experience suffering for many hundreds of years in the worlds of the hungry ghosts. Having been freed from that, he will take birth in the body of an animal. There he will continue to experience sufferings for many hundreds of years. Having been freed again from that, he will again experience sufferings for many hundreds of years in the [animal] realms, as a dog, a pig, an antelope, a monkey, a crow, a cat, a snake, and so on.[1] [2r] Having been freed from those, he will be born as a human, but he will be ridden with diseases such as leprosy and poxes and take bodies that will be ridiculed by everyone, that are blind, deaf, dumb, and deformed. Then he will be born in places that are savage border regions and that provide no opportunities for practicing the dharma."

[At this,] the entire assembly of gods, the chief of the gods, Śakra, and so forth, fainted and fell unconscious. After a long while they awoke from their faints, and the chief of gods Śakra spoke these words to the Bhagavan: "This *devaputra* Vimalaprabha, having done evil acts, whatever they were, he will come to experience such sufferings! Through what method might the Great Compassionate One free him from this?"

The Bhagavan replied, "When the time comes, it will be taught."

And all the gods, the chief of the gods, Śakra, and so forth, prayed with these words: "O Great Compassionate Bhagavan, for the sake of the gods, we, this assembly of gods, request complete buddhahood. The time has come! [Please teach] the supreme of teachings!"

[2v] The Bhagavan replied in these words: "I will explain how the *devaputra* Vimalaprabha initially accumulated the karmic causes and conditions, so listen! In this world realm, in a place called Vaiśali, there was a great king named Immaculate Voice (Dri med sgra; Skt. *Vimalaghoṣa). He had a queen named Loving One (Byams ldan ma; Skt. *Maitrivatī) and a princely son named Jewel Holder (Nor bu 'dzin; Skt *Maṇidhāra). [The prince] had been ordered by his father and mother that as long as he was not ready to rule the kingdom, he should remain within his own entourage and stay in the royal gardens. One day, the prince Jewel Holder spoke these words to his entourage: 'I am the son of King Immaculate Voice. My father has no sons apart

from me. My father enjoys so many entourages, riches, and attendants, while I do not have such entourages and riches. Isn't this unfair?'

"His entourage replied, 'Your father has assumed the sovereignty of a great king. That is why he has such an abundance of attendants and riches. You may be his son, the prince, but so far you have not assumed the throne, and that is why you do not yet have such entourages and riches.'

"The prince said, 'So how should I go about obtaining wealth like that?'

"The entourage replied, 'If your father were killed, you would inherit such a kingdom and wealth.'

"The prince, impressed by this advice, took hold of a sharp sword and killed his father. [3r] Because his heart was so evil as to kill even his own father, his mother, Loving One, also passed away [i.e., from grief]. Then the ministers and entourage, having nobody but the prince, appointed him king.

"[One day] while walking through his royal gardens, enjoying the five sensual pleasures, in a dense and solitary grove, the prince saw a great hermit sage named Needless Love maintaining an ascetic manner. Wearing only bark for clothes and eating only the roots of grasses, he was weak and emaciated. Seeing all this, the prince said to the hermit, 'In my kingdom the king is so excellent that all the people are extremely happy. They enjoy the five kinds of sensory pleasures, yet the likes of you forages for the roots of grasses and wears only bark for clothes! You are so pitiful! You should be enjoying the five pleasures. Go on now!'

"The hermit replied to the prince: 'In reliance on the authentic words of the Buddha Śākyamuni, I mostly practice austerities. These are not painful things, but when I look at you, prince, you have accumulated many sins for the sake of this kingdom and the trifling fame of this life. Immediately after the mere flower of this life passes, you will experience the many sufferings of negative rebirth. The sufferings will be so great!'

"The prince, becoming less sure of himself, spoke these words: 'Hermit, what is this so-called "Buddha" like? [3v] What are these things called virtuous and sinful karma, and positive and negative rebirths? If there is sin in killing just one tiny being, how will the sin of killing one's parents be?'

"The hermit replied to the prince: 'Well, great being, if you wish to listen to my teachings, you should quickly dismount from your excellent horse, join your hands together, and prostrate faithfully. Then I will teach you.' So the prince dismounted from his horse and prostrated to the hermit. As he sat before the hermit, the hermit explained about the characteristics and good qualities of the three precious jewels, about the causes and effects of virtuous and sinful karma, and about the ripening of the sin of immediate retribution of killing one's own parents.

"Therefore, the prince believed him. Because of his extreme regret, he started to vomit forth disease-ridden blood and [soon] died. As he was dying, he had heard the dharma and developed a belief in karma and its ripening. [As a result,] because he felt regret, he took rebirth in the Trāyastriṃśa heaven. [But] when that cause of merit was exhausted, the earlier [negative karma] ripened, and he passed from that life.

"That is how he came to experience such sufferings. The method for one who is to be liberated from those has been taught by all the *tathāgatas* of the past and will also be taught by all the *tathāgatas* of the future. Now I too will explain it for the sake of the *devaputra* Vimalaprabha, and if the *Sarvadurgatipariśodhana-tejorāja* mandala is made, he will be freed from that suffering."

[4r] Then the chief of the gods, Śakra, in that same Trāyastriṃśa heaven, assembled the [requisite] materials and constructed the mandala, whereby the *devaputra* Vimalaprabha was freed from the sufferings of those negative rebirths. Having taken rebirth in the Trāyastriṃśa realm, he, together with the chief of gods, Śakra, went before the Bhagavan. Prostrating at his feet, he gave praise: "Ah the Buddha! Ah the dharma! Ah the *saṇgha*! The blessings of your compassion are inconceivable." Then the enjoyments of the gods became his enjoyments, as they were before.

The above is the narrative setting.

Now the **second topic**, an explanation of what is referred to as the "materials": It is said that "when the great general mandala was constructed, a foundation was raised made out of the five jewels—gold dust, silver dust, and so forth—and that the equipment necessary for a great mandala was originally gathered by the four great kings." [Also] it is said that "for one who is of little means and pure mind from the very core, even if he constructs the mandala out of cleaned earth, sand, and so forth, if he performs purely the visualizations and the dedications, through the compassion and blessings, the *siddhis* will be attained." As for enacting this in the present,[2] one should visualize with pure thoughts the earth pigments and so forth as the five kinds of jewels. Generate with vast intention the arranged implements, *tsakali*, or seed syllables as the noble ones manifested before one.[3] [4v] If the worship is performed with a pure mind, then the *siddhis* will be attained.

Now the **third topic**, an explanation of what is called "the propitiation" (*bsnyen pa*; Skt *sevā*): In the tantra it says, "the deities that arrived into the mandala were propitiated ten billion times, or alternatively, to do it quicker than that, no less than 108,000." Those who rule the mandala—the principal central deity, the *uṣṇīṣa* [buddha]s, the fortunate ones (i.e., the *bodhisattvas*), and the gate protectors on up—will be invited by the master into the place where the mandala has been made for up to seven days, three days, or at least, one day. The protectresses of the mandala and the oath-bound ones will be offered worship and *gtor ma*. *Gtor ma* will be bestowed on the entirety of beings and the karmic creditors. Then the mantra expert enters *samādhi*. By recalling them, he clearly generates the bodily colors of the various deities, the hand implements, the throne, and so forth. Then the mantras and the heart [mantra] are recited 10,000, 1,000, or 108 or more times, and the [deities'] activities are enjoined.

Now the **fourth topic**, an explanation of the etymology: Here, regarding mandala, in Sanskrit it is called a *man-da-la*. To explain that, *man* means the heart (*snying*), while *'da' la* means to receive (*len pa*), because, through being connected to the enlightened heart, one receives the *siddhis* of body, speech, and mind. In Tibetan it is called a *kyil khor*. *Kyil* is taken to be without gaining or losing the awakened essence. [5r] *Khor* is taken as the play of compassion that demonstrates various bodies and teachings for the benefit of sentient beings. In this particular case, *kyil* refers to the principal deity at the center, while *khor* is the illumination of the distinct aspects of his compassion, i.e., the eight *uṣṇīṣa* [buddhas], the bodhisattvas who are the fortunate ones, the directional guardians, the gatekeepers, and so on. In short, the current patron is granted initiation into the enlightened heart and caused to receive the *siddhis* unerringly. As for reckoning the symbols for the five aspects [i.e., families], in Sanskrit they are called the *ragaya*. If translated into Tibetan, they are called the "purification through passion," because when all the appearances of the illustrations of the five aspects are visualized with pure thought as the five kinds of jewels, then the *siddhis* will be attained.

Now the **fifth topic**, explaining the preparatory rites: There are two kinds of preparatory rites—the preparatory rites of the humans and the preparatory rites of the deities. Of those, (i) regarding the preparatory rites of humans, many countless years, months, or days ahead of time, requests for attention (*mkhyen pa gsol*) are made to one who is a master expert in the mandala. Having laid out the substances, the master arranges the offerings (*bab stsal pa*), with not one thing missing, and checks for the date and the best astrology. Timely arrangements constitute what are called "the preparatory rites of humans." (ii) The master's attention having been requested in that way, from that time until the mandala has been prepared and the activities accomplished, the master makes further requests for attention to the deities on behalf of the patron. He performs the recitations and the propitiation and accomplishment. Without stopping, until the activities and the *siddhis* [are accomplished], he maintains the intention and compassion whereby the deities, because of their previous resolutions and compassion, [5v] bestow the blessings and enact myriad kindnesses (*stong rogs*) for the benefit of the patron. This is called "the preparatory rites of the deities."

Now the **sixth topic**, explaining the generation of *bodhicitta*: When the mandala is constructed in the evening (*zho nub*), then that same day the site will be consecrated. The site will be requested from the local rulers, i.e., the local goddess and so on. The platform (*stegs bu*) will be built. It will be smeared with a further layer of cow dung (*'go ma*), the lines laid, and the narrative setting explained. The patron will be advised of the rules (*khrims*). A protective cotton thread is hung [on the patron]. A command to confess all previous sins is given. Oaths not to do evil in the future are conferred. Having eliminated any mental doubts or worries the patron may have,[4] cause them to realize the two kinds of bodhicitta unerringly. This is the generation of bodhicitta.

Now the **seventh topic**, explaining the benefits: In accordance with what has been explained above, the *devaputra* Vimalaprabha, having been freed from his negative rebirths, took the body of a god in the heavens of blissful rebirth and remained in a blissful state of mind (*nyam pag*).[5] In the same way, through the compassion and blessings of all the noble ones, the current patron too, wherever he may be residing, in the realms of negative rebirths or wherever, will have his mind purified today. Therefore, through the patron's preparing the materials, the compassion of all the noble ones, and the master's intention, [the patron] will be led into the mandala, granted the initiations, and cleansed, whereby, without any doubt whatsoever, the *siddhis* will be attained for [rebirth] in the heavens of blissful rebirth. [6r] These are the benefits (*phan yon*).

In the tantra it says, "It is suitable to explain the seven branches in brief: (i) the narrative setting, (ii) the materials, (iii) the propitiation, (iv) the etymologies, (v) the preparatory rites, (vi) *bodhicitta*, and (vii) the benefits." All the above has been a teaching in terms of these seven topics that were the enumerated headings originally [listed].

Now the order of the deities of the mandala, their hand implements, bodily colors, postures, and so forth will be explained a little. The hub at the center of the eight spokes of the wheel is a golden site where a *stūpa* appears. This is the sign of the body of the Bhagavan, the Sarvadurgatipariśodhana-tejorāja Śākyamuni. His golden [color] is taught to be just like the golden site. On a lion throne atop a lotus sits the noble Bhagavan, Śākyamuni, his body colored like refined gold, endowed with a topknot in the peaceful manner of a *bhikṣu*, wearing silk brocade robes, holding a bleached white skull in his hands, and not wavering from the *dharmakāya*.

On the eight spokes outside of that, (i) in the east there appears a single upright five-pointed vajra. This is the hand implement of Uṣṇīṣa-Vajrapāṇi, whose body is white, with a satin mantle [covering] the upper half of his body and a *ti tsi gu*(?) skirt, holding a vajra in his hand, [wearing] a crown of the five gnoses, and bedecked with various jewels. Because he [performs] the activities of defeating all the afflictions and negative realms, he holds a vajra in his hand and sits atop a multicolored lotus throne. [6v] (ii) On the wheel spoke in the intermediate southeastern [direction] is the hand implement of Mahoṣṇīṣa-tejorāśi, light red in color, with a throne, ornaments, and dress as above. In order to purify and liberate the frost and ice[6]—the causes of negative rebirth and the sufferings of the afflicted—with the sun of gnosis, he holds a sun in his hand. (iii) In the south appears an upright sword, the hand implement of Mahoṣṇīṣavijaya, blue in color, with ornaments and dress as above. All the afflictions and negative rebirths having been melted away by the sun of gnosis, to cut at the root of all the sufferings of samsara with the sword of wisdom, there appears an upright sword in the south. (iv) Having cut at the root all the sufferings of samsara with the sword of wisdom, to conquer all demonic and conflicting factions, in the southwestern intermediate direction there appears a victory banner—the hand implement of Jayoṣṇīṣa. Light blue in color, with ornaments and dress as above, having in that way conquered the four demons, he erects the victory banner of power. (v) So as to teach the dharma to limitless beings, in the west there appears an upright wheel—the hand implement of Uṣṇīṣacakravartin. Red in color, with ornaments and dress as above, he turns the wheel of dharma in that way. (vi) In order to fulfill the hopes and wishes of all sentient beings, in the northwest there appears the hand implement of Uṣṇīṣavikiraṇa—a blazing jewel. [7r] Orange in color, with ornaments and dress as above, he fulfills the hopes and wishes of all sentient beings in that way. (vii) In order never to exhaust and to gain mastery over all the activities and the *siddhis*, in the north there appears the hand implement of Uṣṇīṣavidhvaṃsaka—a crossed vajra. Green in color, with ornaments and dress as above, he spontaneously accomplishes all the activities and *siddhis*. (viii) Then to provide all sentient beings of the three realms the refuge and protection of freedom and liberation from suffering and the afflictions, in the intermediate direction of the northeast there appears a white *uṣṇīṣa* umbrella—the hand implement of Uṣṇīṣasitātapatra, and that which crowns the head of all the *tathāgatas*.

Outside of that, they are surrounded by a circular vajra fence. The vajras are uncompounded, displayed because they cannot be destroyed by anything at all. Therefore this mandala, which is constructed for the sake of whatever person (*che ge mo*), is surrounded by a vajra fence that is a sign of receiving the *siddhis* that are spontaneously accomplished without being obstructed by any unfortunate factions, nor searching for opportunities.

Outside of that is a wavy ocean, in the four corners of which are the following: (i) In the southeastern intermediate direction an incense burner (*pog por*) appears—the goddess of the summer season, called Vajradhūpe,[7] that is, Vajra Incense (Rdo rje bdug pa ma), light yellow in color, adorned with various kinds of jeweled ornaments and a crown. [7v] Resting on a lotus seat, with various scents that are the offerings of the summer season, she makes offerings to all the noble ones of the three times. (ii) In the southwestern intermediate direction, a flower tray (*men tog gi gzhong pa*) appears—the goddess of the spring season, called Vajrapuṣpa, that is, Vajra Flower, light blue in color, with jeweled ornaments and accoutrements as above, with a satin mantle for her upper garment and a *ba ti*(?) skirt below. Resting on a lotus seat, with various flowers that are the offerings of the spring season on a golden tray, she makes offerings to all the noble ones of the three times. (iii) In the northwestern intermediate direction, an oil-lamp spade[8] appears—the goddess of the autumn season, called Vajrāloke, that is, Vajra Oil Lamp, light red in color, with jeweled ornaments and accoutrements as above. Holding in her hands a golden spade filled with a luminous fire, with offerings of the autumn season that are like the light rays of the sun, she makes offerings to all the noble ones. (iv) In the northeastern intermediate direction, a conch shell appears—called Vajragandha, that is, Vajra Perfume, light green in color, with jeweled ornaments and accoutrements as above. Holding in her hands a conch shell filled with ambrosial water offerings, with various offerings of the winter season, she makes offerings to all the noble ones of the three times.

(i) On a yellow platform outside of that,[9] [8r] in the first position appears a sword—the emblem of Enlightened Śūraṃgama. To cut all the [mental] continuums of samsara and negative rebirth with the sword of wisdom, a sword appears. (ii) So that all the continuums of samsara and negative rebirth that are in that way severed at the root are transformed into the state of Samantabhadra itself, in the lower eastern position there appears a cluster of jewels—the emblem of Samantabhadra. (iii) Having spontaneously established them thusly in the state of Samantabhadra itself, so that limitless beings may be able to see with faith, in the final upper eastern position there appears a jeweled top ornament—the emblem of Jñānaketu. (iv) Having [produced] in limitless beings a faith in the unmistaken reality, to increase the accumulations of merit and gnosis, in the final eastern position appears a moon—the emblem of Candraprabha-kumāra. These four bodhisattvas of the good age are alike in their attributes, being white in color, with jeweled crowns, adorned with various kinds of ornaments, their upper bodies [draped in] sheer cloth, with *ba ti* skirts below, and sitting evenly upon lotus seats.

(v) In the first southern position appears a jeweled net—the emblem of the bodhisattva Jālinīprabha. Due to the nature of dependent arising, all phenomena become the predispositions (*bag chags*) of sentient beings. To gather all those [beings] entirely into the *dharmadhātu* by means of the net of great compassion, [8v] there appears a jeweled net. (vi) In order to equalize all that the net of great compassion has in this way gathered within the *dharmadhātu*, by means of a skylike I-lessness and selflessness and compassion, in the lower eastern [*sic*] position appears a blazing jewel—the emblem of Ākāśagarbha. (vii) Having equalized them through compassion in that way, so that by means of good view and practice that remain unopposed they are not allowed to fall away, in the final upper position appears a jeweled casket—the emblem of Bhadrapāla. (viii) Having gathered in that way all sentient beings into the *dharmadhātu*, all actions are spontaneously accomplished. Therefore in the final southern position there appears a finger snap—the emblem of Pratibhānakūṭa. These four are alike in their attributes, being blue in color, with jeweled crowns, adorned with various kinds of ornaments, their upper bodies [draped in] radiant gold, with *ba ti* skirts below, and sitting evenly upon lotus seats.

(ix) In the first western position appears a conch—the emblem of the bodhisattva of the good age, Gandhahastin. To proclaim the melodies of the sublime dharma throughout the ten directions for the sake of all sentient beings, there appears a conch. (x) In that way the inexhaustible melodies of the sublime dharma are proclaimed in the ten directions, and to enact the purposes [of beings] throughout the hell realms by means of light rays of compassion, in the lower eastern position [9r] a jeweled light appears—the emblem of Amitābha. (xi) In that way, all of cyclic existence is pervaded by the light rays of compassion. To gather all the *siddhis* through the various means for leading sentient beings, in the final upper position appears a book (*po ti*)—the emblem of Akṣayamati. (xii) In order not to think of anything other than, "How can all the karmic and afflicted predispositions of all sentient beings be exhausted through the various kinds of means that are like that?," in the final western position appears a sword—the emblem of Sarvaśokatamonirghāta[mati] (*Mya ngan kun 'joms*). These four are alike in their attributes, being red in color, with jeweled crowns, elaborated with various kinds of ornaments—bodily ornaments and so forth, their upper bodies [draped in] mantles of radiant white, with *ba ti* skirts below, and sitting evenly upon lotus seats.

(xiii) In the first northern position appears a crossed vajra—the emblem of the bodhisattva of the good aeon, Amoghasiddhi. Having purified all the karmic and afflicted predispositions, without exception, of all sentient beings, at a sign of never parting from the attainment of the sublime *siddhis*, there appears a crossed vajra. (xiv) When one has attained the sublime *siddhis* in that way, having traversed the ten levels, in order to be empowered as a dharma regent of the Buddha, in the lower northern position appears a vase—the emblem of the noble Maitreya. (xv) Having been empowered as a dharma regent, because one cuts at the root all the afflictions and samsara, [9v] in the upper final northern position there appears a vajra club—the emblem of Vajragarbha. (xvi) Having cut the afflictions at the root in that way, in order to lead all into the *dharmadhātu* enlightened heart, in the final northern position appears a hook—the emblem of Sarvāpāyajaha. These four are alike in their attributes, being green in color, their heads and bodies adorned and elaborated with various jewels, their upper bodies [draped in] mantles of radiant red, with *ba ti* skirts below, and sitting evenly upon lotus seats.

(i) On an outer red platform that is cut by that line,[10] to the east is an upright, sturdy vajra—the emblem of Indra, lord of the gods. Gold in color, Indra is at the very top (*thod rdeng*) of Mount Meru, adorned with various kinds of ornaments, on a seat that is a white elephant. Nondual with his queen, Śacī, he sits, surrounded by many assemblies of gods. (ii) In the southeast is a stove, the sign of Agni, the rishi of the gods, with a red-gold body, sitting in the costume of a rishi. In his right hand he holds a stove. In his left hand he holds rosary beads. For his seat he sits on a goat, surrounded by many rishis. (iii) In the south is a skull staff (*thod dbyig*), the symbol of Yāma. Yāma, black in color, holds a skull staff in his hands. For his seat he sits on a water buffalo, surrounded by many assemblies of *mātṛkās* and *pretas*. [10r] (iv) In the southwest there is a sword, the symbol of the *rākṣasa* king, Nirṛta. Nirṛta, dark red in color, holds an upright sword and is ornamented with bones. For his seat he sits upon a *kiṃnara*, surrounded by assemblies of demons. (v) In the west is a noose, the symbol of Varuṇa. White in color, Varuṇa is ornamented with snakes. In his hands he holds a noose. For his seat he sits upon a *garuda*, surrounded by assemblies of *nāgas*. (vi) In the northwest is a banner, the symbol of Vāyu. Gray in color, Vāyu sits in a wind mandala. In his hands he holds a banner. For his seat he sits upon a deer, surrounded by an assembly of *vidyāmantradharas*. (vii) In the north is a jeweled mace, the symbol of the great leader of the *yakṣasas*, Kubera. Green in color, Kubera holds a jeweled mace in his hands. For his seat he sits upon a lion throne, surrounded by many assemblies of *yakṣasas*. (viii) In the northeast is a trident, the symbol of Īśāna. White in color, the king of the *bhūtas*, Īśāna holds a trident in his hands. For his seat he sits upon a great bull, surrounded by many assemblies of *bhūtas*. [10v] (ix) The upper direction is arranged in the east. In the near east is a white *kumuta* [flower], the symbol of the *devaputra* Life-Holding Candra. White in color, he holds in a white *kumuta* in his hands. For his seat he sits upon a swan. (x) In the far east is a red lotus, the symbol of the *devaputra* Life-Holding Sūrya. Red in color, Sūrya holds in his hands a lotus. For his seat he sits upon [a chariot] pulled by two white horses, surrounded by an assembly of the sun and moon and many planets. (xi) The lower direction is arranged in the west. In the far west is a vase, the symbol of Bhūmīdevī. Gold in color, the Earth Goddess Bhūmīdevī holds a vase in her hands. For a seat she sits upon a base, surrounded by many assemblies of *nāgas*.

Beyond the boundaries of these eleven directional protectors, through the compassion of the eight great *uṣṇīṣa* [buddhas], the inner signs emerge on the outside: (i) In order to initiate auspiciously the patron, in the first eastern direction there arises a knot of eternity (*dpal be'u*). This is like the case of the baby[11] of a noble (*dpal*) cow—a calf (*be'u*) that is satisfied and satiated by the milk at her udder. Similarly, so that the compassion and blessings of Mahoṣṇīṣa-Vajrapāṇi may initiate the patron and all sentient beings into satisfaction by means of the taste of the nectar of dharma, there is auspiciousness through this symbol of the mind of Mahoṣṇīṣa-Vajrapāṇi. [11r] In this way, not only is the patron alone initiated by the taste of the ambrosial dharma, but all sentient beings throughout the three realms are [also] initiated.

(ii) In order to turn the wheel of dharma, a wheel—the symbol of the mind of Uṣṇīṣa-Tejorāśi—arises at the last eastern position. In that way, the wheel of dharma is turned, and then, (iii) to create the auspiciousness of protection and refuge for all afflicted sentient beings, in the first south [position] there arises an umbrella—the auspicious sign of the mind of Uṣṇīṣavijayā. In that way, protection and refuge are enacted. (iv) In order to create an abundance of all long life, in the final southern [position], in the last southern [position] there arises a vase—the auspicious symbol for the mind of Uṣṇīṣa-Jayoṣṇīṣa. In that way, all gain mastery over long life, and then, (v) to create the auspiciousness of conquest over the four demons, in the first western [position] there arises a victory banner—the symbol of the mind of Uṣṇīṣacakravartin. In that way, the four demons are conquered, and then, (vi) just as a lotus born out of mud is unsullied by the sins that are the mud, [11v] to bring about an auspiciousness that is utterly unsullied by the sins of samsara, the symbol of the mind of [Uṣṇīṣa]vikiraṇa—a lotus—arises in the last western [position]. In that way, all the sins of samsara are dispelled, and then, (vii) to unerringly proclaim the meanings of the twelve branches of sermons to all limitless beings, in the first northern [position], a symbol of the mind of Uṣṇīṣavidhvaṃsaka—an auspicious conch—arises. In that way, the meanings of the twelve branches of sermons are unerringly realized and taught, whereby (viii) power over all that is desired is gained within the utterly pure *dharmadhātu*. Like a little fish swimming fearlessly within a vast ocean, in the northeastern intermediate direction there arises an auspicious fish—the symbol for the mind of Uṣṇīṣasitātapatra.

At four outer doors that are cut by that line, the great door [guardians] are arranged: (i) At the eastern door appears a hook, like the nature of great compassion. In order to lead forth the life force, the nobility, and all the splendor of the current patron without their falling (*mi 'chor bar*) under the sway of the negative realms, taking negative rebirth, karma, or adversaries, at the eastern door there appears a wrathful one with a body white in color and wielding a hook. [12r] In that way, the nobility and splendor of all sentient beings and the patron are led forth by the hook of compassion without their falling under the power of any karma or adversaries. (ii) So that [the patron] will not fall from that [state into which they are led] and will be absorbed into the expanse (*dbyings*), at the western door there appears a blue wrathful one with a nature of great love and wielding a noose in his hands. In that way, they are made not to fall. (iii) In order to stabilize all the life forces, in the western direction there appears a red wrathful one with the nature of great joy and wielding chains in his hands. In that way, they are stabilized. (iv) Then, to gain mastery over karma and all the *siddhis*, at the northern door there appears a dark-green wrathful one with the nature of great equanimity and wielding a bell in his hands.

In each of the four corners appear a moon and a vajra—power and wisdom. Regarding the vajra, it is the wisdom of realization. Because it is the king of awareness and free (*rang dbang du gyur pa*), it is not slave to karma or controlled (*'phrogs*) by others. It is the symbol of the inexhaustibility of the activities and all the *siddhis*. Regarding the moon, all the life forces of all sentient beings will be like the moon, which is born and increases from new to full. Just so, in order to demonstrate mastery over all the *siddhis*, which are the accumulations of merit and wisdom, a moon and a vajra are arranged in each of the four corners.

The *pañca rang ga* ("the five colors") are called "the five walls" in Tibetan. Inside the palace, which is made not of earth and rocks, as it is here, but of gold, silver, turquoise, coral, *vaidurya*, and so forth, [12v] visualize all the assemblies of the noble ones of the ten directions and the three times, as if they were actually there, sitting atop well-arranged seats. Regarding *muktihara*,[12] tassels and garlands[13] of various jewels, strings of golden bells, and even lines of golden bells[14] are visualized to be ornamenting the palace.

The elephant and the lion that appear at the four gates represent power and fearlessness, arrayed as symbols of the fact that when one accomplishes the *siddhis* that are like this, one will be utterly unafraid of demons and adversaries and will [moreover] be able to overwhelm the demons and adversaries.

Regarding piling up the heaps of five kinds of earth pigments at the four gates and in the center, piling up to the brim the five kinds of jewels is the method for preparing the materials for the [subsequent] unstinting worship of all the noble ones of the three times with pure thought.

Planting the four arrows at the four gates is the basis for the four great kings to protect the mandala's border from the outer rim. The great king of the east is Dhṛtarāṣṭra, white in color, holding a *vina* lute[15] in his two hands, and surrounded by an assembly of *gandharvas*. The great king of the south is Virūḍhaka, blue in color, holding a sword in his hand, and surrounded by assemblies of *kumbhāṇḍa* [demons]. [13r] The great king of the west is Virupakṣa, red in color, holding a vajra in his right hand and a noose in his left, and surrounded by assemblies of attendant *nāgas*. The great king of the north is Vaiśravaṇa, greenish yellow in color, holding a *stūpa* in his hand, and surrounded by attendant *yakṣasa* [demons].

The four swords are the servants of the four great kings, the means for cutting and defeating all the obstructions and mistaken concepts that might interfere with the *siddhis*.

The four daggers are the four great *takṛt*,[16] the nature of the inexhaustible *siddhis*, [set] in the four directions of the mandala. The four mirrors are the nature of clearly displaying all the karmic causes and conditions of sentient beings by means of the four great gnoses. The *dhāraṇī* cords represent the four nonforgetful recollections (*myi brjed pa'i gzung*): not forgetting the deity, not forgetting the mantra, not forgetting the *mudrā*, and not forgetting the great compassion.

The five vases are the nature of the five consorts (*yum*). In this particular case, in Sanskrit they are called the *kalaśa-*vidhāna* (*byi tha na*); they purify all the sufferings of the defilements, karma, and afflictions. In order to gather and receive abundantly all the nobility, splendor, life, and *siddhis*, there are the vases. The water inside is the nature of the great ocean, which is a metaphor for the completely pure *dharmadhātu*. The five sweets (*dngar*) are the nature of the five nectars. The five kinds of medicine are healing medicines. The five kinds of grains are the five nourishing foods. [13v] The five kinds of jewels are the five gnoses. The five scents are the five sense pleasures. The ribbon tied around the neck [of the vase] is the nature of the empowerment. The ornaments at the mouth [of the vase] are the nature of the wish-fulfilling tree. The five kinds of heart [mantras] are the five families of conquerors. The *dhāraṇī* cord is the nature of uninterrupted great compassion.

The display of the outer edges of the mandala as a black ground has the nature of the great compassion of killing (*abhicāra*) that does not reject being violent for the welfare of sentient beings.

The platform's appearance as red has the nature of coercion (*dbang*). Why? Because previously the Bhagavan overpowered the powerful gods and *nāgas* of the four continents—the four great kings, the directional guardians, and so forth—by means of the *Sarvadurgatipariśodhana-tejorāja*, and then conferred on them oaths to ensure that the excellent[17] dharma does not wane and to protect all sentient beings. At that time, all the dharma protectresses and oath holders promised accordingly. Having given the vows, [the Buddha] granted them hand implements as internal signs [of their oaths]. Having brought them under his power, the nature of that coercion is demonstrated [here] as the red platform.

The fortunate bodhisattvas appear on a yellow platform. The yellow is the nature of enhancement. Having in this way overpowered the great kings of the four continents, the directional guardians and so forth, [14r] he enhanced the teachings. He prophesied that all the fortunate bodhisattvas would be bound for just one more lifetime.[18] The increase and enhancement of the nobility, splendor, and power of all sentient beings and the patron that result from those blessings are demonstrated [here].

Inside of and above that, within a great ocean, are the four goddesses of the four times. The ocean is the nature of the *dharmadhātu* without center or limits, within which everything is born and arises, being generated from that by the major elements and the four times. It is demonstrated to be like a mother who gives birth to the range of appearances and all existence.

The circular vajra fence is the nature of the arising of all phenomena from the great peace *dharmakāya*, and their gathering within the sphere (*dhātu*). Regarding the demonstration of the eight spokes, they are the nature of the emanations of compassionate skillful means, which is without middle or limits, extensively illuminating and clarifying (*zur phyin pa*) the welfare of all sentient beings.

In short, the directional guardians, the bodhisattvas of good fortune, the goddesses of the times, and so forth have been initiated by means of the outer *bodhicitta*. All appearances within the outer scope of all sentient beings are likewise initiated by that outer *bodhicitta*, so that they arise in the manner of the complete enjoyment (*longs spyod rdzogs pa*). [14v] The eight great *uṣṇīṣa* [buddhas] have the nature of the inner *bodhicitta*. When one has arrived there [i.e., at their circle], one obtains the initiation of the inner *bodhicitta*, being initiated by the emanation body (*sprul pa'i sku*). The central circle is called the great peace of the *dharmakāya*, the secret *bodhicitta*. In that way, the master grants the excellent initiation of the *dharmakāya*, the secret *bodhicitta*, to the present patron and all limitless sentient beings. Having obtained [the initiation] thusly, they manifestly and completely awaken and are ones who display the *siddhi* of vastly enacting the purposes of all sentient beings in the nature of the spontaneously present three bodies.

[Performing the actual initiation rite:]

Having in that way explained a bit about the appearances of the deities of the mandala, now the patron, be they alive or dead, enters[19] the mandala and performs the initiations and ablutions: Having grasped a vajra in his hand, the master bestows it upon the patron to hold, then will command them to perform prostrations devotedly, one by one [in each direction], beginning from the eastern side. [15r] They come to rest at the eastern door.[20] Covering their eyes with white silk, one commands them with these words:[21] "*Cela*! Generate *bodhicitta*." Then, holding a jeweled ritual dagger in his hands, he commands them to join their hands and pronounce the following [after him]:

> All phenomena are naturally pure, so I too am naturally pure. Ocean of conquerors! Through the gathering of all the oceans of conquerors, may I be united with (*phyor*, [*sic*] for *'byor*) the treasury body."
>
> *Oṃ asame trisame mahāsamaye hūṃ*![22]

To the deities who have entered the mandala:

> May they consecrate me.
> When the jewels, flowers, and so forth
> have established the principal family,
> I have no doubt that attainment will come.

Then they throw the flower or the jewel into the mandala. They are connected with whichever deity it lands on.

Regarding making prayers at the four doors:[23] (i) This is the eastern door of great compassion, called in Sanskrit *purva*. Once one has proceeded to this place, the prayer is offered. Just as the previous *tathāgatas, arhats*, and perfectly enlightened buddhas, when they initially performed the activities of *bodhisattvas*, entered the eastern door of great compassion and found the mirrorlike gnosis, attaining completely perfect buddhahood, [15v] just so, in the same way, the present patron approaches the eastern door of great compassion, then recites this extensive prayer:

> May the afflictive obstructions and the obstructions to omniscience be exhausted. Having completely perfected the accumulations of merit and gnosis, may I attain the result of higher [rebirth] and definitive goodness. And may I finally achieve unexcelled buddhahood. And similarly throughout the land too, may the illnesses of humans and the illnesses of cattle cease, and the harvests and herds always be good. And then may all sentient beings remain in a mental state (*nyam pag*) of leisurely ease.
>
> *Oṃ sarvatathāgata mahāguhya vajrābhiśiñcamām adhitiṣṭha nāma karomi mahāpūja vajradhara.*[24]

Likewise, a prayer is offered at each of the four doors. In Sanskrit, the southern door of great love is called *dakṣiṇa*. In Sanskrit, the western door of great joy is called *padma*. In Sanskrit, the northern door of great equanimity is called *upadarayami*.[25] Command him to apply the [appropriate] mantra for [each] family and recite it.[26]

Then, revealing the four doors, remove the mandala blindfold.[27] Then the master who has left the eastern door and arrived at the western side, to the place where the patron sits,[28] having consecrated the patron, will order him to hold the vajra [again]. If [the patron] is alive, they will enter through the east. If they are dead, they will enter through the west. [Both master and patron] arrive at the center of the mandala, [16r] and the master will hold in his hands the central vase. Four great meditators [i.e., assistants] in the four directions will hold the vases of the four directions. Then, from those four directions, they pronounce [the mantras] (*'dzab*) and recite (*bzlas*) the heart [mantra], and the initiations will be granted. As for the sequence of initiations, one will grant initiation by means of the substances that appear in the scripture: (i) vase, (ii) rosary, (iii) head cloth (*cod pan*), (iv) wheel, and so forth.

The ablutions will be performed. Then grant initiation by means of the eight auspicious substances: First, place a white mustard seed in [the patron's] hand and recite these words:

> This white mustard seed is the great supreme vajra family.
> By means of this great gnosis of equanimity, free of concepts,
> may there be supreme auspiciousness.

Then give them a mirror to hold in his hand:

> This mirror is the ocean of the gnosis of equality.
> By means of this complete realization of the very meaning of equality,
> may there be supreme auspiciousness.

Then grant [the other six] initiations by means of *dūrvā* grass, *bilva* fruit,[29] bezoar, yogurt, a conch shell, and vermillion powder:

> *Dūrvā* increases the life span.
> By gaining mastery over all life force,
> may there be supreme auspiciousness.

> *Bilva* is the fruit of enacting the causes and conditions.
> By completely realizing the very meaning of the dependent arising of causes and conditions,
> may there be supreme auspiciousness.

> Bezoar is the medicine for defeating the poisons [and the obscurations].[30]
> By completely realizing reality, which is the supreme medicine,
> may there be supreme auspiciousness.

> Yogurt is the essence of all dharmas.
> [16v] By realizing the supreme [ripening of the quintessence],[31]
> may there be supreme auspiciousness.

The conch proclaims all the teachings.
By realizing the significance of the music of all the melodious teachings,
may there be supreme auspiciousness.

Red vermillion is the nature of power.[32]
By gaining mastery over all life force,
may there be supreme auspiciousness."

Having granted in that way the initiations for the eight auspicious substances, the eight substances that are the symbols of the minds of the great *uṣṇīṣa* [buddhas], and the thirteen initiation substances, offer prayers, give patience, protect the body, and perform the blessing.

The mantra for digging out the earth for building the mandala platform is: *oṃ vajra khana khana hūṃ phaṭ*. The mantra for beating the earth is: *oṃ vajramungara akoṭṭaya akoṭṭaya hūṃ phaṭ*. For purifying the perfume waters: *oṃ vajra amṛte hūṃ phaṭ svāhā*. The mantra for laying the lines: *oṃ vajra sutra hūṃ phaṭ*. The mantra for staking the ritual dagger: *oṃ vajra kīlaya kīlaya sarvadustan hūṃ phaṭ*. For the white mustard seeds . . . [The rest is missing.]

THREE

Evoking Possession

The Sarvatathāgata-tattvasaṃgraha

> "Do you see the stars shining in the sky?
> Do you hear the dogs barking in Dzokchen Monastery?
> Do you hear what we two are saying?
> What is called 'meditation' is just that."
>
> Then certainty arose within me. Freed from any fetters of right and wrong, I was introduced to the gnosis of sheer awareness and emptiness. I obtained the inner consecration.[1]

THE RITUAL USE of evocative language to transmit a taste of awakening has long been central to Mahāyāna Buddhism, but it has not always been so. Within the genre of ritual manuals, the practice seems to have risen to the fore around the late seventh and eighth centuries. Of course, Buddhists had long been held to have experienced flashes of awakening. Buddha Śākyamuni himself underwent an inconceivable shift in perspective while sitting under the bodhi tree some 2,500 years ago, and his followers sought to replicate this from the very beginning of Buddhist history. Likewise, one might experience serenity (*prasāda*) at the sight of the Buddha, one of his disciples, or a reliquary stupa, or feel distress (*saṁvega*) upon seeing the four pilgrimage sites where the Buddha was born, awakened, taught, and passed away.[2] Such experiences were produced rather passively, but occasionally they were purposely provoked, as when the Buddha is said to have engendered serenity in tormented beings by performing miracles, manifesting a magical image of himself, or carrying on a dialogue with his own projected form.[3] And stories abound of disciples attaining awakening upon hearing the Buddha teach; according to Ashvaghosha's second-century literary masterpiece, the *Saundarananda*, when Nanda heard the Buddha speak about faith, he "was filled with utter joy, as though he had been sprinkled with the elixir of deathlessness. The perfectly enlightened one considered him to have virtually reached the goal by means of faith."[4] Similarly, in the Pāli *Khandavagga*, the Buddha's preaching strikes the gods with distress, "like beasts who hear the lion's roar."[5] Subsequent Buddhist teachers had long sought to facilitate such transformations in their disciples by reciting scriptures, instructing them on contemplative techniques, and so on. In all these ways, spiritually significant affective experiences had long been part of Buddhism. Yet ritual manuals provided an unprecedented literary space for Buddhists to articulate new kinds of intimate ritual encounters between text and reader, and by the turn of the eighth century, a shift had begun in the language of those manuals as new, more evocative forms of expression started to appear. A ritual master using poetic expression *within a ritualized setting* to provoke a particular experience in a disciple was something rarely seen before the advent of the Yoga tantras and their affiliated manuals. Such poetic transmissions would culminate in the early ninth century in the fourth (or "word") initiation and its immediate evocations of awakening, but their roots are visible already in much earlier tantric manuals. Their appearance marked a shift that was part of a much larger nexus of developments within Buddhist practice in the late seventh and eighth centuries. These developments began in India but soon had effects in Tibet, China, and beyond, changing Buddhist practice so thoroughly that today we find it hard to imagine the religion without them.

This chapter turns away from initiation manuals toward the postinitiatory practice of the *sādhana*. No longer immediately dependent on the teacher, the initiate or *sādhaka* would read and perform his *sādhana* to recreate the experience of awakening in his initiation.[6] The teacher is no longer present to evoke awakening through verse and gesture, but at crucial points in the *sādhana*'s proceedings there is a shift in linguistic register from straightforward instruction to poetic uses of metaphor, rhyme, rhythm, and more, all coordinated to produce in the reader an affective experience of union with the deity. Such were the daily meditations of the early practitioner of Yoga tantra.

The two previous chapters traced the rise of the genre of ritual manuals that circulated within and around the *dhāraṇī* sutras. These newly popular *vidhis*, *kalpas*, and so on took root in the mid-fifth century and gained popularity through the sixth century, proliferating rapidly throughout India and beyond. This was unprecedented. Never had so many extracanonical ritual manuals played such a central role in orthodox Buddhist practice. The rites they prescribed were increasingly complex and of a markedly different order from those practiced before. No longer merely recited, *dhāraṇī* spells were now chanted within a carefully constructed ritual space and accompanied by precisely choreographed physical activities within that space. Key to these earliest manuals was an interest in images and image worship, which Buddhists of the period shared with their contemporaries in the other two orthodox religious traditions of early India, Jainism and Brahmanism.

By the mid-seventh century, another shift was beginning across all three traditions, in large part facilitated by the now widespread ritual manuals and their countless innovations: the tantras were starting to emerge at a rapid rate—new scriptures that evinced a sea change in Asian religious practice.[7] With them came an interlocking set of elements involving the inner world of the imagination. In the earlier *dhāraṇī*-based rituals, the officiant would sit before an altar (termed a mandala) and direct their oblations to the buddha at its center. Increasingly, the practice was accompanied, or sometimes replaced outright, by a completely new perspective, an imagined level on which the practitioner *is* the buddha, seated at the center of the mandala and receiving the offerings. When both the physical and the imagined levels of performance were retained, the practitioner might even arrange the prescribed offerings before the image in front of him while visualizing himself as that same buddha, receiving the offerings in a purified form from imagined offering goddesses.

Tantric ritual therefore unfolded on two registers—the outer, which was visible to anyone present, and the inner, which remained invisible to most people—and it was on this inner level that the real rite was held to take place; it was on this imaginary level, from this new perspective of the ritual subject at the center of the mandala, that the rite's true power was generated. The eighth-century tantric commentator Buddhagupta explains that the ritual master, to draw a physical mandala upon the earthen platform, should first imagine the "intrinsically existent mandala" in the space above the platform. Only on the basis of this imagined *true* mandala can its "reflection" be drawn in paints or colored sands.[8] We may see a similar concept in two mandalas depicted at Dunhuang, each with a more elaborate mandala above a simpler mandala altar (fig. 3.1). The outward instructions of the earlier *dhāraṇī*-based ritual manuals were thus augmented with detailed descriptions of what the practitioner should imagine. And imagination in this context was no sad facsimile of reality: it was the root of all phenomena. It was perhaps not a coincidence that the influential seventh-century Indian philosopher Dharmakīrti placed a kind of subjective phenomenology at the heart of his own highly influential philosophical project.

The tantric imaginary, invisible on the physical plane, was also accompanied by a new rhetoric of secrecy. This "more than real" level on which tantric ritual unfolded was invisible, the tantrics claimed, if you had not

FIGURE 3.1 Vajradhatu mandala painting
Source: Guimet 17780, Courtesy of the Musée Guimet

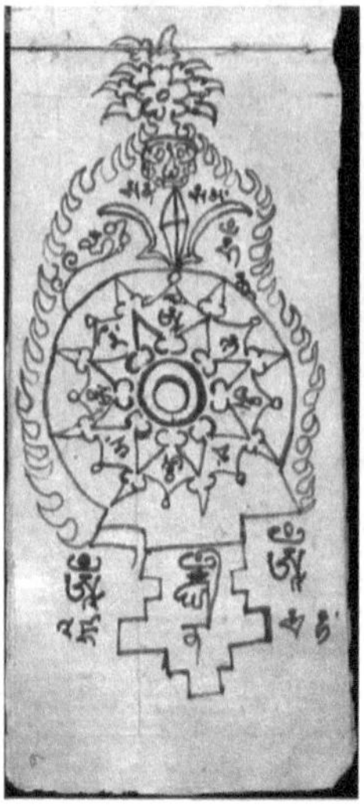

FIGURE 3.2 Mandala with altar
Source: IOL Tib J 510, Courtesy of the British Library

received the proper initiations.[9] Tantric initiation was now requisite before any of these new rites could be explained, and initiates were not to speak about the relevant rites to anyone outside the circle. Unlike the sutras, these Buddhist teachings were not to be propagated freely. Now these most efficacious practices were to be withheld from all but a small group of initiates, and dire consequences were threatened for any who might break this rule. Within the circle, coded language began to be used, and multiple levels of meaning were ubiquitous. A statement made within this highly ritualized context could be understood on an outer or an inner (and sometimes even a further secret) level, with the latter meaning determined through complex systems of mystical associations known only to initiates. Secrecy, initiation, imagination, and self-identification with the Buddha: all these elements worked together to shape this new approach to Buddhist ritual, strongly focused on the tantric subject.

Materials

By the last quarter of the seventh century, a new tantric system was emerging. Eventually encapsulated in the *Sarvatathāgata-tattvasaṃgraha Tantra* (*Compendium of the Realities of All the Tathāgatas*; henceforth *STTS*), the system revolved around the practitioner's imagined union with a buddha.[10] The limits of its influence are hard to define. Writing in the mid-eighth century, Amoghavajra describes the *STTS* as the centerpiece of a corpus of eighteen "assemblies," all of which had been extracted from a supposed 100,000-verse *ur*-text named the **Vajroṣṇīṣa* that his teacher, Vajrabodhi, had lost en route to China. The often-intertwined concepts of a mythic *ur*-text and a corpus of excerpted scriptures that were somehow distinct from previous works of *buddhavācana* was not unique. The seventh-century Chinese pilgrim to India, Yixing, reports on the existence of the related *Vidyādharapiṭaka* in 100,000 verses that already had been lost, of which only a few extracts were extant.[11] And after Amoghavajra's time, references were made to various groups of eighteen tantras, often considered extracts from an *ur*-tantra by the name of *Mayājālā*.[12] Each of these scriptural corpuses shares elements in common, as do the eighteen **Vajroṣṇīṣa* works. As noted in chapter 2, the *Purification of All Negative Rebirths* may be seen as a meeting of the earlier *Buddhoṣṇīṣa* line with the **Vajroṣṇīṣa*, and it received from the latter its system of mantras, *mudrās* (hand gestures), and assorted ritual procedures. Whether these influences came directly from the *STTS* or from a wider range of ritual practices is unclear, but by the mid-eighth century, the *STTS* stood at the center of this influential group of "assemblies."

The *STTS* includes vestiges of its early development that conflict somewhat with the work's overall system. In particular, the fourfold structure of the work, its four *mudrās*, four families, and so on fit uncomfortably with the final product's five families and other fivefold groupings. This is significant, because the *Mahāvairocanābhisaṃbodhi* and other early tantras of the early to mid-seventh century have only three buddha families—the buddha, the *padma*, and the *vajra*, represented by the Buddha with the bodhisattvas Avalokiteśvara and Vajrapāṇi on his proper left and right. Around what must have been the mid-seventh century, a fourth *ratna* family represented by Ākāśagarbha was added, and by the time of the received *STTS* compilation toward the end of the seventh century, a fifth karma family completed the system (though later a sixth *ur*-family would sometimes be mentioned). Other tantras reflect this middle period of four families too, the *Amoghapāśakalparāja* and the *Mañjuśrīmūlakalpa* prominent among them, and early experiments with alternative sets of families are seen elsewhere.[13]

As the *STTS* gained popularity, so did another kind of ritual manual: the *sādhana*. Chapter 2's *Sarvadurgatipariśodhana* initiation manual recommends the propitiation (Tib. *bsnyen pa*; Skt. *sevā*) of the deities as a preparatory rite. Propitiation is the first of two ritual stages, the second being accomplishment (Tib. *bsgrub pa*; *sādhana*). Together, the pair structured much of early tantric practice in both Buddhism and the other Indian religious traditions. Propitiation typically took up the lion's share of the practitioner's time, often requiring extended retreat and involving the recitation of mantras in the thousands or hundreds of thousands. The *Sarvadurgatipariśodhana* initiation manual calls for ten billion recitations, or at least 28,000 if time is short.[14] Such numbers served to ensure purification through intensive engagement by a new initiate before they could perform the other rites in the system.[15] In the end, however, the initiation manual allows for just 10,000, 1,000, or even just 108 recitations, probably more realistic for just preparing to grant an initiation.[16] Having completed the requisite propitiations, the early tantric practitioner would typically be authorized to embark on the second stage of practice, the accomplishment. This could take various forms and basically represented the opportunity for the officiant to direct the now-attentive deities toward a particular purpose.

By the eighth century, this second category, accomplishment, began to overshadow propitiation; *sādhana* became increasingly central to postinitiatory practice. Propitiation was not dropped entirely, and the two categories were even expanded and applied in new interpretive ways, but over time, the *sādhana* stage of practice came to function largely on its own and was formalized as a distinct textual genre, or perhaps subgenre. The manual that is the focus of the present chapter is one such *sādhana*: the *Ārya-tattvasaṃgraha-sādhanopāyikā* (*De nyid 'dus pa' bsgrub pa'i thabs*), a work closely tied to the *STTS*.[17]

No fewer than five copies of the *Tattvasaṃgraha-sādhana* are to be found among the Dunhuang manuscripts. One is complete, while the others range from a single folio to all but one.[18] Unusually for Dunhuang ritual manuals, there is a nearly complete commentary to the *sādhana* with additional ritual notes appended thereto.[19] The commentary is helpful at points but not always reliable; it was probably written later, and not by the *sādhana*'s author. A second *STTS*-based *sādhana*, the *Śrī-vajrahūṃkara-sādhanopāyikā*, focuses on the wrathful vajra-family deity Vajrahūṃkara of the Trailokyavijaya mandala, described in the *STTS*'s second chapter.[20] The work appears in the same manuscript alongside the almost complete copy of the *Tattvasaṃgraha-sādhana* and may date from a slightly later period, as it draws on both the *STTS*'s appended "unsurpassed tantra" (*anuttaratantra*), likely a later addition, and possibly on the *Vajraśekhara-tantra*, a self-professed "further tantra" (*uttaratantra*) that was certainly composed after the *STTS* had been completed.[21] This *Vajrahūṃkara-sādhana* is considerably more elaborate and provides a number of illuminating details. The *Tattvasaṃgraha-sādhana* remains our focus, however, due in part to its apparent popularity and the existence of a commentary but also to its relatively succinct elegance.[22]

Many of the manuscripts containing the *Tattvasaṃgraha-sādhana* show signs of having been penned in the ninth century, particularly the two most complete copies.[23] Although the techniques of paleographic analysis for dating are still not infallible, the weight of evidence is significant. The vast majority of Dunhuang manuscripts containing Mahāyoga texts date to the tenth century. These works, infamous for their focus on ritualized sex and violence (*sbyor grol*), were proscribed by the Tibetan imperial court of the eighth and ninth centuries. But the circle of *STTS*-based works exists in an earlier time, in a realm of tantric practice sanctioned by the court, a Yoga tantra system whose canonical works and commentaries were included in the *Pangtangma* catalogue of officially sponsored translations.[24] If any of the results of paleographic analysis are reliable, then the dates of these manuscripts may reflect the policies and practices of the central Tibetan court.

None of this tells us about the provenance of the original text of the *Tattvasaṃgraha-sādhana*, although we may say with some confidence that it is a translation of an Indic original. That a Sanskrit title is provided in the opening lines right away suggests this. Later Tibetans took to providing Sanskrit titles for their apocrypha, but early Tibetans do not seem to have done so, and among the Dunhuang manuscripts such titles appear to indicate a true Indic origin.[25] The origins of the commentary are more difficult to determine. It may well be a Tibetan composition. In terms of dating, presumably the *sādhana* is from the late eighth century at the latest. So this appears to be a Tibetan translation of an eighth-century Indic *STTS*-based *sādhana* and its Tibetan commentary.

The following analyses will also rely heavily on the *Kosalālaṁkāra*, a commentary on the *STTS* by the late eighth-century scholar Śākyamitra, and to some extent on Ānandagarbha's tenth-century *STTS* commentary, the *Tattvālokakarī*, and his *maṇḍalavidhi*, the *Vajrodaya*.

Opening Comments and Overall Structure of the *Sādhana*

The *sādhana* opens with an homage to Vajrasattva. Though Vairocana is considered the central deity of the *STTS*'s Vajradhātu mandala, Vajrasattva sits immediately before him (as the westernmost deity in the eastern circle surrounding Akṣobhya) and is the first to be emanated from his heart in the narrative account of the original mandala's creation. Throughout much of the early tantric materials, Vairocana and Vajrasattva are so closely aligned as to be almost interchangeable. This is part of a gradual shift in tantric Buddhism away from the buddha family to the vajra.[26] In chapter 2, we saw how in the *Mahāvairocanābhisaṃbodhi*'s initiation sequence, the master first imagines himself as Vairocana to take possession of the site but then consecrates both himself and the initiates as Vajrasattva for the further activities.[27] In this sense, Vajrasattva serves as Vairocana's closest friend and aide (*rājapurohita*?), and he plays a similarly key role in this *sādhana*.

After the homage, it reads: "If one who has received the *samaya* wishes to cultivate [the *samādhi*] and perform the recitations, he should stay in a place appropriately indicated." The practices that follow are therefore solely for initiates who have received and are protecting the vows of *samaya*. While the *sādhana* leaves the vows at that, both the *Vajrahūṃkara-sādhana* and the commentary go to some lengths to discuss a list of fourteen.[28] "Breaking the *samaya* will lead to various obstacles arising in this life and cause all the gods and demons to laugh, and eventually one will be reborn a hell being in [the hell of] weeping and wailing," concludes the commentary, reminding the reader of the bloodthirstiness of the gods and demons held at bay only by the strength of one's vows.[29] The commentary adds that the site may be one established by previous buddhas or just an isolated location. It should be checked in accordance with the Kriyā scriptures, by digging and refilling a test hole:

> If [the hole] is full or there is extra [soil], then it is an indicated site. If it is not full, it is not indicated. If pieces of jewels, flowers, or chunks of flesh come out of the earth, it is an indicated site. If charcoal or bones appear, it is not indicated. Also, if it is within one *yojana* of the *vajrāsana* [i.e., Bodhgāya], it is an indicated place. If it is within one *yojana* from wherever there is a volume of the *Prajñā[pāramitā]*, then it is an indicated place. The vajra family is established as

the family of Oḍḍiyāna. The *ratna* family is accomplished in places that are sources for jewels. Those of the *padma* family gain full accomplishment when they meditate wherever there are lotuses, water springs, and flowers.[30]

Having selected the site, the officiant is ready to begin the practices. The *Vajrahūṃkara-sādhana* intercedes at this point with some preliminaries:

> Should one who has obtained the *ācārya* initiation[31] for the great *maṇḍala* of Trailokyavijaya and the like wish to perform the recitations for Glorious Vajrahūṃkara, one should first perform the *vidyāmantra* observance. On the full moon, one should mentally depict all the *tathāgatas* of all the limitless worlds of the boundless ten directions and perform prostrations before all the *tathāgatas*. Having established the boundaries and so forth, one should worship well the Bhagavan Vajra Śrī Hūṃkara howsoever and recite [his mantra] one hundred times.[32] That is the observance for the *vajra* family.[33]

Although the references to Trailokyavijaya and Vajrahūṃkara are not entirely relevant to our (not specifically vajra family-focused) *sādhana*, this passage suggests that the categories of propitiation and accomplishment continue to play a role in the *STTS* system. A *vidyāmantra* observance, sometimes just *vidyā* observance (*vidyāvrata*), is not discussed in the *STTS* itself, but the tantra's late eighth-century commentator Śākyamitra states that it constitutes the tantra's "preliminary practices."[34] As such, it functions like the *Mahāvairocanābhisaṃbodhi*'s own *vidyāvrata*, which devotes its entire seventeenth chapter to the matter. Buddhagupta's commentary helps to clarify that such a *vidyāvrata* represents the preliminary propitiation, sometimes involving a hundred thousand recitations, to be performed before beginning the *sādhana*.[35]

In the *sādhana* itself, the proceedings may be divided into two main parts (referenced in the analyses below): (1) the meditation on oneself as a buddha along with the subsequent offerings and (2) the four *mudrās* and the mantra recitations. (The four *mudrās* are the *mahāmudrā*, *dharmamudrā*, *samayamudrā*, and *karmamudrā*, four gestures symbolic of the body, speech, mind, and activities of the buddha.) The *Vajrahūṃkara-sādhana* opens with some comments on the overall structure that provide some significant insights. The comments come in two verses, each a quotation from the *STTS* itself. The first reads:

Every day, one should first perform properly the self-consecration (*svādhiṣṭhāṇa*) and so forth,
then accomplish the rest, after which one should perform as one pleases.[36]

In commenting on these lines, Śākyamitra explains that after the self-consecration and "the rest" (Tib. *thams chad*; Skt. **sarvaṃ*), "Having completed the *mudrās* [in the second stage], one performs whichever rites one wishes, be they a mandala rite, a recollection [of the Buddha] (*anusmṛti*), an accomplishment, or sundry minor rites."[37] His first stage of the self-consecrations maps onto the first part of the *sādhana* perfectly. This is followed by completing "the rest," which Śākyamitra glosses as "the *mudrās*," the four that structure the second part.[38] That one then "performs as one pleases" corresponds to the lines that end the stage of the four *mudrās* in the *Tattvasaṃgraha-sādhana*: "Then, binding the *karmamudrā*, perform the recitations or meditations."[39] ("Binding" means to perform the physical gesture.)[40] Thus, the *sādhana* has three parts:

1. Self-consecration (*svādhiṣṭhāna*)
2. Four *mudrās*
3. Recitations or performing other rites ("as one pleases").

The second passage, quoted in the **Śrī- vajrahūṃkara-sādhanopāyikā* immediately after the first, is drawn from chapter 23 (the *anuttaratantra*) of the *STTS*:

Having performed the four ways of offering, [each] in its own four aspects, in accordance with the ritual procedures
at the four sessions, one then accomplishes the activities.[41]

This is still more obscure, but it seems to reference the offerings that end stage 1 and the activities of the *karmamudrā* that end stage 2. In short, there is strong evidence in both the Dunhuang manuscripts and the Indian commentaries that the *Tattvasaṃgraha-sādhana* unfolds according to two principal stages, with a final pseudo-stage of performing further rites, such as granting initiation, as one wishes.[42]

Regarding the *sādhana*'s structure, the *Vajrahūṃkara-sādhana* includes an explicit account of populating the mandala, whereas in the *Tattvasaṃgraha-*

sādhana, the practitioner generates himself as Vajrasattva but the rest of the mandala gets no explicit mention. It is, however, present implicitly, insofar as each ritual act is an instantiation of, and in a sense performed by, a different deity. In this way, the order of the deities in the mandala orders the entire *sādhana*. Thus, after the practitioner transforms into the central deity, the consecration by means of the *jñānasattva*, which installs the four surrounding heads of the buddha families (Akṣobhya and so on), is performed by the *pāramitā* goddesses and the sixteen bodhisattvas. Then the offering goddesses perform the offerings, and finally (moving into part two and the four *mudrās*), the gatekeepers lead in and chain down the deities. All these acts and their corresponding deities follow almost precisely the order in which the same deities are generated in the *Maṇḍalarājāgrī-samādhi* section of the *STTS*.[43]

Vajrāveśa: Entering the Mandala

The proceedings begin with a prostration in each of the four directions. Here, the reader faces the west to prostrate to the eastern vajra family, the north for the southern family, and so on, as if standing before the different sides of the mandala. During each prostration, the reader recites a mantra while imagining the symbol appropriate to that family at a particular point on his body: a vajra at the heart, a jewel at the forehead, a lotus at the mouth, and a crossed vajra at the head.[44]

Next, after taking a seat and performing a brief purification by means of the famous mantra, *oṃ svabhāvaśuddhāḥ sarvadharmāḥ svabhāvaśuddho'ham*, one begins the procedures for uniting with the deity. (In a poetic aside, the commentary adds, "It is suitable to cultivate the deities of the mandala in any of these three [ways]: as flowers falling, as dream images, or with surpassing devotion.)[45] First, one strikes the *vajrabhanda mudrā*, with fingers tightly bound together into a single fist and recites the mantra, "*vajrabandha traṭ*." Then one binds the *vajrāveśa mudrā* ("vajra-possession" or "vajra-entry" *mudrā*) while reciting the corresponding mantra: "*vajrāveśa aḥ*."[46] Here, as the commentary explains, "one imagines that, by means of the *āveśamudrā* together with the mantras, one becomes the deity and gnosis descends."[47] Śākyamitra confirms this understanding: "one may generate the descent of the gnosis . . . thereby imagining oneself in the body of Vajrasattva "[48]

Following this series of acts comes the well-known "five stages of manifest awakening" (*pañcākārābhisaṃbodhikrama*), which transform the practitioner's ordinary body into that of the central buddha, followed by the consecration of that form with the buddha's gnosis. There appears to be some redundancy here, as the foregoing *vajrāveśa* already produced a union with Vajrasattva. Śākyamitra seems to recognize this when he elsewhere explains: "When it says, '*vajrāveśa*,' this possession is a possession by gnosis *but not the possession by the deity* (*sattva*)."[49] So, while the *vajrāveśa* transforms the practitioner into the body of Vajrasattva and effects the possession of the gnosis, it is not a union with one's own deity. Still, Śākyamitra's explanation is not entirely satisfactory.[50]

The Dunhuang *Vajrahūṃkara-sādhana* helps. Just prior to the *vajrabandha* and the *vajrāveśa* sequence, that text instructs the practitioner to prepare and generate the entire ritual space of the mandala through a series of four actions.[51] Only then does one perform the *vajrabandha* and *vajrāveśa*. As in our *sādhana*, all this is then followed by the further generation of oneself as the buddha through the five stages of manifest awakening and the self-consecration. The same two methods for inviting the gnosis to descend may thus be discerned: the *vajrāveśa* for creating the mandala externally and installing its deities through the four actions, and the five stages and self-consecration for installing the deity within/as oneself. Each involves transforming the practitioner into the deity, but each is tied to a different model of worship—one more outwardly focused on the ritual space surrounding the practitioner, the other more inwardly focused on the practitioner himself. The redundancy may have resulted from a meeting of the outward approach of consecrating and worshipping a buddha on an altar and the inward techniques for becoming a buddha oneself.

The *STTS*, in the section corresponding to our *sādhana*'s *vajrāveśa*, makes it explicit that this process can involve the construction of a physical altar, complete with marking out the lines and drawing the deities.[52] Then, having finished constructing the mandala, the master enters it with the *vajrāvésa* and consecrates all the deities, including himself as Vajrasattva.[53] Although the *Vajrahūṃkara-sādhana* describes the creation of such a mandala, it does not mention a physical altar, only a more abbreviated imagined process via its four actions. The *Vajrahūṃkara-sādhana* is thus suspended between worlds, maintaining the external mandala but in an interiorized form. Our *Tattvasaṃgraha-sādhana* does not even mention the mandala, perhaps reflecting the fading importance of physical mandala altars, even as it retains the *vajrāveśa mudrā* and mantra for entering the now entirely implicit external mandala. Such an approach is recognized by Śākyamitra. In referring to the *STTS*'s rather extensive instructions on constructing the physical mandala, he writes:

> This is just for the purpose of illustration. By upholding the [procedures of] the [self-]consecration, the [self-]initiations, the protection, the offerings, and the *samādhi*, one cultivates oneself as Vajrasattva and performs the activities of the mandala. Alternatively, if [one wishes to] abbreviate [the construction of the mandala], one may generate the descent of the gnosis by reciting, "*vajrabandha traṭ*" and "*vajrāveśa aḥ*," thereby imagining oneself in the body of Vajrasattva.[54]

Śākyamitra here seems somewhat dismissive of the passage on constructing the physical mandala. "This is just for the purpose of illustration," he writes. Instead, he suggests moving quickly through this part, abbreviating the extensive procedures by simply performing the *vajrabandha* and *vajrāveśa*—precisely the shortcut in our *sādhana*.

The redundancy in our *sādhana* thus may reflect the changes that tantric practice was undergoing in the eighth century. Two models are at work. In the earlier one, the officiant constructs a mandala as a physical or imagined space, then enters it and invites the consecrating gnosis deities to take their places within the mandala. In the later, the ritual subject transforms into the buddha, then invites the consecrating deities into his body. The ritual subject was gradually taking center stage upon an imagined altar.[55]

The Five Stages of Manifest Awakening: Narrating Consecration

Following the latter model, next come the five stages of manifest awakening. In our *sādhana*, these take a relatively abbreviated form, involving first, the deconstruction of oneself into mind only; second, the cultivation of an imagined moon disc within that empty space; third, the placement of the seed syllable of one's deity upon that moon; fourth, the transformation of the syllable into the symbol of one's deity (e.g., a vajra); fifth, the transformation of that, in turn, into the form of the deity. Though only mentioned in the commentary, each of the last two transformations occurs through the emanation and retraction of light rays. The whole process takes up just two lines of text in the one complete copy of the *sādhana*. Its ritual unimportance relative to what follows has already been suggested by the numerous quotations that refer to this portion of the ritual only in terms of the next procedure, the self-consecrations of the *svādhiṣṭhāṇa*. This may seem surprising given the influence of the five stages and their role in the opening narrative of the *STTS*, where Śarvārthasiddhi, a.k.a. Śākyamuni, is led through them one by one, to transform himself into the buddha Vairocana. As we shall see, however, the *consecration* of images is more important to this tradition than their production.

The *STTS* narrative opens (after an introduction to the nature of Mahāvairocana) on the scene of Sarvārthasiddhi's awakening beneath the bodhi tree. What follows is a tantric reimagining of this iconic moment. All the buddhas descend upon the famous site and rouse the bodhisattva from his nihilistic breath-holding meditation (*āsphānakasamādhi*).[56] They then lead him through a series of five meditations that transform him into the buddha Vajradhātu, who is identical with Vairocana.

The five stages described in our *sādhana* do not match those of the *STTS* narrative. In place of the first-stage deconstruction of the body and the resulting meditation on a mind-only emptiness, the *STTS* has the buddha-to-be generate an initial moon. Then the second stage in our manual produces the seed syllable, and in the *STTS* results in a second moon disc. The tantra's apparent redundancy of two moon discs is treated variously by different commentators. Śākyamitra claims that the initial moon is only a new moonlike sliver that expands into a full moon in stage 2, with the first instantiating the practitioner's purified foundational consciousness (*ālayavijñāna*)

Three Interpretations of the Five Stages of Manifest Awakening

TATTVASAṂGRAHA-SĀDHANA	*VAJRAHŪṂKARA-SĀDHANA*	*STTS*
emptiness	moon 1	moon 1
moon	moon 2	moon 2
syllable	vajra	vajra 1
symbol	Siddhārthasiddhi	vajra 2
deity	deity	deity

made of all the merit they have accumulated over countless aeons, and the second being Samantabhadra, the mind of awakening (*bodhicitta*).[57]

The wrathful *Vajrahūṃkara-sādhana* adheres more closely to the tantra's account and provides all the mantras. The one point of divergence is in the fourth stage. In the *STTS*, the buddha-to-be, the meditating bodhisattva Sarvārthasiddhi, having just produced in the third stage a vajra standing upright upon the full moon disc, is now instructed to make firm the vajra with the mantra, "*oṃ vajrātmako'ham*." According to the *Vajrahūṃkara-sādhana*, by means of this mantra, all the *tathāgatas* throughout the universe enter into the vajra, transforming it back into the body of bodhisattva Sarvārthasiddhi: "The consecrations of all those *tathāgatas* enter that Vajrasattva [probably (*sic*) for *sattvavajra*, i.e., the vajra], which then becomes the form of the bodhisattva Sarvārthasidddhi, who remains there."[58]

Although Sarvārthasiddhi is the protagonist of the *STTS* narrative, the appearance of his form here in the *Vajrahūṃkara-sādhana* is probably based on a misreading. The tantra reads: "Then all the *vajradhātus* of the body, speech, and mind of all the *tathāgatas* dwelling throughout all of space, by means of the consecration of all the *tathāgatas*, entered that *sattvavajra* [i.e., the vajra upon the moon disc]. Then, all the *tathāgatas* granted initiation to that blessed great bodhisattva Sarvārthasiddhi with the vajra-name initiation."[59] The last sentence could be read to mean that the vajra of stage 3 is now, in stage 4, Sarvārthasiddhi, but this is probably not what was originally intended.[60] In the fourth stage of the *STTS*, then, the bodhisattva remains in the form of the vajra that was established in the third stage, only now "stabilized" by the penetration of all the buddhas.

Such a reading of the fourth stage is supported by the larger structure of the *STTS*'s account, for at the heart of the entire narrative lies a powerful interest in consecration, in the installation of awakened mind into the outer shell of the form. In the *STTS*, the five stages therefore unfold in pairs: two moon discs, two vajras, and even two buddhas (as explained below). This is why the form of the fourth stage repeats that of the third. Careful analysis of the tantra's account reveals that, despite its fame as the *locus classicus* for the *five* stages, it is really a story of *six*. The initial moon of stage 1 is made truly a moon in stage 2 by means of the mind of awakening that is Samantabhadra. The initial vajra of stage 3 is made firm (*dṛḍhī*) by the buddhas entering into it in stage 4. ("By means of what power?" asks Śākyamitra, answering his own question, "By means of the consecration of all the *tathāgatas*.")[61]

But the form of the buddha in the "final" fifth stage also requires consecration. For this just reason, immediately upon recognizing his new form as a *tathāgata* in stage 5, Vajradhātu bows to all the *tathāgatas* and requests: "Blessed *tathāgatas*! Consecrate me and make firm this manifest complete awakening!"[62] Thereupon, in something like a sixth stage, the buddhas once more enter into him, awakening him as an *arhat*, a perfectly complete buddha. As Śākyamitra makes explicit, the buddhas enter him through four points on his body—the heart, between the eyes, the throat, and the crown of the head.[63] The moment corresponds precisely, as we shall see in a moment, to the self-consecration that immediately follows the five stages in our Dunhuang *sādhana*. The *STTS*'s account of Sarvārthasiddhi's original performance of the five stages of manifest awakening is thus foremost a narrative of consecration.

Svādhiṣṭhāṇa: Consecrating the Ritual Subject

The reader has now generated himself in the body of Vairocana. The all-important self-consecration that forms the centerpiece of our *sādhana's* first part opens with an explanatory note: "Primarily, the consecrations of the bodhisattvas should be performed with the *mudrā* of one's family."[64] This signals that although the consecration by Sattvavajrī that follows is primary, further consecrations should then be performed using the *mudrās* specific to the remaining sixteen bodhisattvas. And indeed, an instruction on these secondary, rather abbreviated consecrations closes the section below.[65] In any case, one begins by forming (or "binding," Tib. *bcing*) the *mudrā* of one's family. For the central *tathāgata* buddha family, the text explains, one uses the *sattvavajrī-mudrā*. Technically, Sattvavajrī sits to the east of Vairocana and thus represents the vajra family, which once again enjoy a privileged relationship with the *tathāgata* family.[66]

The *sattvavajrī-mudrā* is formed by clasping both hands together into a single fist and raising the two middle fingers to face each other. This, Śākyamitra explains, is a vajra standing upon a moon disc:

> Resting within mind only, that mind only is explained to be like a moon disc. In order to make that firm, moreover, a five-spoked gnosis vajra is placed there; this is the *samaya*; it is established as the form of the gnosis of the buddhas and

> bodhisattvas throughout the Mahāyāna. How so? The vajra clasp is a demonstration of the moon disc, and the two raised middle fingers are taught to be the vajra.[67]

Expressing the identity of this *mudrā* with the *samaya* (the mind of the buddha), one recites the *samaya* mantra: "You are the *samaya*!" (*samayastvaṃ*). One then imagines a moon disc behind one's back. The commentary suggests that the moon is created by circling the *sattvavajrī-mudrā* over one's head.[68] Though our *sādhana* is not explicit on the purpose of this moon disc, the *STTS* suggests that one's own form as the deity is reflected in its mirrorlike surface.[69] Śākyamitra adds that this mirror image is the *jñānasattva* (gnosis being).[70] Thus the consecrating deity is held simultaneously within the *sattvavajrī-mudrā* and the moon disc.

Here some explanation is required. The term *jñānasattva*, the gnosis of the deity, only came into use in the second half of the eighth century. Before then, the term *samaya* or *samayamudrā* carried basically the same meaning. This can be confusing for the modern reader, because later and thus more familiar sources refer to the visualized form of the deity as the *samayasattva* (*samaya* being), into which the mind, the *jñānasattva*, i.e., the deity itelf, enters to enliven it. The early identification of the *samayamudrā* with the *jñānasattva* is clear not only from ritual procedures such as this one, but also from explicit statements in an array of early sources. The ninth-century Vaidyapāda writes, "The so-called *samayamudrā* at one's heart refers to the *samayamudrā* at one's deity's heart, and that is identified as the *jñānasattva*."[71] Similarly, Pelliot tibétain 656 reads: "When the *jñānasattva* comes together with oneself, that is called the *samayamudrā*."[72] For the purposes of our *sādhana's* self-consecration the *mudrā* formed by clasping one's hands with the two middle fingers raised and facing each other, which represents the five-spoked vajra on a moon disc, is the *jñānasattva*. As Śākyamitra concludes: "There is no difference between the *sattvavajrī-mudrā* and the *jñānasattva*."[73] This is in addition to the *jñānasattva* reflected in the moon.

In the *STTS*'s own account of the moon disc behind the practitioner, the *āveśa* (entry) of the *jñānasattva* into the practitioner is effected by reciting a further mantra: "*samayastvam ahaṃ*" ("I am the *samaya* you are"). Śākyamitra explains: "This is to say, 'that which you are, I am,' and 'that which I am, you are." Simultaneously, the image within the moon disc unites with oneself and oneself unites with the image in the moon. "One should cultivate them as indistinguishable, [mixing] simultaneously, like water and milk," adds Ānandagarbha.[74] It is significant that the moon is playing a role often played by a mirror in later image consecration rites. There, the mirror holds the *jñānasattva* until, as in our *sādhana*, the consecration occurs as the two images merge, "just as 'double vision' turns into single vision when one stops crossing one's eyes."[75] In fact, the exchangeability of moon and mirror is entirely natural, as the moon itself functions as a mirror, its light being a reflection of the sun's. As Varāhamihira's sixth-century *Bṛhatsaṃhitā* says, "The rays of the sun reflected on the moon, which is made of water, dispel the darkness of night / Just as if falling on the surface of a mirror, [they dispel darkness] inside a house."[76] Or *sādhana*'s moon disc functions similarly, its surface revealing the true deity, apparent yet empty of independent existence.

Although the *sādhana* instructs its reader to form the moon disc, it does not see the reflection's role in the consecration through to its end; the kind of merging of images just described does not occur. Instead, it focuses exclusively on the *jñānasattva*, or *samaya*, in the form of the *sattvavajrī-mudrā*. The self-consecration is performed by touching the *mudrā* to four places on one's own body, "the heart, between the eyes, the throat, and the crown of the head,"[77] while reciting the mantra "*Sattvavajrī adhitiṣṭhasva mām*" ("O Sattvavajrī, consecrate me!"). Our commentary explains that these four placements (*nyāsa*) purify the mind, body, speech, and activities, respectively.[78] Finally, one generates pride in oneself as the buddha and seals the union by proclaiming, "*samayo'ham*" ("I am the *samaya*"), which plays a similar role to the mantra that seals the union using the moon disc behind the practitioner (i.e., equivalent to "*samayasvtam ahaṃ*").

The same four places on the body already appeared in the context of the tantra's opening narrative, specifically in its final "sixth" pseudo-stage of the buddhas' consecration of Vajradhātu. As Śākyamitra explains, all the *tathāgatas* enter into their freshly minted buddha through these same four bodily points, and significantly, " 'all the *tathāgatas*' here comprise the four *tathāgatas*, Akṣobhya and so on, who are the very essence of the gnosis bodies."[79] Just as our *sādhana*'s consecrations at the four points installs the buddhas' body, speech, mind, and activities into the practitioner, the *STTS* narrative's *tathāgatas* install the heads of the four surrounding buddha families into Vajradhātu. Through this primary act, then, *the core of the mandala is enacted* and poured into the body of the ritual subject. It is immediately followed by the additional consecrations by the sixteen bodhisattvas that surround these central buddhas in the mandala. By the end of the larger self-consecration sequence, the entire inner mandala has been performed, with each ritual act being an instantiation of each buddha and bodhisattva in the subject's body.

Our *Tattvasaṃgraha-sādhana* represents a remarkably well sculpted ritual tradition. Its multiple links with the *STTS*'s opening narrative show careful effort in composition. The five stages of manifest awakening work both within the tantra's narrative and in the system's ritual manuals, but careful analysis reveals that the theme of consecration via its motif of a vajra upon a moon disc is key to both the narrative and early ritual practice. The tantra's opening narrative might even have been written specifically to explain the power of the consecration. Not only do the five stages, with their doubled moons and doubled vajras, only make sense in light of the consecratory act, but the entire sequence sets the stage for the culminating act of all the *tathāgatas*' consecrating Vajradhātu through the four points on his body.[80] And the motif of the vajra upon a moon disc stands (in more ways than one) at the heart of the system. When the *tathāgatas* enter Vajradhātu, they enter through the four points of his body, but they settle at his heart: "Thus he made his request [to be consecrated], and all the *tathāgatas* entered into that *sattvavajra* of Vajradhātu."[81] It suddenly becomes apparent that the vajra upon the moon disc was not just transformed into the form of the buddha in stage 5 but encased within that form; it remains at the buddha's heart. This is confirmed by the eighth-century Indian author Buddhagupta, who writes, "For this reason, both this and other tantras explain that when accomplishing the *samayamudrā*, one binds the *samayamudrā* to be accomplished, then, placing it in the area of one's heart, imagines the mind as a vajra at one's heart."[82] The creation of the consecrated and consecrating vajra upon a moon disc, the *sattvavajra* who is the *sattvavajrī-mudrā*, is thus the focus of the tantra's opening narrative. *This* is the representation of the *samaya*, the gnosis of the buddha. As we shall see, below in this chapter and in the next, this formation was central to tantric ritual of the Yoga and early Mahāyoga classes.

The Four *Mudrās*

Following the self-consecration, the *Tattvasaṃgraha-sādhana* instructs its reader to perform the initiations (Tib. *dbang bskur*; Skt. *abhiṣeka*). These take the form of a ritual donning of the five-buddha crown, as the practitioner binds the *pāramitāmudrās* for each family at five points on the head.[83] This ends the *samādhi* section for uniting with the deity.

Next come the offerings. Under the old Kriyā-style model, these would have been directed to the buddha(s) upon the altar. In the Yoga tantras and our *sādhana*, however, they would presumably be directed to oneself, now as the buddha. Though this is not stated outright, it is implied by the very existence of the offering goddesses, who perform the offerings in place of the officiant. (Of course, the offerings could also be made outwardly at the same time.) The eight offering goddesses are divided into those of the secret and the outward, all listed in the same order seen in the mandala.[84] Their actions accomplished, part one is complete, and the practitioner is ready to proceed into the four *mudrās*.

The *STTS* is one of our earliest sources for the four tantric *mudrās*, being organized around a number of (often interrelated) fourfold divisions: its four sections, four *siddhis*, and four buddha families. (The same four *mudrās* have different meanings in later tantric Buddhism, where the *karmamudrā*, for example, refers to the sexual consort. Such meanings are not relevant in the present Yogatantra context.) Within this context, the four *mudrās* represent the four aspects of the buddha, with *mahāmudrā* the body, *dharmamudrā* the speech, *samayamudrā* the mind, and *karmamudrā* the activities. In our *sādhana*, these four gestures achieve one's union with the deity. Such a union has already been accomplished by means of the five stages and the self-consecration (not to mention the preceding *vajrāveśa*), so why is another now performed?

It must be admitted that a truly satisfactory answer remains elusive. Writing some seven centuries later, the Tibetan scholar Khedrup Delek Pelzang (Mkhas grub dge legs dpal bzang; 1385–1438) remarks in his "Supplement" to his teacher Tsongkhapa's exposition of Yoga tantra, here translated by Jeffrey Hopkins:

> Seal-impression with the four seals is done after you have generated yourself as the pledge-being and caused the wisdom-being to enter into the pledge-being. Seal-impression with the four seals is not done to either the pledge-being alone or the wisdom-being alone because the purpose of seal-impression with the four seals is to make the four—the exalted body, speech, mind, and activities of the wisdom being—inseparable from those four of the pledge-being after they have

> been mixed [through having caused the wisdom-being to enter into the pledge-being], and either of those alone does not have anything to be mixed.[85]

Khedrup Jé suggests that the four *mudrās* are performed to "seal" the identification previously achieved through the mixing of the "pledge being" (*samayasattva*) with the "wisdom being" (*jñānasattva*), i.e., the deity's form generated by the five stages with the gnosis of our *samayamudrā*. There is likely some truth to this explanation of the odd redundancy, but the larger logic of the *sādhana* may also be a contributing factor. That is to say, the second round of creating and consecrating oneself as the deity may have been made necessary by the four remaining deities in the mandala that still have not been performed through any ritual acts, namely, Vajrāṅkuśa, Vajrapāśa, Vajrasphoṭa, and Vajrāveśa.

The first of the four *mudrās*, the *mahāmudrā*, involves summoning the form of the deity using the mantra, "*Vajrasattva āḥ*," then, "*Vajrasattva dṛśya hoḥ*." (The name Vajrasattva, the reader is assured, can be replaced with the name of whichever deity is the focus.) Then the *samayamudrā* is performed. The term itself is not mentioned, nor does the commentary exhibit any awareness of its nature, but the situation is clear enough. The mantrin performs the four *mudrās* and recites the corresponding syllables for the mandala's wrathful gatekeepers: "*Jaḥ hūṃ vaṃ hoḥ*!"[86] The deity is led into the mantrin's body, installed there, bound, and subjugated; this is no gentle entreaty. Each of these four syllables corresponds to one of the four above-named gatekeepers: Vajra Hook, Vajra Noose, Vajra Shackles, and Vajra Possession. Thus, the commentary reads: "By means of the hook and [the syllable,] '*jaḥ*,' he is led into oneself. With '*hūṃ*,' he enters inside. With the shackles and '*vaṃ*,' he is bound, so that oneself and the deity are made indivisible. With the *mudrā* of holding, which is the *āveśa*, and by reciting '*hoḥ*,' he is held so that oneself and the deity are identical."[87] In this way, the ritual acts that mirror the order of the deities in the Vajradhātu mandala are complete.

Yet the proceedings continue. Next is the *dharmamudrā*, which our commentary describes as one's mantra, or just its seed syllable, arranged upon a moon disc at one's heart.[88] And finally one performs the *karmamudrā*, the intensive recitations of the mantra. Śākyamitra provides this summary:

> Having recited the *āveśa* heart [mantra] and performed the *āveśa*, after that, one should recite the heart [mantra] for leading forth the *mahāsattva*. Then recite the

> heart [syllables] for summoning, settling, binding, and overpowering [i.e., *jaḥ hūṃ vaṃ hoḥ*], and do it in one's mind. Having apprehended the *mahāmudrā* and one's own *samayamudrā*, one should transform one's own body into the manner of the *karmamudrā* and remain so [i.e., perform the recitations for some time]. One should also place the *dharmamudrā* on a moon disc and pronounce [the recitations].[89]

After inviting the deity by means of the *āḥ* and the *dṛśya* mantras, one leads the deity into one's heart with the four syllables *jaḥ hūṃ vaṃ hoḥ*. Having in this way joined the *mahāmudrā* and the *samayamudrā* (i.e., the buddha's body with the mind), one enacts the *karmamudrā*, the mantra recitations, with one's own body and with the *dharmamudrā* in the form of the syllable(s) of the mantra upon a moon disc at one's heart. The *dharmamudrā* and the *karmamudrā* therefore come as a package, both facilitating the recitations. This makes some sense, for with the summoning and consecration of the four syllables (which are equivalent to the four gatekeepers), the acts of the mandala deities are already complete. The recitations of the *dharmamudrā* and *karmamudrā* stand apart, as the ritual acts of a now perfected buddha.

Two additional elements mark the divide between the *mahāmudrā/samayamudrā* and the *dharmamudrā/karmamudrā* pairs. First one performs a protection that is accomplished in our *sādhana* by a ritual donning of armor, but in Śākyamitra by the *vajrabandha-mudrā* and mantra. This is done, explains Śākyamitra, in order to "bring together the vajra body, speech, and mind."[90] Second, one worships the perfected buddha with the 108 names.[91] With all this in place, all sources agree that the *karmamudrā* is accomplished by means of multiple recitations of the practitioner's heart mantra, with breaks from maintaining the visualization by reciting the 100-syllable mantra as needed.[92] In terms of time spent, and structurally (as we shall see), the recitations of the heart mantra form the central element of the *sādhana*.

All this represents yet a third method for consecrating oneself as the deity, bringing the *samayamudrā* or the *jñānasattva* into one's body (not counting that of the preliminary *vajrāveśa* discussed above). Already within the self-consecration, two methods functioned side by side: the primary consecration by touching the *samayamudrā* to four places on the body and the simultaneous merging of oneself with one's mirror image in the moon. Now, in the context of the four *mudrās*, yet a third method for drawing the *samayamudrā* into one's heart is employed. Using the four syllables of the four gatekeepers, one forces the deity into one's body. Three methods for installing the *samayamudrā* confirm that this is the *sādhana*'s key concern in preparing for the mantra recitations.

Samaya: Bestowing Awakening

The high valuation given to the *samayamudrā* and *samaya* in general in early Yogatantra ritual is seen in certain Chinese tantric texts from Dunhuang that are also related to the *STTS*. The relevant Chinese manuscripts number twelve, the one complete copy being contained in Pelliot chinois 3913, a codex of eighty-six folios, referred to in scholarship as the *Ritual Instructions for Altar Methods* (*Tanfa yize*; 壇法儀則).[93] The ritual forms presented in these manuscripts are highly sinified but still loosely based on the *STTS* system, which arrived in China with Vajrabodhi and Amoghavajra in the early to mid-eighth century.[94] The first part of these two-part ritual works offers preliminary rites that may be further divided into two primary types: those describing what seems to be an initiation rite and those offering a kind of *maṇḍalavidhi*, that is, instructions for constructing the mandala-altar.[95] The former, which seems to constitute a kind of *abhiṣekavidhi*, or initiation manual, bears the title *The Scripture on Entering the Dharmadhātu Ground: The Profound and Secret Vajradhātu Great Samaya, the Dhāraṇī Great King of Teachings, the Secret Dharma Precept Altar Method for Attaining Buddhahood*. Given that the first two subtitles stand in apposition to each other, we may infer that the author(s) took the *dharmadhātu* ground to be identical with the *mahāsamaya*, a term that elsewhere in the collection is identified as its central teaching.[96] And there is some reason to believe that the Chinese authors of the *Tanfa Yize* saw this all-important "profound and secret *mahāsamaya*" as a *mudrā* specifically associated with the *mind* of the buddha. S. 2272, for example, refers to the teaching as "the secret dharma precept, the profound and secret mind-ground dharma gate, the great *samayayoga* practice, the rite of the mind seal (Ch. 心印; Skt. *cittamudrā*)."[97] Some of Amoghavajra's more canonical works preserved in the Taishō canon similarly attest to the importance of achieving union with this *mahāsamaya*, or the "great *samaya* yoga."[98]

At this point one might object that these Chinese sources are using a different sense of the word *samaya*, as a vow, and that the term's associations with the *samayamudrā* and the buddha's *mind* are not really relevant. In his mid-eighth-century discussion of the *samayamudrā*, however, Buddhagupta addresses these two uses of the term head on, and he reconciles them:

> The secret mind of the great beings is referred to with the term *samaya*. The tantras explain that *samaya* can be for what will be correctly attained or realized, or for the purpose of what is not to be transgressed. Why? The suchness of one's own domain is the *samayamudrā*. The essence that is not transgressed by the great beings has already been explained [above]. Because it is like that, the symbol of the secret mind of the deity is explained as the *samaya*.[99]

For Buddhagupta, then, the *samaya* defines the horizon of the buddha's mind, as both a vow (or vows) not to be transgressed and the mind of awakening to be accomplished.

Here too, the dual valences of *samaya*—as vow and as mind—also involve a tension between *samaya* as multiple (vows) and singular (the mind of the buddha qua the *samayamudrā*). Even though *samaya* often refers to a set of multiple vows (that may be variously numbered), when bestowed, they are singular, transmitted in a ritual act that treats them as a single form, a single *mudrā*.

The connection between the *samayamudrā* and the *samaya* vows is also seen in the *STTS*'s procedure for bestowing the tantric vows in the context of the initiation:

> Then, wearing a red upper garment and covering his face with a red cloth, [the initiand] binds the *sattvavajrimudrā* while [reciting] this heart [mantra]: *samayas tvaṃ* ("you are the *samaya*").
>
> Then [the master] gives him a [flower] garland to hold with his two middle fingers and guides him [into the *maṇḍala*] while [reciting] this heart [mantra]: *samaya hūṃ*.
>
> Then, as soon as [the student] has entered [the *maṇḍala*], [the master] should pronounce: "Now you have entered the family of all the *tathāgatas*. I will generate within you the vajra gnosis, and by means of that gnosis you will attain the accomplishment of all the *tathāgatas*—what need even to speak of the other *siddhis*? And you must not tell anyone who has not seen the great *maṇḍala*, or your *samaya* will be violated!"

> Then the *vajrācārya* himself binds the *sattvavajri-mudrā* and places it, pointing downward, atop the head of the vajra student; he should say, "This is your *samayavajra*; if you tell anyone about it, it will split your head." Then, with that same *samayamudrā*, he [consecrates] some water, pronouncing the pledge heart [mantra] one time, then has the disciple drink it. Now, this is the pledge heart [mantra]:
>
> "Now Vajrasattva himself dwells in your heart. If you speak of this precept, you will instantaneously be destroyed. *Oṃ vajrodaka ṭhaḥ*!"[100]

Here, at the key moment of the initiation, the vajra master deploys the same *sattvavajrī-mudrā* that *sādhana* practitioners use to install the *samaya/jñānasattva* in their heart. In his commentary on this passage, Śākyamitra makes it explicit that the master's generation of this "vajra gnosis" within the student's heart is equivalent to the descent (*vajrāveśa*) of the *jñānasattva*.[101] The master thus places the *mudrā*, which we have already seen represents a vajra upon a moon disc, upon the student's crown, whence it descends to rest at his heart. This is further effected by the drinking of the oath water, which has been empowered with the same *sattvavajrī-mudrā*. Vajrasattva descends at the moment when the student drinks the water. "In order for the gnosis to descend," concludes Śākyamitra, "the *sattvavajrī-mudrā* is placed in the student's heart, and the heart [mantra] is recited."[102] The *samaya* that is the tantric vow (or vows) is thus the mind of the buddha, which takes the form of a vajra upon a moon disc at the practitioner's heart. In this sense, the practitioner of the Dunhuang *sādhana* seeks to reenact his original initiation, to return to the original transmission that he received from his master. In this sense too, the *samaya* is the realization of awakening that is transmitted from teacher to disciple.

Ānandagarbha compares the entry of the deities into one's body at the moment of the *mahāmudrā* consecration (and presumably of receiving initiation) to millions of streams of water from a vase being poured into one's body.[103] A practical version is embodied in the sprinkling of waters (*abhiṣeka*) during initiations. The difference between the processes of earlier initiations, including the *Sarvadurgatipariśodhana* initiation described in chapter 2, and the present *STTS*-based rite is that the waters now enter into the body's interior, to settle at the heart. This crucial difference marks a change in how tantric Buddhists conceived of initiation, and of tantric meditation more generally, from the early to late seventh century. A similar and roughly contemporaneous shift has been discerned within tantric Śaivism, where *āveśa* (entry) began appearing in works such as the *Brahmayāmalatantra* by around the late seventh century; it has been called, "*the* key term that distinguishes Tantric Shaivism from mainstream (esp. Vaidika) Indian religion."[104] In the *STTS* and its surrounding manuals, similar element was emerging within early tantric Buddhism, as initiation changed from emphasizing exterior bathing (*snāna*) to interior possession (*āveśa*).[105]

Evoking Enlightenment: The Rise of Poetry in Buddhist Ritual Manuals

This study has suggested that ritual manuals provided new kinds of intimate literary spaces for Buddhists to engage intensively in religious practice. Initially, manuals focused on physical acts within an arranged ritual space, but over time (across the seventh century specifically) they began to include mental acts as well—imaginal creations and, increasingly, poetic evocations. Chapter 2 examined the ritual master's use of poetic utterances in granting the initiations of the eight auspicious symbols. By the early eighth century, the ritual subject had taken center stage and interiority had become a primary interest. The *Tattvasaṃgraha-sādhana* has revealed how the mind of awakening in the form of the *samayamudrā*, a vajra upon a moon disc, could be installed into the practitioner's heart, either by a teacher during an initiation or by oneself in one's daily practice. In ending this chapter, we consider how the imaginal subject and poetic evocation worked together at this key moment of uniting with buddhahood. Through close readings of the key passages, we see another example of poetry and metaphor at work in early Yogatantra *sādhanas*, how subtle turns of language and imagery are used to create an evocative ritual event. So, let us return to the moment of self-consecration so central to our *sādhana*.

Having established himself in the form of the deity through the five stages of manifest awakening, the practitioner performs the self-consecration of that form, drawing into it the enlivening mind of the buddha. This is accomplished by forming the *sattvavajrī-mudrā*, with both hands clasped together and the two middle fingers extending straight up, face to face: the vajra upon the moon disc. Gazing at this *mudrā*, one pronounces the mantra "*samayastvam*,"then creates a moon disc behind one, in which the *samaya* of the deity is reflected. This image now merges with one's own body while oneself simultaneously merges with it, in a dual movement that commentators are careful to highlight. This merging is effected as one touches the *sattvavajrī-mudrā* to a series of four points on one's body while reciting the Sanskrit mantra, "O Sattvavajrī, consecrate me" (*sattvavajrī adhitiṣṭhasva mām*). With this accomplished, one generates pride in oneself as an actual buddha by reciting, "I am the great *samaya*" (*bdag ni ma ha sa ma ya yin no*).[106] And finally one closes the ritual sequence by reciting, "I am the *samaya*" (*samayo'ham*). The entire consecration thus comprises five distinct procedures, whereby the officiant:

1. Binds the *sattvavajrī-mudrā* while reciting "*samayastvam*" ("You are the *samaya*!");
2. Places a moon disc behind him, reflecting the deity's image as the *samaya* (a.k.a. the *jñānasattva*);
3. Recites "*sattvavajrī adhitiṣṭhasva mām*" ("Sattvavajrī, consecrate me!"), installing the *samaya* into one's body both through the four points and merging with the mirror image in the moon disc;
4. Generates pride, saying, "I am the *mahāsamaya*";
5. Recites, "*samayo'ham*" ("I am the *samaya*!").

The final pronouncement, "I am the *samaya*" (*samayo'ham*), communicates a sense of closure that engenders in the ritual subject a strong experience of being the true deity. Ānandagarbha explains that this "is a display of the accomplishment of the *mahāmudrā* [i.e., the consecrated form] that has been cultivated through faith-filled cultivation of one's union with the Bhagavan, which has finally arisen."[107] The power of the pronouncement to effect this culminating experience resides partly in its allusion to the beginning, its alliterative echoing (Skt. *anuprāsa*) of the earlier statement, "You are the *samaya*!" (*samayastvam*), that opened this particular ritual sequence. The two lines are nearly identical, both semantically and sonically. They also both rhyme and share the same number of syllables: *samayastvam* and *samayo'ham*.

In these ways, the sequence makes use of both the visual image of a mirror (in the form of the moon disc) and an aural echo. These are significant tools, for the Buddhist philosophical views that underpin these rites insist that one is always already divine and that rituals of union are simply ritualized acknowledgments of one's inherent identity with the deity—they are merely mirroring or echoing what is already the case. The mirror is a metaphor for a union that is no union; indeed, metaphor itself (not simile) communicates an identity of two entities that are one. Just as one merges into the deity reflected in the moon and vice versa, the deity merges into oneself, so the two statements, "You are the *samaya*" and "I am the *samaya*" (*samayastvam* and *samayo'ham*), echo each other as sounds that are at once the same and different, the first opening the sequence and the second sealing it.

The image of the mirror is thus itself mirrored in the very structure of the sequence, a chiastic ABCBA, centering on the key moment of union that is no union, where first and second person dissolve in a symmetry that communicates a hidden emphasis. This, the passage seems to say, is the heart of the process; its mysterious import is highlighted by the repetition of the two statements. We might be reminded of God's much commented-upon answer when Moses asks his name: "I am that I am" (*ehyeh ašer ehyeh*).

Chiasmus, or inverted parallelism, is a literary structure known already in ancient Greece. Its "ring structure" has been used by scholars working in a variety of contexts, from the Bible to Sufi scriptures, and more recently in Indian Buddhist narrative literature.[108] Anthropologist Mary Douglas outlines seven formal conventions that characterize the structure. Its name derives from the Greek *chi* (χ), a letter that represents the crossover midpoint of the two sides of the parallel, and as Douglas observes, in a well-formed chiasmus, this turning point is "loaded" with the main message: "The center of a polished ring integrates the whole."[109] Precisely this loading is seen in the mirrorlike symmetry of the self-consecration.

That the author of our *sādhana* was at least somewhat familiar with chiastic structures is apparent from the work's closing rites. Following the *karmamudrā*'s recitations of the heart mantra, the reader is instructed to perform again the eight offerings (which earlier immediately preceded the four *mudrās*), then recite a verse of dismissal (which seems to parallel the *abhiṣeka* of the five-buddha crown), then bind the *mudrās* of the families at each of the four places on the body while reciting the name of the corresponding goddess (Sattvavajrī and so on) followed by *muḥ*, the syllable of dismissal. This last is clearly meant to undo the self-consecration, which involved touching the *mudrās* to these same four places. Together, these acts move backward through the ritual stages of the *sādhana*, returning the reader to his original form. Chiasmus thus structures the entire work, and at the center of this larger loop stand the four *mudrās* and the recitation of the heart mantra.

Returning to the smaller subchiasm of the self-consecration, the practitioner is meant to feel intense devotion toward the deity when they pronounce the opening statement: "You are the *samaya*."[110] The final pronouncement, "I am the *samaya*," may translate the practitioner's initial devotion into a sense of his own authority as the deity himself. This powerful sense of authority may be still further enhanced by the final pronouncement's relationship to another statement. Just before "I am the *samaya*," one generates pride by stating, "I am the *great samaya*!" This is a powerful claim about the mantrin's new sense of majesty, yet it may not provide quite the sense of closure and true unity with the deity that the ritual seeks to impart. It is perhaps for this reason that the final pronouncement, "I am the *samaya*," is both still necessary and so emotionally effective. Its simpler form takes for granted one's identity with the deity. It is no longer a claim but a statement, sure of itself.

Chapter 2 highlighted the use of poetic verse and metaphor at key points in an initiation manual's proceedings. It is notable that our self-consecration passage is not in verse. Indeed, there is almost no verse in the entire *sādhana*, except for a quotation from the *STTS* on a point of terminology near the beginning and a stock verse for dismissing the deities near the end.[111] It would seem that our *sādhana* was designed not for chanting but as a technical work that leads its reader through the intricacies of complex rites. Although the self-consecration examined here does not use an overtly poetic form, its use of metaphor, the richness of its images, and the resonances of its mantras combine to produce a compelling experience of oneself as the deity.

The evocative use of poetic elements at this particular point in the ritual can be taken as another sort of marker, a further hint of a significant moment. When the register changes to the poetic in these early tantric manuals, something important is occurring. The moment when the practitioner is consecrated as the buddha is key for this *STTS*-based ritual system, and it is marked in our text by a shift in linguistic register, a slowing down into a more poetic mode of rhythm, rhyming, chiasmic mirroring, and metaphor deployed to achieve that experience.

The emergence of such poetic moments is highly significant for the history of Buddhist practice, because they were part of a larger set of interests in the ritual subject: in the interior worlds of mind and imaginative processes, in internal bodily spaces, and increasingly in later years in the energies that flow through those spaces. It was surely no coincidence that these interests were accompanied by the idea of teachers transmitting their realization directly to chosen disciples within a ritual setting, and of lineages of these intimate transmissions spanning multiple generations. By the end of the eighth century, the Indian scholar Buddhajñānapāda would write explicitly of "the great pith instruction of the master and nonmeditation itself ('inexpressible, without letters, without words') being transferred from ear to ear," that is, from teacher to disciple.[112] Such immediate transmissions of awakening were closely tied to the intertwined practices of consecration (*adhiṣṭhāna*) and entry (*āveśa*), rites that had become central to the ritual manuals and the tantras of the Yoga class by the turn of the eighth century. As the next two chapters suggest, the adaptation of such methods in the Mahāyoga ritual picked up these elements and ran with them, continuing the trend toward subjectivity, the imagination, and affective moments engendered by poetic expression.

Appendix

Tattvasaṃgraha-sādhanopāyika[1]

A TRANSLATION BASED ON PELLIOT TIBÉTAIN 792, IOL TIB J 417/1, AND IOL TIB J 551, WITH REFERENCE ALSO TO PELLIOT TIBÉTAIN 300 AND IOL TIB J 417/2[2]

Homage to Vajrasattva. If one who has received the *samaya* wishes to cultivate and perform the recitations, he should stay in a place that is appropriately indicated.

First perform the four prostrations: (1) Face toward the west [as if on the mandala's east side] and make manifest all the buddhas and bodhisattvas. Imagine there is a five-spoked vajra on a moon disc at one's heart. Prostrate with one's entire body. With hands folded in the vajra clasp (Skt. *vajrāñjali*; Tib. *rdo rje thal mo*), extend the arms while reciting this mantra: "*Oṃ sarvatathāgata pūjopasthānāyātmānaṃ niryātayāmi, sarvatathāgata vajrasattvādhitiṣṭhasva mām.*"

(2) Then arise again. In the same way, make manifest all the buddhas and bodhisattvas. Face toward the north [as if on the mandala's south side]. Imagine a jewel at one's forehead,[3] Place one's [hands in] the vajra clasp at the heart, and prostrate with one's entire body. While touching one's forehead to the ground, express this mantra: "*Oṃ sarvatathāgata pujābhiṣekāyatmānaṃ niryātayāmi, sarvatathāgata vajraratnābhṣiñca mām.*"

(3) Then arise again. Look toward the east. In the same way, bring to mind all the buddhas and the bodhisattvas. [IOL Tib J 417, 42r][4] At one's mouth imagine a lotus. Prostrate with one's entire body. Place one's vajra clasp at the crown of the head, touch one's mouth to the ground, and recite this mantra: "*Oṃ sarvatathāgata pūjāpravartanāyatmānaṃ niryātayāmi, sarvatathāgata vajradharma pravartaya mām.*"

(4) Then arise again. In the same way, make manifest all the buddhas and bodhisattvas. Face toward the southern direction and prostrate. Place the vajra clasp at one's heart and prostrate with one's head. Imagine a *viśvavajra* at the head and recite this mantra: "*Oṃ sarvatathāgata pūjākarmaṇe ātmānaṃ niryātayāmi, sarvatathāgata vajrakarma kurumāṃ.*" In that way, perform the four prostrations.

Sit. Recite, "**All phenomena are naturally pure. I too am naturally pure,**"[5] [Pelliot tibétain 792, 1v] and thinking that oneself is pure in the ultimate, believe it is so.[6]

Then the methods for **uniting with one's deity** are as follows. First **strike the *vajra-bandha* [*mudrā*] at one's heart** and recite this heart [mantra]: "*Vajra bandha traṭ.*" The characteristics of the vajra clasp and the *vajra-bandha* are:

Pressing one's palms firmly together
and interlacing all the fingers
is called "vajra-clasp" (*vajrāñjali*),
[or too] the *vajra-bandha*, because it is tightly bound.[7]

Then bind the *vajrāveśa* (vajra entry) *mudrā*. Turn the *vajra-bandha* to face upward and rest. [IOL Tib J 417/1, 42v] Place the two thumbs inside the small finger and the ring finger and move them. This is the *vajrāveśa mudrā*. Also recite this heart [mantra]: "*Vajrāveśa aḥ.*"

Immediately after that, examine one's own body.[8] With the intellect, break it down into tiny particles. Then thoroughly analyze how each of those tiny particles has six sides (*drugi tsul*) and rest in mind only.[9] Cultivate that mind, moreover, as a moon disc that is suffused[10] with the accumulation of one's own merit.[11] **Place upon that one's mantra or the letter of one's dharma,**[12] then imagine that one's *mudrā* manifests.[13] Also, imagine that the form of the *mudrā* comes from the subtle particles of the *tathāgatas*.[14] Then imagine that from that [*mudrā*], the form of one's deity is manifestly established.

Then perform the consecrations (Tib. *byin brlab*; Skt. **adhiṣṭhāna*).[15] Primarily, the consecrations of the bodhisattvas should be performed with the *mudrā* of one's family. For the *tathāgata* [buddha] family, bind the *mudrā* of Sattvavajrī: "*Samayastvam*" ("You are the *samaya*!").[16] By means of this [*mudrā* and mantra], place a moon disc that encircles one with light behind. For binding the Sattvavajrī [*mudrā*], raise the middle fingers with level fingertips. With this [*mudrā*], consecrate the four places—the heart, between the eyes, the throat, and the top of the head—together with this mantra: [IOL Tib J 417/1, 41r] "*Sattvavajrī adhitiṣṭhasva mām.*"[17] Then generate pride, saying, "**I am the *mahāsamaya*.**" Then, thinking that one is identical with that *sattva*, who is one's own *mudrā*, [Pelliot tibétain 792, 2r] recite this heart [mantra] and imagine it is so: "*Samayo'ham*" ("I am the *samaya*!").[18]

Then one should cultivate, that is, consecrate the four places using the *mudrās* for the relevant *sattvas* with this mantra: "*Samayasattva adhitiṣṭhasva mām.*"

Then **the initiations** (Tib. *dbang bskur*; Skt. *abhiṣeka*) are granted. (i) **Bind the *mudrā* for Vajradhātviśvara.** Place it atop one's head while reciting this mantra: "*Vajradhatviśvara abhiśiñcamām.*" (ii) **Then again bind the *mudrā* for Sattvavajra.** Place it at one's forehead while reciting this mantra: "*Sattvavajra abhiśiñcamām.*" (iii) **Then bind the *mudrā* for Ratnavajra.** Place it above the right ear while reciting this mantra: "*Ratnavajra abhiśiñcamām.*" (iv) **Then bind the *mudrā* for Dharmavajra.** Place it at the nape of the neck while reciting this mantra: "*Dharmavajra abhiśiñcamām.*" (v) **Then bind the *mudrā* of Karmavajra.** Place it above the left ear while reciting this mantra: "*Karmavajra abhiśiñcamām.*"

(i) Bind the Sattvavajra [*mudrā*] [41v] and place [the tips of] the two forefingers at the third knuckles of the middle fingers: this is for Vajradhātviśvarī. The *mudrā* for Sattvavajra was discussed above. (ii) From that same [Sattvavajra *mudrā*], bend the middle joints and place the two thumbs within to make them like the jewel: this is the Ratnavajrī [*mudrā*]. (iii) From that same Sattvavajrī [*mudrā*], curl [the fingers] like the petals of a lotus: this is for Dharmavajrī. (iv) From that same Sattvavajrī [*mudrā*], insert the middle fingers inside and extend each forefinger and little finger individually: this is for Karmavajra.

These *mudrās* are called "the supreme bodies of the *tathāgatas*." By means of them, the five *tathāgatas* are imagined at the five places. Atop one's head is Vairocana in the *bodhyagra* (supreme enlightenment) *mudrā*. At one's forehead is Akṣobhya in the *bhūmisparśa* (touching the earth) *mudrā*. Above the right ear is Ratnasambhava in the *barada* (supreme giving) *mudrā*. At the nape of the neck is Amitabha in the *samādhyagra* (supreme concentration) *mudrā*. Above the left ear is Amoghasiddhi in the *abhaya* (fearless giving) *mudrā*. In that way one should mentally apprehend the forms of one's deities who emanate howsoever.

This has been [a discussion of] the *samādhi*.

Then the offerings are performed. (i) Bind the *Lāsyāmudrā* and recite this mantra: [Pelliot tibétain 792, 2v] "*Vajralāsye.*" Place two *muṣṭi* (i.e., fists) at one's sides near the ribs, facing inward and turned to face upward [IOL Tib J 417, 40r] and rest them there. Then join them together[19] and lower them to the left side. Pay homage with mind atremble—this means one generates reverence.

(ii) Then hold two *muṣṭi* as if holding a garland and recite this mantra: "*Vajramāle*." (iii) Then bind two *muṣṭi* near one's mouth and fling them open as if words are coming forth, and recite this mantra: "*Vajragīte*." (iv) Then bind two *muṣṭi*, placing the left *muṣṭi* face up in front of oneself and the right *vajramuṣṭi* face down on top of that. Then release the left one first and the right one last. Then circle the hands around the backs of each other, then join the palms and place them atop one's head. This is the Vajranṛtya *mudrā*. Also recite this mantra: "Vajranṛtye." In that way the **secret offerings** are made.

Then perform the [outer] offerings of the *dhūpa* and so forth. (i) Cast two *vajramuṣṭi* downward as if offering incense, while reciting this mantra: "*Vajradhūpe*." (ii) Then cast two *vajramuṣṭi* open in front of one as if tossing handfuls of flowers, while reciting this mantra: "*Vajrapuṣpe*." (iii) Then for the butter lamps, [**40v**] clench two *vajramuṣṭi* again, the thumbs extended upward, while reciting this mantra: "*Vajrāloke*." (iv) Then clench and release the *vajramuṣṭi* at one's heart as if to apply the perfume, while reciting this mantra: "*Vajragandhe*." These are the eight kinds of offerings.

* * *

[Pelliot tibétain 792, 2v.6] Then the *mahāmudrā* should be accomplished. Bind the Sattvavajra *mudrā*.[20] Using the *krodhāṅkuśa* (wrathful hook) with the left [hand], pull the middle finger of the right. Strike, together with this mantra: "*Vajrasattva aḥ. Vajrasattva dṛśya hoḥ*." These are the heart [mantra] for *vajrāveśa* and the heart [mantra] for recollecting the *mahāsattva*[, respectively]. The name should be replaced with that of one's own deity and then recited.[21] Then imagine one's deity before one, and praise him with the 108 names.[22] By means of these mantras, drag, [IOL Tib J 551, 1r] install, bind, and subjugate him: "*Jaḥ hūṃ vaṃ hoḥ*!"

Also, these are the *mudrās*: (i) Turn the left [hand] in *vajramuṣṭi* upside down in front of one. Put the right [hand] in an upward-facing *vajramuṣṭi* on top of that, then bind so that one little finger holds the other like a hook. Extend one's right forefinger and left forefinger and hold them back to back. This is the *aṅkuśamudrā*. (ii) From that same *mudrā*, [**39a**] bend the two forefingers and place them one next to the other, like a loop. (iii) From that *mudrā*, bend the two forefingers to join one to the other like hooks. This is the *vajrasphoṭa* ("vajra shackles") *mudrā*. (iv) Then from that same *mudrā*, join the backs of those two hands.[23] This is the *vajrāveśa mudrā*. In that way the *mahāmudrā* is accomplished.

[Regarding the *dharmamudrā*:] **On a moon disc** at one's heart, **place one's own *dharmamudrā*** [i.e., the syllables].[24] Then the consecrations are granted by means of the *karmamudrā* together with the *samayamudrā*:[25]

Then the protections: By extending the forefingers of two *vajramuṣṭimudrās*, tie the knot at the navel. Then move one's hands to either side of the torso and raise them behind. Then also fasten a knot at the heart. Then, as if [donning] armor, fasten a knot **on each shoulder and at the back of one's neck.** Then fasten another knot behind one's head. Then raise [one's hands] along the two sides and fasten a knot at the temples. Then raise them along the two sides to tie a knot at the nape of the neck. Then circle over the ears. Finally release [the *mudrās*], which one sends forth as if shaking out a silk streamer. Recite the mantra "*oṃ tūṃ.*" **[39v]** Then clap the hands three times gently and recite this mantra: "*Vajra tuṣya ho*!"

Then in order to enact the intention (*dgongs pa*),[26] bind the *vajramuṣṭimudrā*. Place the left *vajramuṣṭi* facing up in front. On top of that, place the right *vajramuṣṭi* upside down and press [them together]. This is the *vajramuṣṭimudrā*. The mantra is "*Vajrasandhi.*"[27] Then recite Vajrasattva's name as one wishes.

[*Karmamudrā*:] **Then, binding the *karmamudrā*,** perform the recitations or meditations.[28] Then, [IOL Tib J 551, 1v] before the aim has been finished, if one wants to relax the *mudrā* or relieve oneself, in order to stabilize one can recite the 100-syllable [mantra]: "*Oṃ vajra sattva samayam anupālaya vajrasattvatvenopatiṣṭha dṛḍho me bhava sutoṣyo me bhava anurakto me bhava supoṣyo me bhava sarvasiddhiṃ me prayaccha sarvakarmasu ca me cittaśreyaḥ kuru hūṃ ha ha ha ha ho bhagavan sarvatathāgatavajra mā me muñca vajrībhava mahāsamayasattva āḥ.*" Then recite, that is, cultivate again as one likes.

CLOSING RITES

When it is time to arise, perform the eight kinds of offerings that have been discussed above. **[46r]** Then recite the words of this prayer for requesting [the deities] to depart:

> **You have enacted the purposes of all sentient beings.**
> You have bestowed [the *siddhis*] in accordance with my accomplishment.
> Please proceed to the buddha realms,
> and return again later.

(i) Bind the *Sattvavajra mudrā*, release it atop one's head, and recite the mantra "*Vajrasattva muḥ*." (ii) Then bind the *mudrā* for Sattvavajra, release at one's heart, and recite this heart [mantra]: "*sattvavajrī muḥ*." Then imagine that the *mudrās* included in the *tathāgata* family are released. (iii) Then bind the *mudrā* of Ratnavajra, release at one's forehead, and recite the mantra "*ratnavajrī muḥ*." Then imagine that the *mudrās* included in the *ratna* family are freed. (iv) Then bind the *mudrā* for Dharmavajra, release at one's throat, and recite this mantra: "*dharmavajrī muḥ*." Then imagine that the *mudrās* included in the *padma* family are freed. [**46v**] (v) Then bind the *mudrā* of Karmavajra, release as it rises from the forehead up to the crown of the head, and recite this mantra: "*karmavajrī muḥ*."[29] Then imagine that the *mudrās* included in the *karma* family are freed. For those remaining, bind the *mudrā* of Vajradhatviśvara, release at the point on the crown of one's head, and recite this mantra: "*vajradhatviśvarī muḥ*."

Then raise the *mudrā* of the *vajraratna* from one's heart and rest at the point of initiation, thereby granting the initiation of all the *mudrās*.[30]

Then recite this mantra: "*oṃ ratnavajrī sarvamudrāṃ abhiṣiñca varakavacena dṛḍhīkuru vaṃ*."[31] In that way, as long as the armor [remains], the garland is bound.[32] Perform the [clapping] palms happily and not forcefully. Then go wherever one wants.[33]

* * *

Ārya tattvasaṃgraha sādhanopāyika, the 100th chapter, is complete.

Sarvatathāgata mahāśubhavajra. The vajra of the great merit of all the *tathāgatas*. Rdzuṃ.

* * *

[Colophon in small print:]
This was written in payment for the monk Byang cub dbyangs. I pray that in this lifetime he be quickly purified of any illness, live a long time, and act for the benefit of sentient beings. And in future times may he melt away and cleanse all his sins, then spontaneously accomplish the three bodies. May it be so for a spiritual friend. This was edited [all] at once.[34]

FOUR

Secretory Secrets

Sexual Yoga in Early Mahāyoga

MEDITATION ON THE foul (*aśubhabhāvanā*) is one of Buddhism's oldest practices. Buddhaghoṣa's fifth-century C.E. *Visuddhimagga* provides a classic account. A monk should proceed to a charnel ground, find an appropriately rotting corpse, and meditate on its aspects, considering how each relates to his own desires and attachments to the body. Sexual desire, Buddhaghoṣa writes, delights in nothing but adventitious adornments that mask the true nature of the body's inherent foulness. "And then," he continues, "when any such bits of it as head hairs, body hairs, nails, teeth, spittle, snot, excrement or urine have dropped off the body, beings will not touch them; they are ashamed, humiliated and disgusted."[1] People lust after such secretions only so long as they remain in their proper place on the body; a simple change of location makes them repulsive, an embarrassment. Early Indian concerns about secretions are expressed elsewhere too. The perhaps sixth-century B.C.E. *Bṛhadāraṇyaka Upaniṣad* even offers a ritual solution:

> A man who engages in sexual intercourse with this knowledge obtains as great a world as a man who performs a Soma sacrifice, and he appropriates to himself the merits of the women with whom he has sex. The women, on the other hand, appropriate to themselves the merits of a man who engages in sexual intercourse with them without this knowledge.
>
> Surely it was this knowledge that made Uddālaka Āruṇi exclaim, as also Nāka Maudgalya Kumārahārita: "Many are the mortals of Brahmin descent who,

> engaging in sexual intercourse without this knowledge, depart this world drained of virility and deprived of merit."
>
> If one discharges semen, whether it is a little or a lot, in sleep or while awake, one should touch it and also address it with this formula:
>
> I retrieve this semen that fell on earth today;
> into water or plants though it may have seeped.
> May I regain my virility, my ardor, my passion;
> let the fire and the fire mounds each return to its place.
>
> As he recites this he should take the semen with his thumb and ring finger and rub it between his breasts or brows.[2]

The *upaniṣadic* rite may not include the incorporation of the fluids back into the body's interior (that would have to await the tantras), but it does illustrate male anxieties about ejaculation resulting in a loss of physical, social, and spiritual power, and about women sapping that power. Early Indians worked hard to maintain their bodily boundaries, not to mention, as Buddhist texts would add, the limits of their selves and even their concepts. Yet none of these boundaries is ultimately possible to control. We are forever leaking, shedding, ejaculating. With feelings of shame, humiliation, or disgust, we fear and mourn these little deaths, but they persist. We learn to tolerate our anxieties through symbolization, a playing and a naming that turns the magic of incantation into the very foundation of symbolic life. As Freud observed of the play of *fort/da*, we find "ways and means enough of making what is in itself unpleasurable into a subject to be recollected and worked over in the mind."[3] Recuperative rites like the *upaniṣadic* one described above are no mere child's play; they are thinking in the truest sense, a visceral and affective exploration of death and life.

The image of tantric deities in *yab-yum*, wrapped in embrace, gained popularity in the second half of the eighth century, but its significance was more complicated than a simple harmony of male and female principles. In its early forms, tantric sex focused less on the practitioner's state of blissful union, though that did play a role, than on the sexual fluids produced. These secretions were seen as pure potentiality. Essentially male, they were also prior to such gendered dualities. *Bodhicitta* (the mind of awakening) made material, these secretions embodied a primordial state that was not yet a thing, yet not nothing—a promise, a vow—neither just physical depletion and death nor yet the life they would become.

Sometimes the *bodhicitta* was mixed with other excretions: female fluids—usually menstrual blood—together with feces, urine, and human flesh. Still, Buddhism was a patriarchal system, and male semen was held to be preeminent.[4] Though early authors affirm that women can achieve awakening by tantric methods, their manuals for ritual union describe the procedures from a male perspective, with the female consort framed as an object of desire, and their rites culminate in the practitioner reincorporating his secreted fluids as a sacrament. Whether this represented an anxious attempt to recuperate male power, as Freud might propose, or a powerful opportunity to disrupt one's carefully maintained identity, as this chapter's *sādhana* suggests, depends on one's theoretical persuasion. In either case, historically, the swallowing of sexual fluids produced through ritualized sexual union was crucial to early Mahāyoga practice of the second half of the eighth century. Later ritual developments would obscure the importance of these secretions in the development of tantric ritual, as manipulations of the breath and bodily energies came to dominate the scene, but remnants of the early sacramental approach may still be detected even in modern-day practice. This chapter attempts to recover those early ritual forms and to provide some sense of their precedents and later effects within tantric Buddhism.[5]

* * *

By the middle of the eighth century, the classification of the Yoga tantras as apart from and above the outwardly focused Kriyā tantras was well established. Over the next few decades, a new classificatory term of Mahāyoga emerged in response to further ritual developments, techniques that were canonized in newly composed or expanded tantras. Thus, the *Guhyasamāja* reached its full seventeen-chapter form by the mid-eighth century, and the *Guhyagarbha* was composed shortly thereafter. Any number of additional titles could be named, but among the Dunhuang manuscripts, these two tantras stand out as the most influential of the early Mahāyoga class.[6]

Central to this new class of tantras were the secret practices of sexual union. The growth of myths and rituals of compassionate violence was also important. Ritual sex and violence were both known in the Yoga tantras, the latter even already in the Kriyā tantras, but with Mahāyoga, sexual union became essential to daily *sādhana* practice in a way that violent rites did not. Some Yoga tantras do include scattered references to secret sexual practices that appear to have functioned in the background. Amoghavajra, in his mid-eighth-century summary of the eighteen Vajroṣṇīṣa scriptures, mentions the existence of secret practices in the fourth, the *Trailokyavijaya-vajrayoga*.[7] And while sexual union is not part of the standard *STTS*-based *sādhana* practice, the *Sarvatathāgata-tattvasaṃgraha* includes several references to such rites, and the only slightly later *Vajraśekhara-tantra* includes further references.

Already in the *STTS*, the sexual practices are usually described under the heading "secret worship" (Skt. *rahasyapūjā*; Tib. *gsang ba'i mchod pa*). A particularly explicit passage occurs in chapter 4:

> Then one should train in the *mudrā* gnosis of the secret worship:
>
> By offering the self-arising worship of the bliss of embracing the entire body, one will quickly become equal to Vajrasattva.
>
> In a powerfully lustful union, by offering to the buddhas the pleasures of grasping the hair, one will become equal to Vajraratna.
>
> By offering the pleasures of the highest kisses with powerful desire and intense bliss to all the buddhas, one will become equal to Vajradharma.
>
> By offering the pleasures of the total union of the two organs in worship, one will become equal to Vajrakarma.[8]

The act of sexual union is here divided into four stages, and the pleasures of each are offered to the buddhas. In return, one gains the realization corresponding to each of the four chiefs of the sixteen bodhisattvas surrounding the center of the Vajradhātu mandala. In this early description of tantric sexual union, the focus is the offering of the pleasures themselves. Other sexual passages found throughout the *STTS* are similarly organized according to various fourfold divisions, from the four *mudrās* to the four ritual activities (of pacification, enhancement, coercion, and violence), with each passage promising further attainments, from the discovery of treasure to accomplishing the welfare of sentient beings.[9]

Interpretations of sexual union as an offering go back at least to the above-cited *Bṛhadāraṇyaka Upaniṣad*. There, the sexual act is described in terms of a fire offering (*homa*): "Her vulva is the sacrificial ground; her pubic hair is the sacred grass; her labia majora are the Soma-press; and her labia minora are the fire blazing at the center."[10] Likewise in the (mid-eighth century?) Buddhist *Vajraśekhara-tantra*, having prepared the site for a fire offering, the *vajrin* bathes, dresses, and ornaments himself. Then, imagining himself as a buddha, he is instructed:

> Being mindful of the pleasure of passion,
> one should not worry about the passion of the desire realm.
> Having roused the woman's fluids,
> one should abandon [the rules about] the seven kinds of copulation.[11]
>
> Having erected the sign (*liṅga*, i.e., the penis),
> one should pacify the organ.
> Being mindful of passion,
> one should properly undertake the fire offering (*homa*).[12]

Compared to the slightly earlier *STTS*, the anatomical detail is greater, with explicit instructions about exciting the male and female sexual organs before beginning, and so on. Just a few pages later a similar level of detail appears, along with additional elements also seen in the Mahāyoga tantras:

> Having extracted the saffron in the *bhaga*,
> one should insert the sign.
> One will obtain the excellent substances
> and accomplish the four aspects.
>
> The *bhaga* is called the "lotus."
> The sign is called the "vajra."
> Having placed the substances upon the lotus,
> one should accomplish with the vajra-churner.
>
> He who is lusty with great desire
> will accomplish the secret.[13]

It is almost as if the passage is introducing readers to the coded language that would become so common in later centuries, explaining that the vagina is the lotus (*padma*) and the penis the vajra. Still, aside from coding the stages and the elements of sexual union with ritual significance, such Yogatantra passages are primarily focused on the pleasures generated and their use as powerful offerings on the path to awakening.[14]

The Manuscript: IOL Tib J 464 and The *Generation of Fortune Sādhana*

The manuscript that is this chapter's focus, IOL Tib J 464, is a small *poti* containing a Mahāyoga *sādhana* bearing the title the *Generation of Fortune Sādhana* (*Skal bskyed ces bya ba'i bsgrub pa'i thabs*) (fig. 4.1). Its five folios are penned in large letters, and its text is made still shorter by the presence of one blank folio side (1v) and one side of ancillary notes (2v). The title is provided only at the end of the text, but its presence suggests the work may be a translation of an Indic original. The manuscript itself is probably from the tenth century; its hand is unknown, but there are no indicators of an earlier date. Most telling is the small marking in the upper left-hand corner of the first folio, where the Hungarian archaeologist Sir Aurel Stein wrote: "Ch. 73. III. 23 [27] 462." Almost all of the Dunhuang manuscripts discovered by Stein, now stored at the British Library, bear similar markings. Although the full significance is yet unknown, the first part (Ch. 73. III) appears to identify one of the bundles in which Stein found the manuscripts. As Tsuguhito Takeuchi has observed, "nearly all of the texts with 'Ch. 73. III.' belong to this [post-Tibetan Empire] period."[15] Despite the manuscript's probable late date, the composition of the text itself probably dates from the second half of

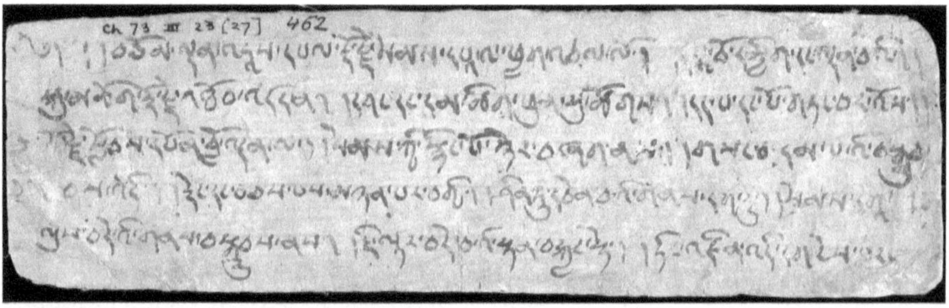

FIGURE 4.1 *Generation of Fortune Sādhana*
Source: IOL Tib J 464, Courtesy of the British Library

the eighth century, for reasons discussed in the introduction to the present study.

Unfortunately, the *sādhana* mentions no tantra or mandala, so it is difficult to know which ritual system may have inspired its rites. The central deity is Vajrasattva, but by the late eighth century he had become quite popular as the buddha that transcends all others. In precisely this spirit, IOL Tib J 583, which contains a collection of Mahāyoga materials, offers the following prayer:

> The five families are of a single mode, inseparable by nature, but
> Due to the need for training, the five families are revealed individually;
> Their omniscient forms are [really] without limits;
> To the inseparable gnosis-body (*jñānakāya*) I pay homage.
>
> Although the aggregate of gnosis is like space,
> Body, speech, and mind are the great identity.
> From the origin of all emanations
> O Vajrasattva, please come.[16]

Accordingly, Vajrasattva is the source, the *ur*-buddha (or perhaps *ādibuddha*) from which all other buddhas emerge to enact their more specific functions. In the *Guhyasamāja*, this role is played by Mahāvairocana, sometimes under the name Bodhicittavajra. In the decades following the consolidation of the *Guhyasamāja*, however, Vajrasattva (and later still Vajradhara) rose to the fore. The shift is nicely illustrated in the Dunhuang *Guhyasamāja* manuscript, the opening lines of which read, "Then the *tathāgata* Akṣobhya, the *tathāgata* Vairocana, the *tathāgata* Ratnaketu, the *tathāgata* Amitābha, and the *tathāgata* Amoghavajra dwelt in the heart of the *tathāgata* Bodhicittavajra,"[17] on which a Dunhuang interlinear note explains: "Then the buddhas of the five families dwelt within the body of Vajrasattva."[18] The note thereby updates the *Guhyasamāja* to match late eighth-century ritual tastes. This was not unusual. In his late eighth-century commentary to the *Mañjuśrīnāmasaṃgīti*, the scholar Vilāsavajra too uses the names of Bodhicittavajra and Vajrasattva interchangeably to refer to the *samaya* that rests at Mahāvairocana's heart.[19]

By the late eighth century, Vajrasattva had become so fundamental to Mahāyoga ritual that his centrality to our *sādhana* tells us little about its affiliations. It is even possible that the author saw his work as free-floating, or only loosely attached to a specific ritual system. Another Mahāyoga *sādhana*, also likely a translation from an Indic original, appears in IOL Tib J 331/1. Like our text, the *Precept for Supreme Goodness* (*Bzang po mchog gi lung*) is a short work, attributed to the eighth-century master Mañjuśrīmitra, and no tantra is named.[20] Taken together, these two works suggest the possibility that large numbers of short, unaffiliated *sādhanas* may have been circulating throughout India and Tibet in the late eighth century. Such works may have been conceived of quite differently from the often-longer *sādhanas* such as the *Guhyagarbha*-based *An Appearance of Suchness: Ornament of the Sacred* (*De kho na nyid snang ba dam pa rgyan*), in IOL Tib J 332/1, works that were more clearly based on a single tantric system.[21]

This said, there is also reason to believe that our *sādhana* may be linked to the *Guhyasamāja*, a tantra particularly influential both within India and at Dunhuang. Its title (*Generation of Fortune*) already may be a reference to the tantra's eighth chapter, an important source for the system's sexual yoga, where verse 3 refers to Mahāvajradhara as "fortunate among buddhas" (*buddhasaubhāgya*) and verse 6 describes the sexual yoga (or *pūjām śreṣṭhām*) as having "the fortune of [awakened] body, speech, and mind" (*kāyavākcitta saubhāgyām*). A connection to the *Guhyasamāja* is lent further support by another version of the same *sādhana* found at IOL Tib J 331/2 (fig. 4.2).[22] Lacking a title, this work is a locally authored Dunhuang elaboration on the earlier *Generation of Fortune Sādhana*. It weaves in additional material seen in other Dunhuang *sādhanas*, regularly breaking the original versification, and at points exerts a concerted effort to reinterpret key elements.[23] Among its insertions is a quotation from the *Guhyasamāja*, immediately following the

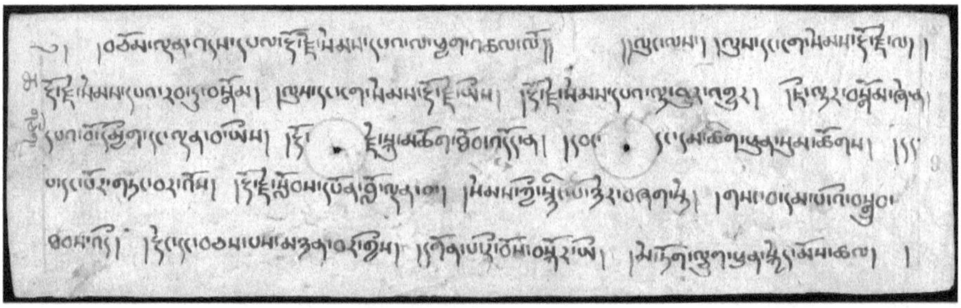

FIGURE 4.2 Extended interpretation of *Generation of Fortune* local to Dunhuang
Source: IOL Tib J 331/2, Courtesy of the British Library

opening homage to Vajrasattva: "In the scripture it says, 'With the vajras of body, speech, and mind, intently cultivate Vajrasattva. As he suffuses one's body, speech, and mind, one becomes like Vajrasattva.' How is [this] to be cultivated?"[24] The compiler of this later version thus frames the entire *sādhana* as an elaboration on this single *Guhyasamāja* verse.[25] Whether the *Generation of Fortune* was originally intended as *Guhyasamāja*-focused remains an open question, but it at least lent itself easily to such an interpretation.

One further manuscript shares certain elements in common with IOL Tib J 331/2. IOL Tib J 554 is an untitled tenth-century Mahāyoga *sādhana* almost certainly compiled at Dunhuang. It was discovered in a bundle along with two other manuscripts, IOL Tib J 552 and 553. The three manuscripts are almost identical in size, paper, and the placement of their two respective ornamental string holes.[26] The three also share some content in common. All open with the five *samādhis* of "the cultivation system of the limitless *sādhana*" (*no pyi kA mtha' dag bsgom ba'i lugs*), followed by the three *samādhis* of the early Mahāyoga generation stage (described below). They also share imagery: a mandala that resembles that of the *Guhyasamāja* and a visualization of Vajrasattva with a *jñānasattva* at his heart, then a tiny vajra, in turn, at his heart, and a still smaller mustard seed-sized *hūṃ* within the center of that vajra. Some of these three works' shared features may be explained through reference to the above-mentioned *Precept for Supreme Goodness*, attributed to Mañjuśrīmitra.[27] Bearing the shelf mark IOL Tib J 331/1, this short item immediately precedes the more elaborate version of our own *sādhana* found at IOL Tib J 331/2. The *Precept* was therefore well known to the Dunhuang-based author of the latter work; indeed, it includes copious interlinear commentary that was at least penned, if not composed, by the same author. Read through the lens of this interlinear commentary, Mañjuśrīmitra's *Precept for Supreme Goodness* describes procedures followed closely by all three *sādhanas* contained in IOL Tib J 552, 553, and 554. Quite possibly an Indian work, it appears to have served as a kind of "root text" for the three *sādhanas*.[28] Of the three, IOL Tib J 554 stands out for including some material seen also in the *Generation of Fortune Sādhana* and in the probably Indic, *Guhyagarbha*-based *An Appearance of Suchness: Ornament of the Sacred*.[29] It is a complex weave of intertextuality, but in short, IOL Tib J 554 shares certain features with IOL Tib J 331/2, which is itself an elaboration on the *Generation of Fortune Sādhana*. All of these overlapping passages will be brought to bear in the readings below.

The ritual notes that appear on the verso of the second folio seem to be in a different hand, and list the ritual elements of a *sādhana*:

> [i] Homage, [ii] analyzing the student's faith, [iii] analyzing the teacher's good qualities, [iv] establishing the site for practice, [v] generating the deity, [vi] consecrations (*byin kyis blab pa*), [vii] initiations (*dbang bskur*), [viii] through the play of method and wisdom, enacting the welfare of beings, [ix] teaching the methods of worship in order to please the deity, [x] performing the worship by means of the four suchnesses (*de kho na nyid bzhi*), [xi] resting (*bzhugs sdu ba*), [xii] teaching that the outer *samaya* is not to be transgressed, and [xiii] the root of merit, the dedication.

It is unclear whether these steps are meant to summarize the *Generation of Fortune Sādhana* or Mahāyoga *sādhanas* in general. All of them can be mapped onto our *sādhana* except the consecrations and initiations. In the *Tattvasaṃgraha-sādhanopāyikā* discussed in chapter 3, both of these elements appear at the same point, immediately after generating oneself as the deity, and in the same order, with the self-consecration effecting the descent of the *samayamudrā/jñānasattva* and the initiations the placing of the five-buddha crown. In the *Generation of Fortune*, the consecration could be mapped onto the moment of reciting the mantra, "*yathā vajrasattvastathāhaṃ*," which parallels the last mantra of the *Tattvasaṃgraha-sādhanopāyikā*'s self-consecration ("*samayo'ham*") and is to be recited immediately upon completing the generation of oneself as the deity. The initiations are somewhat harder to map. It may be that the outline provides a partly idealized view of the actual proceedings.[30]

The *Generation of Fortune*: The Three *Samādhis*

Following the opening homage to Vajrasattva, our *sādhana* begins by emphasizing the importance of receiving the proper initiations, maintaining one's vows, having faith, and studying under "an intelligent *vajrācārya*." It then says to find a solitary but comfortable place, settle in, and begin the meditations. First come the three *samādhis* through which the practitioner transforms themself into the deity. Among the Dunhuang manuscripts, these constitute a definitive element of Mahāyoga meditation. The *Seven Great*

Scriptural Systems (*Spyi'i lung chen po bdun*), a tantric doxographical work found in IOL Tib J 656, says that Mahāyoga "meditation involves cultivating the gradual generation [of oneself as the deity] using the three kinds [of *samādhis*]."[31] Given the triad's ubiquity in the Dunhuang manuscripts, it is likely that they were popular in India too for a brief time around the second half of the eighth century, yet they are almost completely absent from the tantras and commentaries preserved in today's Tibetan canon.[32] Here, it would seem, is a ritual development that never quite made the leap from manual to tantra.

However, the three *samādhis* are well preserved in the ritual literature of the Nyingma school. There, as in the Dunhuang documents, they structure the generation stage (Skt. *utpattikrama*; Tib. *bskyed rim*), the first of the two stages of Mahāyoga practice, before the perfection stage (Skt. *utpannakrama*; Tib. *rdzogs rim*). In brief, the generation stage focuses on transforming oneself into a buddha, the perfection stage on acting as that buddha. In the late eighth century, when the two stages were first introduced, the generation stage corresponded more or less to Yogatantra practice, while the perfection stage represented what was new about Mahāyoga, in particular the rites of sexual union.[33] Our *sādhana* makes no mention of either, though the generation of oneself as the deity via the three *samādhis* is followed immediately by a rite of sexual union. Still, the transition is not explicitly marked (a trend not uncommon even in later *sādhanas*), so it remains unclear whether the *sādhana* reflects a period before the two stages were well known.[34]

The two stages do seem to have come into use around the mid-eighth century. Though they do not play a prominent role in the Mahāyoga *sādhanas* from Dunhuang, at least explicitly so, they are referenced in some manuscripts, often in the context of defining the Great Perfection (*Rdzogs chen*) as beyond both.[35] Outside of Dunhuang, evidence may be seen in the *Guhyasamāja*-related materials surrounding Buddhajñānapāda, an innovative visionary who wrote around the turn of the ninth century.[36] Perhaps the most obvious reference is simply the title of his masterpiece, the *Dvitīyakrama-tattvabhāvanā-mukhāgama* (henceforth just *Dvitīyakrama*), or *Oral Instructions on Training in the Reality of the Second Stage*.[37] Buddhajñānapāda's tantric writings appear not to have reached Tibet before imperial support for translation work collapsed (presumably around 842 C.E.); there is no clear evidence of his influence among the Dunhuang manuscripts.[38] Given that the two stages are nonetheless known there, it seems they were already widely circulating within ritual manuals before Buddhajñānapāda formalized them in his influential writings.

In the *Generation of Fortune*, the first of the three *samādhis*, the thusness *samādhi* (*de bzhin nyid kyi ting nge 'dzin*), which typically culminates in a brief meditation on emptiness, is accomplished through a short visualization: imagining an ཨ syllable atop one's head, light rays emanating from it (and presumably returning) to dissolve one's body and environs into nonconceptual emptiness. Having rested in that state, the reader is next instructed to "cultivate the all-illuminating and the causal," i.e., the second and third *samādhis* (*kun tu snang ba'i dang rgyu'i ting nge 'dzin*). For the all-illuminating *samādhi*, "within the expanse of the space" just cultivated, one imagines a white ཨ, "glittering like Venus" (*pa ba ba* [sic] *sangs ltar 'tser ba*). For the causal *samādhi*, presumably out of this ཨ, a series of four syllables appear (*yaṃ*, *paṃ*, *suṃ*, *bhruṃ*), so that the scintillating ཨ of the all-illuminating represents the coming into being, the opening for the causal *samādhi*'s movement from immaterial to material. As one recites the mantra, "*samayastvaṃ bhruṃ*," these four syllables transform into elemental mandalas—a disc of wind; an ambrosial ocean; earth in the form of Mount Meru, the *axis mundi* of Indian cosmology; and finally from the *bhruṃ*, atop Mount Meru, a jeweled palace, at the center of which sits a jeweled throne upon a lotus pedestal.[39]

The first *samādhi* on thusness is important as the fundamental meditation on emptiness, entered through an imagined dissolution of one's body and the universe, but it is the transition from that nothingness, via the all-illuminating *samādhi*, to the concrete formulas of the causal *samādhi* that is here communicated by means of simile. While our own *sādhana* is brief in its treatment, comparing the emergence of being to the scintillations of Venus, other sources provide further insights into how this second *samādhi* was understood. IOL Tib J 552, one of the aforementioned trio of manuscripts penned on the same size paper, uses a series of similes that emphasize not just what should be cultivated, but how: "How is it to be generated?" asks an interlinear note. "The entirety of these outer and inner appearances and existences are like a ripe *amalakī* fruit held in the palm of one's hand, like seeing the luminous space of dawn emerging from the pitch darkness of an autumn [sky], or substances placed in a clean blue crystal bowl: viewed from outside, they are illuminated from within; viewed from inside, they are illuminated from without."[40]

Here, poetic language is used to produce in the reader a sense of emergence and possibility, presence that is yet absent. All appearances are somehow singular, encased as if resting in one's palm. The *amalakī*, or myrobalan fruit, is a round green fruit that is translucent when ripe, so that the image suggests an experience of surface and luminous depth all at once. This is then compared to the emergence of dawn across a clear, dark sky, when the light seems to come from within space itself. Finally, a third image seems to unite the previous two: objects resting within a dark skylike bowl. The all-illuminating *samādhi* is thus portrayed as a transitional moment between the space of the thusness *samādhi* and the appearances of the causal, a luminous play of surface and depth, inside and outside.

Another Dunhuang manual builds on these themes:

> Like the surface of the sky, appearances are empty, only seeming to appear, and luminous, only seeming to be empty. Like a moon [reflected] in water, gnosis pervades the depths of space without center or limits, so it is called "the all-illuminating *samādhi*," "the emptiness *samādhi*," "the clear bliss of method," "the opening for form," and "the cause for forms to arise." Like the surface of an empty sky, or the reflected forms of the sun, moon, planets, and stars clearly appearing within a clear lake, without identity or characteristics, like an inwardly facing ritual mirror or a lake at dawn: cultivate, without wavering from, the state of the great compassion.[41]

This passage starts right away with the meeting point between depth and surface in the striking image of the surface of the sky. We see an interplay between surface and depth, on the one hand, and appearance and emptiness, on the other. Then the image of a gnosis is at once a mere surface reflection upon shimmering water and a light that pervades the depths of a space that lacks any center or limits. This paradoxical shift is both the cause and the opening for forms to arise. An implicit appearance, the reality of which is still elusive, it is like mere reflections of distant stars, a mirror reflecting itself. Complete in itself, it is a placid lake reflecting light from elsewhere. Such is the state of great compassion on the verge of emanating forth for all beings.

Clearly, the second *samādhi* caught the imaginations of some eighth-century Buddhists. Chapters 2 and 3 have shown how verse and metaphor were deployed at key moments: the granting of the eight *uṣṇīṣabuddha* initiations in a *Sarvadurgati* initiation manual, the moment of union with one's deity in a *Tattvasaṃgraha sādhana*. Now, for the emergence of a visualization, Mahāyoga texts repeatedly use metaphoric language and poetic forms to mark a rite as significant and communicate a certain aesthetic sense of the moment.

Unlike the two Yogatantra works already examined, however, the *Generation of Fortune Sādhana* is composed entirely in verse, with seven syllables per line throughout. If verse marks important moments or sacred speech, this whole text qualifies. Indeed, versification seems to have been typical of Indic Mahāyoga *sādhanas* more generally. Within the Dunhuang archive, the *Guhyagarbha*-based *An Appearance of Suchness* is largely in verse, as is the *Precept for Supreme Goodness*. In any case, if verse is so ubiquitous as to be no longer useful for identifying significant ritual moments, attending carefully to shifts in rhetorical register can still help. In the present context, doing so reveals an interest among tantric authors of the late eighth century in all-illuminating *samādhi* and the process by which buddhas seem to appear out of the most fundamental elements like ཨ, the inherent sound of all the letters of the alphabet, shimmering on the threshold between existence and nonexistence like Venus in the sky. The Mahāyoga manuals from Dunhuang agree on the indescribable significance of this originary, transitional moment out of which the third, causal *samādhi* and thus the mandala emerges.

Having established the mandala palace by means of this third *samādhi*, the practitioner continues to develop the visualization. Upon the throne at the center, a *hūṃ* syllable emanates light-rays in all directions, satisfying the buddhas and all sentient beings. Regathering into the *hūṃ*, a vajra (or another symbol, depending on the practitioner's buddha family) appears. Whether the *hūṃ* itself transforms into the vajra or becomes encased within the central handle of the larger vajra is unclear; as we shall see below, the latter possibility is implied. Once again, light-rays emanate and regather, creating oneself as the deity with one's consort, both in full regalia and sitting in sexual union. In this way, one is now Vajrasattva, a fact recognized with the final mantra, *yathā vajrasattvastathāhaṃ* ("just as Vajrasattva is, so am I").

The Sexual Yoga

The practitioner is now prepared to begin what would become the perfection stage. "Thrusting" the vajra and bell, he recites *hūṃ* three times and brings forth the "jewel sprout," holding it "at the top of the head." Here we enter the realm of secrecy and coded language. "Jewel sprout" (*rin cen myu gu*) probably translates the Sanskrit *ratnāṅkura*, a name for pearls. This is surely the drop of semen, or *bodhicitta*, to be held at the tip of the penis, with the male practitioner remaining on the brink of ejaculation. A note to the *Guhyagarbha sādhana*, *An Appearance of Suchness*, describes this moment of restraint in further detail: "Atop a five-spoked vajra [at the point of union] between the father and the mother, the single syllable [*hūṃ*] is cultivated. At the center of the mother's space, upon an eight-petaled lotus, imagine that from the mother there comes a sun disc: *Jaḥ hūṃ vaṃ hoḥ*! The father's *mudrā* [i.e., drop of semen] is held with the hook, bound with the lasso, restrained with the shackles."[42] The point of sexual union is thus depicted with symbolic imagery: with the penis visualized as a *vajra*, at the tip of which is held the drop of semen, here, it seems, imagined as a *hūṃ* syllable, at the center of the consort's vagina, the sky, upon a sun disc that rests, in turn, upon a lotus flower. (Sun discs often replace moon discs at this point when the deity being generated is wrathful.) To assist the restraint of the drop, and perhaps to invite the entry of the deities into "the bliss mandala" at the point of union, the four syllables *Jaḥ hūṃ vaṃ hoḥ* are recited. These are commonly associated with the four gatekeepers of the mandala: Vajrāṅkuśa (Vajra Hook), Vajrapāśa (Vajra Lasso), Vajrasphoṭa (Vajra Shackle), and Vajrāveśa (Vajra Possession).[43]

The practitioner next consecrates his body with the five syllables. This might require placing (*nyāsa*) the syllables on the body, but other texts suggest it involves a cycling of the breath between the male and female meditators. Either way, the practice is performed while continuing to hold the drop "at the top of the head," as indicated by the line, "by means of the yoga for protecting, firmly protect the *siddhi* identity to the best of one's ability."[44]

When the practitioner can no longer continue the practice, he gazes at his consort and recites "*anurāgayāmi*" ("I am impassioned"), and the consort repeats the same to him.[45] Finally, the *bodhicitta* is emitted: "One unites with great bliss, at which time the *mudrās* are clearly cultivated, the offerings are made, and the emanation is emitted."[46] Buddhajñānapāda ends his description of the parallel moment in his *Dvitīyakrama*: "this is correctly explained by all the best gurus to be the perfection stage."[47] The more elaborate IOL Tib J 331/2 explains that the cultivation of the *mudrās* here refers to the appearance of the mandala at the point of union.[48] The buddhas of the mandala are then worshipped and the *bodhicitta* emitted. Citing the *Guhyagarbha*'s eleventh chapter, *An Appearance of Suchness* likewise seems to equate the worship of the mandala with the emission of the *bodhicitta*:

> Within the mandala of the mother's lotus,
> the blissful mandala of [awakened] mind emanates forth.
> Into all the assembled clouds of buddhas
> it dissolves through this supreme bestowal of ecstatic equality.[49]

In our own *sādhana*, the drop, portrayed as an emanation of the buddha, "the great identity" (*bdag nyid chen po*), is now praised with verses pronounced in the hexatonic *ṣāḍava* (*sha da ba*) melody.[50] The words sung are not provided. They may be something like the verses of praise to *bodhicitta* seen in IOL Tib J 576 (the *STTS*-based concertina discussed above), which were drawn, in turn, from the opening chapter of *Guhyasamāja*: "Kye ma'o! The *bodhicitta* of all the buddhas has emerged! The secret of all the *tathāgatas*, completely nonconceptual and unlocated!"[51]

After this, the *bodhicitta* is offered to the *tathāgatas*, then taken as a sacrament by the practitioner himself. Thus, immediately following the passage above, the *Guhyagarbha-tantra* continues: "That essence of the sun and moon that is accomplishment / Is taken from the mandala with one's vajra-tongue."[52]

In his 1965 study of *The Tantric Tradition*, Aghehananda Bharati suggests that "The main difference between the Hindu and the Buddhist tantric *sādhanā* seems to have been that the Hindu tantric ejects his sperm, the Buddhist Vajrayāṇa adept does not."[53] Writing more recently, David White argues against this theory, referring to "an erroneous paradigm that Buddhist 'Tantric sex' always remained unconsummated, that is, that it ended in coitus interruptus and an ecstatic mystical experience for both partners."[54] The ritual manuals from Dunhuang confirm that already in the eighth century, seminal emission was part of Buddhist tantric sexual yoga. However, White's very next sentence, stating that, while seminal retention "does become the rule in later conformist Buddhist tantric sources, it was not the original practice," appears to require further nuance. The *Generation of Fortune Sādhana* and several other Dunhuang manuscripts indicate that Buddhist *tāntrikas* performed both seminal retention *and* emission with sacramental offering from quite early on.[55] It is true that over time, the sacramental use of sexual fluids faded (except in the second initiation, which will be addressed below), while the practice of retention and its associated manipulations of internal energies grew in importance. (This shift is the focus of the present study's fifth chapter.)

While it is therefore important to distinguish these two periods of ritual development, the earlier and later practices of taking the *bodhicitta* as a sacrament and drawing the semen back into the body's interior both offer methods for recuperating the practitioner's precious bodily fluids. That the sacramental rite was eventually replaced by the practice of drawing the fluids back up the central channel may reflect a continuity of secretory concerns.

All this raises the inevitable question about whether the Mahāyoga practice of sexual union is solely imagined or accompanied by physical union with an actual woman. Although it is impossible to say for sure how the author of our *sādhana* intended his instructions, he certainly leaves open the physical possibility. The sudden burst of coded language is itself suggestive of something, though one might argue it stops there and is just that, mere suggestion. Certainly, two levels of meaning are being exploited in lines such as "Taking up the golden vajra and bell, brandish them with great majesty." That the vajra and bell are Vajrasattva's hand implements allows for this to be a straightforward instruction to hold them in one's hands. Yet the vajra and bell are also common euphemisms for the male and female sexual organs, and the verb "brandish" (*gsor ba*; Skt. **ullālayet*) might also be translated as "agitate" or "thrust," suggesting that the line marks the beginning of sexual intercourse. Throughout the larger passage, the instructions play on these two levels of interpretation, leaving the uninitiated reader unsure how to understand them.

Also telling are certain changes of wording wrought by the elaborated version of our *sādhana* found in IOL Tib J 331/2. Repeatedly, this work pushes the instructions in the direction of the imaginary, away from a physical union. Thus, for example, where the *Generation of Fortune* reads, "In accordance with the ritual procedures, position the jewel sprout at the top of the head," IOL Tib J 331/2 changes the verb "position" (*gzhag*) to "imaginatively conceive" (*brtag*).[56] Then again, where IOL Tib J 464 reads, "Then gaze desirously at the *pāramitā*. She speaks the exhorting words with devotion, and one repeats the exhortation," IOL Tib J 331/2 prefers, "Then gaze desirously at the *pāramitā*. *Imagine* that she speaks exhorting words with devotion."[57]

Finally, when it comes to offering the seminal sacrament, our *sādhana* reads simply, "The offering is made and the accomplishment received," while IOL Tib J 331/2 complicates the process: "From a *banda* [skull-cup] that is endowed with glory and so forth [i.e., bears the indicated characteristics], *for real or in one's imagination*, in accordance with the ritual procedures, perform the consecration, making the offerings and receiving the *siddhi*."[58] Here is an explicit recognition that the rite might be understood as "for real," though clearly the author of IOL Tib J 331/2 sees an imagination-only reading as legitimate.

Since David Snellgrove's early work on tantric Buddhism, scholars have often suggested that interpretations of the sexual yogas trended over time from the real to the symbolic.[59] Generally speaking, the sources seem to bear this out. Explicit instructions to perform sexual yoga in one's imagination are more common after the ninth century than before, though many exceptions may be observed. One appears in Atiśa's eleventh-century writings. In line with the trend toward the symbolic, Atiśa mostly prohibits monastics from taking the second and third initiations, which involved sexual union,[60] but in the end he inserts a caveat: "Provided he understands reality, even a celibate may perform the higher initiations, . . . without [fear of incurring any] fault."[61] Such concessions could have significant results; the generally conservative twelfth-century Tibetan master Katok Dampa Deshek is said to have led 100 couples through the details of ritual union. Dampa's direct disciple Lding po pa writes in the first person, "With a group of 100 couples, we conducted a yearlong retreat on the *Sutra of the Great Gathering [of Intentions]*. The history of this event is secret: *guhya*."[62]

Despite such rather large-scale exceptions, the literature does seem to reflect a trend toward monastic sublimation of tantric sex. This may have been part of a larger shift around the eleventh century, "an all-out doctrinal war against non-monastic officiants," in which "monks were trying to bring back under their authority the religion that [had] now become almost mainstream."[63] IOL Tib J 331/2 provides additional evidence of this general trend. In the documents from Dunhuang offer glimpses of the reworking of sexual rites *in action*. Although many Indian and Tibetan authors of the tenth and eleventh centuries specified that monastics should restrict themselves to performing the sexual yogas in their imagination, the Dunhuang manuscripts include up-close local efforts to alter earlier *sādhanas*.[64]

IOL Tib J 331/2 recommends that the sexual fluids be gathered into a skull cup (*banda*), from which they are then distributed as the sacrament. Other manuscripts on the tantric feast (*gaṇacakra*) recommend further preparations, often by mixing the male semen and the female fluids, typically portrayed as red in color, with three additional profane substances—feces, urine, and human flesh—to produce the fivefold ambrosia, embodying the heads of the five buddha-families. This is offered first to the *vajrācārya*, then to the feast's other participants.[65] Even in such cases, however, the male *bodhicitta*, which embodies Akṣobhya of the Vajra family, is treated as the primary ingredient. In the *Generation of Fortune Sādhana*, no skull cup is mentioned, and the sacramental fluid is bestowed more directly, as also in Pelliot tibétain 841: "When the *bodhicitta* falls, recite, '*a la la ho*!' and imagine that the goddess is pleased. From between the *vajra* and the lotus, with the ring finger of the left hand, take the dew of the lotus and offer it to the noble ones [i.e., the buddhas]. Then oneself and the consort also receive the sacrament."[66]

In such passages, the Dunhuang manuscripts preserve a stage of tantric ritual development that would soon be superseded. From the mid-eighth through ninth centuries, the seminal sacrament was the defining characteristic of tantric practice. The same practice may be seen in canonical works of the period too. The *Guhyasamāja*'s eighth chapter, for example, provides instruction on how to perform worship through sexual union and culminates in the self-administering of the *bodhicitta*: "Thinking of her as a source of blessings, one should imagine worshipping the reality [i.e., the buddhas]. Obtaining the semen from the long-eyed one, he who has a firm mind eats it."[67]

Among the Dunhuang manuscripts, probably the most detailed description of how to take the sacrament appears in IOL Tib J 754, in the context of a tantric feast. The crucial instructions are set off from the rest of the text with an elaborate decorative marker and read:

> Regarding the taking of the *samaya* by the *samaya* beings: From within the lotus skull cup, using thumb and ring finger, three red *hrīḥ* [syllables] are consecutively placed upon the tongue, which is visualized as a moon disc, and swallowed. As the first *hrīḥ* is placed on the tongue, "*oṃ*" is recited, whereby the *hrīḥ* transforms into an *oṃ*. From that *oṃ*, one is filled with the color of Vairocana's body; as it

> passes inside, one's own body is consecrated as his body. Then the middle *hṛīḥ* is placed on the tongue while reciting "*āṃ*," whereby the *hṛīḥ* becomes an *āṃ*. From that *āṃ*, one is filled with the color of Amitābha; as it passes inside, one's own speech is consecrated as his speech. Then the final *hṛīḥ* is placed on the tongue while reciting "*hūṃ*," whereby the *hṛīḥ* becomes a *hūṃ*. From that *hūṃ*, one is filled with the color of Akṣobhya's body; as it passes inside, one's own mind is consecrated as his mind. After swallowing those three *hṛīḥs*, recite the mantra, "*tiṣṭha vajra hoḥ*," the meaning of which is said to be the stabilization of the body, speech, and mind as *svastika*.[68]

This passage deserves some unpacking, for it reveals some continuities between earlier Yogatantra practice and this new practice of swallowing the *bodhicitta*. First, the practice is deemed a "consecration" (Skt. *adhiṣṭhāna*; Tib. *byin gyis brlabs pa*). Second, there is a remnant of the older Yogatantra lexicon in which the *samayamudrā*, or just *samaya* more generally, was used to refer to what is later known as the *jñānasattva*. The passage therefore describes a consecration of the practitioner with the *bodhicitta*, framed a kind of ultimate *samaya*. The *sādhanas* of both Yogatantra and early Mahāyoga alike, then, culminated in parallel consecratory moments.

Following the reception of the sacrament, a moment of silence ends with the next line: "when one comes to know it is time for the dismissal" (*gtong ba 'i dus ni shes pa na*) of the deities in the visualization.[69] Curious here is the exact wording, "when one comes to know." Even a casual reader of the *sādhana* can see very well that the closing rites come next, yet for a moment here, the practitioner does not know it. The reception of the sacrament is followed by a period of not knowing from which the practitioner eventually emerges. It would be easy to pass over this moment too quickly, but it is a significant silence, a gap in the proceedings.[70]

A similar line occurs at the parallel point in the *Mañjuśrīmitra*-attributed *Precept for Supreme Goodness*: "[Perform] the recitations and cultivate, then receive the *siddhi*. . . . Having come to know it is time for the dismissal, one regathers the consort into the gnosis being."[71] Here we have the benefit of a short interlinear note: "in accordance with the number of propitiations or with one's commitment."[72] So the hiatus that follows the reception of the sacrament may include a period of mantra recitation ("propitiations") or may just last for a certain predetermined amount of time. Either way, this is a significant moment, when the reader is meant to rest in meditation.

The Padmasambhava-attributed commentary to the Mahāyoga tantra, the *Lasso of Means* (*Thabs kyi zhags pa*), offers a sense of what is meant to occur at this mysterious moment, though in the context of a group practice (*tshom bu*) that culminates in *gaṇacakra* feasting, singing, and dancing: "When one drinks it down, the supreme accomplishment is attained. . . . By means of that *bodhicitta*, which is Vajrasattva, one passes beyond subject and object and enters into absorption in nonduality, the realm of *mūṃ* [i.e., emptiness]. For this reason, one is called Vajrasattva, he who dwells on the level of Vajra Holder, or he of the thirteenth level. This is the supreme accomplishment."[73] The sacrament thus bestows a direct taste of buddhahood. Ritual falls away and a direct meditation on emptiness emerges. Buddhajñānapāda in his *Dvitīyakrama* describes the reception of the sacrament in these words: "The intelligent one takes up the semen nectar that rests in the lotus and drinks it. In that way, the final reality of all entities becomes profound and luminous."[74]

The Great Perfection

In IOL Tib J 437, the role of the *bodhicitta* as a third entity produced from the union of the father and the mother is spelled out: "The external object is objective phenomena, the feminine Samantabhadrī, a soaring space without center or periphery. The internal subject is subjective perception, the mentally engaging mind, Samantabhadra, the father. The intention of the two, father and mother, is the *bodhicitta*, the revealed mandala."[75] The theme is picked up elsewhere in the same manuscript, in a lengthy description of the sacrament to be recited just before it is bestowed:

> This supreme ambrosia that consecrates the body, speech, and mind,
> from the method and gnosis of the fathers and mothers of the five families,
> is the *bodhicitta* of nondual great bliss.
> Within the secret moon, the immeasurable [palace] of the lotus endowed with the secrets,
>
> The unborn seminal drop of wish-fulfilling ambrosia emanates.
> Out of the very meaning of the *mudrā* that is the supreme fruition of mantra,

the *rasāyana* sweet waters of the vajra nectar
are perfectly displayed within the space of the inexpressible Samantabhadrī.

The great identity of the great perfection, the quintessence of mind,
the excellent medicinal offering beyond birth and death:
when this is offered as a vow-fulfilling treasury,
Lord of Yoga, please accept it as an ornament.[76]

Of particular significance is the appearance of the great perfection (*rdzogs chen*), a term that would grow to become a distinct contemplative system. Although that tradition has roots in late eighth-century Indian Mahāyoga teachings of the sort seen here, it is largely a Tibetan development. The scattered references in Indian sources are often obscure. Used to describe the result of tantric practice, however, it is regularly associated with *bodhicitta*. IOL Tib J 594 contains one of the earliest self-identified Great Perfection texts, the *Small Hidden Seed* (*Sbas pa'i rgum chung*). A brief introduction to the work even describes it as extracted from a larger genre of "scriptures on *bodhicitta*" (*byang chub kyi sems kyi lung*).[77] While *bodhicitta* played a central role in Mahāyāna Buddhism from long before the advent of the tantras, given its crucial role within early Mahāyoga practice at the end of the eighth century, the precise nature of the connection between the early Great Perfection and the sacramental drop deserves further consideration.

An interlinear note to the opening line of this Dunhuang copy of the *Small Hidden Seed* explains that its teachings are "beyond generation and perfection." The same claim is made by the *Cuckoo of Awareness* (*Rig pa'i khu byug*), another short Great Perfection text, contained in IOL Tib J 647: "The *bodhicitta* that is beyond expression is accomplished spontaneously, so the mandala is produced without needing to perform generation and perfection."[78] This also accords with the *Pith Instructional Garland of Views* (*Man ngag lta ba'i phreng ba*), attributed to the late eighth-century master Padmasambhava. There, the great perfection names a third stage that follows the better-known two stages of generation and perfection:

In the method of generation, one generates [the visualization] gradually by means of the three *samādhis*. Accomplishment is gained by establishing and cultivating the mandala step by step. In the method of perfection, on the ultimate level, one

> never wavers from the unarising and unceasing gods and goddesses nor from the nonconceptual middle way, the expanse of reality, but on the relative level, one clearly cultivates the form bodies of the noble ones. Accomplishment is gained by cultivating them as equal yet distinct. In the method of the great perfection, one cultivates the realization of all mundane and supramundane phenomena as primordially and inseparably the nature of the mandala of [the buddha's] body, speech, and mind.[79]

While the *Garland of Views* description of this final stage is largely doctrinal or "gnostic" in flavor, lacking clear reference to any ritual context, the idea that the great perfection followed the perfection stage suggests that, in its earliest days at least, it may have been associated with a specific ritual moment, the state resulting from receiving the supreme sacrament.

Further support for this idea may be gained from another short Dunhuang manuscript. Appended to Pelliot tibétain 841 is a brief interpretation of the three syllables in the word *heruka* (a wrathful form of the buddha that became popular in Mahāyoga tantric writings):

> "He" is the sound of the initial summons. All of the three realms are spontaneously accomplished as the great mandala of the body, speech, and mind, resting without wavering at the center of the sky. Through knowing that all the three realms spontaneously abide as the *mahāmudrā* of gnosis, there is the great delight.
>
> "Ru" is the meaning of resting in the space. The great mandala of gnosis abides indivisibly within the vagina of the consort. To bring the three realms under control by means of the sacrament of the lustful consort, "*ru*" is pronounced; everything is brought into the space of all.
>
> "Ka" is the great *bodhicitta*. The *bodhicitta* [that results] from the nondual union with the consort, equal to the sky, luminously pervades all. The five elements and all the sentient beings of the five continuous ways [of gods, humans, animals, ghosts, and hell beings] dawn as an ocean of compassion; they appear as Samantabhadra.[80]

Earlier in the same manuscript, the viewpoints of Mahāyoga and Anuyoga are juxtaposed, but the term "Atiyoga" (another name for the Great Perfection) does not appear, perhaps because the first folio is missing. Nonetheless, it seems reasonable to understand the three parts in the above passage as referring to Mahāyoga, Anuyoga, and Atiyoga, or their equivalents, the three stages of generation, perfection, and great perfection. It is also perhaps significant that the buddha Samantabhadra, the principal deity for the Great Perfection traditions, is mentioned in the final paragraph.

The early Great Perfection seems to have been linked particularly closely to the *Guhyagarbha Tantra*,[81] which includes four references. Two are explicit in describing it as the sacrament (lit. "*samaya*").[82] The first appears in chapter 19, titled "The Sacrament" and entirely devoted to the topic. After direct reference is made to "the unsurpassed supreme *samaya*" (*bla med mchog gi dam tshig*) and the initiatory bestowal of an ambrosia of sexual fluids, the passage explains: "Resting in the *samaya* of equality, which evenly unites one with equality, the *great perfection* of equality is attained. When it is transgressed, one is not a buddha."[83] We have seen that the bestowal of the sacrament produces a taste of awakening in which the recipient rests for some time. Here the same idea is suggested, and the resulting state is explicitly called the great perfection.

Another reference opens the tantra's thirteenth chapter: "Then, having gathered into one all the mandalas of the vajra body, speech, and mind of all the *tathāgatas* of the ten directions and the four times, the *tathāgata*, with great joy, rested evenly in the *samādhi* of arrayed clouds of the essence that is the extremely secret *samaya* that spontaneously accomplishes all phenomena as the great perfection."[84] The buddha Samantabhadra thusly preaches the entire thirteenth chapter from within the state of the great perfection. The chapter can thus be read as an extended poetic discourse on the supreme sacrament, and its language supports such an interpretation. The chapter ends, for example, with the closing advice, "It should be bestowed upon those worthy recipients who are steadfast in their noble disposition and have offered their bodies and riches. It should never be given to anyone else."[85] This same chapter, moreover, is the subject of the above-cited *Pith Instructional Garland of Views*, one of the first works to define the Great Perfection as a distinct ritual stage. That Padmasambhava, the assumed author, would devote an entire commentary to one chapter is a testament to the importance of the supreme sacrament during this early period of tantric development.

The *Guhyagarbha*'s third reference to the great perfection does not call it a sacrament, but it appears in chapter 14, within a six-verse song of praise to the awakened state taught in the previous chapter: "Oṃ! The great perfection of the body, speech, and mind! The total perfection of the qualities and activities! The primordial, spontaneously perfecting Samantabhadra! The great seminal drop (*thig le*) of the great gathered assembly! Ho!"[86] Given the above-cited reference from chapter 13, in which all the *tathāgatas* are gathered into the singular sacrament, the final line may have a ritual significance that is easy to overlook. Note too the association between the seminal drop and the "great gathered assembly." It is perhaps relevant that the singularity into which "all the mandalas of the vajra body, speech, and mind of all the *tathāgatas* of the ten directions and the four times" are gathered in the opening line to chapter 13 may itself be considered a kind of mandala, "the supreme mandala of the mandala of mind, the space mandala of the secret seminal essence," as the chapter proceeds to explain.[87] This is precisely the same mandala that is praised in chapter 14, and it is the primordial mandala that is the subject of the *Guhyagarbha*'s fourth and final reference to the great perfection: "Gnosis conceived as a center of the four directions, a spontaneously accomplished inconceivable mandala: the yogin who realizes this great perfection practices the great mandala that is the origin of all."[88]

To get a sense of how these references might have been understood by Indian scholars of the late eighth or early ninth century, we may turn to the *Spar khab*, a lengthy commentary on the *Guhyagarbha* attributed to Vilāsavajra. On the above-cited opening line of the crucial thirteenth chapter, we read:

> Everything gathered within the two entities [of cause and effect] is primordially reflexive awareness alone. Therefore, everything is unobstructed and, unborn as anything apart, illuminated as an identity. Being nothing but just the body, speech, and mind, it is the great perfection. Due to imputations that are based on that, the aspects of causality are expressed, but as self-arising gnosis itself, that self-appearance that is devoid of causality is not possible to transgress, so it is called the spontaneously accomplished sacrament (*samaya*).[89]

The great perfection is the embodiment of the ultimate vow, the sacrament beyond time and causality. That this is none other than the drop of *bodhicitta* produced through sexual union becomes clear a few pages later:

> Through the frolicking, when the moon mandala (i.e., semen) manifests at the jewel (i.e., penis), appearing as the mandala of the five gnoses, there is a natural clear light, whereby means unites with wisdom. At that moment, the quintessence

> of everything gathers within the sun mandala, becoming the cause of all without exception. If it is taken with skill in means, everything, including the aggregates and so forth, is spontaneously accomplished as the mandala. That which has the power to perform this consecration manifests at the tip of the pistil; it unites wisdom itself with means. Without the taste of the moon dissipating, yet without it being a focus, they coalesce in an instant, whereby the taste that is free from the two extremes is attained.[90]

The early Great Perfection's close associations with *bodhicitta* and a contemplative state beyond the stages of generation and perfection must be understood within the context of late eighth-century tantric practice, when sexual yoga and the culminating sacrament represented the cutting edge. Against this ritual background, the more gnostic-style reveries of the early Great Perfection sometimes appear in revealing relief. Late eighth-century writings like Mañjuśrīmitra's *Bodhicittabhāvanā* and early Great Perfection texts such as the *Cuckoo of Awareness* make little explicit reference to any ritual setting, but even in such cases, the sacramental moment may have functioned in the background. Before long, the Great Perfection's ritual origins and the importance of the sacrament were left behind, as Mahāyoga practice moved in other directions and the Great Perfection grew into a separate vehicle.

The Secret Initiation

By the tenth century, the *bodhicitta* sacrament was quickly disappearing from Mahāyoga *sādhana* practice, yet it continues to be preserved as an initiation to the present day. Chapter 2 analyzed the Yogatantra initiations of the *Sarvadurgatipariśodhana* tradition. While the eight initiations for the eight *uṣṇīṣa* buddhas were specific to that system, the more standard Yogatantra set of five initiations included the water initiation (*udakābhiṣeka*), the crown initiation (*mukuṭābhiṣeka*), the vajra initiation (*vajrābhiṣeka*), the bell initiation (*ghaṇṭābhiṣeka*), and the name initiation (*nāmābhiṣeka*).[91] Sometimes an additional master initiation (*ācāryābhiṣeka*) would be added to authorize the initiate to grant initiation himself. By the second half of the eighth century, a new "secret initiation" (Skt. *guhyābhiṣeka*; Tib. *gsang dbang*) had developed.

It entailed the guru's copulating with a female consort, then bestowing a drop of the resulting *bodhicitta* upon the initiate for him to swallow, empowering him to perform the secret rites of sexual union. The Mahāyoga ritual manuals from Dunhuang describe more or less the same practice, but as a self-consecration that the practitioner performs at the culmination of the perfection stage. From the point of view of the later tradition, the presence of such a sacramental self-consecration within the context of a daily *sādhana* is unusual. Its presence within the secret initiation, however, is well known.

The later tradition often points to the eighth chapter of the *Guhyasamāja* as a locus classicus for this secret initiation, but read free of later commentaries, the chapter clearly describes a rite of sexual worship (*pūjā*) culminating in a self-consecration.[92] Thus, the nineteenth verse reads:

> So that the abode of the families may be cultivated, it should be cultivated by the wise one.
> With the five qualities that please the senses, he begins making oceans of offerings to that.[93]

Here is a straightforward instruction for a solitary *sādhana* practitioner to prepare the site ("the abode") and make offerings, yet the tantric Candrakīrti's *Pradīpodyotana*, a tenth-century commentary of the Ārya school, assigns these two ritual acts to two distinct ritual actors:

> Regarding "[the abode of] the families . . . ," [the first line] up to, "should be cultivated" is taught so that one [i.e., a guru] who has the wisdom that [the mandala previously constructed] is an abode and a ground for the five families—a yogin who understands the secret initiation—may worship, that is, so he may grant the secret initiation.
>
> [Then:] Following this teaching on the actions of the guru, in order to teach what should be done by the student desiring the secret initiation, it talks about "[the five] qualities that please the senses . . ." and so on.[94]

Here, Candrakīrti explains that *the guru* who will bestow the secret initiation should first construct the mandala-abode, but *the disciple* who is seeking initiation should perform the offerings subsequently described. This is quite clearly not what the tantra's author intended.

Again, in the chapter's penultimate verse, the tantra itself reads:

> Obtaining the semen from the long-eyed one,
> he with a firm mind eats it.[95]

This is the final moment when the practitioner self-administers the drop of sexual fluids. On this verse, however, Candrakīrti writes, "Thinking that all the *tathāgatas* that reside in one's own body are satisfied by this gift of guru to disciple, one should eat it."[96] According to the *Pradīpodyotana*, then, this is the culminating moment not of the postinitiatory sexual worship but of the secret initiation itself. Once more, Candrakīrti's reading runs against the grain of the tantra. The *Guhyasamāja* therefore lacks any mention of the secret initiation (until the supplemental *uttaratantra*, added around the early ninth century).

Which "canonical" tantra is the earliest to name the secret initiation as the culminating ritual? The *Cakrasaṃvara* (*Śrīherukābhidhāna*) reached its received form in the first half of the ninth century and appears to offer an early reference.[97] Its third chapter likely describes such a rite (and certainly was read as doing so by later commentators) in the following verse: "The master, well equipoised, should worship the consort. On the second day he should make the drop (Skt. *tilaka*; Tib. *thig le*) for the disciples with blood thrice enchanted. Having unveiled his [blindfolded] face, he should then show the maṇḍala to the disciple."[98] The passage appears within a larger description of an initiation ritual, complete with the guru removing the disciple's blindfold to reveal the mandala, and so forth. Somewhat less clear is the guru's engagement in sexual union with the consort, where he should "worship the consort," with "consort" translating *mudrā*. The bestowal of the sacrament itself is still more coded. Nonetheless, the passage remains a possible early canonical reference to the secret initiation.[99] Others surely may be found. Outside the tantras, an early reference is in Buddhajñānapāda's *Dvitīyakramatattvabhāvanā-mukhāgama* (vv. 83–85), which likely dates to around the turn of the ninth century: "Then, when the guru is pleased, / He engages in union with her, / Due to which the *sugatas* melt and become the sixteenth part [i.e., the drop]; / This is dropped in the mouth of the disciple."[100] But almost certainly predating this is a line from the *Precept for Supreme Goodness*, the brief Mahāyoga *sādhana* in IOL Tib J 331/1. Although it does not reference the secret initiation by name, it does describe the prerequisite to practice as the "initiation by means of the drop."[101] Given that the *Precept* is attributed to Mañjuśrīmitra, who lived in the second half of the eighth century, this may be our earliest evidence for the secret initiation.

Still, such references from the eighth century are rare, and it seems that the sacrament may have functioned first within the context of *sādhana* practice, as a "secret"—i.e., sexual—take on the earlier consecrations with the *samayamudrā* in the *STTS*, and only later, perhaps around the late eighth century, was enshrined as a distinct initiation. This hypothesis is supported by the evidence from Dunhuang, which reflects a strong interest in the sacrament as the culmination of the sexual yoga but includes no explicit reference to the secret initiation by name.[102] Once it had emerged, the secret initiation became central to the practice of Mahāyoga, and the sexual yogas of the perfection stage in particular. Several sources even suggest that the new initiation initially functioned independently, often performed on its own, apart from the earlier vase initiations (Skt. *kalaśābhiṣeka*; Tib. *bum pa'i dbang*) of the Yoga tantra system, specifically for the purpose of authorizing perfection-stage practice.[103]

The sacramental *bodhicitta* thus eventually came to function as the culmination of sexual yoga in the context of both *sādhana* and initiation. In both settings, it embodied and instilled in its recipient an experience of awakening, and in this sense, this Mahāyoga *samaya* functioned very much like the *samaya* of the Yoga tantras. In the *STTS* the *samaya* is installed within the heart of the initiate by the dual means of placing the *samayamudrā* (a vajra upon a moon disc) atop their head and having them drink the oath water. The Yogatantra practitioner then repeats the consecration in his daily *sādhana*, as he installs the *samayamudrā/jñānasattva* into his own heart. Just so, in Mahāyoga practice the *bodhicitta*—still termed the *samaya*, or supreme *samaya*—is bestowed as an initiation, and "having descended, it enters the lotus at his heart."[104] After this, again, the initiate repeats the consecration at the culminating moment of his *sādhana*-based sexual yoga. In chapter 3, we saw how Sarvārthasiddhi underwent this same consecratory moment in the opening narrative of the *STTS*, as all the *tathāgatas* entered through four points on his body, consecrating him and coming to rest at his heart in the form of the *samayamudrā*, a vajra upon a moon disc. According to the story's logic, this moon disc with the vajra is none other than Samantabhadra, the mind of awakening, *bodhicitta* itself. In Mahāyoga, the sacramental supreme *samaya* is likewise an instantiation of *bodhicitta*, and from this perspective, Samantabhadra's role as the central buddha of the Great Perfection and other early Mahāyoga rituals that focus on *bodhicitta* makes considerable sense. Insofar as the Yogatantra consecratory moment offers the vajra on a moon disc as a metaphor for the mind of awakening, Mahāyoga deploys the drop of semen, a metaphorical substance that is likewise an immediate embodiment of the same *bodhicitta*. The ingested *bodhicitta* is the *jñānasattva* residing at the heart of oneself and all buddhas.[105]

Closing Rites

When the practitioner emerges from the meditative state induced by the sacrament and "comes to know it is time for the dismissal," he is instructed to "regather [the deities] according to one's own tradition (*gtsug lag*)." The details of how to dissolve the visualization are thus left to the reader and the specific teachings he has received. Other Dunhuang *sādhanas* give a sense of what these instructions might have involved. As discussed above, IOL Tib J 552 and 553 are closely related *sādhanas* written by close associates living around Dunhuang in the second half of the tenth century (fig. 4.3). Both are closely tied to the much shorter *Precept for Supreme Goodness*, but each shows the personal interests of its creator, offering a different approach to the key moment of dissolution. Indeed, it is precisely the manuals' closeness that allows us to recognize where they diverge, points of compositional style and poetic license more than mere content.

The visualization to be dissolved is slightly more detailed than but similar to that of our own *sādhana*. It consists of the mantrin as the deity resting in sexual union with a female deity. Earlier in the manuals, we are told that a *jñānasattva*, i.e., a smaller, thumb-sized deity representing the mind of the buddha, what was once called the *samaya*, sits at one's heart. At his heart, in turn, rests a barley seed-sized vajra, a ritual implement that carries much significance in tantric Buddhism. Within the central ball of the vajra, which serves as the implement's handle, rests a still tinier (the size of a mustard seed) *hūṃ* syllable.

At the beginning of the ritual, this visualization is built up from this minute *hūṃ* syllable, step-by-step, into the full-size body of the deity with whom

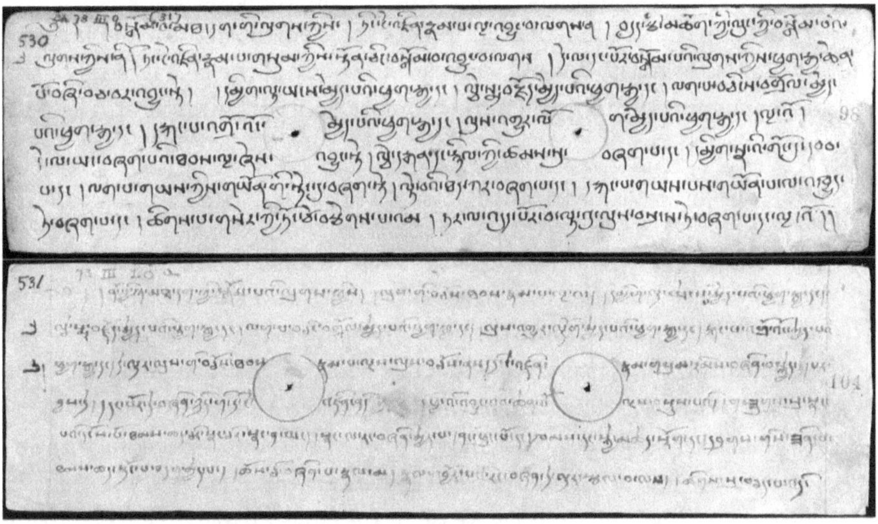

FIGURE 4.3 Two closely related local Mahāyoga *sādhanas*
Source: IOL Tib J 552 and 553, Courtesy of the British Library

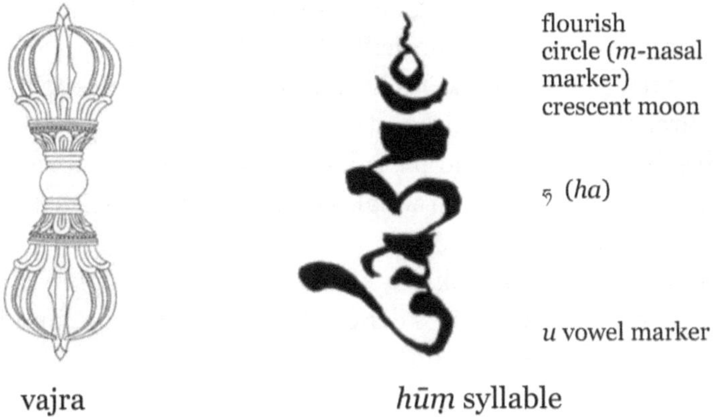

FIGURE 4.4 Vajra and the *hūṃ* syllable

one is identified. Now, to enact the dissolution, both manuals simply reverse this movement, so that one's own divine form dissolves into the vajra at one's heart, which then dissolves into the *hūṃ* at its center, which then dissolves into emptiness. The big difference between the two manuals is how exactly this mustard seed-sized *hūṃ* dissolves into emptiness.

One manual describes the process in considerable detail, leading the reader through the gradual dissolution of each element in the syllable, from the vowel marker at the bottom, through the body of the *ha*, right up to the last disappearing point in which the topmost flourish culminates. The passage reads:

> Then regather in accordance with the systems of yoga, cultivate that, from the lights that were emanated [throughout the universe] to the light of the flourish [atop the *hūm* syllable]—all of it dissolves into both the male and female deities. The female deity dissolves into the male. The male deity likewise dissolves into the *jñānasattva*. The *jñānasattva* further dissolves into the vajra implement. The vajra further dissolves into the *hūṃ* within its handle. The *hūṃ* dissolves into the -u vowel marker [at the bottom of the syllable]. The -u vowel marker further dissolves into the ཧ. The ཧ dissolves into the crescent moon [above]. The crescent moon dissolves into the circle [above that]. The circle further dissolves into the flourish and thus into the thusness *samādhi*, the empty space of phenomena, no-self.[106]

The practitioner is led through a series of smaller and smaller images, from the entire universe to the two deities to just the male deity, to the *jñānasattva* at his heart, to the vajra at *his* heart, to the *hūṃ* syllable at its center, and then through the careful deconstruction of each element of the syllable, up to the subtlest of points atop the highest point of the flourish . . . and into emptiness. A deliberate, gradual, and in the end, delicate movement is communicated.

The second manual takes a somewhat different approach. When the practitioner reaches the final dissolution of the *hūṃ*, they annihilate it in a sudden, roaring rush:

> Having accomplished the aims of all sentient beings, recite "*saṃharaṇa hūṃ*" ("regather *hūṃ*"). Thereby, the principal male deity into the female utterly dissolves. The female deity likewise into the male, utterly dissolves. The [resulting] male deity further into the thumb-sized gnosis deity [at his heart], utterly dissolves. The thumb-sized gnosis deity further into the barley seed-sized vajra utterly dissolves. The barley-seed-sized vajra further into the mustard seed-sized *hūṃ* utterly dissolves. Then recite a long *hūṃ*: "*Hūṃ*!" The *hūṃ*, like a charging

horse of the mind, right up the flourish into the thusness *samādhi* taught earlier, the space of phenomena, utterly dissolves.[107]

"Like a charging horse of the mind" makes clear the dramatic strength and swiftness of the mental event. The thundering hoofs resonate with the extended "*Hūṃ*!" that is pronounced. Each occurrence of the verb "dissolves" is accompanied by the intensifying adverb "utterly," a detail absent from the first manual's more measured account. It is a change, moreover, that alters how the text *sounds*. The adverb "utterly" is pronounced "*tim gi*," thereby doubling the impact of the verb itself, which is similarly pronounced "*tim*." Thus each sentence ends with "*tim gi tim*" (Tibetan being a verb-final language), with this repeated phrase leading up to the final, powerfully pronounced, "*Hūṃ*!" In all these ways, this passage communicates a far more forceful, sudden dissolution into emptiness. The two manuals may have been held to reach a similar result, but they did so by strikingly different means. Both the deliberate delicacy of the first manual's dissolution and the rushing collapse of the second seek to undercut the reader's senses and leave him suspended in a state of emptiness.

Examination of these two passages reveals an interest not only in subjective experience but also in representing that experience. Thus, the use of the simile "like a charging horse" itself draws the reader out of the usual instructional mode typical of most of the manual by surprising them with imagery. The simile tells them not just what to do but *how* to do it. In this regard, the instructions for dissolving the visualization into emptiness resemble those seen earlier for generating the deity out of emptiness. As in the *Generation of Fortune Sādhana*, both IOL Tib J 552 and 553 treat the all-illuminating *samādhi* by instructing the reader to "imagine a white *A* in the space of the sky, glittering like Venus."[108] In all such imagery, the manuals' authors seek to represent not only the ritual procedures but also a certain experience of them, an interest rarely seen in early ritual manuals of the sixth and seventh centuries.

It is significant that poetic imagery is deployed in the Dunhuang manuscripts for leading the reader through both the all-illuminating *samādhi* and the final process of dissolution. The former constitutes the second of the three *samādhis* that structure the generation stage, the methods for cultivating thusness, luminosity emerging from that empty space, and the appearance of the syllables out of which the visualization is constructed. The all-illuminating *samādhi* and the dissolution process both describe the emerging out of and dissolving back into emptiness. Both are focused on experiences in the immediate vicinity of the inconceivability of emptiness. Although our own *sādhana* passes over the two moments quickly, its use of the Venus simile and brief reference to "one's own tradition" signal their significance. In other Mahāyoga *sādhanas* from Dunhuang, the language shifts into a poetic register at both of these points. Such shifts suggest a particular interest on the part of early Mahāyoga authors in representing these originary/final moments, parallel experiences of emanation and regathering that surround the emptiness at one's heart.

The taste of *bodhicitta* is held to engender a similar experience (or "taste") of dissolution. Whereas simile is used to bookend the proceedings with the emanation and reabsorption of the visualization, the crux of early Mahāyoga *sādhana* comes in the middle, the culmination of a far more material procedure. In taking the seminal sacrament, the meditator at once transgresses and transcends his ordinary limits. The timeless moment of silence thus engendered might be described as an encounter with the sublime, an experience at the very edge of the comprehensible.

Appendix

The Generation of Fortune Sādhana[1]

A TRANSLATION OF IOL TIB J464

[1r] Homage to the Bhagavan, noble Vajrasattva.

If a hero endowed with discernment
wishes to attain the supreme vajra body,
the initiations and the *samaya* should be completed:
it is suitable that faith first[2] be enhanced.

To an intelligent *vajrācārya*
one should attend with the essence of one's mind.
Then to this excellent secret *sādhana*
listen with confidence.

In a clean, extremely solitary place,
having established a site pleasing to the mind and comfortable for the body,
lay out a comfortable seat.
Definitively cultivate these [three] *samādhis*.

[2r][3] First, atop one's head,
imagine a white ཨ.
Imagine that light rays [emanate][4] from that.

Dissolving into one's entire body,
it transforms oneself and all one's environs
into the nature of reality.[5]
Then cultivate nonconceptuality.

Meditate in that way [i.e., on the thusness *samādhi*], and
cultivate the all-illuminating and the causal [*samādhis*]:
imagine within the expanse of the space, a white ཨ,
glittering like Venus.

Then imagine the syllables *yaṃ*, *paṃ*,
suṃ, and *bhruṃ* stacked up.
Recite "*samayastvaṃ bhruṃ*."[6]

[3r][7] Imagine that, thereby, from the *yaṃ* comes a wind mandala,
from the *paṃ* comes an ocean of ambrosia,
from the *suṃ* comes a golden base—
a bejeweled Mount Meru.

From the *bhruṃ*, of variegated jewels,
a celestial mansion is cultivated,
ornamented with four doors, outer walls, entryways,
and all the adornments.

The palace of all the *sugatas*,
with inconceivable good qualities and immeasurable dimensions:
cultivate it according to what it says in the scripture.

At the center of that [palace], cultivate a lotus pedestal,
together with a jeweled throne.
[3v] On top of that, upon a moon disc,
concentratively imagine the heart [syllable] *hūṃ*.

Light rays emanate from that,
pleasing the assemblies of conquerors and [achieving] the aims of sentient beings.
[The rays then] fully regather,
whereupon the heart *mudrā* is clearly cultivated.

Imagine that same [symbol] emanates and regathers [light rays],
whereupon just as one recollects one's heart [syllable],
The two *mudrās* [i.e., the central deity and consort] are perfected.
They are completely ornamented.

Then recite this mantra,
whereby nondual pride is generated:
Yathā vajrasattvastathāhaṃ.[8]

Then immediately after that,
[4r] taking up the golden vajra and bell,
brandish them with great majesty,
while saying three times, "*hūṃ*!"

Once more stabilize within that state of majesty.
In accordance with the ritual procedures, the jewel sprout
is positioned at the top of the head.

Oṃ āṃ hūṃ svāhā:
the five great consecrating heart [syllables]
consecrate the five places [in one's body].

By means of the yoga for protecting, to the best of one's ability,
firmly protect the *siddhi* identity.
By means of the four principles,
the recitations should also be performed to the best of one's
abilities.

Then, at the *pāramitā*
[4v] gaze desirously.
She speaks the exhorting words with devotion,
and one repeats the exhortation.[9]

Then, with the signs (*brda*; Skt. **cchomā*) and so forth,
one unites with great bliss,
at which time the *mudrās* are clearly cultivated,
the offerings are made, and the emanation [i.e., the *bodhicitta*] is
emitted.

Having thoroughly cultivated in that way,
by means of the inner and outer praises
and the melodies (*glu*) of the *sādava* and so forth,
in a manner of supreme yearning,
strongly praise the great identity (*bdag nyid chen po*).

The offering is made, and the accomplishment received.

When one comes to know it is the time for the dismissal,
[6r] with [arms] crossed, snap the fingers
and recite, "*Jaḥ hūṃ baṃ hoḥ*!"
Regather [the deities] according to one's own tradition (*gtsug lag*).

With the observances (**vrata*) of a great hero,
this yoga of vajra union
is not to be forsaken, even at the cost of one's life;
nor should one allow it to deteriorate in any of one's daily activities.

For the benefit of those feeble-minded *siddhas*
who do not have the fortune to hear the tantra,
I have explained this *sādhana*.
By this means, I pray that the Blessed One, Vajrasattva's,
mind be pleased.

Whoever cultivates like this
is said to be like Vajrasattva.

The *Generation of Fortune Sādhana* is complete.

FIVE

Circles of Blazing Breaths

A Manual for Mantra Recitation

ALTHOUGH SOME EARLY ritual manuals were written by famous, elite scholars from major monasteries, most were cobbled together, scrawled, and altered by community priests exercising interests specific to their own time and place. Likewise, among the Dunhuang manuscripts, a few tantric manuals are titled, tightly organized, and composed in regular verse, but many are scrappy local compositions. Chapters 3 and 4 looked at manuals that are likely translations of Indic originals. The present chapter turns to a *sādhana* composed in Tibetan, as well as two commentaries that are even more local, probably unique to the environs of Dunhuang itself. The root text is a patchwork creation typical of early tantric ritual manuals, some lines reflecting influences from Chinese Chan, others from Indic manuals and commentaries. As such, our text at once reflects regional interests and offers significant insights into the broader development of early Indian tantric ritual.

The poses and the breathing techniques of yoga so popular today are rooted in the subtle body physiologies of the tantras, systems that developed in support of tantric sexual rites a millennium ago. Though Buddhist sexual yoga of the eighth century culminated in swallowing a sacramental drop of semen figured as *bodhicitta*, in the ninth century, this all-important sacrament began to give way to new ritual interests. As complex systems of *cakras*, breath energies (Skt. *prāṇa*; Tib. *rlung*), and subtle channels (Skt. *nāḍī*; Tib. *rtsa*) were mapped onto the practitioner's body, tantric sexual yoga increasingly centered on the body's blissful energies and manipulating them to intensify meditations on emptiness and awakening.

For the most part, the manuals from Dunhuang reflect a period of ritual development that preceded the subtle body technologies. Sexual yoga and the so-called perfection stage are present, but only in their sacramental forms. One ritual element, however, was a prelude to what was to come: the circulation of breath between the practitioner and his sexual partner. Perhaps because it was still being taught in secret, transmitted orally from guru to disciple, the breath-cycling practice is hinted at only briefly in just a few Dunhuang manuscripts, but it is elaborated upon in this one short *sādhana* and its two closely linked commentaries. The practice is markedly different from the more complex methods of channels and *cakras* that would soon emerge, and though in later centuries it continued to function alongside those systems, its breath circulations represent an early method for manipulating the energies within the body while engaging in sexual union. In this sense, it was part of the larger ongoing shift toward the body's interior, which would culminate in the subtle body and meditations on the slightest changes of the breath. This chapter examines the short *sādhana* in question, with a view to the more complex developments that were on the horizon, just beyond the Dunhuang manuscripts.

The ninth century witnessed a gradual decline in the seminal sacrament's significance within sexual yoga. The origins of the secret initiation, which seems initially to have functioned independently from the vase initiation to authorize perfection-stage sexual practice, have been addressed in chapter 4. After the channels and winds had taken center stage, however, the sacrament continued to be used in other, closely related contexts, most notably in the secret initiation and as part of the tantric feast. But it was soon supplemented by two further initiations—the wisdom-gnosis initiation (Skt. *prajñājñānābhiṣeka*; Tib. *shes rab ye shes kyi dbang*) and the fourth initiation (Skt. *caturtābhiṣeka*; Tib. *dbang bzhi pa*). These effectively downgraded the secret initiation, maintaining it as an important yet inadequate step on the path. The resulting set of four initiations was circulating by the early to mid-ninth century, with the locus classicus being the *Samājottara-tantra*, a later supplement to the *Guhyasamāja-tantra* that sometimes circulates as its eighteenth chapter. "In this tantra," the *Samājottara* reads, "the initiations are divided into three types. The initiation of the vase is the first, the secret initiation is the second, wisdom-gnosis is the third, and the fourth is likewise that again."[1] Here, the third initiation of wisdom-gnosis almost certainly was meant to refer to the guru leading his disciple through the stages of sexual yoga. The last phrase is less clear, which may reflect the still-nascent state of the fourth initiation at the time of the *Samājottara*'s composition. Nonetheless, the passage soon became the *locus classicus* for all four initiations, with the fourth (after some debate) understood as the guru's verbal introduction to the direct experience of the goal of awakening.[2] Today, these four initiations remain the standard set for Yoganiruttara (Unexcelled Yoga) practice, with the seminal sacrament preserved as a mere shadow of its former, eighth-century self.

A Multicultural Text: Pelliot tibétain 634 and 626

Among the tantric manuscripts from Dunhuang is a circle of interrelated works, all of which appear to have been composed locally. All date to the late tenth century and were of interest to Dunhuang-based practitioners of both Mahāyoga and Chan Buddhism. In these materials, we catch a rare glimpse of interreligious dialogue on the ancient Silk Road. These seven items are:

- Pelliot tibétain 626 and 634: Two commentaries on an unnamed Mahāyoga *sādhana.*
- Pelliot chinois 3835V, a Chinese copy of a similar, though not identical, Mahāyoga *sādhana* to that seen in Pelliot tibétain 626 and 634.[3]
- IOL Tib J 689, 1774, and Pelliot tibétain 121, 19–21: Three copies of a short Chan text called the *Brief Precept* (*Lung chung*), attributed to the Chan patriarch Bodhidharma.
- Pelliot tibétain 699: A commentary on the *Brief Precept.*

At the heart of this group are two short works—a succinct and untitled Mahāyoga *sādhana* and a short Chan meditation text sometimes referred to as the *Brief Precept.*[4] The former manual and its commentary in Pelliot tibétain 634 are the primary focus of this chapter, with occasional references to the further comments offered by Pelliot tibétain 626. At least some portions of the root *sādhana* may be of Indic origin; as we shall see, some parallel passages appear in other sources. The two commentaries in Pelliot tibétain 634 and Pelliot tibétain 626, however, reflect a mix of Indian tantric and Chinese Chan interests and were therefore probably composed in Tibet or around

Dunhuang. The commentary on the Chan *Brief Precept* preserved in Pelliot tibétain 699 appears to have been composed under the influence of our Mahāyoga root *sādhana*.[5] Finally, the Chinese-language ritual described in PC3835V closely mirrors our *sādhana*, though portions of it also appear in other Chinese manuscripts that are heavily sinicized and in some cases linked to Chinese Chan lineages.[6] Given all this intertextuality among such idiosyncratic manuscripts, it is likely that our two commentaries were composed in or around Dunhuang. That neither provides a title for the *sādhana* or any authorship attribution further suggests that the work may have been composed in Tibet, or perhaps even at Dunhuang as well.

The two commentaries were penned by a single hand in the late tenth century, the same hand as the commentary to the *Brief Precept* seen in Pelliot tibétain 699.[7] We are left with the distinct possibility that all three commentaries were composed by the same, Dunhuang-based individual, someone with interests in both Mahāyoga and Chinese Chan. The two Mahāyoga commentaries provide different, though usually complementary information. They are also formatted differently, Pelliot tibétain 626 being an in-line commentary, with the words from the root *sādhana* written in red ink, and Pelliot tibétain 634 providing its comments in copious and meticulously written interlinear notes (fig. 5.1). The most intact version of the root *sādhana* is thus obtained by extracting it from the latter manuscript:

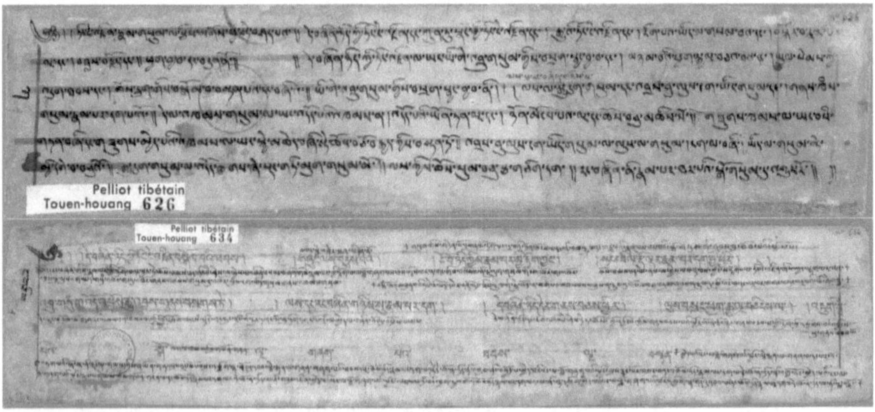

FIGURE 5.1 Mahāyoga *sādhana* with commentaries
Source: Pelliot tibétain 626 and 634, Courtesy of the Bibliothèque Nationale

The method for cultivating the thusness *samādhi*,
as gathered from scripture:

Though [one is already] essentially nonconceptual,
as with silver ore, in order to purify,
the three seed [syllables] radiate light, incinerating the causes, the effects, and the places;
one is purified in both one's practice and nature.

In order to dwell in that thusness,
with a straight body, bind the five *mudrās*,
and display the five gates of entry—the five methods for resting.
Gazing at the mind (*sems lta*) is the method, not locating is wisdom.

[The mind] is not anything; one does not think anything,
not mentally engaging in or conceptualizing features;
one's sphere of activity is pure, so do not abide anywhere.
Comprehend the state of the three liberations.

Method is not separating, like taking *hala*.
Wisdom is unwavering, like applying an antitoxic cure.

Mindfulness is unerring, as for [rain]drops, like gatekeepers.
Alertness is recognition, like a watchman for thieves.

Vipaśyanā is effulgent, like a lamp.
Śamatha is unwavering, still, like a deep lake.

Those[8] six [lines above] are divided into pairs:
the stages of entry, remedy, and settling the intellect.

Śamatha and *vipaśyanā* are balanced, like a lamp in a vase,
unmoving and clear, like a clear lake.

Then, the method for cultivating the all-illuminating *samādhi*:
Not moving from the space, knowing whatever occurs in its vividness,
compassion, even throughout all, the space of desirelessness,

opening like the sky, becoming the cause for emanations to arise,
not desiring the two extremes, free from all without abandoning anything.
Thus it is said.

The method for cultivating the causal *samādhi*:
From the syllable *A*: *e tang khang lang ram*.
Purifying the five poisons through the empowerments of their natures, the five mothers,
the *samādhis* of the five entireties (Skt. *kṛtsna*; Tib. *zad par*) are cultivated.
Thus, the five great elements are cultivated in a stack.

Then the **techniques for the recitations for the activities are taught:**
As if mindfulness, the vital breath, and its restriction were speaking, speaking!
As if the earrings, necklace, and limbs were swaying, swaying!
As if on the base, the vajra and seed syllables were blazing, blazing!
The vowels, *anusvāras*, intersyllabic dots are so perfect!
Holding these three aspects in mind at once, one's mind,
without distraction and stupefaction, is aware with mindfulness and luminosity.[9]

Second *samādhi*:
Within a state of *dharma*, performing the *mudrās* and singing the songs,
from the seed syllables of speech that are the mind itself,
the secret mantra should be listened to in one's mind,
whereby the secret mantra is pure, and the recitations clear.

Third *samādhi*:
(i)The unchanging syllables strung together as a garland,
(ii) [resound] constantly like the sound of a bell.
(iii) There is a projecting and gathering of light, with a manner of a [spinning] firebrand.
(iv) Gathering back, one presses down with the word.
(v) The method for leading is joined with a mute *hūṃ*.

Fourth *samādhi*:
When it has cycled, one aspires faithfully,
paying homage in a manner of realization, and

embracing apprehended and apprehender within a state of nonduality:
may the merit of sentient beings increase.

The *samādhi* is complete.

As reflected here, the text is written almost entirely in verse. Two kinds of language may be distinguished—the evocative instr5uction and brief explanatory markers (in bold). The evocative instruction is all in verse. The markers often use no verse at all, as in: "Then, the method for cultivating the all-illuminating *samādhi*." Sometimes, though not always, the explanatory markers use verse that breaks the meter, as in the lines, "Those six [lines above] are divided into pairs: / the stages of entry, remedy, and settling the intellect," which use seven-syllable verse in place of the nine-syllable verse seen before and after. In any case, taken together, the explanatory markers, found in both Pelliot tibétain 634 and Pelliot tibétain 626, provide a clear structure:

A. The three *samādhis* of the generation stage:
   1. Thusness *samādhi*
   2. All-illuminating *samādhi*
   3. Causal *samādhi*
B. Techniques for the recitations:
   1. Mental illumination [of the deity]
   2. Second *samādhi*: fulfillment of speech
   3. Third *samādhi*: five kinds of cycling
   4. Fourth *samādhi*: completing the recitations and homage

The ritual thus proceeds through seven steps—the first three *samādhis* of the generation stage, which end with establishing the mandala palace atop the elemental discs, and another four *samādhis* for the mantra recitations of the perfection stage. (It is never explicitly stated that the "mental illumination [of the deity]" is the first of the latter four *samādhis*, but the implication is clear enough.)

Each of these seven steps offers evocative instructions written almost entirely in verse—nine-syllable verse for the generation of the deity, then seven-syllable for the final *samādhis* on the recitations. As discussed in chapter 4, by the second half of the eighth century, other Mahāyoga *sādhanas* were being composed entirely in verse. Thus, the *Generation of Fortune Sādhana* was translated into seven-syllable lines, mostly arranged into four-line verses. But most of that work's content was relatively straightforward instruction: do this, do that, interrupted by poetic simile and song only at occasional moments; the ཨ syllable of the all-illuminating *samādhi* was "glittering like Venus," and "the inner and outer praises" were to be sung using specific melodies while resting in sexual union. Such a pattern of more poetic language being deployed at key moments in the ritual has been observed in all the tantric ritual manuals examined so far. The present *sādhana* is conspicuous for its pervasive use of simile, poetic language that shapes the reader's experience at every step of the ritual.

The shift from nine-syllable to seven-syllable lines following the generation stage likely reflects the composite nature of the *sādhana*. The point where the shift occurs almost matches the content-based division of the text into two parts (i.e., the three *samādhis* of generation and the four *samādhis* of recitation). Unfortunately, the seven-syllable lines of the first half extend too far, into the first six lines of the verses on recitation. So, while the shift in meter probably indicates a composite text, an easy explanation for why it occurs where it does eludes us.

That said, the first and second halves of the text are distinct in one other regard. There seem to exist no parallel passages for the first half of the text on the three *samādhis*, in canonical tantras or any other works, yet several parallel passages for the second half on recitation are found. In this way too, then, the two parts of the text may be distinguished, with the first half more idiosyncratic, looking in part toward Chinese Buddhism, and the second half more likely pieced together out of the Indic ritual writings circulating in Tibet following the collapse of the empire in the mid-ninth century.[10]

The Three *Samādhis*: The Thusness *Samādhi*

The method for cultivating the thusness *samādhi*,
As gathered from scripture:

Though [one is already] essentially nonconceptual,
as with silver ore, in order to purify,

the three seed [syllables] radiate light, incinerating the causes, the effects, and the places;
one is purified in both one's practice and nature.

Within the *sādhana*'s first half, the initial thusness *samādhi* is particularly idiosyncratic in style. It is also the longest of the three *samādhis*, filling the first two and one-third (out of six) folio sides. Most tantric manuals open and close with a meditation on emptiness, so that the ritual emanates out of emptiness and dissolves back into it. (Hence the closing poetic dissolutions of the *hūṃ* syllable described in IOL Tib J 552 and 553, discussed at the end of chapter 4.) In the *Tattvasaṃgraha-sādhanopāyikā* of chapter 3, after some initial prostrations and purifications, the proceedings open with a brief philosophical analysis of the self and its component parts: "With the intellect, break it down into tiny particles. Then thoroughly analyze how each of those tiny particles has six sides and rest in mind only." The result is a *cittamātra* (mind-only) version of emptiness, out of which a moon disc subsequently emerges, "suffused with the accumulation of one's own merit." The *Generation of Fortune Sādhana* in chapter 4 begins with a visualization sequence wherein a white ཨ descends from atop one's head into one's body, dissolving oneself and one's environs into the nonconceptual *dharmatā*. In *An Appearance of Suchness*, one begins by contemplating a poetic verse on the miraculously unoriginated nature of all phenomena:

Ema! Fantastic, marvelous phenomena:
the secret of all perfected buddhas.
All originates from the unoriginated;
yet in that originating itself, there is no origination.[11]

To open, the reader pronounces "Ema!" (in the canonical version, "Emaho!"), a cry of amazement at the wondrous fact of phenomenal existence. These phenomena, already in their very immediacy, exclaims line 2, are the secret of all buddhas. This is an unexpected equivalence. Ordinarily, one would imagine the secret of all buddhas to be obscure and difficult to comprehend, requiring careful thought, yet here such thinking collapses, as one sees anew that the ordinary phenomena are in and of themselves the secret. This revelation demands that the reader see differently, let go of truth being elsewhere. Narrative and memory collapse as the reader is brought into the immediacy of the present, and the next two lines take this still further, cutting away any attempt to subject these suddenly wondrous phenomena to one's will. They originate from the unoriginated, yet that very origination is without beginning. They come out of emptiness, yet their emergence never begins. Here again, narrative and time are undercut, leaving phenomena suspended within a state of surprise.[12]

In the opening sequences of tantric *sādhanas*, be they the first of the three *samādhis* of the generation stage, the first of the *pañcākārābhisaṃbodhikrama*, or part of some other system, language is deployed carefully—analytically, visually, poetically—to lead the reader into a meditation on emptiness. This may involve a series of deconstructive reflections, a visualized dissolution, or a poetic reverie on the paradoxes of existence. This place of evocation is where Buddhist philosophy meets tantric ritual.[13] It is also where some Chan meditators found a point of contact. In its explanation of the aforementioned Tibetan Chan *Brief Precept*, the commentary in Pelliot tibétain 699 draws upon several elements in our Mahāyoga root *sādhana*, all in the section on the opening thusness *samādhi*. If the Great Perfection grew out of the *end* of tantric ritual, out of perfection-stage sexual yoga, here we see how some recognized Chan in the *beginning*, in the first of the three *samādhis* of the generation stage.

Our root *sādhana* introduces the thusness *samādhi* by claiming that the methods employed were gathered from a yet-unidentified scripture (*gzhung*). Pelliot tibétain 634 explains that what follows relates to what is always already nonconceptual, and yet, because we beings cycle through samsara under the influence of the three poisons, we must extract that nonconceptual liberation (more specifically, the "three gates of liberation," emptiness, signlessness, and wishlessness) from the dross of the afflictions, like smelting silver out of ore. Already, then, simile is being deployed, leaving the reader with the image of their own mind being a pure, reflective surface that is revealed as the dross of conceptuality falls away.

Now the reader is led into the meditation. The three syllables of body, speech, and mind are introduced: *oṃ aṃ hūṃ*, imaginatively placed at the crown of one's head, one's mouth, and one's heart. Light rays emanate out, purifying the universe, and regather, "incinerating the causes, the effect, and the places" on one's body. (Pelliot tibétain 626 adds that this emanation and regathering should be performed three times.) In this way, one enters the nonconceptual state of thusness, the "gnosis of awareness" (*rig pa'i ye shes*), as our commentator writes.[14]

In order to dwell in that thusness,
with a straight body, bind the five *mudrās*,
and display the five gates of entry—the five methods for resting.
Gazing at the mind (*sems lta*) is the method, not locating is wisdom.

[The mind] is not anything; one does not think anything,
not mentally engaging with or conceptualizing features;
one's sphere of activity is pure, so do not abide anywhere.
Comprehend the state of the three liberations.

Next, a four-line verse instructs the reader to compose his body in the five *mudrās*, with the right hand on top of the left, the right leg on top of the left, a straight back, eyes resting down the length of the nose, and tongue pressed against the roof of the mouth. The same five *mudrās* appear in other Mahāyoga manuscripts from Dunhuang, so we can assume ours derive from Mahāyoga ritual literature of the period.[15] Nonetheless, the commentary on the Chan *Brief Precept*, found in Pelliot tibétain 699 and penned in the same hand as this work, also uses them.[16]

If the five *mudrās* come from Mahāyoga writings and are used for interpreting Chan, the next paragraph reveals the opposite—likely a case of a popular Chan contemplation method appearing in a Mahāyoga work. Now settled into the proper physical posture, the reader is told to gaze at the mind (*sems lta*). Nothing is seen, whereby one settles into nonconceptuality and comprehends the three gates of liberation. The dross has fallen away, and the shining silver of a buddha's body, mind, and speech (which Pelliot tibétain 626 identifies with the three gates) is revealed.

Gazing at the mind (Ch. *kanxin*; 看心) is a practice closely associated with Chan texts of the Northern School. There, it is often identified with gazing on the unlocalized (*kan wu suo chu*; 看無所處),[17] and sure enough, the relevant line in our *sādhana* reads: "Gazing at mind is method; not locating (*mi gnas*) is wisdom." We can be sure that our scribe, and very likely the author of the commentary, were aware of the Chan roots of this practice, as the *Brief Precept* includes the line: "In gazing at one's own mind, the essence of mind is utterly nonexistent."[18] This verse confirms that our Mahāyoga commentary and probably at least the first part of the *sādhana* itself look both ways, primarily to the Indian Mahāyoga ritual tradition but also toward local Chinese Buddhism.[19]

> Method is not separating, like taking *hala*.
> Wisdom is unwavering, like applying an antitoxic cure.
>
> Mindfulness is unerring, as for [rain]drops, like gatekeepers.
> Alertness is recognition, like a watchman for thieves.
>
> *Vipaśyanā* is effulgent, like a lamp.
> *Śamatha* is unwavering, still, like a deep lake.

Next comes a set of three two-line verses, each line offering a simile for one aspect of how to sustain the comprehension gained from gazing at the mind. The following line explains that "those six can be divided into pairs." The first pair of similes serve as gates of entry into method and wisdom, the second pair as the remedies of mindfulness and alertness, and the final pair to settle the mind into *vipaśyanā* and *śamatha*.

Our text's use of simile to discuss gazing at the mind itself may reflect the influence of Chan Buddhism. Simile and analogy are common in pretantric Buddhist texts, regularly used to describe meditation practices. A particularly relevant example is where Buddhaghoṣa's fifth-century *Visuddhimagga* explores a series of similes in its treatment of breath meditation. Like a gong that fades after being struck, one's breaths become progressively subtle until they cease; like a gatekeeper, one watches the breath as it enters and exits, not worrying about it when it is inside or outside the body.[20] There is nothing extraordinary, then, about our *sādhana*'s use of simile in discussing a meditation practice. That the list of six similes appears in this specific context, however, might still be significant. The thusness *samādhi* is the most formless meditation within the *sādhana*. As a meditation that has no object, a nonconceptual method inseparable from whatever is occurring in the present, it is inevitably difficult to describe. Chan tradition, moreover, at least rhetorically resists the reification of any practice, so to describe gazing at the mind is already to tread on dangerous ground. By deploying simile, our author can approach the *samādhi* at a slant, gaze at the mind by looking elsewhere.[21]

The commentary goes into some detail on these similes, reframing each as a syllogism (*prayoga*). Since Bhavaviveka's time, Buddhist logical syllogisms were typically composed of three parts: the subject (*dharmin*), the probandum to be affirmed (*sādhya*), and the reason for its being so (*hetu*). Here, however, our commentator replaces the final element with a "compatible analogy" (*mthun ba'i dpe*), thereby reframing the six similes as a series of propositions, less to prove a claim than simply to facilitate reflection on different aspects of one's cultivation of thusness. Both Pelliot tibétain 634 and Pelliot tibétain 626 offer brief reflections on their respective propositional reframings. Pelliot tibétain 626 explains, "Regarding this method of breaking those [lines] down into component parts, moreover, the subject, the probandum, the compatible analogy, and the reason of scripture are all being combined."[22] Pelliot tibétain 634 says, "The three [syllogistic elements] are bound together by reason of scripture."[23] These reflections thus provide the reason these analogies are true, namely, by reason of scripture (Tib. *lung*; Skt. *āgama*). Resorting to scripture for proof of a proposition was a controversial move in some Buddhist circles. The seventh-century philosopher Dharmakīrti insisted on only two kinds of valid cognition (Tib. *tshad ma*; Skt. *pramāṇa*): direct perception and inference. In so doing, he meant to limit how scripture could be used, targeting the non-Buddhist Mīmāṃsakas and Sāṃkhyas, who often turned to the Vedas for proof of their arguments. Yet for certain kinds of inferences, where the object is radically inaccessible, Dharmakīrti did allow for the use of scriptures that had passed three tests of trustworthiness.[24] The scriptural sources behind our own analogies remain obscure, but perhaps that is not so important. The analogies really are less about the fact that the identifications being made—of the method and not separating, mindfulness and unerringness, *vipaśyanā* and effulgence, and so on—are true than about *how* they are so. Each analogy thereby offers a brief meditation that defines the reader's experience of the thusness *samādhi*.

The first pair of lines explain that, as one rests in unlocated mind, one does not reject ordinary samsara but accepts it as a kind of a vaccine, so that the illness and its cure—samsara and nirvana—are one. Thus, the method is not to separate from samsara, and wisdom is unwavering because there is nothing from which to waver. The second pair compares mindfulness to raindrops and gatekeepers, and alertness (Tib. *shes bzhin*; Skt. *samprajāna*) to a watchman. Thus, one minds the five sense doors (of sight, hearing, smell, taste, and touch), watching undistracted by thoughts of what happened in the past or might happen in the future, like a gatekeeper who looks right through the rain without getting caught up in watching the individual drops descend. One remains alert, like a watchman whose attention only increases as the thieves of the senses approach. Finally, the third pair compares the effulgence of *vipaśyanā* to a lamp and *śamatha* to the stillness of a deep lake. Both our commentary and Pelliot tibétain 626 play on the fact that the flame of *vipaśyanā*'s lamp might be extinguished by the waters of *śamatha*'s lake. Thus, one should rest in the luminosity of *vipaśyanā*, "without sinking too far into the wetness of *śamatha*, which is like darkness," warns Pelliot tibétain 626.[25]

Those six [lines above] are divided into pairs:
the stages of entry, remedy, and settling the intellect.

Śamatha and *vipaśyanā* are balanced, like a lamp in a vase,
unmoving and clear, like a clear lake.

Following the explanatory line that summarizes the foregoing six lines of analogy, a final pair of lines explains this potential problem by emphasizing that *śamatha* and *vipaśyanā* should be balanced, like a calm, clear lake and reflections on its surface. With this image, the commentary on the thusness *samādhi* ends. It provides a smooth transition to the following lines, which move the reader on to the all-illuminating *samādhi*.

The Three *Samādhis*: The All-Illuminating and Causal *Samādhis*

Then, the method for cultivating the all-illuminating *samādhi*:
Not moving from the space, knowing whatever occurs in its vividness,
compassion, even throughout all, the space of desirelessness,
opening like the sky, becoming the cause for emanations to arise,
not desiring the two extremes, free from all without abandoning anything.
Thus it is said.

In chapter 4, we saw how several Dunhuang manuscripts wax poetic on the moment of the all-illuminating *samādhi*, evoking a paradoxical experience of both surface and depth. Indeed, IOL Tib J 437 uses precisely the image with which the thusness *samādhi* ends—"the reflected forms of the sun, moon, planets, and stars clearly appearing within a clear lake"—and describes the all-illuminating *samādhi* as "the opening for form" and "the cause for forms to arise." Our present *sādhana*'s treatment of this transitional moment is similar: "opening like the sky, becoming the cause for emanations to arise," to which the commentator adds, "the great omniscient wisdom opens a gap in the clouds, and the syllable of oneself, a white ཨ syllable endowed with causal consciousness, arises brightly in the sky." Appearance and emptiness are beginning to separate, even as they remain one.

> **The method for cultivating the causal *samādhi*:**
> [2v] From the syllable *A*: *e tang khang lang ram.*
> Purifying the five poisons through the empowerments of their natures, the five mothers,
> the *samādhis* of the five entireties (Skt. *kṛtsna*; Tib. *zad par*) are cultivated.
> Thus, the five great elements are cultivated in a stack.

With the third of the three *samādhis* of the generation stage, the ཨ syllable from the all-illuminating produces the elemental syllables, as in the *Generation of Fortune Sādhana*. As the five poisons are purified through the empowerments of the five mothers, existence is consumed by each of the five elements, resulting in a stack of elemental colored discs, arranged in order from subtle to coarse—from space to wind, fire, water, and earth.[26] The last element of earth results in a celestial palace atop Mount Meru, explains the commentary, and so end the three *samādhis*.

"Then the techniques for the recitations for the activities are taught." With this explanatory marker, we move into the perfection stage.[27]

The Four *Samādhis* for Recitation

It is odd that the causal *samādhi* ends with the mandala palace atop Mt. Meru having been produced, but its enlightened inhabitants are nowhere mentioned. In other manuals, the causal *samādhi* culminates in the development of a series of emanating and regathering light rays, with each cycle effecting another transformation, first of the central deity's heart syllable (typically a *hūṃ*) into a symbol (typically a vajra), then of that symbol into the body of the deity (which is identical with oneself). In the present *sādhana*, these stages are not spelled out, but they are assumed as the first of the four perfection-stage *samādhis* transports the reader into the story, into the immediate presence of the deity. And it is a vivacious presence:

As if mindfulness, the vital breath, and its restriction were speaking, speaking!
As if the earrings, necklace, and limbs were swaying, swaying!
As if on the base, the vajra and seed syllables were blazing, blazing!
The vowels, *anusvāras*, intersyllabic dots are so perfect!

dran pa srog dang rtsol ba gsung gsung ltar /
snyan ca 'gur chu yan lag 'gul 'gul ltar /
gzhi la rdo rje yig 'bru 'bar 'bar ltar /
gug skyed klad kor tsheg dang zur phyin pa /[28]

The four lines provide an exceptional example among the Dunhuang *sādhanas* of poetic conjuring. In a pattern not always possible to reproduce in translation, each nine-syllable line flashes a series of three two-syllable images at the reader, then a doubled exclamatory verb ("speaking, speaking!") and a final "as if" that infuses the entire scene with a dreamlike quality, reminding the reader these images are mere perception. (The English translation requires the "as if" to come at the beginning of each line.) Only the final line lacks these lines' doubled exclamations and the "as if," thus providing a sense of closure through both form and content with its last words: "so perfect!" The flashing, layered images are ones of energy, movement, and light. Nowhere is the deity itself described, yet it is very much already present, and perhaps its solidity lies precisely in this givenness. The poetry exploits the changeability of thought, working at the evanescent surface of the imagination to seduce the reader's attentions with the movements of the deity's speech, body, and mind. Yet precisely in doing so, the verse draws the reader into its underlying imaginal reality, for these are the expressions *of someone*, the adornments *on someone*, the blazings *within someone*. Even as the imagery draws our attention to the surface, it assumes an underlying depth, the presence of the deity itself.

Other *sādhanas*, from Dunhuang and elsewhere, go to great lengths to describe the mandala and its inhabitants, from the decorations around the gates to the items held in each deity's hands.[29] Such detail, almost excessive, may have been meant to emphasize the extraordinary complexity and thus orthodoxy of the iconography, but also to lead the reader through a kind of meditative journey, dwelling on each element for a moment to build a complete picture. Here, however, is a silence that invites the reader to fill it, to participate in constructing the imaginative world of the mandala. As the reader's attention is drawn to the earrings, necklace, limbs, and their swaying (repeated twice to emphasize the movement), the implicit existence of the deity's body between and beneath them is the reader's to imagine.

The meaning of the lines is also quite unclear, and in this way too the gaps—this time semantic—imply an underlying world, the commentarial background of the verse. Of course, tantric ritual in general is known for its obscure and coded language that requires oral and written commentary to understand; most tantric ritual operates within an atmosphere of esotericism and layered meanings. But the present *sādhana*, with its unusually poetic instructions, takes this a step further, weaving its spell of secrecy through not only the obscure content of its words but also its formal features. By flashing disconnected images at the reader, each line invites the reader to inhabit the gaps between them, while the commentaries help to structure these silences, providing further semantic layers and aesthetic depth to the *sādhana's* poetry.

Both commentaries begin by labeling each line, though they do so differently. Pelliot tibétain 626 summarizes the first line as a general description of the vision's overall mood and themes, while the second produces "the mental illumination of mindfulness of the body," the third produces that of mind, and the fourth that of speech. Curiously, Pelliot tibétain 634 (written in the same hand) offers a different analysis, with the first line about speech, the second body, and the third and fourth mind. (Pelliot tibétain 634 seems preferable from a technical perspective.) Either way, once the reader is aware of these commentaries, the coded references behind the poetry begin to pervade the experience of reciting the semantic gaps in the lines themselves.

The two commentaries also approach the images differently. Pelliot tibétain 626 tends to analyze the lines image by image, while Pelliot tibétain 634 prefers a more wholistic approach. This difference continues throughout the two texts, suggesting that the former may have been written for the purpose of study and the latter, formatted with the root verses clearly visible, to facilitate ritual use. On the first four lines of the first *samādhi*, Pelliot tibétain 626 reads:

> Then it says, "mindfulness, the vital breath, . . ." This is an overall [description]. "Mindfulness" is the vibrant awareness (*rig rig*) in the veins of one's eyes (*spyan rtsa*).[30] "The vital breath" is the subtle stirrings (*kyib kyib*) of the breath. "Its restriction" is being on the verge of vocalizing.
>
> Then it says, "the earrings . . ." This is the mental illumination of mindfulness [of the body].[31] From the wheels on the feet up to the topknot on the head, all is dazzling (*sbrid be re re*) with ornamentation.
>
> Then it says, "on the base, the vajra and seed syllables . . ." This is mental illumination of mindfulness of the mind. The moon disc at one's own heart is not a real support. The vajra does not touch it; it is illuminated within [the moon], as in the surface of a mirror. At the center of the vajra vase[32] are inscribed the seed syllables. Just as colors dwell within a clear crystal, it is internally luminous when viewed from the outside.
>
> Then it says, "The vowels . . ." This is the mental illumination of mindfulness of speech. The seed syllables shine with a [quality of] *visarjana* [i.e., radiance].[33]

Key here is that the verse describes not only the buddha's image but also the reader's own subjective experience of being that deity. According to Pelliot tibétain 626, the subjective aspect of the description is present already in the first line. One is experiencing a mindful knowing in the very veins of one's eyes, the stirrings of one's breath, and one's energetic restrictions, just on the verge of pronouncing the mantra. Pelliot tibétain 634 adds that this intense visualization is "not like looking for a tree in the fog."

Elsewhere it becomes clear that the visualization involves a string of three or five syllables circling at one's heart; Pelliot tibétain 626 has *oṃ aṃ hūṃ*, Pelliot tibétain 634 *oṃ aṃ hūṃ svā hā*. These are the focus of the last two lines of the four-line verse, and both commentaries offer evocative descriptions of the delicacy and ethereality of the elements that constitute the reflective apparatus of a moon disc and vajra, within which the syllables shine forth like the colors of a rainbow glowing within a crystal. The moon "is not a real support"; it is nothing so substantial. The vajra does not even touch it but is reflected within its mirrorlike surface. Even as the commentaries unpack the terse poetry of the verse, then, both continue to use the poetic language of metaphor and playful terms that use the ringing of repeating syllables to conjure specific experiences: *rig rig* (vibrant awareness), *kyib kyib* (subtle stirrings), and *sbrid be re re* (dazzling).[34] Pelliot tibétain 626's use of the Sanskrit *visarjana* (presumably in the sense of "radiance"), a term probably unknown to most Tibetan readers, is unusual and may be less about evoking a specific experience than about infusing the meditation with an atmosphere of esotericism.

That Pelliot tibétain 634 does not mention the Sanskrit word is yet another difference between the two commentaries that *might* suggest they were written by different authors. They differ on how to apply the trio of body, speech, and mind to the four lines quoted above, yet they agree that each line is about "the mental illumination" (*yid la gsal ba*) of mindfulness (Pelliot tibétain 626) or awareness (Pelliot tibétain 634) of each component. They also use the same language throughout and contain many additional parallels. In the end, and given that they are penned by the same hand, they more likely represent two attempts by a single author—probably local to Dunhuang and quite possibly our own scribe—to compose a commentary on the same root *sādhana*.[35]

This begs the question of the *sādhana*'s own origins. Its lack of a title might be a sign of a native Tibetan composition, and the likely influence of Chan in the first half is another clue. But was it written in central Tibet or around Dunhuang? The second half, on the perfection stage, includes a number of passages for which parallels may be found in other works preserved in other collections belonging to the Nyingma school. Pelliot tibétain 634 even opens by stating that the *sādhana* is "extracted from scripture." In fact, every one of the six lines that compose the first *samādhi* of the perfection stage appears elsewhere. The closest parallel is in the *Compendium of All Knowledge Sutra* (*Kun 'dus rig pa'i mdo*), the so-called "root tantra" of the Nyingma school's Anuyoga class. Chapter 30 is dedicated to the vajra song, and there are all but one of our six lines, though with two fewer syllables per line. These same five parallel lines are also reproduced, almost verbatim, in the context of a vajra song in a *sādhana* based on the same tantra, the *Sādhana for the Wrathful Vajra Family* (*Khro bo rdo rje rigs kyi bsgrub thabs*), attributed to the (ninth-century?) Indian master Bde ba gsal mdzad.[36] The last three of the six lines also appear in the *Attitude for the Recitations for Kīlaya* (*Phur pa'i 'dzab dgongs*), constituting a verse recited, "in order to hold that object in mind,"[37] the object being the

ROOT SĀDHANA (PELLIOT TIBÉTAIN 634, 2V.2–3R.1)	*COMPENDIUM OF ALL KNOWLEDGE* (TOH. 831), 105B.5–6	*SĀDHANA FOR THE WRATHFUL VAJRA FAMILY*, 558.1–2	*ATTITUDE FOR THE RECITATIONS FOR KĪLAYA*, 230.2–4
dran ba srog chags brtsal ba' gsung gsung lta	*srog rtsol dran rig gsung gsung ltar*	*srog rtsol dran rig gsung gsung ltar*	
snyan ca 'gur chu yan lag 'gul 'gul lta	*mgur chu yan lag 'gul 'gul ltar*	*'gur chu yan lag 'gul 'gul lta*	
gzhi la rdo rje yig 'bru 'bar 'bar lta	*rdo rje yi ger 'bru 'bar ltar*	*rdo rje yig 'bru 'bar 'bar ltar*	
gug skyed glad skor tshag dang zur phyin zhing	*gug skyed klad kor tsheg par phyin*	*gug skyed klad kor tsheg dbar phyin*	*gug skyed klad kor tsheg bar zur phyin te / ljags la pad+ma'i 'bru dgu gsal bar bsgom*
rnam gsum gcig tu yid la zhen sems pa'			*rnam gsum dus gcig yid la gsal la gyur pa*
ra ri khal khol myed par dran gsal rig	*ra ri khal khol sgrib med pa / ye shes don la mkhyen rig rgyas*	*ra ri khal khol bsgrib med pa / ye shes don la mkhyen gsal rig*	*bdag ye shes sems dpa' kI la ya 'bru dgu / ra ri ka khol med par dran gsal zhing*

nine syllables of the Kīlaya mantra upon one's lotuslike tongue. All sources thus use the lines to describe acts of recitation. The parallels are most clearly visualized in a chart.

Unfortunately, none of this tells us where our root *sādhana* was composed. It might have been compiled in central Tibet, where other tantric manuals may have been more numerous, but the *Compendium of All Knowledge* or other text(s) from central Tibet could have traveled to Dunhuang, where our scribe or another local author extracted the relevant lines. Until further evidence surfaces, we can only conclude that the text was probably composed in Tibetan.

Second *samādhi*:

Within a state of *dharma*, performing the *mudrās* and singing the songs,

from the seed syllables of speech that are the mind itself,
the secret mantra should be listened to in one's mind,
whereby the secret mantra is pure, and the recitations clear.

The second of the perfection-stage *samādhis* does not follow sequentially from the first but focuses in on the nature of the moon, vajra, and syllables. The moon, we read, is a reflection of the form that results from the transformation (Skt. *āśraya parāvṛtti*; Tib. *gnas gyur ba*) of the foundational consciousness; the vajra comes from the transformation of one's mind (Skt. *manas*; Tib. *yid*); and the syllables come from the afflicted mind (Skt. *kliṣṭamanas*; Tib. *nyon mongs pa'i yid*). Pelliot tibétain 634 is careful to specify that each element is a "reflection" of the form that results from the transformations of these different levels of consciousness. Our commentator thereby reinforces the sense of emptiness that the meditator is to maintain throughout his visualizations. The last two lines of the second *samādhi* add that the recitations of the syllables are performed silently, "in one's mind."

The third *samādhi* introduces a transition from this silent recitation of the garland of syllables at the heart to another exercise focusing more on sexual union. Its five lines read:

(i) The unchanging syllables strung together as a garland,
(ii) [Resound] constantly like the sound of a bell.
(iii) There is a projecting and gathering of light, with a manner of a [spinning] firebrand.
(iv) Gathering back, one presses down with the word.
(v) The method for leading is joined with a mute *hūṃ*.

The commentaries agree that each line explores a different aspect of a new direction taken by the cycling garland. The first line dwells on the movement of the syllables and the second on the sounds, with each syllable resonating sympathetically ("like the sound of a bell") with one's silent reading of it.[38] Pelliot tibétain 634 explains that the syllables in question number five: *oṃ āṃ hūṃ svā hā*, whereas Pelliot tibétain 626 elsewhere mentions only three: *oṃ āṃ hūṃ*.

At this point, Pelliot tibétain 626 explains that the garland is no longer restricted to one's heart and descends to the tip of the vajra (i.e., penis): "The 'garland' that is assembled from the seed syllables descends down one's vajra path and cycles: *kwa ra ra*!"[39] From there, the syllables enter the consort's lotus (i.e., vagina): " '[There is a projecting and gathering] of light . . .' refers to the cycling of light. It arises in the secret vajra path. Descending into the space of the consort's pure lotus, within a sleeve of light, the sparklike light rays of the five seed syllables rise up: *dwa ra ra*!"[40] As we shall see, from the consort's lotus, the garland ascends her spine to cycle back into the male practitioner. The resulting circle of light is the focus of the third line. Pelliot tibétain 634 explains it in similar terms, spelling out the metaphor of the ember and the sparks more explicitly: "Glowing like the sparks in a fire scattered by a blacksmith's bellows, the five seed syllables are light rays, [circling] like sparks in a five-colored sleeve opening. Just so, the five seed syllables, resounding with their respective sounds, should be successively recited."[41] In this way, the individual syllables are compared to sparks, like the root verse's ember at the end of a firebrand. As those five-colored sparks whirl through the body, they become lines ("light rays"), as when one spins a firebrand (or perhaps a sparkler) at night.

The next line (line 4 of the third *samādhi*) adds a further detail: "Gathering back, one presses down with the word," which Pelliot tibétain 634 explains in these terms: "The secret substance is the *hūṃ vajradhṛk*. If it were just the *hūṃ*, it would bring no benefit. So, extracting the heart [syllable] of the five families, it is further ornamented to make *hūṃ vajra dhṛk*. Pressing [the substance] down with the wheel at the center of one's navel makes it arise in the vajra path. It descends into the space of the consort and mounts her spine."[42]

The secret substance is certainly the drop of *bodhicitta*. As the seed of the buddhas, the *bodhicitta* might be assumed to be identical with the letter *hūṃ*, the seed syllable from which the *ur*-buddha, Vajrasattva, is born. Here, however, the drop is identified with the elaborated form, *hūṃ vajra dhṛk*, the additional syllables being appended to set it moving and make it efficacious. In this form, the substance is then pressed down with the *cakra* at the navel, sending it to the tip of the vajra (i.e., penis), whence it enters the consort's vagina, then rises up along her spine. That Pelliot tibétain 634 mentions only the spine without referencing any central channel may well reflect our commentator's lack of familiarity with the technology of subtle channels that does not seem to have reached Dunhuang before Cave 17 was closed.[43]

Taken together, Pelliot tibétain 634 and 626 offer a glimpse of a breathing practice that played a central role in perfection-stage sexual union in late eighth-century India. The details these two manuscripts provide are unique among the Dunhuang documents, though a few other references do appear.[44] A related sequence is seen in Pelliot tibétain 42: "Then, perform in accordance with what it says in the *nopika* [i.e., *sādhana*]: From a garland that is the essence of the mantras (**mantrahṛdaya*), from 108 up to ten million [recitations] are recited. Without breathing, the extremely subtle speech is fully illuminated. The recitations that are performed in that way arise from the gnosis of the *samādhi*."[45] Once again, a form of silent mantra recitation is to be performed while in sexual union, but the specifics are scant.

A little more information perhaps may be gleaned from IOL Tib J 464, which describes the practice of sexual union as follows:

> Once more stabilize within that state of majesty.
> In accordance with the ritual procedures, the jewel sprout
> is positioned at the top of the head.
>
> *Oṃ āṃ hūṃ svāhā*:
> The five great consecrating heart [syllables]
> consecrate the five places [in one's body].
>
> By means of the yoga for protecting, to the best of one's ability,
> firmly protect the *siddhi* identity.
> By means of the four principles,
> the recitations should also be performed to the best of one's abilities.[46]

As explained in chapter 4, the first verse here refers to restraining the drop of *bodhicitta* at the tip of the vajra. Regarding the second verse, it is unclear whether this is a reference to a practice of *nyāsa*, placing the five syllables at five points on the body, or to the kind of cycling practice seen in the texts presently under discussion, such that a garland of five syllables consecrates the five bodily places as it cycles through them.[47] The third verse reminds the reader to continue restraining the drop (the "*siddhi* identity"), while performing the recitations for as long as one can, by relying on the four principles (*de nyid rnam bzhi*).

These four principles are probably those mentioned in some ritual notes inserted on the verso of folio 2 of IOL Tib J 464, where they are said to be the means for "performing the worship" (*de kho na nyId bzhi 'I tshul gyIs mchod pa gyi ba*).[48] For a discussion of the foursome, if they are the same, we have to look outside Dunhuang, specifically to the Kriyā/Ubhayā tantra, the *Meditation Supplement in Progressive Stages* (*Dhyānottarapaṭalakrama*). There they are enumerated as the principles of: (1) oneself, (2) the deity, (3) recitation, and (4) meditation, and again they serve to structure the practice of mantra recitation.[49]

The relevance of these four principles to our own root *sādhana* is further strengthened by some close parallels between two lines from the third *samādhi* and the *Meditation Supplement*. As already observed, other lines from our root *sādhana* also appear in other texts, so we may not be looking at a singular correspondence here. Indeed, parts of our third *samādhi* also appear in the above-cited and unattributed *Attitude for the Recitations for Kīlaya*. Nonetheless, the parallels do provide a further link to the *Meditation Supplement*.

Returning at last to the final line of our third *samādhi*, line 5 reads: "The method for leading is applied with a mute *hūṃ*." Pelliot tibétain 634 explains that this fifth line is about the cycling of the breath: "One projects forth the above-mentioned *hūṃ*, then without expressing its sound, one inhales the *hūṃ* back inside. Think that it dissolves with fragrance into one's left nostril." Keeping in mind that he last had the syllables climbing up the consort's spine, our commentator here seems to suggest that it is drawn back into the male practitioner with an inhalation, possibly through the left nostril. From there, the syllables presumably move back down through the male practitioner, through his vajra, and back into the consort, continuing the cycling as he recites the mantra and restrains emission for as long as he can.

ROOT *SĀDHANA* (FROM PELLIOT TIBÉTAIN 634), 3R.2–3:	*MEDITATION SUPPLEMENT*, 224A.7–224B.1:[50]	*ATTITUDE FOR THE RECITATIONS FOR KĪLAYA*, 231.2:[51]
The unchanging syllables strung together as a garland [resound] constantly like the sound of a bell.	The unchanging strung-together syllables [resound] unceasingly like the sound of a bell.	The fine string of nine syllables [resounds] constantly like the sound of a bell.
yi ge myi 'gyur 'phreng bar rgyus / dril bu sgra ltar rgyun myi chad /	*yi ge brgyus la mi 'gyur rnams / dril bu'i sgra bzhin ma chad par /*	*yi ge 'bru dgu'i phra brgyus pas / dril bu'i sgra ltar rgyun mi chad /*

Interpreting our two commentaries is not without its difficulties. First there is the problem of sequence: is only one act of cycling being described, i.e., that between sexual partners, or two, i.e., first at one's heart and then between partners? Given that neither commentary mentions sexual union before the third *samādhi* and both agree that the structure of moon disc, vajra, and syllables resides at one's heart, it seems two successive acts are probably described. During the first and second *samādhis*, the mantra is recited while focusing on one's heart,[52] and during the third, the cycling between partners takes place.[53]

This raises a second problem: how to understand the use of the mantra, *hūṃ vajradhṛk*. Pelliot tibétain 626 provides little guidance, but Pelliot tibétain 634 clearly states that this mantra is used, along with pressing down on the navel *cakra*, to propel the *bodhicitta* through the vajra path and into the space of the consort. The very next line reads, "The method for leading is applied with a mute *hūṃ*," and Pelliot tibétain 634 only mentions the *hūṃ*, not the full *hūṃ vajradhṛk*. It seems, then, that *vajradhṛk* provides the force necessary to propel the *hūṃ* from the heart down to the point of union, whence it can begin cycling between the partners along with the other four syllables in the string: *oṃ āṃ hūṃ svā hā*.

Subtle Yogas and Vajra Recitations

We appear to have here a version of what became known as "subtle yoga" (Skt. *sūkṣmayoga*; Tib. *phra mo'i rnal 'byor*), a practice central to the Jñānapāda and Ārya schools of *Guhyasamāja* exegesis. The *Guhyasamāja*'s sixth chapter is the locus classicus for the perfection-stage subtle yoga (chapter 3 for the generation-stage version). Here too, the details are less than clear. Verses 8 and 9 offer these instructions:

> Resting at the center of the expanse of space, a moon disc should be cultivated.
> Having cultivated the form of a buddha, commence the subtle yoga.
>
> At the tip of the nose, imagine a white mustard seed. As the animate and the inanimate within the white mustard seed,
> cultivate the abode of supreme gnosis, created by means of secret mantra.[54]

Fortunately, we may catch a glimpse of how these lines were understood in early Tibet from the interlinear comments in the manuscript copy of the *Guhyasamāja*:

> [On verse 8:]
>
> Visualize one's own body to be like space, and at the center of that space, briefly visualize the likeness of a clear moon, unobscured and unobstructed. If one is unable, just imagine a tiny mirror. Atop that sits oneself. Having transformed from that into the body of the deity, rest there. The moon and the seed syllable for generating one's body [as the deity] may vary according to what is suitable, that is, in accordance with one's own mind.
>
> [On verse nine:]
>
> While resting in the *mahāmudrā* in that way, clearly cultivate a white mustard seed at one's heart, then move it from within, that is, move it up to one's nose. Cultivate such that, having risen to one's nose, it remains at the tip of the nose. Habituate to that. Cultivate the entire container and its inhabitants to be contained within the mustard seed.[55]

As in our root *sādhana*, the reader is instructed to generate himself as a buddha upon a moon disc in the midst of space. Then, while maintaining this visualization, he commences the subtle yoga. Verse 9 has him first move "a white mustard seed" from his heart to the tip of the "nose." Here, "nose" is widely understood to be code for penis.[56] If we take the verse as roughly equivalent to our own root *sādhana*'s third *samādhi*, we might understand this to parallel the moment when the focus shifts from the practitioner's heart to the tip of the vajra. And in the Dunhuang notes on the *Guhyasamāja* verses that immediately follow, gathering and projection is performed where our *sadhana* has it cycling between partners. On verse 12, for example, we read: "In habituating to that, perform the retention of this method for extended union, while enacting gathering and projection."[57]

In prescribing a "subtle yoga" that combines projection and regathering while maintaining a small object (be it a mustard seed, a jewel, a vajra, or whatever) at the tip of one's nose, the *Guhyasamāja* may have been influenced by a still earlier practice seen in the *STTS*. There, a "subtle vajra" (Skt. *sūkṃavajra*; Tib. *rdo rje phra mo*) is placed at the tip of one's actual nose (not the penis).[58] The practice is introduced in chapter 3, where it seems to involve holding a minute vajra at the tip of one's nose until stability is attained. (Curiously, in the same work, subtle yoga is occasionally associated with a secret [*rahasya*] rite involving sexual union of some sort.)[59]

The subtle vajra of the *STTS* may have inspired the subtle yoga of the *Guhyasamāja*, though each has its own way of maintaining the tiny visualized image at the nose/penis while projecting and gathering light rays. In neither case, however, does mantra recitation play much of a role, at least explicitly. Only in the somewhat later writings of the Jñānapāda and Ārya schools of *Guhyasamāja* exegesis do we find a method for performing the subtle yoga's projection and regathering that centers on mantra recitation, a method named vajra recitation (Skt. *vajrajāpa*; Tib. *rdo rje'i bzlas pa*). In both schools, the primary focus is on the three syllables, *oṃ āḥ hūṃ*, which are recited (or heard to resound) as one breathes in, holds the breath, and breathes out, respectively.[60] Both schools have the practitioner perform the vajra recitations in the context of sexual union, and both Buddhajñānapāda and early Ārya school works such as the *Caryāmelāpakapradīpa* and the *Pañcakrama* see vajra recitation as the perfection-stage version of the subtle yoga.[61] The major difference between our own *sādhana* and these two later traditions and is that neither of the later schools involves a cycling of syllables between the sexual partners. It may be that our root *sādhana* describes a sexualized form of subtle yoga that, with its focus on a vajra recitation–like mantra recitation, represents a developmental midpoint (without intending too linear a model) between the relatively simple subtle yoga described in chapter 6 of the *Guhyasamāja* itself and the vajra recitations of the Jñānapāda and Ārya schools, with their noncircular breathing practices.

But where does the idea of cycling one's breath upon a garland of syllables between oneself and another come from? Similar practices are seen elsewhere in Indian ritual, though not always in a sexual context. Perhaps most common are image consecration rites that involve infusing the vital breath into a statue or some other container. Such vital breath consecration (*prāṇapratiṣṭhā*) rites may have been a relatively late development. Both Varāhamihīra's sixth-century *Bṛhatsaṃhitā* and the seventh-century *Niśvāsatattvasaṃhitā* include detailed descriptions of consecration rites, but nothing about the breath.[62] References that can be securely dated to before the eleventh century are difficult to find, and some modern scholarship has suggested that breath consecration may even have originated in tantric writings.[63] In such rites, the priest recites the appropriate mantras while transmitting the vital breath from his heart into the deity. The transmission of the syllables may be effected in various ways, through breathing, touching, or scattering flowers. Vital breath consecration may be rooted in early methods for possessing or animating the bodies of others.[64]

Within Buddhist texts, an early precursor to this cycling practice appears in the *Meditation Supplement*. This is particularly significant given the multiple links to this text already observed in our root *sādhana*. As seen above, the two works share lines in common and are connected indirectly through IOL Tib J 464 and the four principles, which appear to have originated in the *Meditation Supplement*. In this same Kriyā tantra, the cycling of breath is between oneself and a deity visualized in front. In fact, the above-cited parallel lines appear in verse 12 of the same section on cycling, which begins:

> [1.] For the site for the deity's form,
> having first prepared the preliminary offerings,
> the wise one who rests in yoga
> imagines the *sugata* in front [of himself].
>
> [2.] Subsequently, free oneself from the [sensory] branches,
> completely abandoning opening or closing [one's senses].
> Subtle, clear without wavering,
> the mind's activity abides in front [i.e., in the deity].
>
> [3.] Resting oneself in this way,
> cultivate with a consciousness of the mantra.
> Binding [one's mind], remain in the *samādhi*;
> thoroughly bind the vital breath and its restriction.
>
> [4.] Immerse oneself in the sound, the mind, and the ground.
> Abide in the ground of the unchanging secret mantra.
> Without allowing the branches to diminish, recite the secret mantra;
> when resting, rest in oneself.
>
> [5.] Unchanging and endowed with the letters.
> Changing from ground to ground, in that way,
> think that the purification of the mind
> is what is imagined, for the sake of one's mantra.

[6.] Drawing in by regathering [the breath],
the mind that has bound the vital breath and its restriction,
through awareness of the mantra, is united with the mantra.
Mental recitations should be undertaken.[65]

Buddhagupta, in his eighth-century commentary to the *Meditation Supplement*, clarifies some of the more obscure verses. On binding the "the vital breath and its restriction" in verse 3, for example, he explains that the vital breath (*srog*) refers to the winds that move in and out of the body's orifices. "To restrict them," he writes, "in this context, means to stop them emerging and entering."[66]

On verse 4, Buddhagupta explains that "the sound, the mind, and the ground" in which the meditator immerses himself correspond to the garland of syllables, *bodhicitta qua* the moon disc, and the "ground" of the *tathāgata*. In the same verse, the branches are identified as the four branches of reciting, associated even today with the Caryā tantras. These are one's own deified body, speech, and mind (i.e., one's form as the buddha, the syllables, and the moon disc) and the Buddha in front.[67]

On verse 5 and "changing from ground to ground" is the following crucial explanation:

> In order to distinguish further the details of that, it says: "Changing from ground to ground." The ground from which [it moves] is the ground of the completely perfected buddha. The ground to which [it moves] is the ground of oneself, the body of one's own buddha. One views the mind, which takes on the aspect of the moon disc at the heart of one's own form, which has become one's own deity, endowed with the syllables of the secret mantra, and one recites until the end of the exhalation. Next, one views in the same way again the ground of the completely perfected Buddha. From that, the mind regathers once more, so that it comes to rest again in the ground that is the body of one's own deity, during which one performs the recitations.[68]

Accordingly, the breath and the syllables move from one's own heart into that of the deity, then return. All the while, verse 6 reminds us, the meditator is restricting the subtle winds and reciting only in one's mind.

As Buddhagupta was aware, the recitation practice described in the *Meditation Supplement* received an update in the presumably slightly later *Mahā* *vairocanābhisaṃbodhi*, a tantra that dates from around the mid-seventh century.[69] That work's fifth chapter offers a meditation that is largely identical to that of the *Meditation Supplement*, even using similar language.[70] The real variation comes in chapter 6. Verse 23 has the reader create himself as the Buddha with a second buddha—the "second ground"—no longer in front, but on a moon disc at his heart. Further details unfold over the next few chapters, but the idea is an alternative, inwardly focused recitation technique, wherein the syllables recited revolve within the heart of the buddha at one's own heart: "Imagining that the sound abides in him, one should recite in equipoise."[71] The *Mahāvairocanābhisaṃbodhi* thus offers two alternatives, an outward and an inward recitation method. This may well be why Buddhgupta opens his commentary by observing: "Although this *Vairocanābhisaṃbodhi-vikurvati-adhiṣṭhāna-tantra* is a Yoga tantra, insofar as it is mainly for means and wisdom, in order to appeal to those disciples who are oriented toward [outward] activities (**kriyā*), it also teaches some practices that accord with the Kriyā tantras. Therefore, it may be labeled and proclaimed as a Kriyā tantra or as a tantra of both (*ubhayā*)."[72]

If the *Mahāvairocanābhisaṃbodhi* took the *Meditation Supplement*'s recitation method inward, authors of Mahāyoga manuals like the root *sādhana* at Dunhuang soon moved it into the realm of sexual union. Such were the kinds of transformations made by first Yoga, then Mahāyoga tantric authors in many areas. The language of our *sādhana* suggests that its author (or someone whose writings he copied) was aware of the earlier cycling practices in the *Meditation Supplement*. Before long, however, the vajra recitation practices of the Jñānapāda and Ārya schools offered still other forms. Methods for cycling breath between sexual partners continued to be incorporated into later manuals for centuries to come, but in our root *sādhana* we see such practices "in the making," still exhibiting early characteristics that would later fall away.[73]

The Future: Whispers of Channels and Winds

During the ninth and tenth centuries, still other techniques for manipulating the body's subtle winds developed, but along radically different lines. Already in the early ninth-century writings of Buddhajñānapāda there are references to the channels that run up the center of the practitioner's torso, as well as a sexual practice that closely resembles what would become the yoga of "inner heat" (Skt. *caṇḍālī*; Tib. *gtum mo*).[74]

Over the course of the ninth century, such practices began to spread. These were dark years for institutional Buddhism in Tibet, as monasteries were shuttered and translation projects defunded. We get a sense of how the new perfection-stage technologies were percolating through tantric communities from the writings of one Tibetan who continued to travel back and forth between Tibet and India. Nupchen Sangyé Yeshe offers a snapshot of the latest teachings in his *Lamp for the Eye in Contemplation*:

> Generally speaking, there are two kinds of pith instructions—those for [meditation] with a support and those without a support. For those without a support, there are the pith instructions of the whispered lineages (*snyan khung brgyud pa*), which involve the cultivation of thusness without intellectualizing; these are specific to Atiyoga.
>
> [The pith instructions for meditation] with a support include those for both the upper and the lower [doors]. Relying on the upper door involves abiding at the four places, of the *śiraścakra* [and so on]. In general, in cultivating that, one imagines or [actually] arouses the karmic fires and winds through diverse individual methods. One milks the sky cow, at which point the gnostic nectar descends and bliss is experienced.[75] There are many diverse scriptures, each with its own individual way of thinking about the channels, seminal drops, lights, and so forth.
>
> In particular, for the sake of those who have either great karmic formations or the [necessary] fortune, there are the pith instructions on the dying process. Within the casket of the innermost secret gnosis (i.e., at one's heart), the afflicted mind is imagined as a moon. Atop that, the foundation (*ālaya*) free of elaboration is illuminated as a thumb-sized *prabhākara* (i.e., sun).[76] Atop that, as the essence of gnosis, imagine that the likeness of a white *hūṃ* syllable of awakened mind is born. Eventually, through one's habituation to those three [elements], they will disappear. Alternatively, at the time of cessation,[77] the three [elements] commingle one by one with the winds; as one exhales and inhales, one gathers each into the next. Finally, when [the moon and the sun] have been gathered into the *hūṃ*, one imagines a thumb-sized gnosis *heruka* and exhorts him within the great Akaniṣṭha. After one has been absorbed into the thumb-sized [*heruka*], upon emerging, neither phenomena nor selves are perceived, whereby one's negative karma is interrupted. Regarding the point through which the mind

emerges, there are the pith instructions on its moving through the nose[78] and so on, or alternatively, the pith instructions on its arising through the utterly empty cranial aperture.

In short, engaging the winds of the upper and the lower [doors] may be distinguished. Because both of those may have a flavor of worldliness or of transcendence, one should experience them and bring them to completion.

Relying on the lower door involves thoroughly searching out a wisdom consort who accords with scripture, as explained above. Having offered her for the delight of the guru who will provide the explanations, one completes the stages. One completes the outer and inner [stages], experiences the wisdom gnosis initiation with one who is moon-endowed, and experiences the great bliss [initiation] with one who is sun-endowed.[79] Then one familiarizes oneself with those, experiencing the flavor of worldliness and the flavor of the gradual path of transcendence. Next, initially the gnosis of supreme bliss is shaky, then there is attainment, and having stabilized one's engagement, one attains *anuyoga*.[80] Then, even without a support [i.e., a consort], there is no diminishment [of one's experience], so one should habituate to gnosis without a support.[81]

For such pith instructions, one must rely on the oral instructions of one's guru in accordance with the scriptural traditions of the masters Vimalamitra, Buddhagupta, Padma[sambhava], and so on.[82]

After briefly touching on meditation without a support, those secret techniques that were transmitted through "whispered lineages" and closely associated with Atiyoga, Nupchen turns to the practices with a support. These he divides into those of the upper door and the lower door, two categories that would continue to be prevalent in later tantric writings. Generally speaking, those of the lower door focus on union with a consort, seminal emission, and consumption of the sacrament, while those of the upper door involve the channels and winds and the practice of inner heat.[83] Nupchen turns first to the upper door, focusing on the *cakras* and "milking the sky cow," i.e., the practice of inner heat (Tib. *gtum mo*; Skt. *caṇḍalī*). Already by the time Nupchen was writing, presumably around the turn of the tenth century, "diverse individual methods" for accomplishing this were in circulation. Apparently also an upper-door practice, the practice for dying he describes involves imagining three increasingly subtle levels of one's mind in the forms of a moon disc, a sun disc, and a *hūṃ* syllable. The more experienced meditator may make these disappear immediately, or one may follow a more gradual path whereby, through meditative breathing, each level of mind gathers into the next until one's now rarified gnosis merges into the heart of a deity, leaving one purified.[84] Nupchen's account of the lower door moves through finding an appropriate consort, receiving the requisite initiations, then cultivating the realizations corresponding to each initiation, culminating in the meditation without a support that is based on the fourth initiation of great bliss. All of these instructions, he concludes, should be received orally from one's guru, in accordance with one of several transmission lineages that had already taken root in early Tibet, especially those founded by the eighth-century Indian masters Vimalamitra, Buddhagupta, and Padmasambhava.

The existence of such lineages of oral teachings is significant. Given Nupchen's discussion, it seems the perfection-stage practices of our root *sādhana* would fall into the lower door category, though explicit mention of consuming the sacrament is absent from the fourth *samādhi* that brings the work to a close.[85] In the tenth century, when this *sādhana* was probably composed, the upper door meditations, with their inner heat and systems of *cakras*, had not yet found their way to Dunhuang. Indeed, even in India, the *Hevajra Tantra*, which encapsulated many of these complex practices, was not composed until the tenth century. Nonetheless, from Nupchen's writings, we get a sense that much more was going on in the ninth century than one might think from reading the canonical tantras. Not only local ritual manuals but alsoral instructional lineages on the channels and winds were being passed from master to disciple within India and, to a more limited extent, even in central Tibet. Only gradually did such doctrines begin to be put into writing, first in the personally held ritual manuals that circulated informally and later in the tantras.

With these new teachings of the upper door came a new way of understanding sexual yoga. No longer were the seminal fluids so central, and the consort herself began to be eclipsed. David White has observed a parallel shift in Śaiva sources, "one that would gradually reduce the Yoginī to the internal energy, the *śakti* or *kuṇḍalinī* located within the body of the initiated male practitioner."[86] From the perspective of the consort, our cycling rite offers an active role for the woman involved. As breath cycling gave way to the technologies of channels and winds, however, the focus of sexual yoga shifted to the raising of the feminine energy from the bottom of the central channel and the descent of the male energy from the crown of the head.

"Behind this," as White again discerns regarding parallel later developments on the Śaiva side, "we can detect a still earlier phase of the Kubjikā traditions, in which motion would have been rotary before being projected upon a vertical axis."[87]

As these vertical elements were eventually written into new tantras such as the tenth-century *Hevajra*, the disjunction between the perfection stage of the eighth century and that of later works became increasingly clear.[88] Before long, commentators who remained loyal to the early tantras were being forced to read the later techniques into the earlier. Thus the circa eleventh-century Vīravajra, when faced with the absence of channels and winds in the *Cakrasaṃvara-tantra*, reinterprets an account of eating the sacramental fluids, which appears in the opening verse to the tantra's forty-second chapter, as follows: "The hero and yoginī, being purified by the four [steps of] service and worship (*sevāsādhana*), having drunk the flower water—i.e., transmitted uterine blood and semen—into the aperture of the central channel (*avadhūti*), should meditate in concentration upon the upward diversion [of these fluids]."[89] No longer do the practitioners swallow the sacrament to bring it into their hearts; now, that drinking is a suction of the fluids through the male vajra and up the central channel.

In Tibet, the same disjunction between the earlier and later perfection-stage techniques became the stuff of polemics. In the thirteenth century, Rok Bande ridiculed his New School (Gsar ma) contemporaries for their fascination with the latest trends: "They see as amazing the doctrines of the channels, drops, and so on—doctrines that have a lot in common with the doctrines of the non-Buddhists."[90] A century later, Longchen Rabjam followed a similar path to Vīravajra's when he defended the Nyingma school's *Guhyagarbha-tantra* against New School critics who found it lacking. On the tantra's verse that comes at the conclusion of the sexual yoga (within the larger context of a tantric feast), "That essence of the sun and moon that is accomplishment / is taken from the mandala with one's vajra-tongue,"[91] Longchenpa writes:

> That essence of the sun and moon is taken with the tongue, which is the secret vajra, into the mandalas of the four *cakras* within the channels. Filled gradually from below, all the places on the body are permeated, and it is resolved as gnosis. Regarding this, some people assert that it is taken while imagining the tongue

> of [oneself] illuminated as the deity to be a vajra, then swallowed inside. This is not so. They do not understand the meaning of union.[92]

Here again, a later author is seen interpreting away the swallowing of the sacrament that marked the culmination of sexual yoga in the late eighth century as a coded instruction for drawing the fluids up the central channel. The *Guhyagarbha*, Longchenpa assures his readers, had the whole system of channels and winds well in place.

Such a reading is unlikely to have been intended by the *Guhyagarbha*'s author(s). Today's Buddhist faithful might argue that we cannot know for sure, as tantric writings are so often transmitted alongside oral teachings. Certainly, the presence of no longer extant ritual manuals and other extracanonical writings cannot be discounted. As this study has amply demonstrated, a tantra may not exhibit a given rite, yet manuals based on that same tantra may nonetheless include it. Ritual manuals constitute a highly flexible genre that is ever open to local innovation. And at an even less visible level, there is the possible existence of oral instructions. We have seen how difficult our own root *sādhana*'s perfection-stage verses are to comprehend without commentary. Tantric ritual writings consistently point beyond themselves, whether poetically to assumed deific presences or hermeneutically to secret explanations. In this sense, tantric ritual manuals are intentionally incomplete. Drawing their affective and rhetorical power from gaps and silences, they are ever supplemented by appended notes, marginal jottings, drawings, and knowledge from elsewhere. If ritual manuals are ever-changing, the oral instructions that often accompany their transmission are still more fluid, forever being tailored to each student and each moment when they are offered. Locally produced ritual manuals of the sort discovered at Dunhuang bring us a step closer to such teachings, to the lived religious practices of medieval Buddhists, but it is important to recognize they still hold us at a remove. The eighth and ninth centuries constituted a time of remarkable innovation in tantric practice. New ideas permeated everywhere. With ancient manuscripts personally penned by distant meditators, we gain some sense of what it was like, but inevitably we remain wandering through our own time and place.

Appendix

Samādhi Sādhana *with Commentary*

A TRANSLATION OF PELLIOT TIBÉTAIN 634

[1r] **The method for cultivating the thusness samadhi, as gathered from scripture:**
[This] relates to the naturally nonconceptual. All phenomena are primordially unborn. Therefore, one's intellect rests in the naturally nonconceptual. So why is there cycling as long as there are phenomena? There is cycling because of the causes, the three poisons. What cycles? The results [of those poisons]—the body, speech, and mind—cycle. Where do they cycle? They cycle through the three realms. The body, speech, and mind ripen as the four kinds of rebirth in the many three realms—this is the topic.

* * *

Though essentially nonconceptual,
in order to purify, as with silver ore,
Though all phenomena are primordially uncreated, it is not realized through the view, so one strongly cultivates nonconceptuality with concentration (*samādhi*). To exemplify with an appropriate metaphor, if one has ore that is a cause for silver, when it is melted by an expert blacksmith, the silver will come out, but if it is not melted and hammered, the silver will not come out. Similarly, if the antidote is applied using the three syllables, which are like the blacksmith, then the afflictions, which are like the dross, are removed, and the resulting three gates of liberation, which are like the extracted silver, are obtained.

* * *

The three seed [syllables] radiate light, incinerating the causes, the effects, and the places;
In that way [the poisons] are vanquished. At the crowns of oneself and all sentient beings an *oṃ*, at their mouths an *aṃ*, at their hearts a *hūṃ*. The *hūṃ* is white like a stainless white pearl. These radiate light, and from that . . .

* * *

one is purified in both one's practice and nature.
In order to dwell in that thusness,
That is to say, in order to dwell in that thusness and the gnosis of awareness (*rig pa'i ye shes*) by means of the *dharmadhātu*.[1] Well then, how does one dwell? One dwells in the space of nonconceptualization and nonfixation.

*   *   *

With a straight body, bind the five *mudrās*,
and display the five gates of entry—the five methods for resting.
The five gates of entry [i.e., the five *mudrās*] are as follows: put the right hand on top of the left; put the right leg on top of the left; straighten the posture; rest the eyes along the nose; press the tongue on the roof of the mouth. There are the five methods for resting: in order to settle the intellect in a state in which the suchness of pure *dharmatā* is unwavering and unmoving, the posture is straightened. In order to settle the intellect in a state in which the suchness of pure *dharmatā* is without going or coming, the right leg is placed on the left. In order to settle the intellect in a state in which the suchness of pure *dharmatā* is without subject or object, the hands are in the *mudrā* of equality (*mnyam pa'i phyag rgya*). In order to settle the intellect in a state in which there is no fixating vision of the pure *dharmatā*, the eyes rest down the nose. In order to settle the intellect in a state in which the suchness of pure *dharmatā* is without expression, the tongue presses on the roof of the mouth. Those are the five.

*   *   *

[1v] **Gazing at the mind (*sems lta*) is method; not locating is wisdom.**
Gazing at the mind is the method, and not locating it is wisdom.

*   *   *

It is not anything; one does not think anything,
What is this mind? It is not anything. Because it is without categories, it has no class of the gods, no class of *nāgas*, and no servant class whatsoever. Because it has no colors, it is not white, red, yellow, or green. Well then, what is it? It is absolutely nothing. Deconstructing the mind with the mind, it is not established as the mind. Therefore, the mind is nothing at all. Then place the intellect on the nonappearance (*mi gsal ba*) of the intellect. [Thus, the two phrases

in this line teach:][2] (i) the method for analyzing the mind and the method for analyzing objects; and (ii) the method for settling the intellect regarding mind and the method for settling the intellect with regard to objects.

* * *

not mentally engaging with or conceptualizing features,
"Features" refers to the objective aspects. "Mentally" refers to the mind. And it says, "not engaging with the objective aspects within the mind." What does that mean? One does not engage with the objective aspects within the mind. By scrutinizing the mind with the mind, as described above, mind is not established as mind and objects are not established as objects. Because there is no appearance or designation of the object in the mind, this is called "not mentally engaging with the aspects." Where does the intellect settle? The intellect settles in nonconceptuality.

* * *

the sphere of activity (*spyod yul*) is pure, so do not abide anywhere.
"Activity" (*spyod*) refers to the mind. "Sphere" (*yul*) refers to the objective aspect. Having scrutinized the mind with the mind as described above, mind is not established, so mind is pure. Objects are not established as objects, so objects too are pure. Well then, where does the intellect settle? It settles in nonabiding.[3]

* * *

Comprehend the state of the three liberations.
The method for analyzing the mind is applied to the [buddhas'] body, speech, and mind.[4] The method for analyzing objects is applied to the body. The method for analyzing both body and mind is applied to speech.

* * *

The method is not separating, like taking *hala*.[5]
Method is the subject. The predicate is its not separating. The compatible analogy for establishing that is *hala*. By means of the method that is great compassion, samsara itself is united with nirvana without separation.[6] For example, in the island kingdom of Siṅghala, the rocks are all gold and silver. For food, they eat the poisonous *hala*. Right from the start, when the babies have entered into their mothers' wombs,[7] the poisonous *hala* that is eaten

[by the mothers] enters into their wombs through the [umbilical] blood. And after they are born, [the children] are able to clean it by means of their blood from eating the poisonous *hala*.[8] If they drink it, even though others[9] see it as poison, they see it as an excellent food.

* * *

Wisdom is unwavering, like applying an antitoxic (*nad myed*) cure. Wisdom is the subject. The predicate is its being unwavering. The compatible analogy for establishing that is the antitoxic medicine. By means of wisdom that is the understanding of someone who has completely understood, samsara itself is established as unwavering nirvana. The compatible analogy is the application of a vaccinatory medicine. Similarly, by means of a measure (*srang*) of antitoxic medicine, the poisonous *hala* is extracted (*phyung*) as a noxious distillation (*gnag nur*), so that the *hala* itself comes to have the nature of a medicine. In the same way, through great compassion [of the buddha],[10] samsara, having been set aside (*bzhag*), is experienced in the manner of nirvana, whereby it is established as nirvana, and thus one is a buddha, right?[11]

Here, in combining the three [elements of the syllogism], the logic of scripture (*lung gi gtan tshig*) [is being used].

* * *

Mindfulness is unerring, as for [rain]drops, like a gatekeeper. Mindfulness is the subject. The predicate is its being unerring. The compatible analogy for establishing that is the five gatekeepers. Similarly, when a sense (*tshor ba*) of the three times, which are concepts of one's own conceptualizing mind, arises, one cultivates not conceptualizing earlier and not conceptualizing later. An experience of nonconceptuality arises vividly. Just as in the analogy of one not being mistaken with regard to the drops when rain is falling from the sky, similarly, one does not in any way conceptualize earlier or later, which are karmic errors.[12]

* * *

Alertness is recognition, like a watchman for thieves. Alertness is the subject. The predicate is that it is recognition.[13] The compatible analogy for establishing that is a watchman, the similarity of which establishes alertness as recognition. Like the analogous watchman when a thief is approaching the barn, when errors come like the thief, one thinks, it's all happening![14]

* * *

***Vipaśyanā* is effulgent,[15] like a lamp.**
Vipaśyanā is to be established as effulgence. The analogy is placing a lamp inside a dark hole in a wall. Just like a lamp placed in a hole in a wall, *vipaśyanā* projects the light of wisdom. That [*vipaśyanā*] focuses, by means of *samādhi* that is suffused with the wetness of *śamatha*, and illuminates.[16]

* * *

***Śamathā* is unwavering, still like a deep lake.**
Like the analogy of a lake that is unwavering at the edges, undisturbed in the middle, *śamatha* is like an invalid (*nad pa*), while the light of *vipaśyanā*'s wisdom, like a lamp, is luminous and stirring.[17]

* * *

Those six [lines above] can be divided into pairs.
They may be divided into the pairs of method and wisdom, mindfulness and alertness, and *vipaśyanā* and *śamatha*.

* * *

[2r] **The stages of entry, remedy, and settling the intellect.**
Entry refers to method and knowledge; remedy refers to mindfulness and alertness; settling the intellect refers to *vipaśyanā* and *śamatha*.

* * *

The *śamatha* and *vipaśyanā* should be balanced, like a lamp in a vase.
Vipaśyanā and *śamatha* are the subject. The predicate is their balance. The compatible analogy for establishing that is a lamp.

* * *

Since it is unmoving and clear, it is like a clear lake.
In the analogy, when there is an opening in the clouds in the sky, the reflections of multitudes of stars are illuminated in a clear lake. Similarly, in the

śamatha that is suffused with wetness like the clear lake, the reflections of *vipaśyanā* are taken as clear light by wisdom.

* * *

Then, regarding the method for cultivating the all-illuminating *samādhi*: How does the so-called "all-knowing" know all? It knows the meanings of the two kinds of phemomena, of samsara and nirvana. Because one knows the phenomena of nirvana, without wavering from the thusness *samādhi*, one comes to know the phenomena of samsara. The all-knowing wisdom having been born, one knows, vividly and without obscuration, the subtle aspects of the contaminants of all beings—all the imprints (*bag chags*) of wheels on the feet, head, and hands.

* * *

Not moving from the space, knowing whatever occurs in its vividness, compassion, even throughout all, the space of desirelessness,
Great compassion is continuously generated. Displayed in this way, it is not a partial compassion being generated. All sentient beings remain pervaded by compassion. Space is realized as the space of thusness, the *dharmadhātu*.

* * *

opening like the sky, becoming the cause for emanations to arise,
This is like when, in the sky, as a gap in the clouds opens, the moon and many stars are revealed. Similarly, in the thusness *samādhi*, which is like the sky, the great omniscient gnosis opens a gap in the clouds, and the syllable of oneself, a white *A* endowed with causal consciousness, arises brightly in the sky, dwelling as the cause.

* * *

not desiring the two extremes, free from all without abandoning anything.
The two extremes are samsara and nirvana. The knowledge that is their consummation is not attached to being apart from the extreme of samsara. The means that is great compassion is not attached to being apart from the extreme of nirvana. "All" means being free from the extreme of samsara.

* * *

Thus it is said.

* * *

Regarding the method for meditating on the causal *samādhi*:
[2v] **From the syllable A: *e tang khang lang ram*.**

In the skylike thusness *samādhi*, a door is suddenly opened by the great omniscient gnosis. The white ཨ syllable of oneself, endowed with the cause of consciousness, dwells as the cause. In the midst of space, it arises, shining white. This is "the syllable ཨ."

* * *

Purifying the five poisons through the empowerments of their natures, the five mothers,[18]
the *samādhis* of the five entireties (Skt. *kṛtsna*; Tib. *zad par*) are cultivated.

The five poisons are desire, anger, ignorance, pride, and jealousy. The five great elements are gathered in stages, *saṃharaṇa*, whereby the five seed syllables are cultivated in a series, like blazing jewels strung on a golden thread.

* * *

Thus, the five great elements are cultivated in a stack.

Then the five seed syllables, "*oṃ aṃ hūṃ svā hā*," emanate light all at once, the five seed syllables ringing forth, each with its own sound.

* * *

Then the techniques for the recitations for the activities are taught:
As if mindfulness,[19] the vital breath, and its restriction were speaking, speaking!

One engages in the mental illumination of the awareness of speech: the non-conceptual cultivation is not a dark meditation, like looking for a tree in the fog or like being in the shadow of some gloomy cairn or pine tree. The cultivation of the deity's body is to be held and apprehended with a consciousness that is mindful and lively. One cultivates the traveling series on the verge of orally vocalizing.

* * *

As if the earrings, necklace, and limbs were swaying, swaying!
One engages in the mental illumination of the awareness of body: the earrings, choker, anklets, necklace, and all the rest give off imagined light rays that scatter throughout the universe in the ten directions, like in the *Vidyādharapiṭaka*, where there appear moving mongoose purses that are shaken, and when a mongoose purse is shaken, it spits out a series of jewels.

* * *

As if on the base, the vajra and seed syllables were blazing, blazing!
The vowels, *anusvāras*, intersyllabic dots are so perfect!
One engages in the mental illumination of the awareness of mind: at one's heart rests a delicate, smooth moon disc lying flat. On that disc rests a vertical[20] vajra, around which the seed syllables are revolving. [The moon disc] is not a real support. The vajra does not touch it. The syllables are not of writings in sutras. Though they are close, their closeness is clear; each is illuminated distinctly, like the colors that radiate within clear crystal.

* * *

Holding the three aspects in the mind at once, one's mind
without distraction and stupefication, is mindful, bright, and aware.[21]
[The three aspects] may be taken as referring to the three aspects of mental illumination of the awarenesses [i.e., of speech, body, and mind], or, alternatively, to the triad of the moon, vajra, and seed syllables.

* * *

[3r] **Regarding the second *samādhi*:**
Within a state of *dharma*, the *mudrās*, and singing songs,
Of the ultimate *dharma*, the accomplishment *dharma*, and the explanatory *dharma*, the ultimate *dharma* is awareness in the expanse. The explanatory [*dharma*] is to join with the *mudrās*, that is, to be aware of oneself in the *mahāmudrā*.

* * *

from the seed syllables of speech that are the mind itself,
By transforming one's *ālayavijñāna*, the form of the mirrorlike wisdom is attained; the reflection of this form is the moon. By transforming one's

manas, the form of the discriminating wisdom is attained; the reflection of this form is the *vajra*. By transforming one's *kliṣṭamanas*, the form of the equality wisdom is obtained; the reflection of this form is the syllables. Each is clear in its appearance.

* * *

the secret mantra should be listened to in one's mind,[22]
At one's heart, the moon, *vajra*, and seed syllables appear. One's tongue is thought to be a moon disc, on top of which is held a five-spoked vajra. One should read the seed syllables at one's heart that appear along with the moon and vajra.

* * *

whereby the secret mantra is pure, and the recitations clear.
If one practices in this way, the secret mantra of speech will be pure, and the mental recitations will be clear.

* * *

Regarding the third *samādhi*:
(i) The unchanging syllables strung together as a garland,
The manner of all these syllables is such that the sounds [of the individual letters] do not change but the seed syllables move. How so? For the single *oṃ*, the sound does not change.

* * *

(ii) [resound] constantly like the sound of a bell.
There is the cycling by sound, such that the syllables move, though *oṃ* does not change into *aḥ*; *hūṃ* does not change into *svā*; *svā* does not change into *hā*; they remain in a series.

* * *

(iii) There is a projecting and gathering of light, with a manner of a [spinning] firebrand.
This applies to the cycling of light: glowing like the sparks in a fire scattered by a blacksmith's bellows, the five seed syllables are light rays, [circling] like sparks in a five-colored sleeve opening. Just so, the five seed

syllables, resounding with their respective sounds, should be successively recited.

* * *

(iv) Gathering back, one presses down with the word.

This is to be applied to the cycling by the word: the secret substance is the *hūṃ vajradhṛk*. If it were just the *hūṃ*, it would bring no benefit. So, extracting the heart [syllable] of the five families, it is further ornamented to make *hūṃ vajra dhṛk*. Pressing [the substance] down with the wheel at the center of one's navel, it arises in the vajra path. It descends into the space of the consort and mounts her spine.

* * *

[3v] **(v) The method for leading is applied with a mute *hūṃ*.**

This is to be applied to the cycling of the breath: one projects forth the above-mentioned *hūṃ*, then without expressing its sound, one inhales the *hūṃ* back inside. Think that it dissolves with fragrance into one's left nostril.

* * *

Regarding the fourth *samādhi*:

When it has cycled, one aspires faithfully,

When it is time to dismiss the garland, think that it has been 108, that is, the seed syllables revolving around the vajra. First there was the mental illumination of the awarenesses; second, perfecting the heart [mantra]; third was the luminosity; and fourth, the propitiations (*bsnyen pa*) are completed and the activities performed. In one revolution of the garland, the sins of 108 aeons are purified all at once.

* * *

paying homage in a manner of realization, and

One who is in that way endowed with the gnosis of realization realizes objects to be uncreated space, with an awareness that the mind that apprehends apprehended objects as uncreated objects is [itself] without self.

* * *

winding up apprehended and apprehender into a state of nonduality: nay the merit of embodied beings increase.

The father, endowed with the gnosis of realization, completes the accumulation of merit, while the mother, the selflessness of the apprehending mind, completes the accumulation of gnosis. Thereby the father, who is endowed with the piercing vajra of insight (*vipaśyanā*), dwells in a manner of entry, while the mother, who is endowed with the *samādhi* of the cleansing wetness of calm abiding (*śamatha*), rests before the father in a manner of paying homage. Viewing in this way, this is how the devoted pray.

* * *

The *samādhi* is complete.

Conclusions

THIS BOOK OFFERS a history of early tantric Buddhist ritual as seen through the lens of the Dunhuang manuscripts. Among the tantric manuscripts held in this remarkable collection, there are precious few tantras but hundreds of tantric ritual manuals. As chapter 1 explains, the genre of ritual manuals began to spread in the second half of the fifth century, gaining increasing popularity alongside *dhāraṇī* sutras through the sixth. This new genre provided a literary space for Buddhists to engage their tradition in increasingly complex ways. Operating outside the strictures of the more canonical sutras and other words of the Buddha (*buddhavacana*), their authors were relatively free to compose their own manuals, to tailor Buddhist rituals to local needs and interests, to weave disparate rites into new wholes, and even to experiment with new ritual techniques. Ritual manuals were therefore a highly creative force in Buddhism from at least the sixth century on.

The early *dhāraṇī*-based manuals were very much human-authored affairs. Written in prose, they provided straightforward instruction on how to construct an altar and arrange it with offerings, where to place a buddha image, how to recite the *dhāraṇī* spell, and often how to distribute the resulting blessings. The author's instructions were addressed directly to the reader, one human Buddhist to another, speaking in the imperative about what one should do. By the early seventh century, however, some *vidhis* began to be embedded within the sutras themselves. No longer framed as mere human-authored writings that circulated alongside or were appended to the sutras, these were presented as teachings by the Buddha himself for his future disciples to follow in their practice. Around the same time, multiple ritual manuals began to be collected into stand-alone sutras, offering panoplies of rites for all sorts of purposes. (The well-known *Susiddhikara* is one such work.) Such compilations were framed as works of *buddhavacana* and eventually were retroactively labeled as the first tantras (typically under the rubric of Kriyā tantra).

Also in the seventh century, as tantric Buddhism proper was emerging, new kinds of practices entered the genre: initiations (*abhiśeka*), fire offerings (*homa*), elaborate new meditations, and more. Perhaps the most significant change in Buddhist ritual during this pivotal century was its gradual interiorization. This took several forms. The *Mahāvairocanābhisaṃbodhi-tantra* had one imaginatively transform oneself into a deity to worship the deity (or mandala), and by the end of the century, in works like the *Sarvatathāgata-tattvasaṃgraha*, identification with the deity had become key to initiation and postinitiatory *sādhana* practice alike. Such unions were effected through careful consecratory (*adhiṣṭhāna*) methods for *āveśa*, techniques for merging the deity into the practitioner's body.

Additionally, the external ritual acts of the earlier manuals and mandala altars began to give way to interiorized acts of the mind and imagined mandala palaces. Increasingly, the imagination was where the "real" ritual unfolded, whether accompanied by parallel acts in the physical world or not. This inward shift was accompanied by an interest in the body's interior. The above-mentioned merging of the deity with the practitioner, for example, was also an *insertion* of the deity into the body. As consecration became a vital trope in late seventh- and eighth-century Buddhist ritual, the manuals of the Yogatantra class focused in particular on the image of a vajra upon a moon disc as the ultimate instantiation of awakening itself. Through initiation and then again in the practioner's postinitiatory act of self-consecration, this image was imagined to be inserted in an act of *āveśa* (possession) into the body, where it would come to rest at the heart. In the context of initiation, this was partly accomplished by an accompanying swallow of *samaya* water. This *samaya*, or *samayamudrā*, was the mind of awakening and would rest at the heart for as long as the practitioner's vow was observed.

A few decades later, starting in the mid-eighth century in the writings of early Mahāyoga, this trope was sexualized. So-called "secret" reinterpretations of the consecration rite focused on a drop (Skt. *bindu*; Tib. *thig le*) of sexual fluids produced through ritualized sexual union. This secret "mind of awakening" (*bodhicitta*) was swallowed at the culmination of both the secret initiation and the practitioner's subsequent *sādhana* practice. This taking of the sacrament formed the central concern of the earliest perfection-stage practices, and again, after being swallowed, the secret drop would come to rest in the practitioner's heart. The importance of the *bodhicitta* sacrament to early tantric sexual yoga would become obscured in the ninth and tenth centuries as the subtle body techniques of the winds and channels took center stage, but the manuals from Dunhuang offer a window into this crucial period. Furthermore, recognizing the significance of this "supreme *samaya*" allows us to discern developmental continuities between these early Mahāyoga sexual rites and the earlier *Sarvatathāgata-tattvasaṃgraha*-based system's consecratory acts of *āveśa* and the vajra and moon disc of the *samayamudrā*.

Alongside all these ritual developments, new uses of ritual language may be discerned within the genre. Whereas the earlier *dhāraṇī*-based manuals were written largely in prose, use of poetic language gradually increased across the seventh and eighth centuries. In the manuals of the so-called Yoga tantras (the *Sarvadurgatipariśodhana-tantra* and the *Sarvatathāgata-tattvasaṃgraha-tantra* being two influential examples), a switch from prose to verse or the sudden use of metaphor, rhyme, rhythm, and other literary devices may be seen at specific points in the proceedings. For example, in the *Sarvadurgatipariśodhana*-based initiation manual examined in chapter 2, a switch to verse accompanies the ritual master's bestowal of the eight empowering objects, eight symbols of the mind of the buddhas. In the *Sarvatathāgata-tattvasaṃgraha*-based *sādhana* studied in chapter 3, a shift in register marks the moment of consecration, as the practitioner brings the *samayamudrā* (a.k.a. *jñānasattva*) into himself.

If our evidence from Dunhuang is any indication, this trend culminated in the second half of the eighth century and the manuals of the Mahāyoga class. The two Mahāyoga *sādhanas* examined in chapters 4 and 5 are composed entirely in verse, while others, such as the Buddhagupta-attributed *sādhana*, *An Appearance of Suchness: Ornament of the Sacred*, were copied directly and largely word for word from the *Guhyagarbha-tantra* or other tantras. As the distinction between guru and buddha dissolved, the line between human-authored and buddha-authored manuals was similarly weakening. As extractions of tantras, in the literal or the figurative sense, tantric ritual manuals, though still recognized as human-authored, now held and transmitted the sacrality of *buddhavacana*. The growing use of evocative language within ritual manuals was thus also entangled with the rise of the tantric subject—and tantric author—as divine. The Mahāyoga tantric practitioner was now a buddha, and as such could not only incorporate sexual pleasure and violent aggression into the path to awakening but also use poetic language and aesthetic experience to enrich the path.

Chapter 5 examined a spectacularly poetic Mahāyoga *sādhana* that not only is written entirely in verse but also lacks the kind of detailed instruction seen in the Yogatantra manuals. Instead, the text evokes a series of experiences, leaving the reader to fill in the gaps with the implicit ritual acts and inward imaginings. Loaded with similes, the text is as concerned as much with *how* one experiences the ritual as with *what* one is to do. Its evocations mark an extreme of poetic language among the tantric manuals from Dunhuang.

The same *sādhana* also provides rare detail on a breathing practice to be performed while in sexual union. No mention is made of ingesting the sacramental *bodhicitta*, so central to other early Mahāyoga practices (though it may be implied). Rather, the ritual dwells on mantra recitations performed in conjunction with an elaborate cycling of the breath between the meditator and his female consort. Intertextual connections suggest some may have understood this as a sexualized take on earlier breath-cycling meditations from the seventh-century *Mahāvairocanābhisaṃbodhi* and its circle of texts. Before long, similar practices were developed by the Jñānapāda and Ārya schools associated with the *Guhyasamāja-tantra* and popularized as the so-called vajra recitation. All these are early indications of the coming shift to perfection-stage sexual yogas that would focus on the *cakras*, channels, and winds of the subtle body, yogas that are well known even today in tantric Buddhist practice.

This, then, is a story of how tantric Buddhism developed within the genre of ritual manuals, which initially circulated alongside *dhāraṇī* sutras and offered simple rites of image worship and spell recitation. These ritual manuals provided an intimate literary space for Buddhists to innovate and tailor their practices for their own needs, in which individuals could creatively interact with their religious tradition. Tantric Buddhism dissolved the boundaries between buddha and meditator, and the resulting manuals produced a uniquely tantric subject, rooted in the imagination, whose daily meditations were carefully shaped by the evocative language of tantric *sādhanas* and other kinds of ritual writings. The manuscripts from Dunhuang tell this much of the story, and then there is silence. More was to come, but that remains for other sources to tell.

Notes

Introduction

1. This statement should be qualified by the existence of several sutras that purport to include the teachings of a buddha other than Śākyamuni, the *Avataṃsaka* being a good example. But in such narratives, Śākyamuni is usually still the main speaker.
2. In India, the *tripiṭaka*—the "three baskets" of sutra, *vinaya*, and *abhidharma*—was held to encompass the entirety of *buddhavacana*. As such, it was passed down through the centuries, but its actual contents varied by school. Still today, the canons recognized in East Asia and Tibet are multiple and varied. The idea of a Buddhist canon is therefore complex, not without problems, and deserving of a study in its own right. For some thought-provoking initial considerations of "the very idea of the Pali canon" (and that of a more practical "ritual canon") in Sri Lanka and Southeast Asia, see Steven Collins, "On the Very Idea of the Pali Canon," *Journal of the Pali Text Society* 15 (1990): 89–126.
3. Think, for example, of the recent proliferation of new tantric ritual manuals in the West, written by Tibetan teachers for foreign audiences.
4. Here, I do not count what I would call *dhāraṇī-sūtras* that are preserved in the "tantra" (*rgyud*) section of today's *Bka' 'gyur*, such as the *Suvarṇaprabhāsottama*, the *Bhadracārya-praṇidhānarāja*, or the *Aparimitāyurjñāna-nāma-mahāyāna-sūtra*. The three tantras I have in mind are the *Prajñāpāramitānayaśatapañcāśatikā*, the *Mañjuśrīnāmasaṃgīti*, and the *Guhyasamāja*.
5. See Jacob P. Dalton, *Taming of the Demons: Violence and Liberation in Tibetan Buddhism* (New Haven, CT: Yale University Press, 2011), especially chapters 2 and 3.
6. The foregoing theories may be seen in (i) Alexis Sanderson, "The Lākulas: New Evidence of a System Intermediate Between Pāñcārthika Pāsupatism and

Āgamic Śaivism," *The Indian Philosophical Annual* 24 (2006): 143–217, and Dominic Goodall, ed., *The Niśvāsatattvasaṃhitā: The Earliest Surviving Śaiva Tantra*, vol. 1: *A Critical and Annotated Translation of the Mūlasūtra, Uttarasūtra and Nayasūtra* (Pondichéry: Institut Français de Pondichéry; Paris: École française d'Extrême-Orient; Hamburg: Asien-Afrika-Institut, Universität Hamburg, 2015); (ii) Steven Neal Weinberger, "The Significance of Yoga Tantra and the *Compendium of Principles (Tattvasaṃgraha Tantra)* Within Tantric Buddhism in India and Tibet," (PhD diss., University of Virginia, 2003), and Ronald M. Davidson, *Indian Esoteric Buddhism: A Social History of the Tantric Movement* (New York: Columbia University Press, 2002); and (iii) David Gordon White, *Kiss of the Yoginī: "Tantric Sex" in Its South Asian Contexts* (Chicago: University of Chicago Press, 2003).

7. Such is the wording used by both Hugh B. Urban, "The Extreme Orient: The Construction of 'Tantrism' as a Category in the Orientalist Imagination," *Religion* 29 (1999): 123, and Richard D. McBride, "Is There Really 'Esoteric' Buddhism?" *Journal of the International Association of Buddhist Studies* 27, no. 2 (2004): 329. McBride suggests that such is also the conclusion of Donald S. Lopez, Jr., *Elaborations on Emptiness: Uses of the Heart Sūtra* (Princeton, NJ: Princeton University Press, 1996), 78–104, but here he overreads Lopez, who concludes simply by raising the possibility and observing that the term has been the product of Indian and Tibetan Buddhist imaginings as much as of "the Western mind."
8. Li-Kouang Lin, "Punyodaya (Na-T'i), un propageteur du tantrisme en Chine et au Cambodge à l'époque de Hiuan-tsang," *Journal Asiatique* 227 (1935): 84 n. 2 (rendered into English from the French).
9. For a translation of the complete passage, see Stephen Hodge, *The Mahā-vairocana-abhisaṃbodhi Tantra, with Buddhaguhya's Commentary* (London: Routledge Curzon, 2003), 10.
10. The idea of a long-lost *ur*-corpus, of which the new ritual works were mere excerpts, appears in Indian writings too. Thus, the Indian monk Atikūṭa, who arrived in China in 651, references a similar collection named the *Sutra of the Great Vajra Seat of Awakening (Jin'gang dadaochang jing)*; see Koichi Shinohara, *Spells, Images, and Mandalas: Tracing the Evolution of Esoteric Buddhist Rituals* (New York: Columbia University Press, 2014), 29, and Paul Copp, *The Body Incantatory: Spells and the Ritual Imagination in Medieval Chinese Buddhism* (New York: Columbia University Press, 2014), 215–16. Shinohara notes that the colophon to Yaśogupta's c. 570 Chinese translation of the *Sutra of the Divine Spell of the Eleven-Faced Avalokiteśvara* (T. 1070) also claims that work to be an extraction of the same *Sutra of the Great Vajra Mandala*, which would push the concept of an *ur*-corpus back into the sixth century. Jizang (549–623) and Xuanzang (602–664) also reference some sort of canon of spells; see Copp, *The Body Incantatory*, 212. All scholars agree that such voluminous and "probably imaginary" works "may never have existed in [their] entirety" (Shinohara, *Spells, Images, and Mandalas*, 30). That the concept of a *Vidyādharapiṭaka* was common in India by the eighth century is suggested by the term's appearance in chapter 6 of Śāntideva's *Śikṣāsamuccaya* (English translation by Cecil Bendall, *Śikshā-samuccaya: A Compendium of Buddhist Doctrine compiled by Śāntideva Chiefly from Earlier Mahāyāna Sūtras* [London: John Murray, 1922], 140). By the second half of the eighth century, still further mythic

collections such as the *Vajraśekhara* and the *Māyājāla* began to be referenced in Indian tantric writings; see Kenneth W. Eastman, "The Eighteen Tantras of the Vajraśekhara/Māyājāla," *Transactions of the International Conference of Orientalists in Japan* 26 (1981): 95–96, and Rolf W. Giebel, "The Chin-Kang-Ting Ching Yu-Ch'ieh Shi-Pa-Hui Chih-Kuei: An Annotated Translation," *Journal of Naritasan Institute for Buddhist Studies* 18 (1995): 107–201.

11. Thus, Śubhākarasiṃha (637–735) calls the *Mahāvairocanābhisaṃbodhi* a sutra, while Buddhagupta (c. 700–790) calls it a tantra (on the latter's dates, see Hodge, *The Mahā-vairocana-abhisaṃbodhi Tantra*, 22). Similarly, the *Sarvatathāgata-tattvasaṃgraha* is termed a sutra in its mid-eighth century Chinese translation but a tantra by Buddhagupta. The latter also labels several early texts Kriyā and Yoga tantras; see Jacob P. Dalton, "A Crisis of Doxography: How Tibetans Organized Tantra During the 8th–12th Centuries," *Journal of the International Association of Buddhist Studies* 28, no. 1 (2005): 122–23. This study uses Buddhagupta as the reconstruction of the Tibetan *Sangs rgyas gsang ba* rather than the sometimes-favored Buddhaguhya. For a review of the evidence on this matter, see Nicholas Schmidt, "The Jewel's Radiance: A Translation of '**Ratnabhāsvara*,' an Extensive Commentary on the *Vajravidāraṇa-nāma-dhāraṇī*" (MA thesis, Centre for Buddhist Studies at Rangjung Yeshe Institute, Kathmandu University, 2018).
12. Michel de Certeau, *Heterologies: Discourse on the Other* (Minneapolis: University of Minnesota Press, 1986), 82.
13. Sanderson, "The Lākulas," 148–50. Portions of the *Niśvāsasamhitā* have been called "the earliest surviving Śaiva tantra," but it too reached its final form in the seventh century; see Goodall, *The Niśvāsasamhitā*, 71. On the relatively late appearance of "tantra" as a common term, see 30–31.
14. See Davidson, *Indian Esoteric Buddhism*, 25–74, and Alexis Sanderson, "The Śaiva Age: The Rise and Dominance of Śaivism During the Early Medieval Period," in *Genesis and Development of Tantrism*, ed. Shingo Einoo (Tokyo: Institute of Oriental Culture, University of Tokyo, 2009), 252–303.
15. As is well known, Sanderson ("Vajrayāna: Origin and Function," in *Buddhism Into Year 2000*, ed. Dhammakaya Foundation [Bangkok and Los Angeles: Dhammakaya Foundation, 1994), 87–102; " The Śaiva Age," 189–92) and Davidson (*Indian Esoteric Buddhism*, 386 n. 105) have disagreed over the nature of textual borrowings between Śaivism and Buddhism. These issues, and those surrounding Ruegg's concept of a pan-Indian religious substratum ("Sur les Rapports entre le Bouddhisme et le 'substrat religieux' indien et tibétain," *Journal Asiatique* 252 [1964]: 77–95; "Review of David Snellgrove, *Indo-Tibetan Buddhism: Indian Buddhists and Their Tibetan Successors*," *Journal of the Royal Asiatic Society* 1 (1989): 173; *The Symbiosis of Buddhism with Brahminism/Hinduism in South Asia and of Buddhism with "Local Cults" in Tibet and the Himalayan Region* [Vienna: Verlag der Österrischeischen Akademie der Wissenschaften, 2008]), do not directly bear on the present study. Sectarian boundaries were being renegotiated across India, and tantric ritual on all sides was considerably enriched by the resulting exchanges.
16. Both also cite the writings of Indian Marxist historians of the 1980s and early 1990s on the changing societal patterns of the early medieval period, such as

Brajadulal Chattopadyaya, *The Making of Early Medieval India* (Delhi: Oxford University Press, 1994), and Ram Sharan Sharma, *Urban Decay in India (c. 300–c. 1000)* (New Delhi: Munishiram Manoharlal, 1987) and *Early Medieval Indian Society: A Study in Feudalisation* (Calcutta: Orient Longman Limited, 2001), and others.

17. For a review of attempts to date Tibet's control of Dunhuang, see Zhengyu Li, "Shazhou Zhenyuan sinian xianfan kao" 沙州貞元四年陷蕃考 [A Study of the Fall of Shazhou to Tufan in Zhenyuan 4], in *Duhuang yanjiu* 敦煌研究 [Dunhuang Research] 104, no. 4 (2007): 98–103.
18. In my own research, I have yet to identify a single Mahāyoga tantric manuscript that can be dated to before the tenth century. Based on handwriting and other paleographic markers, I have argued elsewhere that some of the Yogatantra materials, particularly those based on the *Sarvatathāgata-tattvasaṃgraha*, may date from somewhat earlier, perhaps as early as the mid-ninth century. On dating the Tibetan Dunhuang manuscripts according to handwriting style, see Sam van Schaik, "Dating Early Tibetan Manuscripts: A Paleographical Method," in *Scribes, Texts and Rituals in Early Tibet and Dunhuang*, ed. Brandon Dotson, Kazushi Iwao, and Tsuguhito Takeuchi (Weisbaden: Reichert Verlag, 2013), 119–35.
19. On a possible indirect reference to the secret initiation in IOL Tib J 331/1, 1r.2, see the discussion in chapter 4.
20. Despite its insistence on the importance of local variations, this study offers a rather linear narrative of the development of early tantric Buddhist ritual. Surely this is a fault, and further nuancing of its story may be necessary as additional materials are consulted. Given the still-nascent state of tantric studies, however, a narrative of some sort is needed, even if it must remain partial or even be found by future scholars to be misleading in some regards.
21. As Matthew Kapstein, "New Light on an Old Friend: PT 849 Reconsidered," in *Tibetan Buddhist Literature and Praxis*, ed. Ronald Davidson and Christian Wedemeyer, Proceedings of the Tenth Seminar of the IATS 2003, vol. 4 (Leiden: Brill, 2006), 9–30, has observed, Pelliot tibétain 849 may represent an exception to this rule, as it appears to reflect a stage of Indian development closer to the manuscript's own tenth-century date, and other exceptions may yet be identified.
22. On the official copying efforts, see Kazushi Iwao, "The Purpose of Sūtra Copying in Dunhuang Under the Tibetan Rule," in *Dunhuang Studies: Prospects and Problems for the Coming Second Century of Research*, ed. Irina Popova and Liu Yi (St. Petersburg: Slavia, 2012), 102–5; on the recent discovery in Lhasa, see Sam van Schaik's references to the work of Pasang Wangdu and others (https://earlytibet.com/2011/03/14/secrets-of-the-cave-iii-the-cave-of-monk-wu/); and on Heshang and Facheng (a.k.a. Chos grub), see Luis O. Gomez, "The Direct and Gradual Approaches of Zen Master Mahayana: Fragments of the Teachings of Mo-ho-yen," in *Studies in Ch'an and Hua-yen*, ed. Robert Gimello and Peter Gregory (Honolulu: University of Hawai'i Press, 1983), 69–167, and Jonathan A. Silk, "Chinese Sūtras in Tibetan Translation: A Preliminary Survey," *Annual Report of The International Research Institute for Advanced Buddhology at Soka University* 22

(2019): 227–46, respectively. For more on the close religious relationship between Dunhuang and central Tibet, see Dalton, *Taming of the Demons*, 8–10.

23. *Sgra sbyor bam po gnyis pa*, 73.14–20 and *Dkar chag 'phang thang ma*, 45.
24. IOL Tib J 470, r1. *dgos ched ni sna nam ldong khyu'i don du 'am / phyi rabs kyi rnal 'byor pa blo la myi gsal zhing the tsom dang sdug par gyur pa'i gnas bsal ba'i don gsungs.* On dating Dpal dbyangs, see Kammie Takahashi, "Lamps for the Mind: Illumination and Innovation in dPal dbyangs's Mahāyoga" (PhD diss., University of Virginia, 2009), 148.
25. *Rnam thar rgyas pa*, 29a.4–6. *ci skad bshad la tshul bzhin du cho ga dag pas dal du bzhug cing / sngags kyi sgo gsum gyi dam tshig 'bogs pa la sogs pa / theg pa la rims kyi gzhol ba / sngags gzhung tshad ma rnams gtso bor byas.*
26. *Rnam thar rgyas pa*, 29b.5–6. *dpe cha spyir bzhes / phyin chad de ltar ma spyod ces lan gsum bsgo / skyed ma mchis na rgyal ba'i bka' khyad du bsod pa po lags ces dpral bar yi ge bris te phyogs gzhan du dbyung ngo.* For a fuller discussion of these edicts, see Jacob P. Dalton, "Power and Compassion: Negotiating Religion and State in Tenth-Century Tibet," in *The Illuminating Mirror, Tibetan Studies in Honour of Per K. Sørensen*, ed. Olaf Czaja and Guntram Hazod (Wiesbaden: Dr. Ludwig Reichert Verlag, 2015), 101–18.
27. IOL Tib J 351/3, 28v.8. *Dge slong Rdo rje bris.*
28. IOL Tib J 790, v1.10. *rtsang rje dge slong gtsug gi gyal bas bris.*
29. Pelliot tibétain 792, 3r.3. *ban de byang cub dbyangs kyi sku yon du bris te.*
30. IOL Tib J 463/1, r11.2. *'rge slong 'dru hu rIn 'chen rdzags 'gyIs skyur nas 'rtan la 'phap ste/ yi dam du 'gyIs/ 'phyag dar ste bris.* Here, I read *'dru hu* (elsewhere in the manuscript, *tru 'hu*) as *dru gu*, which would suggest the scribe was Uyghur. Another colophon from the same manuscript is discussed in chapter 1, n. 15, and for more on this use of *yi dam*, see the same chapter, n. 18. While there were probably more Tibetans in Dunhuang during the period of Tibetan occupation until 848 C.E., it is possible that some of the above-cited names attached to ninth-century manuscripts are Tibetan names taken by non-Tibetan persons during or shortly after that period.
31. For the name's two occurrences, see Pelliot tibétain 103, 5r.7 and 10r.6. The manuscript's third work was penned by Ban de Dge slong Shes rab rgyal mtshan (7r.6). The Chinese character commonly used for the same Kuchean family name is *bai* (白), originally pronounced with a hard -g ending. My thanks to Al Dien of Stanford University for his assistance in identifying the possible origins of this name.
32. IOL Tib J 470, r1. *phu shi meng hwe'i 'gyog kyis bris.* In reconstructing the Chinese here, I follow the lead of Sam van Schaik, "The Sweet Sage and *The Four Yogas*: A Lost Mahāyoga Treatise from Dunhuang," *Journal of the International Association of Tibetan Studies* 4 (2008): 24–25, who further acknowledges the assistance of Kazushi Iwao.
33. IOL Tib J 321, 84b.5. *Kam cu pa Bo'u ko gis bris.*
34. For several tantric manuscripts that may be connected to Khotan, see Jacob Dalton, Tom Davis, and Sam van Schaik, "Beyond Anonymity: Paleographic Analyses of the Dunhuang Manuscripts," *Journal of the International Association of Tibetan*

Studies 3 (2007): 1–23. There are exceptions to the rule just stated, i.e. tantric manuscripts written in Chinese, as discussed in chapter 6 and Amanda K. Goodman, "The Vajragarbha Bodhisattva Three-Syllable Visualization: A Chinese Buddhist *Sādhana* Text from Tenth-Century Dunhuang," *Buddhist Road Paper* 2, no. 7 (2022).

35. For the "brethren," see Pelliot tibétain 321, 1r.1 and 7v.3–5. For the "*vajrācārya*," see 7v.3, and for the "vajra king," see 7v.4. Pelliot tibétain 283, r1, ll. 15–16, a text closely related to that in Pelliot tibétain 321, clarifies that the latter term refers to the *vajrācārya* (*slobs dpon rdo rje rgyal po*). For the "patron," see Pelliot tibétain 321, 10v.4 and 11r.1. All these references are just examples; many others could be noted in both Pelliot tibétain 321 and Pelliot tibétain 283.

36. Pelliot tibétain 321, 9r.1. *gong ma mnyes pa'i rtsal shugs chungs pas / gso sbyong thams cad du ma chud pas bsgribs pa*. More or less the same passage appears in *Dpal he ru ka snying rje rol pa'i rgyud gsang ba zab mo'i mchog*, 192a.7–192b.7 (compare Pelliot tibétain 321, 8r.4–9v.3), but there the phrase on the *poṣadha* reads instead: *gnod sbyin mi tshud pa'i sgrib pa* (192b.4).

37. Pelliot tibétain 36, v3.3–4.5. For the rest of the original manuscript, see IOL Tib J 419 and Pelliot tibétain 42.

38. Two of the longest ritual manuals from Dunhuang are *gaṇacakra* manuals; see Pelliot tibétain 321 and the ritual compendium Pelliot tibétain 36/IOL Tib J 419/ Pelliot tibétain 42, as well as Pelliot tibétain 283 and Pelliot tibétain 332/2. A shorter fragment is found in Pelliot tibétain 323, and others are likely to be found. A sixth chapter on Pelliot tibétain 321 was originally going to be included here, but it is a long translation and, relative to its length, adds little to my central arguments. The chapter is therefore being published as a separate, forthcoming article.

39. IOL Tib J 464, 1r.4: *shin tu dben ba'i gnas dag su*. IOL Tib J 331/2, 1r.5: *dgon pa rI bos bskor yl/ me tog lcug phran skyid mos tshal*.

40. For another discussion of the codicology of Tibetan Dunhuang manuscripts, see Brandon Dotson and Agnieszka Helman-Ważny, *Codicology, Paleography, and Orthography of Early Tibetan Documents* (Vienna: Wiener studien zur tibetologie und buddhismuskunde, 2016), 34–41. On the Chinese manuscripts, see Imre Galambos, *Dunhuang Manuscript Culture* (Berlin/Boston: Walter de Gruyter GmbH, 2020), 23–36.

41. Note should be made of the (roughly 20.5 x 72 cm) *potis*, containing professionally scribed copies of the *Śatasāhasrikāprajñāpāramitā-sūtra*, which should be distinguished from the more numerous smaller *potis* containing a wider variety of texts. Together with the hundreds of professionally copied *Aparimitāyur-nāma-mahāyāna-sūtras*, which appear most commonly in horizontal scrolls (as do some copies of the *Śatasāhasrikāprajñāpāramitā*, on which see Iwao, "The Purpose of Sūtra Copying in Dunhuang Under the Tibetan Rule"), these make up a large portion of the Tibetan Dunhuang collection. On the *Śatasāhasrikāprajñāpāramitā* manuscripts, see Marcelle Lalou, "Les manuscrits tibétains des grandes *Prajñāpāramitā* trouvés à Touen-houang," in *Silver Jubilee Volume of the Zinbun-Kagaku-Kenkyusho Kyoto University* bétains trouvés

à Touen-houang," *Rocznik Orientalistyczny* 21 (1957): 149–52; "Manuscrits tibétains de la *Śatasāhasrikā-prajñāpāramitā* cachés à Touen-houang," *Journal Asiatique* 252 (1964): 479–86; and Brandon Dotson, "The Remains of the Dharma: Editing, Rejecting, and Replacing the Buddha's Words in Royally Sponsored Sutras from Dunhuang, 820s to 840s," *Journal of the International Association of Buddhist Studies* 36/37 (2013–14 [2015]): 5–68.

42. On IOL Tib J 401, see Sam van Schaik, *Buddhist Magic: Divination, Healing, and Enchantment Through the Ages* (Boulder: Shambala, 2020); on Pelliot tibétain 37, see Sam van Schaik, "The Uses of Implements Are Different: Reflections on the Functions of Tibetan Manuscripts," in *Tibetan Manuscript and Xylograph Traditions: The Written Word and Its Media Within the Tibetan Cultural Sphere*, ed. Orna Almogi (Hamburg: Department of Indian and Tibetan Studies, Universität Hamburg, 2016), 221–42; on IOL Tib J 437/Pelliot tibétain 324, see Jacob P. Dalton, "Mahāyoga Ritual Interests at Dunhuang: A Translation and Study of the Codex IOL Tib J 437/Pelliot tibétain 324," in *New Studies of the Old Tibetan Documents: Philology, History and Religion*, ed. Yoshiro Imaeda, Matthew Kapstein, and Tsuguhito Takeuchi (Tokyo: Research Institute for Languages and Cultures of Asia and Africa, 2011), 293–313. That the latter work has the generation stage practice second makes it an odd piece that cannot really be termed a *sādhana* proper. Taken together, the two parts look a bit like a *vajrācārya*'s personal ritual notes.

43. Jean-Pierre Drège, "Les cahiers des manuscrits de Touen-houang," in *Contributions aux études sur Touen-houang*, ed. Michel Soymié (Genève: Droz, 1979), 18, observes that the earliest Chinese booklet is dated 899; in the same article (p. 28) he suggests the influence of Nestorianism or Manichaeism. See also Galambos, *Dunhuang Manuscript Culture*, 32.

44. See F. W. Thomas and L. Giles, "A Tibeto-Chinese Word-and-Phrase Book," *Bulletin of the School of Oriental and African Studies* XII, no. 3 (1948): 753–69.

45. Recall the above-cited copy of the *Questions and Answers of Vajrasattva*, penned by the Chinese official Fushi Meng Huai Yu (see IOL Tib J 470, and by association its unsigned source manuscript, Pelliot tibétain 837), another example of a vertical scroll that may have been created under the influence of Chinese cultural interests. Such a manuscript suggests (admittedly on thin evidence) that some of the other tantric treatises listed here may have been copied by culturally Chinese Buddhists. Whether the same may be said of the tenth-century tantric ritual manuals remains unclear but quite possible.

46. Gregory Schopen, "On the Absence of Urtexts and Otiose Ācāryas: Buildings, Books, and Lay Buddhist Ritual at Gilgit," in *Écrire et transmettre en Inde classique*, ed. Gérard Colas and Gerdi Gerschiheimer (Paris: École française d'Extrême-Orient, 2009), 189–91, citing de Jong, observes that, contra the shibboleth that the verse portions of such Mahāyāna sutras predate the prose, recent work on old Sanskrit manuscript material has shown that the opposite sometimes may have been the case. Then too there are the earliest Chinese translation of the Larger *Sukhāvatīvyūha*, which does not include the verses (Vincent Eltschinger, "Pure Land Sūtras," in *Brill's Encyclopedia of Buddhism*, vol. 1, ed. Jonathan A. Silk [Leiden: Koninklijke Brill NV, 2015], 215) and Zacchetti's observations regarding

verse summaries such as the *Ratnaguṇasaṃcayagāthā* representing "a mature stage of development of the Prajñāpāramitā literature" (Stefano Zacchetti, "Prajñāpāramitā Sūtras," in *Brill's Encyclopedia of Buddhism*, vol. 1, ed. Jonathan A. Silk [Leiden: Koninklijke Brill NV], 184). A similar pattern is seen in early *jātakas*, where verses are added later (see Naomi Appleton, *Jātaka Stories in Theravāda Buddhism* [Surrey, England: Ashgate, 2010], 43, citing Hinüber). Note too J. W. De Jong, "Recent Japanese Studies on the Lalitavistara," *Indologica Taurinensia* 23, no. 4 (1997–1998): 289–49, where a more complex relationship is observed between the prose and metrical portions of the *Lalitavistara*.

47. Edward Conze, *The Perfection of Wisdom in Eight Thousand Lines and Its Verse Summary* (Bolinas, CA: Four Seasons Foundation, 1973), 202. Thanks to Sonam Kachru for pointing me to this line and similar ones in later Mahāyāna sutras.
48. Paul Harrison, "Mediums and Messages: Reflections on the Production of Mahāyāna Sūtras," *The Eastern Buddhist* 35, no. 2 (2003): 124.
49. Many aspects of the inward shift that Buddhist ritual underwent in the seventh and eighth centuries were not without precedent. Early Buddhist texts themselves represented their contemplations as internalizations of Vedic sacrifice, as did the Āraṇyakas and Upaniṣads, which included many elements of later yogic practice. For two overviews, see J. C. Heesterman, *The Inner Conflict of Tradition: Essays in Indian Ritual, Kingship, and Society* (Chicago: University of Chicago Press, 1985), 26–44, and Gavin Flood, *An Introduction to Hinduism* (Cambridge: Cambridge University Press, 1996), 75–84.
50. Eric Greene, *Chan Before Chan: Meditation, Repentance, and Visionary Experience in Chinese Buddhism* (Honolulu: University of Hawai'i Press, 2021), 205–48, even suggests that critiques of meditative visions were part of what defined early Chan, and similar warnings may be found scattered throughout writings on tantra and the Great Perfection, even as those same texts dwell at length on meditative experiences.
51. Such an argument is suggested by Robert H. Sharf, "Visualization and Mandala," in *Living Images: Japanese Buddhist Icons in Context*, ed. Robert H. Sharf and Elizabeth H. Sharf (Stanford, CA: Stanford University Press, 2001), 196, though his argument is more complex than this summary reference suggests. The Śaiva *Brahmayāmala*, 71.97 (*naṭavat paśya*), as discussed by Judit Törzsök, "Theatre, Acting and the Image of the Actor in Abhinavagupta's Tantric Sources," in *Around Abhinavagupta: Aspects of the Intellectual History of Kashmir from the Ninth to the Eleventh Century*, ed., Eli Franco and Isabelle Ratié (Berlin: LIT Verlag, 2016), 471, recommends that tantric ritual be performed by the ritualist while "seeing himself as an actor," feet astride the two worlds of actor and character, sentient being and awakened deity.
52. *Sarvabuddhasamāyogaḍākinījālasaṃvara-nāma-uttaratantra*, 9.243cd–248ab (= Toh. 366, 178b.1–4). *śamyatālasamājais tu gītavāditanartitaiḥ || śṛṅgāravīrakaruṇāhāsaro ṣabhayānakāḥ | bībhatsādbhutaśāntāś ca rasamudrārthasiddhidāḥ || śṛṅgārādirasāsa ṅgaviśvamudrāpranartanaiḥ | sarvātmamudrāyogātmā sarvāveśaḥ prasidhyati || śṛṅgāre vajrasattvas tu vīre vīras tathāgataḥ | karuṇāyāṃ vajradharo hāse lokeśvaraḥ paraḥ || vajrasūryas tu vai roṣe vajrarudro bhayānake | bībhatse śākyamunibuddhaḥ sarvārallis tathādbhute ||praśānte śāśvato buddhaḥ sarvaduḥkhopaśāntaye.* I thank

Peter Szánto for sharing his edition of these verses. This passage from the eighth-century *Sarvabuddhsamāyoga* appears to be the earliest documented example of the nine moods of Indian aesthetics appearing in any Buddhist scripture, as first noted by Kimiaki Tanaka, "*Navarasa* Theory in the *Sarvabudd hasamāyogaḍākinījālasaṃvara-tantra* Reconsidered," *Tōhō* 10 (1994): 323–31. From that point, they quickly spread throughout tantric literature; see, for example, the *Vajramāla*, 265b.2, which is explicit about the moods being drawn from the world of Indian drama (Tib. *gar*). For a discussion of the nine moods in tantric Buddhism more generally, see James F. Hartzell, "Tantric Yoga: A Study of the Vedic Precursors, Historical Evolution, Literatures, Cultures, Doctrines, and Practices of the Eleventh-Century Kasmīri Saivite and Buddhist Unexcelled Tantric Yogas" (PhD diss., Columbia University, 1997), 593–601. Probably writing in the late ninth century, Gnubs chen Sangs rgyas ye shes suggests that the nine moods may be applied to the nine vehicles of the Buddhist dharma, for teaching disciples of middling or higher wisdom (*Mun pa'i go cha*, vol. 51, 291.3).

53. *Dgongs pa 'dus pa'i mdo*, 151a.2. *mthun 'jug byis pa'i spyod pa.*
54. Sheldon Pollock, *A Rasa Reader: Classical Indian Aesthetics* (New York: Columbia University Press, 2016), 15, 21.
55. Giebel, "The Chin-Kang-Ting Ching," 179–80.
56. IOL Tib J 332, 2v.1–3. *bdag nyid bcoM ldan 'das 'bu ta he ru ka / 'bar ba' chen po gar dgu dang ldan ba' / sgegs po / dpa' 'o / 'jigs su rung ba'i cha byad can / dgod pa dang / gshe ba dang / 'dzin par byed pa dang/ snying rje chen po dang / shin tu rngam ba dang / don dam par zhi ba chos nyid kyi sku las ma g.yo pas / 'jig rten chags 'jig kyi dus ltar drag pa gcig gsal bar bsgoms ste.*
57. This same period witnessed a "revolution" in aesthetics, as *rasa* theory began to be used to discuss not only drama but also poetry, while simultaneously the focus was shifting from the affect of the actor/character in a drama to that of the audience hearing the poem. Thus, Pollock writes, "The aesthetic revolution in the tenth century brought to the fore the aesthetic subject—the audience and its response" (*A Rasa Reader*, 27). And too, regarding the place of the ninth affect of peace, he writes: "The dispute over the peaceful rasa, the emotion of emotionlessness, speaks not only to the difficult extension from performance, where it could not be represented, to narrative, where it could, but also to the movement from formalism, where it could not be embodied, to reception, where it could be felt" (15).
58. de Certeau, *Heterologies*, 83 [with my addition].

1. Ritual Manuals and the Spread of the Local

1. Although the Dunhuang manuscripts shed some light on "lived religion," the truth of this statement is relative to other, more canonical works, which tend to be more Buddha-focused and prescriptive. The manuscripts do have their own limits in this regard; they are not entirely descriptive and remain in many ways prescriptive. For precisely this reason, much of the richest evidence of

"lived religion" examined in this chapter is extratextual, in the manuals appended to sutras, the physical features of the manuscripts, the colophons, marginal drawings, and so on. Here and throughout this study, I distinguish text from manuscript: a text is a more abstract object that may (or may not) have a title, was carefully composed by an author, and can be copied and thus transmitted across time and space. Such texts are contained within manuscripts, specific exemplars usually penned by an individual hand, on a particular kind of paper, in a certain form, and so on. In this sense, the kinds of marginalia, colophons, drawings, and the like in the Dunhuang manuscripts may be called "extratextual."

2. See Jacob P. Dalton, "How Dhāraṇīs WERE Proto-Tantric: Liturgies, Ritual Manuals, and the Origins of the Tantras," in *Tantric Traditions on the Move*, ed. David B. Gray and Ryan Overbey (New York: Oxford University Press, 2016), 199–229, though much of the material found therein is included in the present chapter.
3. On the problems inherent in the Japanese Shingon classification of Esoteric Buddhism into "pure" and "miscellaneous," see Ryiūchi Abé, *The Weaving of Mantra: Kūkai and the Construction of Esoteric Buddhist Discourse* (New York: Columbia University Press, 1999), 152–57, 165–77, and 182. Abé even calls for the outright abandonment of the scheme in critical scholarship. Further complicating the picture, however, is the fact that some *dhāraṇī* sutras also appear in the tantra section (*rgyud sde*) of today's Tibetan canon.
4. See Michel Strickmann, *Mantras et mandarins: Le bouddhisme tantrique en Chine* (Paris: Gallimard, 1996), 130, and *Chinese Magical Medicine* (Stanford, CA: Stanford University Press, 2002), 103–9. For Strickmann, the main point of similarity between *dhāraṇīs* and tantras is their shared emphasis on worldly gods and demons. Such an emphasis, however, is by no means specific to *dhāraṇīs*. As Peter Skilling, "The Rakṣā Literature of the Śrāvakayāna," *Journal of the Pali Text Society* 16 (1992): 109–82; Gregory Schopen, *Bones, Stones, and Buddhist Monks* (Honolulu: University of Hawai'i Press, 1997); Robert Decaroli, *Haunting the Buddha: Indian Religions and the Formation of Buddhism* (New York: Oxford University Press, 2004), and others have noted, Buddhists were widely concerned with ghosts and worldly gods from early on.
5. See Robert H. Sharf, *Coming to Terms with Chinese Buddhism* (Honolulu: University of Hawai'i Press, 2002), 263–78, and "Buddhist Veda and the Rise of Chan," in *Chinese and Tibetan Esoteric Buddhism*, ed. Yael Bentor and Meir Shahar (Leiden: Brill, 2017), 85–120; Ronald M. Davidson, *Indian Esoteric Buddhism: A Social History of the Tantric Movement* (New York: Columbia University Press, 2002), 117 and 368 n. 12; Richard D. McBride, "Is There Really 'Esoteric' Buddhism?" *Journal of the International Association of Buddhist Studies* 27, no. 2 (2004): 329–356, and "Dhāranī and Spells in Medieval Sinitic Buddhism," *Journal of the International Association of Buddhist Studies* 28, no. 1 (2005): 85–114. The larger issue of the place of tantric Buddhism in East Asia is not entirely settled, and scholars such as Charles D. Orzech, "The 'Great Teaching of Yoga,' the Chinese Appropriation of the Tantras, and the Question of Esoteric Buddhism," *Journal of Chinese Religions* 34 (2006): 29–78; and Robert Gimello, "Manifest Mysteries: The Nature of the Exoteric/Esoteric Distinction in Later Chinese Buddhism"

(unpublished paper delivered at the Annual Meeting of the American Academy of Religion, 2006), have argued that whatever the case may have been for "esoteric" teachings in earlier periods, Chinese Buddhists from the eighth century on often did see something like "tantric" teachings as distinct from and superior to other strains of Mahāyāna, referring to them as "yoga teachings" (*yuqie jiao*), "great teachings of yoga" (*yuqie dajiao*), "teachings of the adamantine vehicle of yoga" (*yuqie jin'gangsheng jiao*), and sometimes even "esoteric teachings" (*mijiao*).

6. Thus even without the influence of East Asian scholarship, Waley coined the term "Dhāraṇī Buddhism" to describe the Buddhism of Dunhuang from the fifth to eighth centuries; Arthur Waley, *A Catalogue of Paintings Recovered from Tun-Huang* (London: British Museum, 1931), xiii–xiv. Within Buddhist writings too, as already observed in the introduction to this study, references to the *Vidyādharapiṭaka* (Spell-Holder Basket) abound from the seventh century on.
7. On *dhāraṇī* as unique to Mahāyāna Buddhism, see Jan Nattier, *A Few Good Men: The Bodhisattva Path According to The Inquiry of Ugra (Ugraparipṛcchā)* (Honolulu: University of Hawai'i Press, 2003), 291–92 n. 549. In the same note, Nattier discusses early uses of the term as a mnemonic device.
8. For some recent scholarship on the ritual uses of *dhāraṇī*, see Gregory Schopen, "The Bodhigarbhālaṅkāralakṣa and Vimaloṣṇīṣa Dhāraṇīs in Indian Inscriptions," *Wiener Zeitschrift für die Kunde Südasiens* 29 (1985): 119–49; Skilling, "The Rakṣā Literature of the Śrāvakayāna"; Paul Copp, "Manuscript Culture as Ritual Culture in Late Medieval Dunhuang: Buddhist Seals and Their Manuals," *Cahiers d'Extrême-Asie* 20 (2011): 193–226; and Koichi Shinohara, *Spells, Images, and Mandalas: Tracing the Evolution of Esoteric Buddhist Rituals* (New York: Columbia University Press, 2014).
9. The same may be said of many Buddhist sutras, but the *dhāraṇī* sutras made this fact central to their project, as is recognized already by Winternitz (in J. K. Nariman, *Literary History of Sanskrit Buddhism [From Winternitz, Sylvain Levi, Huber]* (Delhi: Motilal Banarsidass, 1992 [1919]), 116: "Many dharanis are only a kind of philosophical Sutras, the doctrines of which they are intended to present in a nutshell, but in the process it becomes less a question of the substance of the doctrine than words which are mysterious and unintelligible."
10. The term "liturgy" often refers to texts that are for public recitation within a group but is used more broadly here to indicate texts that are assembled for the purpose of ritual recitations that may be public or private.
11. Yukei Matsunaga, "A History of Tantric Buddhism with Reference to Chinese Translations," in *Buddhist Thought and Asian Civilization*, ed. Leslie S. Kawamura and Keith Scott (Emeryville, MA: Dharma Publishing, 1977), 170. Arlo Griffiths, "Written Traces of the Buddhist Past: *Mantras* and *Dhāraṇīs* in Indonesian Inscriptions," *Bulletin of the School of Oriental and African Studies* 77, no. 1 (2014): 186, observes, "none of the Indonesian inscriptions presented here comprises any part of the prose that frames the mantras or *dhāraṇīs* in their respective source texts."
12. IOL Tib J 396, 1r.5. *yi ger 'dri 'am / glegs bam la bri ste.* For the canonical equivalent, see *Jayavatī-nāma-dhāraṇī*, 213b.5.

13. On the use of *sku yon pa* (lit. "gift person") to refer to scribes writing on behalf of others, see Brandon Dotson, "The Remains of the Dharma: Editing, Rejecting, and Replacing the Buddha's Words in Royally Sponsored Sutras from Dunhuang, 820s to 840s," *Journal of the International Association of Buddhist Studies* 36/37 (2015): 11–12.
14. For the canonical Chinese and Tibetan versions of the former sutra, see T. 2897 and Toh. 1067, respectively. For some preliminary notes on it, see Gregor Ahn, "Das Sutra der 'Acht Erscheinungen': Bemerkungen zu den tibetischen Versionen," in *Religionbegenung und Kulturaustausch in Asien: Studien zum Gedenken an Hans-Joachim Klimkeit*, ed. W. Gantke, K. Hoheisel, and W. Klein (Wiesbaden: Harrassowitz, 2002), 63–71.
15. IOL Tib J 463, v2.2–4: *rke slong tru 'hu rin cen gyis / myi 'phed pa'i 'par pa'i pa 'og rtson krus gyis . . . phags pa snang rgyad dang / tshe dpag myed pa zhengs sol / pa'i sod nams gyis stobs gyis . . . pha dang / ma snga raps das pa yang mto ris gyi gnas su skye par smon*. As already discussed in the introduction, n. 30.
16. Though Skilling, "The Rakṣā Literature of the Śrāvakayāna," 138, notes there are seven sutras that can appear as part of the *Pañcarakṣā* collection. For more on the *Pañcarakṣā*, see also Pentti Aalto, "Prolegmena to an Edition of the Pañcarakṣā," *Studia Orientalia* 19 (1954): 5–48, and *Qutut-tu Pañcarakṣā Kemekü Tabun Sakiyan Neretü Yeke Kölgen Sudur* (Wiesbadan: Otto Harrassowitz, 1961); and Gergely Hidas, "*Mahāpratisarā-mahāvidyārājñī*, the Great Amulet, Great Queen of Spells. Introduction, Critical Editions and Annotated Translation" (PhD thesis, Oxford University, 2008). At least one copy of this collection is found among the Dunhuang manuscripts. Unfortunately, the collection has been split into at least six different manuscripts (five in London and one in Paris). The shelf marks, in the order they should be read, are: IOL Tib J 399, IOL Tib J 397, Pelliot tibétain 535, IOL Tib J 398, IOL Tib J 388, and IOL Tib J 394. One of the five titles is missing. The four present are the *Mahāsāhasra-pramardana*, the *Mahāśītavana*, the *Mahāpratisarā-vidyārājñī*, and the *Mahāmantra-anudhārī*. Calculating the length of the missing sutra, we see that it roughly matches that of the popular *Mahāmayūrīvidyārājñī*. The collection may have been deposited in Cave 17 due to damage, but not before the most popular of the five works, the *Mahāmayūrīvidyārājñī*, was extracted for continued use. The order of the five texts in this Dunhuang *Pañcarakṣā* is not that seen in the later canonical collections. In the *Ldan dkar ma* and the *Dkar chag 'phang thang ma*, the *Gzungs chen po lnga*, known elsewhere as the *Pañcarakṣā* (nos. 329–333) are listed as: 1. *Rma bya chen mo*; 2. *Stong chen mo rab tu 'joms pa*; 3. *Rig pa'i rgyal mo so sor 'brang ba chen mo*; 4. *Gsil ba'i tshal chen mo*; 5. *Gsang sngags rjesu 'dzin pa*. And still a different order is found in the Tibetan canon (Q. 177–181; Toh. 588–563). However, another example of the *Pañcarakṣā* in precisely the same order appears in a manuscript discovered at Tabo and probably dating from between the ninth and eleventh centuries. For these dates, see the conclusions of Paul Harrison, "Preliminary Notes on a *gZungs 'dus* Manuscript from Tabo," in *Suhllekhā: Festgabe für Helmut Eimer*, ed. M. Hahn, J.-U. Hartmann, and R. Steiner (Wisttal-Odendorf: Indica et Tibetica Verlag, 1996), 49–68. An index to a *dhāraṇī* collection, this manuscript

lists the *pañcarakṣā* in an order that matches the Dunhuang manuscript. Here, then, may be a standard set of *dhāraṇīs* in the order that circulated in early Tibet.

17. IOL Tib J 311, 1r.1: *log shig tu phyungs te / yI dam du klag pa*.
18. IOL Tib J 311, 21r.4: *wang btsun shes rab dpal gyI g.yar dam lags* so. The manuscript appears to have belonged to a subsequent owner, as another line written in a different hand has been inserted beside this one: *kwag dar ma 'I yi dam / lags s+ho*. On the etymological connections between *g.yar dam* and *yi dam*, see Dan Martin, "Review of *Facets of Tibetan Religious Tradition and Contacts with Neighbouring Cultural Areas, Orientalia Venetiana Series* no. 12," *The Tibet Journal* 29, no. 1 (2004): 93. Several of the *dhāraṇi*-based liturgical collections from Dunhuang include colophons stating that the liturgies contained therein are to be recited as their owner's "daily commitment" (*yi dam*). These collections may have been intended for recitation in toto. In addition to the present example, see also IOL Tib J 312/4, 21r.4; IOL Tib J 353/1, 3r.1; and IOL Tib J 463/1, r11.2. For a different example of *yi dam* being used in this sense, see Pelliot tibétain 996, 2r, where the late-eighth-century Tibetan monk Nam ka'i snying po is said to have observed a *yi dam* of abiding in the *dhūtā-guṇas*; Pelliot tibétain 996, 2r.4–5: *dbyangs pa'I yon tan gI chos yI dam du blangs te* (with *dbyangs sic* for *sbyangs*).
19. Pelliot tibétain 49/4, l. 34–35: *'phags pa kun tu bzang po zhes bya ba'i gzungs las/ sngags dang cho ga logs gcig tu bkol te phyung ba rdzogs s+ho*.
20. Many of the Dunhuang *dhāraṇī* collections are incomplete, so their order is difficult to discern, but for some particularly clear examples of this order, see IOL Tib J 316 and 366 and Pelliot tibétain 22, 23, 24. Cases of the invitation appearing in the middle of the collection also do occur; see IOL Tib J 466 (discussed below) for an example. Skilling, "The Rakṣā Literature of the Śrāvakayāna," 122, notes a similar pattern in the *paritta* texts: "In all of these collections," he writes, "the canonical *paritta* texts are set within ancillary opening and closing verses (*paritta-parikamma*, etc.)." Skilling also points out that "If a collection of Sri Lankan *parittas* were published along with all such preliminaries, admonitions, ceremonies, and rites, in both contents and length it would resemble one of the composite *Pañcarakṣā* texts, minus, of course, the *mantras*" (144). Several *dhāraṇīsaṃgraha* from Dunhuang include an offering *dhāraṇī* or prayer immediately following the invitation; see the entry to IOL Tib J 369 in Jacob Dalton and Sam van Schaik, *Tibetan Tantric Manuscripts from Dunhuang: A Descriptive Catalogue of the Stein Collection at the British Library* (Leiden: Brill, 2006), 102. In the same article, Skilling notes that no fewer than ten Śrāvakayāna *rakṣā* texts are classified as *Kriyā* tantras (161).
21. The separate *dhāraṇī* section appears only in those *bka' 'gyur* collections stemming from the *Tshal pa* edition. See Helmut Eimer, *Der Tantra-Katalog des Bu ston im Verglieich mit der Abteilung Tantra des tibetischen Kanjur* (Bonn: Indica et Tibetica Verlag, 1989), 40 n. 7.
22. For a discussion of these final *gāthās*, see Skilling, "The Rakṣā Literature," 129–37, where Skilling demonstrates how many of them are extracted from earlier sutras. He also translates from the index (*dkar chag*) to the *Golden Tanjur* a justification for including in the canon the closing *gāthās*: "In order to make fruitful

the work that has [just been] completed [the copying of the *Tanjur*], the dedications (*bsngo ba* = *pariṇamanā*), aspirations (*smon lam* = *praṇidhāna*), and blessings (*bkra śis* = *maṅgala*) [follow]" (Skilling, "The Rakṣā Literature of the Śrāvakayāna," 131).

23. Pelliot tibétain 22, R1.8: *zab mo rgyal ba'i bka' la kun gson cig*. While several Dunhuang versions share this ending (e.g. Pelliot tibétain 24, r4.4 and Pelliot tibétain 26, r2.3–4), others end differently, though with a similar sentiment; see, for example, IOL Tib J 316, v3.2–3: "All those who live in this universe, listen!" (*'jig rten 'khams 'dir gnas pa kun gson cig*). Further work is necessary to determine the relationships among the multiple versions of this much-varied work. My comments here are only meant to represent its general form and ritual purpose.
24. Pelliot tibétain 25, 1v.4: *skabs 'dir mdo sde 'am zhal . . . gsungs pa'i tshigs bcad klag*. Unfortunately, the folio is damaged in the middle of the line. Although this line does not appear in the canonical versions, what follows it is present (compare *Rgyud gsum pa*, 3b.4). Lalou mistook these final lines for the beginning of a new text. See Marcelle Lalou, *Inventaire de Manuscrits tibétains de Touen-houang*, 3 vols. (Paris: Libraire d'Amérique et d'Orient 1939–1961), vol. I, 9.
25. The standard Nyingma narrative of the origin of the tantras begins with a King Dza who receives the teachings after a series of seven dreams over the course of seven nights. That narrative shares elements in common with the legend of how the *Karaṇḍavyūha Sūtra* first arrived in Tibet by descending into the hands of King Lha tho tho ri. On these early myths see Rolf A. Stein, *Tibetan Civilization* (Stanford, CA: Stanford University Press, 1972), 51; Samten Karmay, "King Tsa/Dza and Vajrayāna," *Mélanges chinois et bouddhiques* 20 (1981): 192–211; Dudjom Rinpoche, *The Nyingma School of Tibetan Buddhism*, 2 vols., trans. Gyurme Dorje (Boston: Wisdom, 1991), vol. 1, 508. Another possibly related version of the story appears in the Chinese work, T. 1332, which describes a ritual in which the ruler climbs to the top of a tall building and pays respect to the buddhas of the ten directions. Shinohara, *Spells, Images, and Mandalas*, 12, suggests that the ruler climbs to a height so that he can more directly address the buddhas in their distant lands. In a note (232 n. 32), Shinohara also highlights the possibly related story of Sumāgadhā, Anāthapiṇḍatha's daughter, who addresses the distant buddha from atop a tall tower. The narrative in IOL Tib J 711 may have emerged from this same narrative mix; see Jacob P. Dalton, *Taming of the Demons: Violence and Liberation in Tibetan Buddhism* (New Haven, CT: Yale University Press, 2011), 62–64.
26. After this, the rest of the commentary proceeds through the *Invitation* prayer, discussing each god and demon named, until the end where it returns to the ritual setting within which the invitations are to be read. Final advice is dispensed on which substances are to be offered to particular gods or demons the reader seeks to invoke. And special attention is given to the *nāgas*, whom we might conclude were of particular concern for these early Tibetans.
27. On these manuscripts and their scribing, see Dotson, "The Remains of the Dharma."

28. In discussing the same manuscript for its mention of King Khri Srong lde brtsan, Van Schaik and Doney have made similar observations regarding its format and possible date. See Sam van Schaik and Lewis Doney, "The Prayer, the Priest and the Tsenpo: An Early Buddhist Narrative from Dunhuang," *Journal of the International Association of Buddhist Studies* 30, no. 1–2 (2018): 175–217.
29. On the former contexts, see Schopen, *Bones, Stones, and Buddhist Monks*, 207–8 and 231–33. On the latter, see Jonathan Silk, *Managing Monks: Administrators and Administrative Roles in Indian Buddhist Monasticism* (Oxford and New York: Oxford University Press, 2008), 80–81.
30. For a translation of the relevant passage, see Sylvain Lévi, "Sur la récitation primitive des texts bouddhiques," *Journal Asiatique* 11, no. 6 (1915): 401–47 and 432–34, and J. Takakusu, *A Record of the Buddhist Religion as Practiced in India and the Malay Archipelago* (Oxford: Clarendon Press, 1896), 152–53, as referenced by Schopen, *Bones, Stones, and Buddhist Monks*, 232.
31. IOL Tib J 466, 2r.20. For more on the *tridaṇḍaka* in India and its melodic recitation in particular, see Gregory Schopen, "On Incompetent Monks and Able Urbane Nuns in a Buddhist Monastic Code," *Journal of Indian Philosophy* 38, no. 2 (2010): 118.
32. IOL Tib J 466, 2v.2–3. *phywa'i rgyal thabs mnga' brnyes shing / chab srId gnam gyI lde mtshon can / 'phrul rje khrI srong lde brtsan.* Translation following that of van Schaik and Doney, "The Prayer, the Priest and the Tsenpo," 195. See also Lewis Doney, "Imperial Gods: A Ninth-Century *Tridaṇḍaka* Prayer (*rGyud chags gsum*)," *Central Asiatic Journal (Special Issue: Old Tibet and Its Neighbors)* 61, no. 1 (2018): 188.
33. For a brief discussion of the item, see Sam van Schaik, "The Uses of Implements Are Different: Reflections on the Functions of Tibetan Manuscripts," in *Tibetan Manuscript and Xylograph Traditions: The Written Word and Its Media Within the Tibetan Cultural Sphere*, ed. Orna Almogi (Hamburg: Department of Indian and Tibetan Studies, Universität Hamburg, 2016), 226–28.
34. Ryan Overbey, "Vicissitudes of Text and Rite in the *Great Peahen Queen of Spells*," in *Tantric Traditions in Transmission and Translation*, ed. David B. Gray and Ryan R. Overbey (New York: Oxford University Press, 2016), 257–83, analyzes the developments seen across the various Chinese translations of this sutra. As he explains, T. 984 is the first to include a ritual manual, though still with no image worship. Overbey also observes that T. 988, an earlier, fifth-century translation, includes a list of decorations for creating an elaborate ritual space but no instructions on how they are to be arranged. For the ritual manual section in the (eighth-century) Tibetan translation, which almost matches that of T. 984, see *Mahāmāyūrīvidyārājñī*, 116b.1ff.
35. Gimello, "Manifest Mysteries," 2. Divākara (613–688) completed his translation (T. 1007) in 685 or 686, and Vajrabodhi's (T. 1075) dates from 723 and Amoghavajra's (T. 1077) from between 742 and 774. Kieshnick has observed the same pattern, though perhaps not that it was already beginning to take shape in the sixth and seventh centuries: "With the three great Tang ritual specialists Amoghavajra, Vajrabodhi, and Śubakarasiṃha [*sic*] . . . it was no longer enough to chant a common spell; spell-casting now required expertise in a vast body of

technical, esoteric lore" (John Kieshnick, *The Eminent Monk: Buddhist Ideals in Medieval Chinese Hagiography* [Honolulu: University of Hawai'i Press, 1997], 89–90). Further evidence lies in related observations made in passing by other scholars. Skilling has noted the ritual "annexes" in the later recensions of the *Mahāsamāja-sūtra*, as well as in the Tibetan *Bhadrakarātrī* and the Central Asian Sanskrit *Nagaropama-sūtra* (Peter Skilling, *Mahāsūtras*, 2 vols. [Oxford: Pali Text Society, 1994–1997], vol. 2, 533–35). In personal correspondence, October 18, 2004, he also confirms that early on, "In the Theravada lineage the texts—*paritta* and other *rakṣās*—were memorized and also written, but the rites rarely. . . . It seems the specifics of the rite are transmitted orally and by example."

36. The *Mahāpratisarāvidyārājñī*, perhaps dating to the late sixth or early seventh century, is a good example of a *dhāraṇī* sutra with ritual techniques (specifically for drawing a *dhāraṇī* amulet) relatively well integrated. It also includes, however, a final ritual section for curing the ill (also discussed in chapter 2) that serves as a kind of appendix. For more on this sutra, see Hidas, "*Mahāpratisarā*."
37. Schopen, "The *Bodhigarbhālaṅkāralakṣa*," 144. For some additional observations on these texts using the Dunhuang manuscripts, see Christina Scherrer-Schaub, "Some Dhāraṇī Written on Paper Functioning as Dharmakāya Relics: A Tentative Approach to PT 350," in *Tibetan Studies: Proceedings of the 6th Seminar of the International Association for Tibetan Studies*, 2 vols. (Oslo: Insitute for Comparative Research in Human Culture. 1994), vol. 2, 711–27. For the Tibetan translations of the two sutras named, see Toh. 599 and 625, respectively.
38. Schopen, "The *Bodhigarbhālaṅkāralakṣa*," 145. However, the situation is not quite as simple as Schopen makes out, for the former work does nonetheless include a short manual involving a square mandala altar (*Samantamukha-praveśa*, 257a.7–257b.5) and make repeated reference to a "ritual manual for the recitations" (*bzlas brjod kyi cho ga*) that should be performed (see 255a.6 and 258a.3); it is perhaps the latter that the **Sarvaprajñā* provides.
39. *Dkar chag 'phang thang ma*, 23–24. For more on this catalogue, see Georgios T. Halkias, "Tibetan Buddhism Registered: Imperial Archives from the Palace-Temple of 'Phang-thang,'" *The Eastern Buddhist* 36, nos. 1 & 2 (2004): 46–105.
40. Deleanu notes a similar, perhaps even clearer, difference between the Indian and Chinese understandings of early Mahāyāna meditation texts: "From a thematic point of view, the *śrāvakabhūmi* belongs to the substantial corpus of texts dedicated to the presentation and elucidation of the [*sic*] spiritual cultivation. As far as I know, there is no traditional Indian term denoting this genre. The Chinese Buddhists, faced with an impressive number of such translations (as well as apocrypha), coined terms like *chanjing* 禪經 'meditation scripture.'" Florin Dealeanu, *The Chapter on the Mundane Path (Laukikamārga) in the Śrāvakabhūmi: A Trilingual Edition (Sanskrit, Tibetan, Chinese), Annotated Translation and Introductory Study*, 2 vols. (Tokyo: International Institute for Buddhist Studies, 2006), 157.
41. As we shall see in chapter 3, a similar change occurred for the Buddhist *sādhana*, which began as part of the *sevā-sādhana* pairing and gradually, perhaps around the late seventh century, emerged as a subgenre of stand-alone ritual manuals.

42. The shift from the earlier recitation-based practices to those also focusing on an image has been observed by Shinohara, *Spells, Images, and Mandalas*, 13–14.
43. Sharf, "Buddhist Veda and the Rise of Chan," 100, writes, "In contrast [to ordination spaces], altars or *maṇḍalas* used in the worship of deities were often elevated." It may have been truer in China than in India that the mandala-altars made for worshipping buddhas in early *dhāraṇī-vidhis* were "often" elevated. Most passages describing such altars are not entirely clear, but they rarely mention the raising of a platform. Modern-day practice in South Asia makes no such distinction and leaves us to conclude that altars are more often at ground level. This said, the *Uṣṇīṣavijayā* rituals studied in chapter 2 do seem to be distinguished by a preference for platforms. In the same article, Sharf (101–2) also suggests that the seventh-century Chinese scholar Daoxuan's image of the monastic ordination space as an elaborate structure with a stupa at its center was formed under the influence of the bodhisattva precept platforms. I would suggest that said influence may also have come from the nascent tradition of tantric initiation, even if not recognized as such and filtered through Chinese interests in the bodhisattva precepts. (Atikūṭa performed his mandala initiation ceremony at Huirisi monastery in 651, sixteen years before Daoxuan's death in 667, so such tantric ideas were already beginning to circulate in China at the time.) I accept Sharf's overall point that Chinese Buddhists of the seventh and especially eighth centuries seem to have conflated the precept ceremony with tantric initiation and therefore may not have recognized the influences of tantric Buddhism as such; indeed, such tantra was only just starting to gain its own identity at the time in India.
44. *Jayavatī-nāma-mahāvidyārāja-dhāraṇī*, 187b.1. *ba'i lci bas dkyil 'khor bskus*. Similar instructions to smear cow dung on the ground are seen regularly; see for example *Vajrapāṇyabhiṣeka-mahātantra*, 75a.2, and *Mañjuśrīmūlatantra*, 269a.5.
45. *Mahāvairocanābhisaṁbodhi*, 162a.2. *gzhi rab tu 'thas par bcags te / ba'i lci ba sa la ma lhung ba dang ba'i gcin du bsras pas byug go*; corresponding to Stephen Hodge, *The Mahā-vairocana-abhisaṃbodhi, with Buddhaguhya's Commentary* (London: Routledge Curzon, 2003), 90.
46. Pelliot tibétain 49/4, ll. 143–154. *cho ga ni ri mo mkhan khrims brgyad bzung bas / ras tshon sna tshogs dang / ma 'dres pa dkar po la / sangs rgyas bcom ldan 'das gi sku gzugs bri / 'phags pa spyan ras gzigs dbang phyug gi gzugs ral pa dang / cod pan can ri dags e ne ya'i pags pa thogs pa / gu lang gi cha byad 'dzin pa / rgyan thams cad gis brgyan par 'bri 'o / de nas sgrub pa pos / sku gzugs de'i spyan sngar / ba lang gi lci ba'i skyil 'khor bgyis te / men tog bkram la spos chab kyis bltam ba'i bum pa brgyad bzhag ste / mchod pa brgyad dang / mchod pa sna drug cu rtsa bzhi dang / sha khrag ma mchis pa'i gtor ma sbyar la / a ga ru'i bdug spos kyis bdug cing / rig sngags brgyad stong bzlas par bgyi 'o / nyi zhag gsum mam / nyin zhag gcig du zas dkar po sna gsum 'tshal zhing / dus gsum du khrus bgyis la / gos gtsang ma bgos te bzlas par bgyis 'o / de nas sku gzugs gi spyan sngar / bdag 'bar bar mthong bar 'gyur te / de mthong nas / dga' bar 'gyur ba nas / 'phags pa spyan ras gzigs dbang phyug nyid gshegs te / bsam ba thams cad rdzogs par mdzad pa'i bar du 'gyur ro / ldong ros sam lug pu myig la sngags kyis btab ste/ myig bskus na / myi snang bar 'gyur te / nam ka la 'gro bar 'gyur ro / don yod pa'i ye shes zhes bya ba'i ting nge 'dzin kyang thob par 'gyur / ci 'tshal ba de yang 'grub*

par 'gyur te / 'di ni bsgrub pa 'o. The eight precepts (*aṣṭaśīla*) appear in the *Vinaya* as abstinence from (1) killing; (2) stealing; (3) sexual activity; (4) lying; (5) alcohol; (6) eating after noon; (7) dancing, singing, and wearing perfumes and jewelry; and (8) sitting on high seats. The final lines that follow this *vidhi* are slightly different in the Dunhuang version compared to both the canonical Tibetan and the received Sanskrit, perhaps indicating the late addition of these lines that were written to tie the *vidhi* back into the rest of the sutra. See R. O. Meisezahl, "The *Amoghapāśahṛdaya-dhāraṇī*: The Early Sanskrit Manuscript of the Reiunji, Critically Edited and Translated," *Monumenta Nipponica* 17 (1962): 312 and 328.

47. Shinohara, *Spells, Images, and Mandalas*, 53.
48. T. 972, 365a6–9. For more on the passage, see chapter 2.
49. *Vajravidāraṇa-nāma-dhāraṇīvyākhyāna-vajrāloka*, 163b.7–164b.2. While the attribution of this commentary to Padmasambhava is unproven, its Indian pedigree is clear enough from its grammatic forms.
50. For a description and translation of an *upasampada kammavaca*, see Dickson 1874, reprinted in H. C. Warren, *Buddhism in Translation* (Cambridge, MA: Harvard University Press, 1896), 393–401. My thanks to Charlie Hallisey and Peter Skilling for their assistance on these points. The short (just one folio side) *Daśaśikṣāvidhi* (*Bslab pa bcu'i cho ga*) is preserved in the modern *Bstan 'gyur*, where it is attributed to the omnipresent Nāgārjuna. Its content consists of the triple refuge, a prayer that the gathered readers (*bdag ming 'di zhes pa gyi bdus*) henceforth refrain from a list of negative behaviors, another that they train in the teachings, and a final one that, once again, they refrain from a still further list of negative behaviors. The lines are punctuated with a prayer that their "master" (Skt. *ācārya*; Tib. *slob dpon*) think of them. Unfortunately, the origins of this brief work remain obscure.
51. Daniel B. Stevenson, *The T'ien-t'ai Four Fourms of Samādhi and Late North-South Dynasties, Sui, and Early T'ang Buddhist Devotionalism* (PhD diss., Columbia University, 1987), 440–41. On the *saptapūjā*, see too Kate Crosby and Andrew Skilton, *Śāntideva: The Bodhicaryāvatāra* (Oxford: Oxford University Press, 1995), 9–13, where the worship is traced to the second century C.E.
52. Richard Gombrich, "The Monk in the Pāli Vinaya: Priest or Wedding Guest?," *Journal of the Pali Text Society* 21 (1995): 197. Gombrich makes this point in disagreeing with an earlier piece by Gregory Schopen ("The Ritual Obligations and Donor Roles of Monks in the Pāli *Vinaya*," later republished in Schopen, *Bones, Stones, and Buddhist Monks*, 72–85), in which the latter suggests that monks' roles in life-cycle rites were more central than most scholars assume.
53. Dating of the *Consecration Sutra* according to Ōmura Seigai, as cited by Michel Strickmann, "The *Consecration Sūtra:* A Buddhist Book of Spells," in *Chinese Buddhist Apocrypha*, ed. Robert E. Buswell (Honolulu: University of Hawai'i Press, 1990), 80 and 110 n. 12. On this sutra, see also Davidson, *Indian Esoteric Buddhism*, 127–29, and more recently, "Some Observations on an Uṣṇīṣa Abhiṣeka Rite in Atikūṭa's *Dhāraṇīsaṃgraha*," in *Transformation and Transfer of Tantra/Tantrism in Asia and Beyond*, ed. István Keul (Berlin: Walter de Gruyter, 2012), 77–97. In the

later paper (79–80), Davidson largely dismisses the significance of the *Consecration Sutra*'s short *abhiṣeka* rite within the "lineal continuum" of rituals that led to the tantras. Observing, "the purpose of the rite is the transmission of a text, instead of entry into the mandala," he suggests that it should be understood as "a Chinese ritual primarily based on literary examples and perhaps on hearing Indian narratives of royal consecration." Nonetheless, it remains a witness to the gradual rise of ritual manuals and more complex ritual forms from the fifth century on. Also important to consider is the so-called *Yogalehrbuch* and the fifth-century meditation manuals studied by Yamabe. While the received Chinese translation of the *Yogalehrbuch* dates from the fifth century, as Yamabe recognizes, "the dating of the *YL* itself is not definite" (Nobuyoshi Yamabe, "The Significance of the '*Yogalehrbuch*' for the Investigation into the Origin of Chinese Meditation Texts," *Buddhist Culture* 9 [1999]: 4). The possibility of Buddhist meditation manuals circulating in India before the fifth century must be taken seriously. Such hypothetical works again raise the question of what exactly qualifies as a ritual manual. In any case, the facts that such manuals no longer exist and our earliest extant evidence of them dates from the fifth century are significant. For more on Chinese ritual manuals from Dunhuang, see Copp, "Manuscript Culture as Ritual Culture in Late Medieval Dunhuang," and "Writing Buddhist Liturgies in Dunhuang: Hints of Ritualist Craft," in *Language and Religion*, ed. Robert A. Yelle, Courtney Handman, and Christoph I. Lehrich (Berlin: De Gruyter, 2019), 68–86.

54. See the *Da jiyi shenzhou jing*; T. 1335. Unfortunately, this ascription, as is the case with many by such Chinese translators (see Strickmann, "The *Consecration Sūtra*," 79) is not necessarily reliable. Tanyao was a highly reputed monk of the sort that might attract false attributions. The Taishō lists him as the translator of three works in all. For his other two translations, he worked as part of a two-man team, whereas for the *Dhāraṇī of Great Benefit* he is said to have worked alone. Moreover, both of his other works are thoroughly exoteric in content. My thanks to Koichi Shinohara for his help on these points. Similarly, Yi-liang Chou, "Tantrism in China," *Harvard Journal of Asiatic Studies* 8 (1945): 242, discusses a third-century Chinese translation of the *Mātaṅgī-sūtra* that contains "directions for the worship of stars and some simple rites for sacrificing to them . . . including instructions for necessary ceremonies during the recitation of the dhāraṇīs. One of these rites is performed by lighting a great fire and throwing flowers into it at the end of the recitation." This sutra was translated into Chinese at least four times, and the *homa* rites appear only in the latest of these (T. 1300), which dates from the middle or end of the fifth century. On dating the latter, see Strickmann, *Mantras et mandarins*, 435 n. 88, citing the work of Hayashiya Tomojirō. Once again, my thanks to Koichi Shinohara for his help.

55. Hodge, *The Mahā-vairocana-abhisaṃbodhi*, 8, mistakenly dates the manual in question to a 342 CE translation of the *Mahāmāyūri*, but no such appendix is to be found in that location. Hodge identifies the text with T. 1331, which is actually the abovementioned *Consecration Sūtra*. Instead, a *vidhi* section containing

precisely the same ritual procedures Hodge describes is found as an appendix to Sanghabhara's translation (T. 984).

56. On the development of similar ritual spaces within Brahmanical circles, see Shingo Einoo and Jun Takasima, eds., *From Material to Deity: Indian Rituals of Consecration* (New Delhi: Manohar, 2005). It seems the *gṛhya-pariśiṣṭhas*, which are the focus of much of Einoo's work, predated the Buddhist *dhāraṇī* manuals and may have served as a developmental bridge between the earlier Vedic and the later (Brahmanical and Buddhist) tantric rituals. Such questions are beyond the scope of the present study.
57. Following the dating of Stephen Hodge, "Considerations on the Dating and Geographical Origins of the *Mahāvairocanābhisambodhi-sūtra*," in *The Buddhist Forum*, 6 vols., ed. Tadeusz Skorupski and Ulrich Pagel (London: School of Oriental and African Studies, 1995), vol. 3, 65.
58. See his *Dhyānottarapaṭala*, 11b.1–3. Nyangral makes a similar distinction; see *Slob dpon padma'i rnam thar zangs gling ma bzhugs* (Chengdu, China: Si khron mi rigs dpe skrun khang, 1989), 63.
59. Under "distinct tantras" he lists works like the *Mahāvairocana-abhisaṃbodhi* and the *Vajrapāṇyabhiṣeka*. He also lists the *Vidyādharapiṭaka* and the *Bodhimaṇḍa*, neither of which has been firmly identified. In his *Piṇḍārtha*, 4a.6, he further adds to this subclass the *Trisamayarāja*, and the *Trikāyauṣṇīṣa*. The *Susiddhikara*, 184b.5–6, even references the existence of "*kalpas* and *dhāraṇī-vidhi*" as sources for alternative ways of performing certain rites.
60. Around this same time, i.e., the early seventh century, alongside the compiling of multiple ritual manuals into single works, a parallel development began within the iconographic sphere, with multiple deities (rather than *vidhis*) being gathered into more complex mandalas (rather than *saṃgrahas* or *tantras*); see, for example, Atikūṭa's mid-seventh-century *Tuoluoni ji jing* (T. 901), which has been discussed extensively by both Davidson, "Some Observations," and Koichi Shinohara, "The All-Gathering Maṇḍala Initiation Ceremony in Atikūṭa's Collected Dhāraṇī Scriptures: Reconstructing the Evolution of Esoteric Buddhist Ritual," *Journal Asiatique* 298, no. 2 (2010): 389–420, and *Spells, Images, and Mandalas*. In the same article, Davidson (23) refers to Atikūṭa's work as the "earliest surviving tantric documents." Though it too is titled the *Dhāraṇīsaṃgraha*, Atikūṭa's work is different from the liturgical collections in the present chapter, though the title reflects, once again, the continuities between early *dhāraṇī* ritual compilations and the first tantras.
61. See, for example, Matsunaga, "A History of Tantric Buddhism;" Skilling, *Mahāsūtras*; Donald S. Lopez, Jr., *Elaborations on Emptiness: Uses of the Heart Sūtra* (Princeton, NJ: Princeton University Press, 1996), 78–104.
62. As Ronald Davidson observes, despite *dhāraṇī* ritual manuals' generic influences on the tantras, such manuals continued to be written after the rise of the tantras, and much of this material was unaffected by their methods. "Sources and Inspirations," in *Esoteric Buddhism and the Tantras in East Asia: A Handbook for Scholars*, ed. Charles Orzech (Leiden: Brill, 2011), 23.
63. Of course, the fifth- and sixth-century authors of *dhāraṇī* ritual manuals had no idea that a new genre of *buddhavācana* would emerge in the seventh and

eighth centuries, but insofar as any historical narrative is possible only from some kind of teleological perspective, even if the historian is careful not to think anachronistically about any given period, ritual manuals may be said to be proto-tantric. The same appears to have been the case for early tantric Śaivism. Discussions of tantric Śaiva material in early works such as the *Niśvāsatattvasaṃhitā*, for example, speak of multiple, no longer extant *kalpas* or *mantrakalpas* that circulated as supplements to tantric literature proper. (I thank Shaman Hatley for his observations on this point.) Richard Davis has similarly noted a proliferation of *paddhatis* (ritual manuals that "follow in the footprints" of the Śaiva *āgamas*) from at least the tenth century; see Davis, *Ritual in an Oscillating Universe: Worshiping Śiva in Medieval India* (Princeton, NJ: Princeton University Press, 1991), 15–16.

64. Davidson, *Indian Esoteric Buddhism*, 117.
65. Davidson, "Sources and Inspirations," 23, and *Indian Esoteric Buddhism*, 118.
66. Ram Sharan Sharma, "Early Medieval Indian Society: A Study in Feudalisation," *Indian Historical Review* 1, no. 1 (1974): 2, writes that "The Gupta period saw a strong feudalization of the state apparatus which is not to be found in Mauryan times." Sharma goes on to trace the feudalization process back to the first century CE, when the practice of making land grants to the brahmins first began, though it did not become widespread, especially among secular recipients, until somewhat later; see Brajadulal Chattopadhyaya, *The Making of Early Medieval India* (Delhi: Oxford University Press, 1994), 11.

2. From *Dhāraṇī* to Tantra

1. The missing mantras may be reconstructed in part by comparison with IOL Tib J 384, r3.1.
2. The handwriting is a well-penned and somewhat generic *dbu can* that matches none of van Schaik's ninth-century styles; nor is there any double *tsheg*. The genitive and ergative *'i/'is* particles are sometimes, though not always unattached. While none of these factors is decisive, they generally point to a tenth-century date. On paleographic dating of Dunhuang manuscripts, see Sam van Schaik, "Dating Early Tibetan Manuscripts," and Brandon Dotson, "Misspelling 'Buddha': The Officially Commissioned Tibetan *Aparimiāyur-nāma mahāyāna-sūtras* from Dunhuang and the Study of Old Tibetan Orthography," *Bulletin of the School of Oriental and African Studies* 79, no. 1 (2016): 129–51. I have suggested the importance of the intersyllabic double *tsheg* (:), which can also become a lowered "midline" *tsheg*, as a marker of a ninth-century date. Indeed, I have found this to be the most reliable marker proposed so far. Occasional exceptions may be found; the Tibetan script on Or. 8210/S.95, for example, belongs to the tenth century, as it is penned on the verso of a Chinese almanac dated to 956 C.E. (see Jacob P. Dalton and Sam van Schaik, *Tibetan Tantric Manuscripts from Dunhuang: A Descriptive Catalogue of the Stein Collection at the British Library* [Leiden: Brill, 2006], 347), yet it exhibits a few (still rare) double *tshegs*. But a survey of the fifty-one

manuscripts identified by Tsuguhito Takeuchi, "Old Tibetan Buddhist Texts from the Post-Tibetan Imperial Period (Mid–9 C. to Late 10 C.)," in *Old Tibetan Studies*, ed. Cristina Scherrer-Schaub (Leiden: Brill, 2012), 205–14, as postimperial works reveals that the double *tsheg* is used rarely, if ever, in any of them. Further work needs to be done on how common the double *tsheg* is across all imperial-period manuscripts, but it is evident that manuscripts with a preponderance of double *tshegs* date from before the tenth century.

3. *Sarvadurgatipariśodhana*, 60a.7. *sdug bsngal gcig nas gcig tu brgyud ba myong zhing myong bar 'gyur ro.*
4. Under the patronage of Empress Wu Zetian (624–705), it is said to have been translated into Chinese no less than four times within a nine-year period, between 679 and 688. On the translation and deployment of the sutra under Empress Wu, see Jinhua Chen, "*Śarīra* and Scepter: Empress Wu's Political Use of Buddhist Relics," *Journal of the International Association of Buddhist Studies* 25, nos. 1–2 (2002): 103ff. Chen provides a list of all ten of the Chinese translations; see 105 n. 188. Most influential has been the translation by Buddhapālita, completed in 683. At least four copies of the sutra in Tibetan also appear among the Dunhuang documents (Pelliot tibétain 6/3, 54, 74, and 368; the latter is the only complete copy), and several early Sanskrit manuscript copies are extant, of which I have only been able to consult "The Los Angeles Manuscript" transcribed and translated by Gregory Schopen in an unpublished, if remarkably well-penned, document (my thanks to Paul Copp for providing the latter). On the *Uṣṇīṣavijayā* in Pāli, see Peter Skilling, *Buddhism and Buddhist Literature of South-East Asia: Selected Papers*, ed. Claudio Cicuzza (Bangkok: Fragile Palm Leaves Foundation, 2009).
5. IOL Tib J 712, 4r.2–3. *a la la sangs rgyas / a la la chos / a la la dge 'dun.*
6. Instead of the exclamation, "*a la la*," Pelliot tibétain 368, verso lines 42–43, reads "*kye ma'u*" for: *kye ma'u / sangs rgyas kye ma'u / chos kye ma'u / gzungs 'di 'dra ba / 'jigs rten du mngon bar byung.* However, both the canonical sutra (*Uṣṇīṣavijayā-dhāraṇī*, 248a.2) and Pelliot tibétain 54, 15v.1 (which apparently represents a different Tibetan translation from that found in Pelliot tibétain 368) read *a la la.* The Sanskrit reads *aho.*
7. *Samantamukha-praveśa*, 255b.1. *a la la sangs rgyas / a la la rig sngags / a la la chos.* For the list of animals, see 252b.4–5. The sutra also includes a rite in which one recites the *dhāraṇī* twenty-one times over dirt that is then scattered over the bones of the deceased to free them from negative rebirths, resembling a rite in the *Uṣṇīṣavijayā*; compare *Samantamukha-praveśa*, 258b.5 to Toh. 597, 247b.1–2. That it was known in early Tibet is indicated by Pelliot tibétain 78 and 336, which mention its title and two copies of its extracted spell, respectively, as well as IOL Tib J 435, a work on *stūpas* that includes the spell (at 2r.4–3v.4). This *Samantamukha-praveśa* is the same work discussed in chapter 1 for its close relationship with the *Sarvaprajñā-dhāraṇī.*
8. For this list, see IOL Tib J 384, v8.2–3: "first as a monkey, second as a tiger and a lion, third as a tawny bear and a red bear, fourth as a crow and a *sgeg ga*(?); fifth as a dog and a pig; sixth as a snake" (*'gro ba ris drug la / sbre'u sde gcig / stag dang seng ge dang gnyis / dom dang dred dang gsum / bya rog dang skeg ga dang bzhi / khyi*

dang phag dang lnga / sbrul dang drug). In IOL Tib J 384, the patricidal prince is named Ajātaśatru (Ma skyes dgra), the fifth-century B.C.E. Indian king of Buddhist legend infamous for his supposed patricide (for more on this figure in Buddhist literature, see Michael Radich, *How Ajātaśatru Was Reformed: The Domestication of "Ajase" and Stories in Buddhist History* [Tokyo: The International Institute for Buddhist Studies of the International College for Postgraduate Buddhist Studies, 2011]). The *Vajravidāraṇa-dhāraṇī* focuses on him in its own framing narrative.

9. For a discussion of the eight copies, see Yoshirō Imaeda, "The *History of the Cycle of Birth and Death*: A Tibetan Narrative from Dunhuang," in *Contributions to the Cultural History of Early Tibet*, ed. Matthew Kapstein and Brandon Dotson (Leiden: Brill, 2007), 109–14.
10. Imaeda, "The *History of the Cycle of Birth and Death*," 119.
11. That the *Story* (or "*History*," as Imaeda translates the term *lo rgyus*) is a postmortuary tale may be the *only* factor that links it to the *Sarvadurgatipariśodhana*. In contemporary Tibetan and Newar Buddhist circles, the *Uṣṇīṣavijayā-dhāraṇī* tends to be used for long-life rituals and the tantra for funerary rites, a difference partly reflected in the two works' different framing narratives; in the *dhāraṇī*, the god is soon to die and the rituals are taught to prolong his life span, while in the tantra, the god died seven days earlier and the rites are taught to ensure a better rebirth. However, the *dhāraṇī* also encourages its use in funerary settings. Its funerary associations are expressed most eloquently in the arrangement of the south wall of Dunhuang Cave 3, with a Tangut painting of an *Uṣṇīṣavijayā* mandala, an Amitāyus buddhafield, and a *Sarvadurgatipariśodhana* mandala, read from left to right.
12. Observing that the actual spell of the *Uṣṇīṣavijayā* is not supplied in the *Story*, Imaeda concludes that perhaps "The [*Uṣṇīṣavijayā*] formula announced by Śākyamuni in our *History* was later replaced by the fundamental formula of the *Sarvadurgatipari śodhanatantra*, which, as we have noticed earlier . . . , is plausibly the source of inspiration for the framework of our *History*" (Imaeda, "The *History of the Cycle of Birth and Death*," 169). Imaeda's conclusions in this regard, which he himself presents as tentative, are based on a reading of the *Story*'s final line, *bsngo' ba*. The latter verb can mean "to dedicate," as in the final dedication of merit seen in so many Buddhist works, or "to substitute," which Rolf A. Stein, "Un document ancien relatif aux rites funéraires des Bon-po tibétains," *Journal asiatique* 258 (1970): 155–85, has shown was sometimes used to refer to the substitution or transformation of Buddhist for non-Buddhist funerary rites. J. W. De Jong, "Review of Yoshiro Imaeda, *Histoire du cycle de la naissance et de la mort*," *Indo-Iranian Journal* 25 (1983): 224, argues instead for a Buddhist reading of the term as a dedication of merit, yet Imaeda, "The *History of the Cycle of Birth and Death*," 167 n. 87, insists on his substitution reading. Even if we accept that reading, the idea that the *Lha yul du lam bstan pa* was meant to complete the work begun by the *Story*, and thus that its *Sarvadurgati* mantra is meant to replace the *Story*'s *Uṣṇīṣavijayā* spell, remains questionable. It may be true that the two Tibetan works traveled in similar circles, sometimes in the same manuscript, and that early Tibetans

looked to both the tantra (as evident in other sources) and the *dhāraṇī* for their narratives and rituals in replacing the Bon funerary practices, but these are no reasons to complicate the *History*'s clear connections to the *Uṣṇīṣavijayā-dhāraṇī*.

13. The one Sanskrit manuscript I have been able to consult (Schopen's abovementioned copy of the Los Angeles Manuscript) consistently reads just "rebirths" (*gati*) rather than "negative rebirths" (*durgati*).
14. Ronald M. Davidson, "Some Observations on an Uṣṇīṣa Abhiṣeka Rite in Atikūṭa's *Dhāraṇīsaṃgraha*," in *Transformation and Transfer of Tantra/Tantrism in Asia and Beyond*, ed. István Keul (Berlin: Walter de Gruyter, 2012), 82.
15. The *Sarvadurgatipariśodhana-tantra* may be seen as the product of this earlier *uṣṇīṣa* system, represented in part by the *Uṣṇīṣavijayā-dhāraṇī*, meeting the somewhat later **Vajroṣṇīṣa* (sometimes referred to in Western scholarship as the *Vajraśekhara*) cycle that rose to prominence in the eighth century (and that is the focus of the present study's third chapter). On Vajroṣṇīṣa being a preferable reconstruction of the Chinese *Jingangding*, see Rolf W. Giebel, "The Chin-Kang-Ting Ching Yu-Ch'ieh Shi-Pa-Hui Chih-Kuei: An Annotated Translation," *Journal of Naritasan Institute for Buddhist Studies* 18 (1995): 109, and Ronald M. Davidson, "Sources and Inspirations," in *Esoteric Buddhism and the Tantras in East Asia: A Handbook for Scholars*, ed. Charles Orzech (Leiden: Brill, 2011), 24.
16. The Chinese writing above the diagram identifies the altar as such. Earlier studies of this diagram include Susan Whitfield, *The Silk Road: Trade, Travel, War, and Faith* (Chicago: Serindia, 2004), 274; Sarah Fraser, *Performing the Visual: The Practice of Buddhist Wall Painting in China and Central Asia, 618–960* (Stanford, CA: Stanford University Press, 2004), 154–55, fig. 415; Wladimir Zwalf, *Buddhism, Art and Faith* (London: British Museum Publications Limited, 1985), no. 324; Roderick Whitfield, *The Art of Central Asia: The Stein Collection in the British Museum*, 3 vols. (Tokyo: Kodansha International, 1982–1985), vol. 2, fig. 81; Arthur Waley, *A Catalogue of Paintings Recovered from Tun-Huang* (London: British Museum, 1931), no. 74; Aurel Stein, *Serindia*, 5 vols. (Oxford: Clarendon Press, 1921), 893, 974.
17. See *Uṣṇīṣavijayā-dhāraṇī*, 247a.3ff. Although this translation is the main version of the sutra used in the modern Tibetan tradition, it oddly lacks the main *vidhi* procedures that involve an altar. (The passage is missing from the *Sde dge par phud* for idiosyncratic reasons: a folio side from the next volume (vol. *ba*) has mistakenly been inserted in place of the folio side that should contain the relevant portion of the text. Nonetheless, the passage was probably never there; even in the Narthang and Peking *Bka' 'gyurs* it is missing. For the relevant point in the Narthang, see *rgyud*, vol. *pa* (92), 389.2, and for the Peking, see Q. 198, *rgyud*, vol. *pha*, 231a.5). To get a sense of the altar rite in question, one must look to the Sanskrit (f. 20), Buddhapālita's Chinese (T. 967, 351c–352c), or the Tibetan Dunhuang version (Pelliot tibétain 368, verso, ll. 29–37), all of which more or less agree on the procedures. Another canonical Tibetan translation, listed under the title *Sarvatathāgatoṣṇīṣavijaya-nāma-dhāraṇī-kalpa-sahita*, does include the passage (see 233a.4f–233b.1), though with the *mudrā* introduced before the description of the altar (as in the Sanskrit but not in the Buddhapālita or the Tibetan Dunhuang versions), and with a cloud of offerings (again, as in the Sanskrit but not Buddhapālita, who has visions of flowers instead, while the Tibetan

Dunhuang has unspecified offerings—see translation below). This Tibetan "*kalpa-sahita*" (presumably [*sic*] for *saṃhita*) translation also has eight pages of additional ritual material appended (see 234a.1, from "*gzhan zhig la bris*"), which is probably the appended *kalpa* mentioned in the title. Among the other translations clustered in this part of the *Sde dge bka' 'gyur*, Toh. 594 and 595 share a similar *nidāna*, featuring Amitayus and Avalokiteśvara, then focus quickly on more or less the same ritual material. Toh. 596 is a shorter sutra that also shares the *nidāna*, though in a slightly edited form, and a brief *vidhi* probably extracted from 594. Finally, Toh. 598 is also a short work with basically the same *nidāna* that offers an elaborate mandala altar with many deities arranged upon it for the purposes of reciting the spell. In short, the main two translations are Toh. 597 and 594.

18. *Uṣṇīṣavijayā-dhāraṇī*, 247b.1–3. *gzungs yungs kar dag la lan nyi shu rtsa gcig yongs su brjod de / de dag gi rus gong rnams kyi steng du gtor na de dag dmyal ba "am / dud 'gro'i skye gnas sam / gshin rje'i 'jig rten nam / yi dwags sam / de las gzhan ngan 'gro rnams su skyes par gyur kyang rung ste / de dag gzungs 'di'i mthus ngan 'gro de dag las thar bar 'gyur ro / de dag las thar nas kyang lhar skye bar 'gyur ro.*
19. Pelliot tibétain 368, verso, ll. 29–37. *gzungs "di dran bar byos la / dkyil kor gru bzhi gyiste / men tog sna mang po dang / pog sna mang pos mchod cing gsol la / pus mo' g.yas pa'i lha nga sa la tshugste / de bzhin gshegs pa thams shad mngon bar rmigste / phyag byos la / de nas de'i phyag rgya thal mo sbyar te / 'dzub mo gnyis gyi thog ma bgug nas / mthe bo gnyis gyi 'og tu mnan la / bam tol gdab pa'i thabsu byos shig / de nas de'i tshe gzungs brgya' rtsa brgyad slos shig / de bslas ma thag du bye ma dung phyur brgya' stong phrag drug cu rtsa brgyad gyi / 'ga' 'ga' klung gi bye ma dang bnyam ba'i de bzhin gshegs pa rnams la / des rim gro dang byas sti stang byas shing / de bzhin gshegs pa kun la / mchod pa ched pos mchod par 'gyuro / de thams shad gyis kyang legso zhes bya ba'i tshig 'byungo / de bzhin gshegs pa thams cad / nyid las 'byung ba'i bur sem shan de rig par byos shig / ma bsgribs pa'i ye shes dang ldan zhing / byang cub sems pa'i sems gyis / brgyan pa thob par 'gyuro / lha'i dbang po gzungs 'di bsgrub pa'i cho ga dang / yo byad gyi thabs de byas na sems shan dmyal ba lastsogs pa'i rgyud kun las thar cing thag la / de las thar par 'gyuro / tshe ring bar 'ongo.* For the phrase *bam tol gdab pa*, the *Story of the Cycle of Birth and Death* here reads *ban tol* (Imaeda, "The *History of the Cycle of Birth and Death*," 165), which De Jong, "Review of Yoshiro Imaeda," 224, corrects to *bem tol*, as in *bem rtol rgyab*, "to snap the fingers."
20. The back formation of the Sanskrit for this title in the Sde dge edition cited here reads *kalpa-sahita* (Tib. *rtog pa dang bcas pa*), but I prefer *kalpasaṃhitā*, as it appears in the Cone edition.
21. *Sarvatathāgatoṣṇīṣavijaya-nāma-dhāraṇī-kalpa-sahita*, 234a.6–234b.3 (compare the almost identical passage in Toh. 595, 239a.2–6): *sa la ma lhung ba'i lci bas maN+Dala gru bzhir byas la me tog dkar po bkram ste / mtshams bzhir zhun mar gyi mar me bzhi bzhag la / a ga ru dan du ru ska'i bdug pa byas la / de bzhin du dri'i chus gang ba'i snod me tog dkar pos brgyan te / gzungs kyi snying po can gyi mchod rten nam sku gzugs dbus su bzhugs su gsol la / de la g.yon pa'i lag pas reg ste g.yas pa'i lag pa phreng ba 'dzin pas nyi ma re re zhing len nyi shu rtsa gcig rtsa gcig dus gsum du bzlas pa byas la / de'i chu khyor ba gsum 'thungs na nad med pa dang / tshe ring ba dang / dgra yongs su nyams pa dang / 'dzin blo rno ba dang / ngag btsun par 'gyur ro / skye ba nas skye bar*

skye ba dran par 'gyur ro / de'i chus khang pa dang / phyugs kyi ra ba 'am / rta'i ra ba 'am / rgyal po'i khab tu gtor na / rkun ma dang / sbrul dang / gnod sbyin dang / srin po la sogs pa'i 'jigs pa mi 'byung zhing nad kyis yongs su gdungs par mi 'gyur ro / mgo la gtor na de nad de las grol bar 'gyur ro / de ltar tshe dpag tu med pa'i phan yon che ba'i gzungs 'ang gang dang gang du rab tu sbyar na / de dang de ru zhi ba chen por 'gyur ro / so shing la lan nyi shu rtsa gcig yongs su bzlas te / 'chos na nad med pa dang / blo rno ba dang / tshe ring bar 'gyur ro.

22. The *Kalpasaṃhitā* is said to have been translated by Chos kyi sde and Ba ri, making it a late eleventh- or early twelfth-century translation. (Toh. 595 provides no information.) However, the *Dkar chag 'phang thang ma*, 23, does include an **Uṣṇīṣavijayā-dhāraṇī-vidhisaṃhitā* (*cho ga dang bcas pa*).
23. That is, Vairocana, Vajrapāṇi, Mañjuśrī, Sarvanivāraṇaviṣkambhī, Kṣitigarbha, Avalokiteśvara, Maitreya, Ākaśagarbha, Samantabhadra. On these eight, see Kimiaki Tanaka, *Indoniokeru mandara no seiritsu to hatten*, 58–66 (Tokyo: Shunjusha, 2010), as well as Pratapaditya Pal, "A Note on the Mandala of the Eight Bodhisattvas," *Archives of Asian Art* 26, nos. 71–73 (1972/1973), and Phyllis Granoff, "A Portable Buddhist Shrine from Central Asia," *Archives of Asian Art* 22 (1968/1969): 80–95. Kimiaki Tanaka, *An Illustrated History of the Maṇḍala: From Its Genesis to the Kālacakatantra* (Somerville, MA: Wisdom, 2018), 66, says the oldest text to feature an eight-bodhisattva mandala is a Chinese translation completed in 663 C.E., the *Shizizhuangyanwang pusa qingwen jing*. Amoghavajra's manual may be dated to 764.
24. Taishō 972, 365a6–9. My thanks to Koichi Shinohara for helping me with this passage.
25. See Hanjin Horiuchi, *Kongochokyo no Kenkyu* (*Sarvatathāgata-tattvasaṃgraha-nāma-mahāyāna-sūtra*) (Koyasan University, Mount Kōya, Japan: Mikkyo Bunka Kenkyujo, 1983), v. 2182 or *Sarvatathāgatatattvasaṃgraha*, 108a.4–5. The same lines open the Dunhuang *Vajrahūṃkara-sādhana* that appears in IOL Tib J 417/ Pelliot tibétain 300, where they structure daily practice; for more on this, see chapter 3.
26. For an analysis of this manual and the works that may have influenced it, see Koichi Shinohara, "The Ritual of the Buddhoṣṇīṣa Vijaya Dhāraṇī Maṇḍala," *Hualin International Journal of Buddhist Studies* 1, no. 2 (2018): 143–82.
27. Found today in T. 848 and T. 1796, respectively.
28. See T. 973, 376a1–27, for the relevant descriptions.
29. For the eight *uṣṇīṣa* buddhas, see Stephen Hodge, *The Mahā-vairocana-abhisaṃbodhi Tantra, with Buddhaguhya's Commentary* (London: Routledge Curzon, 2003), 115. Their iconographies, which match precisely those seen in Śubhākarasiṃha's *Uṣṇīṣavijayā* manual, appear in chapter 13 of the same work; see Hodge, *The Mahā-vairocana-abhisaṃbodhi*, 294.
30. This is not to say that Śubhākarasiṃha's manual was the singular model for the Sarvadurgati mandala or to deny the possibility that Śubhākarasiṃha might have known of the Sarvadurgati when he designed his mandala. The tantra may date from around the turn of the eighth century.
31. That the etymology of *dkyil 'khor* is included *alongside* that of "mandala" is a possible indication of the work's Tibetan origins.

32. Perhaps a reference to *Sarvadurgatipariśodhana-tantra*, 68b.7ff.
33. IOL Tib J 712, 4r.7. *da ltar mdzad pa 'di yang.*
34. IOL Tib J 712, 5v.4–6v.1. *da ni don bdun pa phan yon 'chad de / gong du bshad pa ltar / lha 'i bu dri ma myed pa'i 'od ngan song las thar nas / bde 'gro mtho ris su lha'i lus blangs nas / bde ba nyam pag du gnas pa de bzhin du / deng gi yon bdag kyang / de dang mthun bar 'phags pa thams cad kyi thugs rje dang / byin rlabs kyis / ngan song gi gnas la bstsogs te gang na gnas na yang / deng sems dag pas / yon bdag gis rgyu sbyar ba dang / phags pa thams cad kyi thugs rje dang / slobs pon gi dgongs pas / dkyil 'khor nas phyung / dbang bskur / khrus bgyis pas / bde 'gro mtho ris su / the tsom rnam 'ag yang ma mchis par / dngos grub thog pa 'di ni / phan yon lags te.*
35. See Rolf A. Stein, "Du récit au rituel dans les manuscrits Tibétains de Touen-houang," in *Études Tibétaines dédiées à la mémoire de Marcelle Lalou* (Paris: Adrien Maisonneuve, 1971), 479–547; Cathy Cantwell and Robert Mayer, "Enduring Myths: *Smrang*, *Rabs* and Ritual in the Dunhuang Texts on Padmasambhava," *Revue d'Etudes Tibétaines* 15 (2008): 289–312; Brandon Dotson, "Misspelling 'Buddha': The Officially Commissioned Tibetan *Aparimiāyur-nāma mahāyāna-sūtras* from Dunhuang and the Study of Old Tibetan Orthography," *Bulletin of the School of Oriental and African Studies* 79, no. 1 (2016): 129–51. The Dunhuang documents include a number of examples. Just among the Buddhist texts, see for example IOL Tib J 343 and IOL Tib J 377 (on both the narrative setting and benefits of water offerings), IOL Tib J 338 (on the narrative setting and benefits of *caitya*), IOL Tib J 422 (on pacificatory fire offerings), IOL Tib J 711 (on the narrative setting of the *Invitation to the Great Gods and Nāgas*), Pelliot tibétain 307 (on the Seven Mothers/*Ma bdun*), and Pelliot tibétain 44 (on Phurpa), as well as the funerary texts discussed by Dotson; still others could surely be added to the list.
36. Brandon Dotson, "The Dead and Their Stories: Preliminary Remarks on the Place of Narrative in Tibetan Religion," in *Zentral-Asiatische Studien* 45, ed. Peter Schwieger et al. (Andiast: International Institute for Tibetan and Buddhist Studies, 2016), 83.
37. Dotson, "The Dead and Their Stories," 83, quoting Pelliot tibétain 1136, l. 60: *gna' phan da yang phan gna' bsod da yang bsod.* On such statements, see also Stein, "Du récit au rituel," 504, and Brandon Dotson, "Complementarity and Opposition in Early Tibetan Ritual," *Journal of the American Oriental Society* 128 (2008): 45.
38. *Vairocanābhisambodhi-vikurvitādhiṣṭāna-mahātantravṛtti*, vol. *tu*, 157b.1–3: *rnam par snang mdzad ni sgrub pa po lta bur blta la / . . . rang gi lha'i sku'i gzugs su snang bar 'gyur ro zhes ma 'ongs pa'i gdul ba'i 'gro ba rnams la bstan pa yin no.*
39. IOL Tib J 338 and 343 provide two examples of discussions on "the narrative setting and the benefits" (*gleng gzhi dang phan yon*) for the building of stupas and performing water offerings, respectively, though they may well have been composed under the influence of Tibetan interests.
40. Stein, "Du récit au rituel," 482.
41. IOL Tib J 384, 3.4–5: *gdan la bzhugs nas / chag shing phyag du bzung nas / dkyil khor gyi lo rgyus bshad.*
42. The distribution of the story in printed form is a part of *Sarvadurgati* funerals in today's Newar Buddhism; thanks to my student, Kris Anderson, for her observations in this regard.

43. Dotson, "The Dead and Their Stories," 96, distinguishes between the Buddhist "charter myth" and the pre-Buddhist Tibetan "antecedent tale," seeing the former in works such as the *Story of the Cycle of Birth and Death*, where "the Buddha does not perform the funeral rite for Rin chen's father, nor does he embody a paradigm for subsequent ritual practitioners, but rather gives instructions to tantrikas." Given the factors cited above, the difference thus defined may not always be so clear. See also Cantwell and Mayer, "Enduring Myths," 292–94.
44. For these lines, see IOL Tib J 712, 2r.2 and 2v.7. The narrative includes, of course, much reported speech in which the Buddha sometimes speaks of future events or lifetimes.
45. IOL Tib J 712, 4v.4. The past tense *zhugs* that follows in the same line may be explained as part of a sequence of events. It is followed by a continutative *te* particle, so the past tense is probably used in a similar way to those verbs immediately preceding a gerundive *nas*.
46. See IOL Tib J 712, 5v.2, 6v.6, and 8v.4.
47. For the present analysis, I am focusing on the Sanskrit. The canonical Tibetan translations use the present tense in these if-then statements, though the Dunhuang translation prefers the imperative, as in, "one should perform [the recitation] 1,000 times" (Pelliot tibétain 368, verso, l. 17: *lan stong byos shig*).
48. *Mahāpratisarāvidyārājñī* translation following Gergely Hidas, "*Mahāpratisarā-mahāvidyārājñī*, the Great Amulet, Great Queen of Spells: Introduction, Critical Editions and Annotated Translation" (PhD thesis, Oxford University, 2008), 232; for the corresponding Sanskrit see 167–68: *nāśaya nāśaya sarvapāpāni me bhagavati / rakṣa rakṣa māṃ sarvasattvāṃś ca sarvatra sarvadā sarva bhayopadravebhyaḥ*.
49. For translations of spells extracted from their sutras, see IOL Tib J 311/1, 312/4, 372/2; 322, 348, and 388 (and many others). For partly translated spells appearing within their sutras, see IOL Tib J 141/3, IOL Tib J 311, 312/4, 372/2, and Pelliot tibétain 49/4, perhaps indicating some confusion regarding where the spells begin and end. By the time of the canonical version of the sutras, the spells are left entirely untranslated, as is the common practice in both Tibetan and Chinese translations today. Finally, for a commentary on a *dhāraṇī* spell, see IOL Tib J 97, 43b.1–47b.3.
50. IOL Tib J 712, 5r.8–5v.1. *las dang dngos grub la bar du myi gcod par / dgongs pa dang / thugs rje bzung bar mdzad pas / lha rnams kyang sngon gi smon lam dang / thugs rjes / yon bdag de 'i don du / byin rlabs stsol cing / stong rogs mdzad*. As explained in greater detail in chapter 3, the shifting relationship between propitiation and accomplishment in early tantric Buddhism is complex. In the present context, even though it says the master should perform both the propitiation and the accomplishment as preliminaries, I understand the granting of the initiation, which follows the master's propitiations, to be equivalent to, or part of, the *sādhana* and its accomplishment of the *siddhis*. Such a reading is supported by Śākyamitra's comment on the *Sarvatathāgata-tattvasaṃgraha*; see chapter 3, n. 37. This is likely why propitiation, and not accomplishment, is addressed separately in our manual's third topic.
51. IOL Tib J 712, 15r.1–2. *je la byang cub du sems bskyed / de nas lag du rin po che'i phur pa thogs nas / thal mo sbyar te . . .*

52. A translation of the popular mantra, *oṃ svabhāvaśuddhāḥ sarvadharmāḥ svabhāvaśuddho'ham.*
53. The preceding lines constitute a common verse, versions of which appear in IOL Tib J 331/2, 3v (in a similar context); IOL Tib J 332, 6v.7–7r.1; and the *Dgongs pa 'dus pa'i mdo*, 159a.6–7, where Rudra requests initiation (for a translation of the latter, see Jacob P. Dalton, *Taming of the Demons: Violence and Liberation in Tibetan Buddhism* [New Haven, CT: Yale University Press, 2011], 196).
54. Compare IOL Tib J 384, r5.2 (*e sa me / dri sa me / ma ha sa ma ya*), where the mantra is said to be for opening the doors to the mandala, an idea seen elsewhere too. See Tadeusz Skorupski, *The Sarvadurgatipariśodhana Tantra, Elimination of All Evil Destinies: Sanskrit and Tibetan Texts with Introduction, English Translation and Notes* (Delhi: Motilal Banarsidass, 1983), 316 n. 17.
55. Again, the preceding two lines are seen elsewhere; compare *Sarvabuddhasamāyogaḍākinījālasamvara-nāma-uttaratantra*, 183a.6.
56. IOL Tib J 712, 15r.1–2. *chos sku* ([*sic*] for *kun*) *rang bzhin dag pas na / bdag kyang rang bzhin rnam par dag / rgyal ba rgya mtsho kun 'dus pas / sku 'i dbyig tu bdag phyor* (*sic* for *sbyor*) *cig / aoṃ ri sa me / ma ha sa ma ye hung / dkyil 'khor la ni 'khor lor bshad / de nyid dam tshig yin bar bshad / dkyil 'khor gshegs pa'i lha rnams kyis bdag la byin kyis brlab tu gso l/ rin cen men tog la bstsogs te / gtso bo rigs te bsgrubs na ni / thob 'gyur 'di la the tsom myed.* A *shad* is missing between *kyis* and *bdag.* Compare a slightly reordered and more elaborate version in Or. 8210/S. 421, recto, lines 13–31.
57. These initiations immediately follow the more standard set of Yoga tantra initiations—vase, rosary, crown, wheel, and so on. Little is said about the performance of that set, except that they are bestowed using empowered vases in the middle of the mandala in accordance with the scripture; see IOL Tib J 712, 16r, 1–2. That the initiations with the eight auspicious substances correspond to the eight *uṣṇīṣas* is indicated by IOL Tib J 712, 16v.3. The two groups of initiations may reflect the meeting of the **Vajroṣṇīṣa/Vajraśekhara* and the earlier *uṣṇīṣa* buddha system (identified by Davidson; see n. 14 above) within the *Sarvadurgatipariśodhana-tantra.* Other *Sarvadurgati* initiation manuals from Dunhuang take various approaches. IOL Tib J 384 lacks the standard initiations, though it includes one or two of them, e.g., the crown, among its list of eight substances. IOL Tib J 579, which shows more signs of *Sarvatathāgatatattvasaṃgraha* (*STTS*) influence, includes the *pañcākārābhisaṃbodhikrama* and has the eight substances only in a larger list of empowering substances bestowed prior to the standard, *STTS*-style initiations of the five buddhas, the primary focus.
58. Compare the eight auspicious substances and their respective powers that appear in later tantric literarture, such as Dge rtse Paṇḍita's *Gu ru drag po ye shes rab 'byar gyis sgrub khog*, vol. *ca*, f. 119. See also Yael Bentor, *Consecration of Images & Stūpas in Indo-Tibetan Tantric Buddhism* (Leiden: E. J. Brill, 1996), 342–45.
59. IOL Tib J 712, 16r.3–16v.2. *yung dkar rdo rje 'i rigs mchog chen po ste / rtog bral mnyam nyid ye shes chen po 'dis / des kyang 'dir ni bkra shis mchog 'gyur cig . . . dung ni gsung rabs ma lus sgrogs pas na / gsung dbyangs thams cad sgra brnyan don rtogs pas / des*

kyang 'dir ni bkra shis mchog 'gyur cig / li khri dmar pa dbang gi rang bzhin te / tshe dbang thams cad dbang du 'dus pas kyang / des kyang 'dir ni bkra shis mchog 'gyur cig.

60. The precise relationship between metaphor and metonymy vis-à-vis tantric ritual substances is a complex question that raises the issue of whether an object symbolizes or simply *is* the awakened mind. In the case of the *bodhicitta* sacrament so central to chapter 4, for example, it is more of a metonymic (if such a word is even appropriate) relationship. For a preliminary discussion of the metonymic character of Indian ritual, see Laurie L. Patton, "Poetry, Ritual, and Associational Thought in Early India and Elsewhere," in *Figuring Religions: Comparing Ideas, Images, and Activities*, ed. Shubha Pathak (Albany: State University of New York Press, 2013), 179–98. Though Patton writes about Vedic ritual, much of what she says applies to some tantric rituals too. The author of our manual, however, in the manual's closing sentence, describes the consecratory substances as "symbols" (*rtags*) of the minds of the eight *uṣṇīṣa* buddhas, thus framing them as more metaphors than metonymy.
61. The patron does pronounce a passage one other time, though not in verse. The words are recited before each of the mandala's four doors as the patron circumambulates the structure near the beginning of the proceedings. They form a prayer for the afflictions to be exhausted, for higher rebirth and buddhahood, for the health of the livestock and for harvests to be good, and for all beings to be at ease. Here, then, a shift into verse marks the patron's first encounter with the sacred space and symbolism of the mandala. A similar prayer also appears in Or. 8210/S. 421, ll. 1–6. See too Pelliot tibétain 37/2, which follows an incomplete copy of the funerary text, the *Dug gsum 'dul ba* (studied by Imaeda, "The *History of the Cycle of Birth and Death*"), and similarly directs the master to circumambulate the *Sarvadurgati* mandala, stopping at each door. The text shares some lines in common with our own; compare, for example, Pelliot tibétain 37/2, 4r.1–4 to IOL Tib J 712, 15r.4–15v.1.
62. IOL Tib J 712, 14v.5–6. *yon bdag gson gshin gang lags kyang rung ste / dkyil 'khor nas dbyung zhing / dbang bskur khrus bgyi bar 'byung ste.*
63. IOL Tib J 712, 15v.7. *gson po zhig na ni / shar du dbyung/ gum ba lags na nub du dbyung.*
64. Toh. 483, 61b.4. *shi ba'i lus dkyil 'khor du bcug ste / dbang bskur na / de sems can dmyal bar skyes na yang de ma thag tu rnam par thar nas lha'i rigs su skye bar 'gyur ro.*
65. *Dba' bzhed*, 31b.2–3. *de nas phyis ngan song sbyong rgyud la brten nas / kun rig dang gtsug tor dgu'i dkyil 'khor la brten nas / shid rnams byas so.* The passage further specifies that "For those who die by the sword, funerals were performed on the basis of the Wrathful Sun mandala. For those who have died by curse, [spirit-appeasement] rituals such as knife-taming rites were performed together with sutra passages" (*grir shi ba la khro bo nyi ma'i dkyil 'khor la brten nas shid byas / de'i gtad yar da gri 'dul la sogs pa rnams mdo sde'i khungs dang sbyar nas mdzad*). For a description of a Khro bo nyi ma mandala, see Skorupski, *The Sarvadurgatipariśodhana Tantra*, 370 n. 324.
66. Pasang Wangdu and Hildegard Diemberger, *dBa' bzhed: The Royal Narrative Concerning the Bringing of the Buddha's Doctrine to Tibet* (Wien: Verlag der Osterreichischen Akademie der Wissenschaften, 2000), 103 n. 422.

67. The tantra itself also includes funerary fire offering (*homa*) rituals, and it is possible the funerary initiation functioned alongside these methods for corpse disposal.
68. *Sba bzhed*, 45, as first noted by Giuseppe Tucci, *Minor Buddhist Texts: Part II* (Rome: Istituto italiano per il Medio ed Estremo Oriente, 1958), 26–27. Unfortunately, this crucial passage is missing from the earlier *Testament of Wa*, so we must take this account with a grain of salt. Is description does accord with several other later sources as well as the plans of later restorations to the temple, based on which Kapstein has argued that we can take the account as at least somewhat reliable. Matthew Kapstein, *The Tibetan Assimilation of Buddhism* (Oxford: Oxford University Press, 2000), 61.
69. See the recently discovered manuscript of the so-called *Rgyal rabs zla rigs ma*, 11v.6–7: *skar chung gi gtsug lag khang bzhengs nas / gdan ma lcang 'tshal du kun rig rtsa ba'i dkyil 'khor bzhengs.*
70. As observed of the *Dkar chag ldan kar ma* by Kapstein, *The Tibetan Assimilation of Buddhism*, 62–63. Since Kapstein's book was published, the slightly later *Dkar chag 'Phangs thang ma* has also emerged, and it too features the *Sarvadurgatipariśodhana* prominently; see Rta mdo, *Dkar chag 'phang than ma. Sgra sbyor bam po gnyis pa* (Beijing: Mi rigs dpe skrung khang, 2003), 61). Padmasambhava (if we accept the attribution), when discussing Buddhism's power to overcome negative rebirths in his commentary to the *Thabs kyi zhags pa'i rgyud*, calls attention to the *Sarvadurgatipariśodhana*'s successes with Vimalamaṇiprabha (see IOL Tib J 321, 8a.2–3).
71. See Amy Heller, "Ninth-Century Buddhist Images Carved at lDan Ma Brag to Commemorate Tibeto-Chinese Negotiations," in *Tibetan Studies: Proceedings of the Sixth International Seminar of the International Association for Tibetan Studies*, 2 vols, ed. Per Kværne (Oslo: Institute for Comparative Research in Human Culture, 1994), 1: 335–49 and appendix, 1: 12–19; "Early Ninth-Century Images of Vairochana from Eastern Tibet," *Orientations* 25, no. 6 (1994): 74–79; "Eighth- and Ninth-CenturyTemples and Rock Carvings of Eastern Tibet," in *Tibetan Art: Towards a Definition of Style*, ed. J. C. Singer and P. Denwood (London: Laurence King, 1997), 86–103; "Buddhist Images and Rock Inscriptions from Eastern Tibet," in *Tibetan Studies: Proceedings of the Seventh Seminar of the International Association for Tibetan Studies*, ed. H. Krasser, M. T. Much, E. Steinkellner, and H. Tauscher (Vienna: Austrian Academy of Science, 1997), 1: 385–403; Kapstein, *The Assimilation of Tibetan Buddhism*, 63–64.
72. First studied by Marcelle Lalou, "Notes à propos d'une amulette de Touen-houang: les litanies de Tārā et la Sitātapatrādhāraṇī," *Mélanges chinois et bouddhiques* (Brussels: Imprimerie Sainte Catherine, S. A., 1936), vol. 4, 134–49. For the mantra, compare Skorupski, *The Sarvadurgatipariśodhana Tantra*, 126.
73. The writing at the top is a prayer to a list of twenty buddhas for protection from poison, weapons, fire, and water; the surrounding writing is a prayer to the three jewels and the mantras and *dhāraṇīs* of all the gods for protection from illness and harmful demons; the bottom calls upon Sitātapatra by means of the *Uṣṇīṣasitātapatre-aparājitā-nāma-dhāraṇī.*

74. Eight lines of faded and unfortunately illegible writing in the same hand run across the center of the manuscript. And the handwriting in Pelliot tibétain 389 is seen on several Tibetan Chan manuscripts, including the famous Pelliot tibétain 116 (see Sam van Schaik, *Tibetan Zen: Discovering a Lost Tradition* [Boston and London: Snow Lion, 2015], 30, on some important editorial notes to that manuscript that are likely in the same hand), and it is often accompanied by pictures drawn in a generally similar style. This scribe's interests in working across the Sino-Tibetan divide raises further questions about his possible connections with the Chinese *Sarvadurgati* amulets discussed immediately below.
75. Pelliot chinois 4519 also has visible folds on it, so was probably an amulet. Regarding the surrounding texts, see the identifications made in the online catalogue on gallica.bnf.fr. For more on this item, see Christian Luczanits, "Ritual, Instruction and Experiment: Esoteric Drawings from Dunhuang," in *The Art of Central Asia and the Indian Subcontinent in Cross Culture Perspective*, ed. Anupa Pande and Mandira Sharma (New Delhi: National Museum Institute–Aryan Books International, 2009), 145.
76. Pelliot chinois 3937 is also a *Sarvadurgati* mandala drawn in a generally similar style, but with Śākyamuni at the center and the surrounding deities arranged in horizontal rows outside of the mandala proper. This makes a closer match with the nine-deity *uṣṇīṣa* buddha mandala described in our own Dunhuang manual (and others), which also centers around Śākymuni. The tantra's first chapter contains a mandala with All-Seeing Vairocana at its center (*Sarvadurgatipariśodhana-tantra*, 62a.6ff); however, it lacks the eight *uṣṇīṣa* buddhas. A mandala with these eight is at the beginning of chapter 2 (71a.6ff.) but has Śākyamuni at its center. Unlike the amulets discussed above, Pelliot chinois 3937 appears to have served as a guide for painters, as we can see dots of the appropriate colors in many of the deities, and just enough of each decoration to serve as a template for what more needed to be filled in. A similar artist's template for the Vajradhātu mandala is found at Pelliot chinois 4518 (33).
77. IOL Tib J 579, 15r.6–7. *de nas dbang gyI dkyil 'khor gyi dbus su / myi de rtsa ba'i dkyil 'khor la kha bstan nas . . .* The main mandala in our manual is raised, as becomes clear in some appended notes on the mantras to be used in making ritual preparations, the first of which is "digging out the earth for constructing the mandala platform" (IOL Tib J 712, 16v.5. *dkyil 'khor gi stegs bu brtsig pa'i sa brko ba'i sngags*).
78. *Vairocanābhisambodhi-vikurvitādhiṣṭāna-mahātantravṛtti*, 150b.3, as translated by Hodge, *The Mahā-vairocana-abhisaṃbodhi*, 142. ("Initiation mandala" = *dbang bskur ba'i dkyil 'khor* [**abhiṣeka-maṇḍala*].) The tantra itself refers to it just as the "second mandala" (*Mahāvairocanābhisaṁbodhi*, 173b.2: *dkyil 'khor gnyis pa*). A secondary mandala, termed a "water mandala," also appears in the seventh-century *Dhāraṇīsaṃgraha* of Atikūṭa (T. 901). Atikūṭa's secondary mandala is discussed by Koichi Shinohara, *Spells, Images, and Mandalas: Tracing the Evolution of Esoteric Buddhist Rituals* (New York: Columbia

University Press, 2014), 45–46; see also 33, where Shinohara refers to it as the "*abhiṣeka* platform."

79. Hodge, *The Mahā-vairocana-abhisaṃbodhi*, 145. Over time the initiation mandala faded from use. This may suggest the involvement of a smaller number of initiates than in later centuries.

80. On this trend, see John R. McRae, "Daoxuan's Vision of Jetavana: The Ordination Platform Movement in Medieval Chinese Buddhism," in *Going Forth: Visions of Buddhist Vinaya*, ed. William M. Bodiford (Honolulu: University of Hawai'i Press, 2005), and Robert H. Sharf, "Buddhist Veda and the Rise of Chan," 98–102. Meanwhile, the *Mahāvairocanābhisaṃbodhi*, with its full-blown mandala and initiation rites, may be dated to at least as early as 674 C.E., when the Chinese monk Wuxing is said to have collected a copy while in India; see Kazuo Kano, "Vairocanābhisaṃbodhi," in *Brill's Encyclopedia of Buddhism*, ed. Jonathan A. Silk (Leiden: Brill, 2015), 382. There is no question that the work was in formation for some time before this, and Hodge dates it to "perhaps around 640 C.E. or a little earlier" (see Hodge, *The Mahā-vairocana-abhisaṃbodhi*, 11 and 14–15). Given what we have seen of the antecedence of ritual manuals, and ritual experimentations more generally, to their encapsulation in large-scale tantras, we may assume that Buddhists were exploring related practices for some decades before this date, probably from the very beginning of the seventh century.

81. On the rise of image worship and *pūjā* in non-Buddhist orthodox circles, see (among others) Phyllis Granoff, "Reading Between the Lines: Colliding Attitudes Towards Image Worship in Indian Religious Texts," in *Rites hindous, transferts et transformations*, ed. Gérard Colas et Gilles Tarabout (Paris: Écoles des hautes études en sciences sociales, 2006), 389–421, and Shingo Einoo, "The Formation of the Pūjā Ceremony," *Studien zur Indologie und Iranistik (Festschrift für Paul Thieme)* 20 (1996): 73–87. For a broader picture of mandalas, particularly in the *gṛhyasūtras* and *gṛhyapariśiṣṭas*, see Shingo Einoo, "The Formation of Hindu Ritual," in *From Material to Deity: Indian Rituals of Consecration*, ed., Shingo Einoo and Jun Takasima (New Delhi: Manohar, 2005), 24–33.

82. For the treatment of a sick person, see *Mahāpratisarāvidyārājñī-dhāraṇī*, 133b.6ff, with the Sanskrit by Hidas, "*Mahāpratisarā-mahāvidyārājñī*," 179–81, and translated on 236–37. For a Tibetan-authored example, inspired by the *Mahāsāhasrapramardana-sūtra*, see IOL Tib J 401, 24v.7–8, where a woman who wants to have a child is brought into the center of a prepared mandala. (For an English translation, see Sam van Schaik, *Buddhist Magic: Divination, Healing, and Enchantment Through the Ages* [Boulder: Shambala, 2020], 161.) For the *Candanāṅga vidhi*, see IOL Tib J 337/1, r5.2. As observed in Dalton and van Schaik, *Tibetan Tantric Manuscripts from Dunhuang*, 65, the healing rite is absent from the canonical translation, though a different *vidhi* section does appear.

83. Sanskrit birchbark manuscripts of the *Mahāpratisarā* date from the early seventh century and probably indicate still earlier sixth-century versions, but the dating of the appended *vidhi* that contains the healing rite remains a question (Hidas, "*Mahāpratisarā-mahāvidyārājñī*," 7 and 35). And given the *Candanāṅga*'s

references to "secret mantra" and accomplishing *siddhis*, it may not much predate the eighth century. See IOL Tib J 337, r4.3, and, because the Dunhuang copy is so incomplete, *Candanāṅga-nāma-dhāraṇī*, 37b.4.

84. *gsol* sic for *sol*; *kab* sic for *bkab*. This last phrase is added as an interlinear note: *dkyil 'khor zhal kab gsol.*

85. This shows this is primarily a funerary text, as it focuses on entry through the west. The same leaning is also seen in IOL Tib J 384, r4.6–r5.1, which may be even more specifically funerary in that it lacks the entire blindfolding and flower-tossing sequence.

86. IOL Tib J 712, 15v.6–16r.2. *de nas sgo bzhi bstan lags nas / dkyil 'khor zhal kab* ([*sic*] for *bkab*) *gsol* ([*sic*] for *sol*) */ slobs pon shar phyogs kyi sgo nas zhugs te / nub phyogs na yon bdag sdod pa'i sar phyin pa dang / yon bdag la byin kyis brlabs nas / rdo rje la 'jur stsal te / gson po zhig na ni / shar du dbyung / gum ba lags na nub du dbyung / dkyil 'khor gi dbus su phin pa dang / slobs pon dbus kyi bum pa phyag tu bzhes/ phyogs bzhi 'i sgom cen bzhis / phyogs bzhi 'i bum pa blang / phyogs bzhi nas / 'dzab dang snying po bzlas shing dbang bskur / dbang bskur ba'i rim pa / bum pa dang 'phreng ba dang / cod pan dang / 'khor lo la bstsogs pa dbang rdzas gzhung las 'byung bas dbang bskur / khrus bgyi.*

87. Davidson, "Sources and Inspirations," 23.

88. Shinohara, *Spells, Images, and Mandalas*, 148. Shinohara summarizes the *Guhya-tantra*'s initiation proceedings on 148–49. On dating the *Guhya-tantra*, he notes on 275 n. 4 that the only extant Chinese translation is Amoghavajra's mid-eighth century rendition (T. 897), but Yixing, who died in 727 yet cites it extensively in his commentary to the *Mahāvairocanābhisaṃbhodhi*, must have had an earlier translation, presumably dating to the late seventh or early eighth century.

89. Shinohara,' *Spells, Images, and Mandalas*, 156.

90. For these three references, see *Mahāvairocanābhisaṁbodhi*, 162a.3, 164a.7, and 172b.2–3. For an English translation of the relevant passages, see Hodge, *The Mahā-vairocana-abhisaṃbodhi*, 90–91, 100, and 138. The last reference seems of particular significance for the proceedings and is returned to in the *Mahāvairocanābhisaṃbodhi's* fourteenth chapter; see Hodge, *The Mahā-vairocana-abhisaṃbodhi*, 301–2. Immediately following this purification at the gate, the disciple tosses the flower while still identified with the deity. This is unlike the Dunhuang manual (see passage translated above), where the disciple only prays for the deities of the mandala to grant their consecrations as the flower is thrown. Nonetheless, in both cases, the flower-tossing ceremony is marked as an important moment (in our own manual it is marked by the poetic prayers of the patron, in the *Mahāvairocana* by the preparatory *adhiṣṭhāna*).

91. See *Mahāvairocanābhisaṁbodhi*, 173b.2–138b.2 (corresponding to Hodge, *The Mahā-vairocana-abhisaṃbodhi*, 142–47).

92. *Vairocanābhisambodhi-vikurvitādhiṣṭāna-mahātantravṛtti*, vol. *cu*, 152b.2–3: *slob ma de dbang bskur bar bya ba'i tshe / 'dir dngos su ma gsungs kyang dkyil 'khor du 'jug pa'i tshe na rdo rje sems dpa'i skur bsgyur te / de las gzhan pa'i skur bsgyur bar ma gsungs pas rdo rje sems dpa'i skur bsgyur te dbang bskur bar bya'o.* See Hodge, *The Mahā-vairocana-abhisaṃbodhi*, 146.

Appendix: A *Sarvadurgatipariśodhana* Initiation Manual

1. An extra "dog" is crossed out.
2. I.e., what follows is no longer about the mythic original performance by the gods and so forth, but about the ritual instructions for the reader's performance.
3. In other words, the implements, initiatory images (*tsakali*), or seed syllable specific to each deity may be used as symbols for those deities and arranged within the constructed mandala.
4. *rnam 'ag yang*: this phrase appears elsewhere too; see, for example, 5v.7. The *'ag* seems to function in the same way as *ga*.
5. *nyam pag*: Perhaps [*sic*] for *nyams bag*, this term is used again in a similar sense later in this manuscript; see f. 15v.3. The same spelling (*nyam pag*) is also used, in a different sense, on a wood slip discussed by Frederick William Thomas, *Tibetan Literary Texts and Documents Concerning Chinese Turkestan*, 4 vols. (London: Royal Asiatic Society, 1951), 2: 392, and in Pelliot tibétain 1042, l. 52, discussed by Marcelle Lalou, *Rituel bon-po des funérailles royales (fonds Pelliot tibétain 1042)* (Paris: Société Asiatique, 1953a), 353 n. 2, where it seems to refer to a kind of pastry. See too Joanna Bialek, *Compounds and Compounding in Old Tibetan. Vol. 2: A Corpus Based Approach* (Marburg: Indica et Tibetica Verlag, 2018), 97.
6. *cha brom*, [sic] for *'khyags rom*.
7. For some reason the name of this goddess and of Vajrāloka below appear in the vocative form, while Vajrapuṣpa and Vajragandha appear in their nominative forms.
8. *Khyong bu*, [*sic*] (or alternate spelling) for *kyong bu*.
9. Compare the sixteen bodhisattvas that follow to the somewhat different list in Skorupski, *The Sarvadurgatipariśodhana Tantra, Elimination of All Evil Destinies: Sanskrit and Tibetan Texts with Introduction, English Translation and Notes* (Delhi: Motilal Banarsidass, 1983), 312.
10. *de'i re kas bcad pa'i phyi rim*. Probably from *rekha* = line in Skt.
11. *phyi*, [*sic*] for *byi*.
12. *muktihara* (*drwa ba*) = the swooping hanging garlands and *ardhahara* (*drwa phyed*) = the straight hanging-down garlands between the swoops of the *muktihara*.
13. *chun phyang*, [*sic*] for *chun 'phang*.
14. *tsong tsong bres pa* appears in the *Rnying ma rgyud 'bum* version.
15. *pyi bang*, [*sic*] for *pi wang*
16. *ta krid*: short for *antakṛt*, death, or terminator.
17. *nam*, [*sic*] for *dam*.
18. A slightly loose translation of *skye ba gcig gis thogs pa* (Skt. *caramabhaviko*).
19. . . . *nas dbyung*: Here and elsewhere, clearly means "enter into" (rather than "emerge from"). Compare Q. 116, 55b.8, where it mentions entering (*bcug*) a corpse (*shi ba'i lus*) into a mandala by means of initiation, whereby anyone born in hell will be immediately freed.
20. Dittography: *shar phyogs kyi*.
21. This last phrase, "offers these words" (*tshig 'di skad brjod du stsal*), is mistakenly repeated twice (see 15r.1).

22. Best guess, based on the Tibetan: *Aoṃ sa me / tri sa me / ma ha sa ma ye hung.*
23. The text backs up here, to the prostrations at the doors, to provide the appropriate prayers for that procedure.
24. Compare the prayer and mantra that opens S. 421, ll.1–10.
25. This last one doesn't make much sense; it might be related to *uttara.*
26. The preceding couple of paragraphs and the prayer are performed in conjunction with the four prostrations above. They appear to be inserted here slightly out of order, as they interrupt the proceedings.
27. *gsol,* [*sic*] for *sol; kab,* [*sic*] for *bkab.* This last phrase is added as an interlinear note: *dkyil 'khor zhal kab gsol.*
28. This shows that this is primarily a funerary text, as it focuses on entry through the west. The same leaning is also seen in IOL Tib J 384, r4.6–r5.1. The latter, though, may be even more specifically funerary, in that it lacks the entire blindfolding and flower-tossing sequence.
29. Here I have corrected this from "*bilva* wood" (*shing byil ba*) to "*bilva* fruit" (*shing tog byil ba*, or *bil ba*).
30. Damage to the manuscript here (16r.7) makes this word illegible. I have assumed "obstructions" based on other parallel lists.
31. Another gap in the manuscript, probably meant to be *snying po'i bcud du smin.*
32. Red being the color associated with the ritual activity of coercion. Dge rtse Paṇḍita's *Gu ru drag po ye shes rab 'byar gyis sgrub khog* says it gathers all the power, not life force, which might make some sense, since life force was covered above by *dūrvā.*

3. Evoking Possession

1. Third-hand account of Smyo shul Lung rtogs bstan pa'i nyi ma's (1829-1901) encounter with his teacher, Dpal sprul rin po che (1808–1887), by Mkhan po ngag dga', *Kun mkhyen ngag gi dbang po'i rang rnam* (Hongkong: Tianma tushu youxian gongsi 天马图书有限公司, 2001), 79: *nam mkha' la skar ma shar ba mthong ngam / rdzogs chen dgon du khyi zug pa thos sam / rang re gnyis kyis gtam smra ba go'am gsungs so sor lan phul bas 'o sgom zhes pa de yin gsungs pas bdag kyang kho thag nang nas chod / yin min gyi sgrog las grol rig stong rjen pa'i ye shes de dus ngo 'phrod pa yin / de yang khong gi byin rlabs las 'phrod pa yin.*
2. Regarding seeing the pilgrimage sites, see *Dīgha Nikāya II.*141, 142, as cited in Ananda K. Coomaraswamy, "*Samvega:* Aesthetic Shock," in *The Essential Ananda K. Coomaraswamy* (Bloomington, IN: World Wisdom, 2004 [1943]), 177. *Saṁvega* < √*vij*, to shudder with excitement or fear. For more recent and more text-based observations on *saṁvega* and the role of emotions in early Buddhism, see Maria Heim, "The Aesthetics of Excess," *Journal of the American Academy of Religion* 71, no. 3 (2003): 531–54; Andrea Arci, "Between Impetus, Fear and Disgust: 'Desire for Emancipation' (Saṃvega) from Early Buddhism to Pātañjala Yoga and Śaiva Siddhānta," in *Emotions in Indian Thought-Systems*, ed. P. Bilimoria and A. Wenta (Delhi: Routledge, 2015), 199–227, and Lajos Brons, "Facing Death from a Safe

Distance: Saṃvega and Moral Psychology," *Journal of Buddhist Ethics* 23 (2016): 83–128.

3. See Andy Rotman, *Thus Have I Seen: Visualizing Faith in Early Indian Buddhism* (Oxford: Oxford University Press, 2008), 69. *Prasāda* is almost always passively experienced. Rotman mentions the possibility of a student cultivating *prasāda*, though "this too appears to be more of a reflex act than a practiced, proactive response" (70).
4. Aśvaghoṣa, *Handsome Nanda*, trans. Linda Covil (New York: New York University Press, 2007), 243.
5. Bhikki Bodhi, *The Connected Discourses of the Buddha: A Translation of the Saṃyuta Nikāya* (Boston: Wisdom, 2000), 914.
6. Although third-person plural pronouns were used in chapter 2 to refer to the patron/initiate, in the present chapter and those following, all of which focus on *sādhanas*, third-person male singular pronouns will be used in referencing the reader. As Yael Bentor, "Women on the Way to Enlightenment," in *From Bhakti to Bon. Festschrift for Per Kvaerne*, ed. H. Havnevik and C. Ramble (Oslo: Novus Press, 2015), 89–96, shows so well, tantric authors considered women capable of performing many of the rites described and thereby attaining awakening. Nonetheless, as Bentor also observes, the *sādhanas* themselves are all written from the point of view of a male practitioner.
7. Again, many of these earliest "tantric" works (the *Mahāvairocanābhisaṃbodhi* and the *Sarvatathāgata-tattvasaṃgraha* among them) were initially referred to as sutras and only came to be called tantras in the eighth century.
8. *Vairocanābhisambodhi-vikurvitādhiṣṭāna-mahātantravṛtti*, 314a.6–314b.1; see Stephen Hodge, *The Mahā-vairocana-abhisaṃbodhi Tantra, with Buddhaguhya's Commentary* (London: Routledge Curzon, 2003), 103.
9. Here I reference the title of David Shulman's history of the imagination in South India, *More Than Real: A History of the Imagination in South India* (Cambridge, MA: Harvard University Press, 2012). Ronald Davidson, "The Problem of Secrecy in Indian Tantric Buddhism," in *The Culture of Secrecy in Japanese Religion*, ed. Bernhard Scheid and Mark Teeuwen (Oxon and New York: Routledge, 2006), 60–77, discusses the links between secrecy and the disjunction between perception and reality, or the outer and the inner, which he notes go back to the Mahāyāna sutras.
10. On dating the *STTS*, see Kazuo Kano, "Sarvatathāgatatattvasaṃgraha," in *Brill's Encyclopedia of Buddhism*, ed. Jonathan A. Silk (Leiden: Brill, 2015), 373–74.
11. Latika Lahiri, *Chinese Monks in India* (Delhi: Motilal Banarsidass, 1986), 65. As Koichi Shinohara, *Spells, Images, and Mandalas: Tracing the Evolution of Esoteric Buddhist Rituals* (New York: Columbia University Press, 2014), 29 and 239 n. 8 observes, Atikūṭa, writing in the mid-seventh century, describes his *Dhāraṇīsaṃgraha* as just one part of a larger work known as the **Vajramahāmaṇḍalasūtra*, and Yaśogupta (active second half of the sixth century) names a similarly titled work as the source for his translation of the *Eleven-Faced Avalokiteśvara Dhāraṇī* (T. 1070).
12. See, for example, Jñānamitra's late eighth-century *Āryaprajñāpāramitānayaśata pañcāśataka*, 273a.3 (*sarba buddha sa ma yo ga la sogs pa sde chen po bco brgyad*), as

cited by Rolf W. Giebel, "The Chin-Kang-Ting Ching Yu-Ch'ieh Shi-Pa-Hui Chih-Kuei: An Annotated Translation," *Journal of Naritasan Institute for Buddhist Studies* 18 (1995): 114. On later lists of the eighteen Mayājālā tantras, see Kenneth W. Eastman, "The Eighteen Tantras of the Vajraśekhara/Māyājāla," unpublished paper presented to the 26th International Conference of Orientalists, Tokyo, Japan, May 8, 1981. A summary can be found in *Transactions of the International Conference of Orientalists in Japan* XXVI (1981), 95–96, and Jacob P. Dalton, "Preliminary Remarks on a Newly Discovered Biography of Gnubs chen sangs rgyas ye shes," in *Himalayan Passages: Tibetan and Newar Studies in Honor of Hubert Decleer*, ed. Benjamin E. Bogin and Andrew Quintman (Somerville, MA: Wisdom, 2014), 119 n. 20. Some valuable identifications of Amoghavajra's descriptions with texts in today's Tibetan canons are also made by Steven Neal Weinberger, "The Significance of Yoga Tantra and the *Compendium of Principles* (*Tattvasaṃgraha Tantra*) Within Tantric Buddhism in India and Tibet" (PhD diss., University of Virginia, 2003).

13. On the *Amoghapāśakalparāja*, see Shaman Hatley, "Converting the Ḍākinī: Goddess Cults and Tantras of the Yoginīs Between Buddhism and Śaivism," in *Tantric Traditions in Transmission and Translation*, ed. David B. Gray and Ryan Richard Overbey (Oxford: Oxford University Press, 2016), 63; on the *Mañjuśrīmūlakalpa*, see David L. Snellgrove, *Indo-Tibetan Buddhism*, 2 vols. (Boston: Shambhala, 1987), 197. Atikūṭa's *Dhāraṇīsaṃgraha* is divided into five deity groupings, those of the buddhas, Prajñāpāramitā, Avalokiteśvara, Vajra, and the heavenly gods, with the buddha at the center, Avalokiteśvara deities to the north, and Vajras to the south (no mention of the Prajña deities; see Shinohara, *Spells, Images, and Mandalas*, 33 and 241 n. 40). Though this does not fit with the positioning of these groups in different directions, the order of the groups roughly maps onto the Vajradhātu mandala, with the inner circle inhabited by buddha(s), to the surrounding *pāramitās*, to the bodhisattvas (sometimes the term used to refer to the Avalokiteśvara group), to the Vajra deities who protect the boundaries, to the mundane gods of the *laukika* world at the edges.
14. IOL Tib J 712, 4v.2.
15. On the importance of propitiation, see for example *Subāhuparipṛcchā*, 118a.4ff.
16. IOL Tib J 712, 4v.5.
17. The title appears in transcribes Sanskrit and Tibetan in the opening line of Pelliot tibétain 792, 1r, and again in Sanskrit at the end as: *a rya da twa sang gra ha sa dha na o pa'i ka' le'u brgya pha rdzogs so* (Pelliot tibétain 792, 3r.2). This last reference to the work as the "Hundred-Chapter *Ārya Tattvasaṃgraha-sādhanopāyikā*," or perhaps the "hundredth chapter," remains a mystery to me.
18. For the complete copy, see Pelliot tibétain 792 and IOL Tib J 551, which together make a single *poṭhi*-style manuscript of densely packed writing across eight folio sides (though the last side is blank). A second, nearly complete copy (probably missing only its first folio) is scattered across three shelfmarks: IOL Tib J 417, Pelliot tibétain 300, and IOL Tib J 519. (At this time, IOL Tib J 519 is missing from the British Library, but a transcription was published before it disappeared; see Kimiaki Tanaka, *Tonkō: Mikkyō to Bijutsu (Essays on Tantric Buddhism in Dunhuang: Its Art and Texts)* (Kyoto: Hōzōkan, 2000), 245–46. In my entry

in Jacob P. Dalton and Sam van Schaik, *Tibetan Tantric Manuscripts from Dunhuang: A Descriptive Catalogue of the Stein Collection at the British Library* (Leiden: Brill, 2006), I mistook the first folio of IOL Tib J 417/2 (f. 38 using the British Library's numbering system) for the first folio of IOL Tib J 417/1. This means that 417/1 is missing its first folio, not its second.) Beyond these, three further incomplete copies have been identified: one consisting of seven folios of densely packed Dunhuang *dbu med* (IOL Tib J 448 and Pelliot tibétain 270) that is incomplete at its beginning and end, and two with just one folio each (Pelliot tibétain 265 and 271).

19. The commentary is found in IOL Tib J 447 and is penned in the same hand and on the same size paper as one of our more complete copies of the *sādhana* itself, i.e., IOL Tib J 448.
20. The text is complete in fifteen folios (thirty sides) and is spread across IOL Tib J 417, Pelliot tibétain 300, and IOL Tib J 519.
21. See *Vajraśekhara*, 148b.5–7. On its possible use of the *Vajraśekhara*, see n. 28. For some further comments on the relative dating of these two *sādhanas*, see n. 80.
22. Very similar procedures to those seen in our Dunhuang manuscripts also appear in Amoghavajra's writings (e.g., T. 874) and in the considerably later *Vajrodaya* and the *Kriyāsaṃgraha*; compare Tadeusz Skorupski, *Kriyāsaṃgraha* (Tring, UK: Institute of Buddhist Studies, 2002), 76–85.
23. For a paleographic analysis of the manuscripts in question, see Jacob P. Dalton, "On the Significance of the *Ārya-tattvasaṃgraha-sādhanopāyikā* and Its Commentary," in *Chinese and Tibetan Esoteric Buddhism*, ed. Yael Bentor and Meir Shahar (Leiden: Brill, 2017), 325–29. In terms of dating these to the ninth century, the shakiest cases are those of IOL Tib J 448 and the *sādhana* commentary, IOL Tib J 447. Both are written in the "headless official" style that Sam van Schaik, "Dating Early Tibetan Manuscripts: A Paleographical Method," in *Scribes, Texts and Rituals in Early Tibet and Dunhuang*, ed. Brandon Dotson, Kazushi Iwao, and Tsuguhito Takeuchi (Weisbaden: Reichert Verlag, 2013), 119–35, dates to the ninth century. However, IOL Tib J 507/ Pelliot tibétain 353 is written in a similar and quite likely identical hand, and its contents are distinctly Mahāyoga in style (including mentions of the *Gsang ba'i sngags tan tra rdzogs pa chen po'i mdo* and the three *samādhis* of the Mahāyoga generation stage). Then too there is IOL Tib J 401, also in a similar hand. This is a codex, a format not generally seen in Dunhuang manuscripts from before the tenth century. It also includes some lines in a second hand that belongs to an identified scribe who wrote during the second half of the tenth century. Although this scribe could well have written these lines on an inherited older manuscript, they give one further pause.
24. See Rta mdo, *Dkar chag 'phang than ma*, 61, where the *STTS*, with its *uttaratantra* as well as Śākyamitra's *Kośalālaṃkāra* commentary and other works, are listed as imperially approved works.
25. Such pretensions are evidenced in Chinese works earlier on, even in the esoteric Dunhuang manuscripts. See, for example, the opening frame in Pelliot chinois 3913, translated by Amanda K. Goodman, "The *Ritual Instructions for Altar Methogs* (*Tanfa yize*): Prolegomenon to the Study of a Chinese Esoteric Buddhist

Ritual Compendium from Late-Medieval Dunhuang" (PhD diss., University of California, Berkeley, 2013), 64. Whether this frame was composed in Dunhuang or elsewhere remains unclear. On Chinese Taoist texts masquerading as Buddhist at Dunhuang, see also Christine Mollier, *Buddhism and Taoism Face to Face: Scripture, Ritual, and Iconographic Exchange in Medieval China* (Honolulu: University of Hawai'i Press, 2008), 112–13.

26. Snellgrove, *Indo-Tibetan Buddhism*, 134–41.

27. In his commentary to the *Mahāvairocanābhisaṃbodhi*, Yixing explains that the officiant transforms himself into Vairocana when performing the role of *ācārya* and Vajrasattva when looking after the practicalities of creating the mandala; see Shinohara, *Spells, Images, and Mandalas*, 159.

28. Both sources agree, these include (1–3) going for refuge to the three jewels; (4) honoring one's teacher; (5–7) caring for one's vajra, bell, and *mudrā*; (8–11) giving the four gifts of wealth, fearless protection to the unfortunate, the dharma (at least by reciting one verse each day for the gods and demons), and love for all sentient beings; and (12–14) upholding the dharmas of the outer [sciences], the inner [secret mantra], and the three vehicles; see IOL Tib J 447, r2.8–5.2 and Pelliot tibétain 300, 6v.4–7r.1. The list's wording in the *Vajrahūṃkara-sādhana* is remarkably similar to that of the (slightly more elaborate) discussion in the *Vajraśekhara* (183a.7–183b.3), though in that source the lines are presented as not what the disciple should recite but what the master says, i.e., in the second person rather than the first. In later practice, the master might recite the lines and the disciples repeat them. Compare also basically the same passage in the *Sarvadurgatipariśodhana-tantra*; see Tadeusz Skorupski, *The Sarvadurgatipariśodhana Tantra, Elimination of All Evil Destinies: Sanskrit and Tibetan Texts with Introduction, English Translation and Notes* (Delhi: Motilal Banarsidass, 1983), 146, translated on 18–19.

29. IOL Tib J 447, r5.4–6. *dam tshigs rab ba ni tshe 'di yang bgegs sna tshogs 'byung la / lha 'dre kun gyi bzhad gang du yang 'gyur la / yun du yang 'o dod cher 'bod pa'i sems can dmyal bar 'gro'o.*

30. IOL Tib J 447, r7.8–8.3. *gang 'am lhag na/ sa brtags pa yin / ma gang ma brtags / sa'i nang nas rln po che dum bu dang men tog dang sha dum byung na brtags / sol ba dang rus pa byung na ma brtags / yong ni rdo rje'i gdan tshad dpag tshad gcig tshun cad brtags pa'i gnas / shes rab 'bum pa ga la yod pa dpag tshad gcig tshun cad brtags pa'i gnas / rdo rje'i rigs ni u rgyan gyi rigsu 'grub rin po che'i rigs ni rin po che 'byung khung gi gnas na 'grub/ pad mo'i rigs ni pad mo dang chu myig dang men tog yod par bsgoms na nye bar 'grub.* Note that, despite our commentary's nod to the Kriyā techniques for site preparation, Śākyamitra's *Kosalalālaṁkāra*, vol. *yi*, 88a.4–5, likewise describes clearing the soil of charcoal and bones and leveling the ground.

31. In the later tantric tradition, the *ācārya* initiation authorizes the initiate to perform initiations himself, as a "vajra master." On what distinguishes this initiation, according to Ānandagarbha (*Vajrodaya*, 46a.4-46b.1), in the brief form of the ritual (*saṃkṣiptakrama*; Ānandagarbha also describes the medium and extensive forms), the *ācāryābhiṣeka* involves applying the *nyāsa* of Vajrasattva and so forth on the body of the initiand, placing an image of Vajrasattva on his

head, reciting the mantra *oṃ mahāsukha vajrasattva jaḥ hūṃ vaṃ hoḥ suratas tvam* 108 times and a giving a water *abhiṣeka*. This is followed by a *stuti* of the 108 names, bestowal of *anujñā* by means of five verses, and a *vyākaraṇa* by means of a panegyric and a prophecy. Finally, there is a *guhyābhiṣeka*, which is actually part of the *ācāryābhiṣeka* and different from the later Mahāyoga- or Yoginī-tantra-type *guhyābhiṣeka*, i.e., no sexual intercourse, nor imagining thereof; it is just the verbal imparting of the *maṇḍalatattva* and *devatātattva* and the rites/duties of the *ācārya*. It is unclear to me why this initiation is required just to perform the *Vajrahūṃkara sādhana* that follows.

32. "Recite [his mantra] 100 times (*brgya bslas*) here could be read instead as "chant the hundred names," particularly since 100 times does not seem much. However, Buddhagupta's comments on the *Mahāvairocana's vidyāvrata* (Hodge, *The Mahā-vairocana-abhisaṃbodhi Tantra*, 318) suggest it is the mantra of the practitioner's tutelary deity, here Vajrahūṃkara. In that context, however, Buddhagupta recommends either 100,000 recitations or six months of retreat.
33. IOL Tib J 417, 2r.3–5. *khams gsum las rnam par rgyal ba'i dkyil 'khor chen po las stsogs pa'i / slob dpon gyi dbang thob pas / rdo rje dpal hung zhes pa/ bslas par 'dod na / thog mar rig sngags gyi brtul zhugs byas te / zla ba phyed du/ phyogs bcu mtha yas mu myed pa'i 'jig rten gyi khams gyi / de bzhin gshegs pa thams chad yid gyis bris la / de bzhin gshegs pa thams chad la phyag ba'o / mtshams bcing ba las stsogs pa byas nas/ bcom ldan 'das / rdo rje dpal hung zhes pa la / ji lta bus rab du mchod de/ brgya' bslas so / rdo rje rigs gyi brtul zhugso.*
34. *Kosalālaṁkāra*, vol. *yi*, 96a.6: *sngar spyad pa ni rig pa'i brtul zhugs so.*
35. Hodge, *The Mahā-vairocana-abhisaṃbodhi Tantra*, 318. Despite sharing a rather general interest in nonduality, this *vidyāvrata* is probably better distinguished from the transgressive one that became so well known in later tantric writings (contra Christian Wedemeyer, *Making Sense of Tantric Buddhism: History, Semiology and Transgression in the Indian Traditions* [New York: Columbia University Press, 2013], 159–63, especially 161).
36. IOL Tib J 417, 38r.2. *ji ltar thog ma'i dus rtag par/ bdagis byin brlab stsogs de bzhin / byas nas thams chad bsgrub par te / de nas phyin cad ci bder ro.* In translating this and the next verse, I have done my best to balance the original Sanskrit against the different translations, perhaps with only mixed results that will satisfy none. Compare Horiuchi Hanjin, ed., *Kongochokyo no Kenkyu* (*Sarvatathāgata-tattvasaṃgraha-nāma-mahāyāna-sūtra*) (Koyasan University: Mikkyo Bunka Kenkyujo, 1983), v. 253 (*pratyahaṃ prāg yathā-kālaṃ svādhiṣṭhān'ādikaṃ tathā / kṛtvā tu sādhayet sarvaṃ tataḥ paścād yathā-sukham iti*) and *Sarvatathāgatatattvasaṃgraha*, 30a.7 (*dang por nyin re'i dus bzhin du / rang la byin gyis brlab la sogs / byas nas thams cad bsgrub bya ste / de yi 'og tu ci dgar bya*).
37. *Kosalālaṁkāra*, vol. *yi*, 107a.5–6. *phyag rgya bsgrub ste rdzogs nas dkyil 'khor gyi las sam / rjes su dran pa'am bsgrub pa'am / las phran tshegs dang / de dag las gang 'dod pa de bya'o.*
38. In fact, the *STTS* passage under examination comes early in the section on the four *mudrās*, and Śākyamitra reads it as a segue into the section. Thus he writes, "Because how to accomplish that has not been taught yet, it says, 'regarding

that,' and so on, so that is what is being taught" (*Kosalālaṁkāra*, vol. *yi*, 107a.6–7: *de ji ltar bsgrub par bya ba ma gsungs bas de la zhes bya ba la sogs bas de ston pa yi to*).

39. IOL Tib J 551, 1r.7. *de nas kar ma'I mu tra bcingste / 'dzab bam bsgom ba gyis shig*. Our commentary in IOL Tib J 447 elsewhere explains that these recitations are to be performed variously, depending on the buddha family with which one is associated; see IOL Tib J 447, r6.5–9, where one recites mentally for the buddha family, through one's nose for the vajra family, in a whisper for the padma family, and out loud for the karma family. The *Śrī-vajrahūṃkara-sādhanopāyikā* (Pelliot tibétain 300, 4v.5), which focuses on the vajra family, adds the visualization of a tiny white vajra atop one's tongue while reciting the mantra.

40. The tenth-century commentator Ānandagarbha further elaborates on the above passage differently: " 'After which, one should perform as one pleases' means that one cultivates the *mahāmudrā* and so forth, and then, if one is tired, one rests and recites and cultivates some more without binding the *mudrās*. Then, when one is no longer tired or weary, one once again recites and cultivates while binding the *mudrās*" (*Tattvālokakarī* [Toh. 2510], 147a.7–147b.1. *de'i 'og tu ci dgar bya / zhes bya ba ni phyag rgya chen po la sogs pa bsgom pa dang / bzlas pas dub na ngal bso zhing phyag rgya ma bcings par yang bzlas pa dang bsgom pa bya ba'o / de nas skyo zhing dub pa dang bral ba na slar yang phyag rgya bcings la bzlas pa dang bsgom pa bya ba'o*). Contrary to Śākyamitra's reading, Ānandagarbha seems to understand "perform as one pleases" as a reference to the breaks the practitioner may take during mantra recitation. The *sādhana* does make allowance for such moments of drowsiness or distraction (during the *karmamudrā* phase toward the end of the entire text), and it recommends reciting the 100-syllable mantra in order to stabilize one's practice (see IOL Tib J 551, 1v.1–2). Why Ānandagarbha parts ways with Śakyamitra on this point remains unclear, but he does agree that the four *mudrās* structure the second stage as they do in the Dunhuang *Tattvasaṃgraha-sādhana*, after which comes a third pseudo-stage in connection with performing the mantra recitations.

Just prior to the passage under discussion here, the *STTS* describes these stages as "the great activities of *sādhana*, *siddhi*, and *siddha*" (Horiuchi, *Kongochokyo no Kenkyu*, v. 253: *athātra sarvakalpānāṃ sādhanaṃ siddhir eva ca / siddhānāṃ ca mahat karma pravakṣyāmy anupūrva- śaḥ*), which may correspond to the ritual stages of (i) the *svādhiṣṭhāna* and offerings; (ii) the four *mudrās*, which accomplish the *siddhis;* and (iii) the final performance as one pleases.

41. IOL Tib J 417, 38r.2–3. *rnam pa bzhi su mchod pa ni/ tshul bzhir yang ni cho ga bzhin / dus bzhir yang ni sbyar nas su/ las su byas nas bsgrub par ro*. The authors of the **Śrī-vajrahūṃkara-sādhanopāyikā* may have separated the "activities" (*las*) from the "accomplishment" (*bsgrub pa*) to make three stages and thereby bring this verse more into line with the passage cited above, but given the Sanskrit and the canonical Tibetan, this is likely a misreading, and Śākyamitra clearly agrees with the canonical interpretation; see Śākyamitra's *Kosalālaṃkāra* (Toh. 2503), vol. *ri*, 103a.1. Compare Horiuchi, *Kongochokyo no Kenkyu*, v. 2182 (*caturvidhābhiḥ pūjābhiḥ sadā-yogāc caturvidham / catuḥ-kāla-prayogeṇa kurvan karmāṇi sādhayet*) and *Sarvatathāgatatattvasaṃgraha*, 108a.4–5 (*dus bzhi yi ni tshul dag tu / mchod pa*

rnam pa bzhi yis ni / rtag tu ldan pa rnam bzhir yang / byas nas las rnams bsgrub par bya). On the sixteen kinds of offerings (4x4), see Śākyamitra's *Kosalālaṃkāra*, vol. *ri*, 102b.5–103a.2, where he lists the four kinds of offerings (*pūjā*) as those of *bodhicitta*, *gaṇa*, *dharma*, and *samādhi*.

42. In Dalton, "On the Significance of the *Ārya-tattvasaṃgraha-sādhanopāyikā*," where my analysis of these two passages also appears, I argue that the Shingon tradition's "eighteen methods" (*jūhachi geiin*) correspond to our stage 1, the "invocation procedures" (*nenju hō*) to our stage 2, and the "dispersed invocations" (*go kuyō*) to our third pseudo-stage. The ritual forms described in our *sādhana* are seen in Amoghavajra's writings too, and clearly he followed a system that was fundamentally the same as our own.
43. The one difference is that in the *STTS*, the four *pāramitās* come after the sixteen bodhisattvas. This is a little odd, given their prominence in the consecration rites (see below). However, in the *STTS*'s subsequent instructions on constructing the mandala altar, where all the deities are again listed, the four *pāramitās* appear in the same order as in our *sādhana*. It is possible that this discrepancy may reflect the later addition of both the opening Sarvārthasiddhi narrative, i.e., the *ādiyoga-nāma-samādhi* section, and the *maṇḍalarājāgrī-samādhi* to the ritual core now embedded in the *karmarājāgrī-samādhi* section. For more evidence on this possibility, see below, n. 55.
44. The commentary adds that following each prostration, the primary bodhisattva in the retinue accompanying each buddha approaches the master and places another version of the implement at the same point, thereby consecrating it. Hence, the commentary reads in each case, "the symbol will always reside there"; see, for example, IOL Tib J 447, r9.3 or r10.1. Śākyamitra explains differently what prostrating to each family gives you; see *Kosalālaṁkāra*, vol. *yi*, 98r.1–4.
45. IOL Tib J 447, r12.7–8. *man 'dal gyi lha men tog bab pa dang / rmyi lam du brnyan pa dang / lhag par dad pa 'di gsum gang bsgom yang rung ste.*
46. The *STTS* similarly describes the *vajrabandha* followed by the *vajrāveśa*; see Horiuchi, *Kongochokyo no Kenkyu*, vv. 299–300 or *Sarvatathāgatatattvasaṃgraha*, 34a. The *Vajrahūṃkara-sādhana* (Pelliot tibétain 300, 8r.5–8v.3) replaces this relatively simple *vajrāveśa* (*rdo rje dbab pa*) rite with a more complex series. In that work, *vajrāveśa* is translated as "vajra invitation" (*rdo rje spyan drang ba*), which is also how the term is translated in the canonical Tibetan translation of Śākyamitra's commentary. *Spyan 'dren* often translates *āvāhana*, as noted by Yael Bentor, "On the Symbolism of the Mirror in Indo-Tibetan Consecration Rituals," *Journal of Indian Philosophy* 23 (1995): 58. Like our *sādhana*, the *Vajrahūṃkara-sādhana* includes the recitation of the syllable *aḥ*, which effects the *āveśa* in the *STTS*'s account (see Horiuchi, *Kongochokyo no Kenkyu*, v. 300).
47. IOL Tib J 447, r13.8. *a vyI sha 'i phyag rgya dang sngagsu bcas pas bdag ltar gyur pa la ye shes dbab par bsam mo.*
48. *Kosalālaṁkāra*, vol. *yi*, 89b.1: *dis ye shes dbab pa bskyed de/ bdag nyid rdo rje sems dpa'i skur bsam mo.*
49. *Kosalālaṁkāra*, vol. *yi*, 126b.4–5: *rdo rje dbab pa zhes bya ba la / dbab pa 'di ni ye shes dbab pa yin gyi / sems dpa' dbab pa ni ma yin no* (my italics).

50. What follows is an attempt at explaining the redundancy, but a tentative one.
51. See Pelliot tibétain 300, 7v.2–8r.3: (i) repairing any broken vows; (ii) forming the mandala circle using a *vajra-cakra mudrā* and mantra; (iii) purifying one's sins by means of another *mudrā* and mantra (for the mantra in the *STTS*, see Horiuchi, *Kongochokyo no Kenkyu*, v. 841, or *Sarvatathāgatatattvasaṃgraha*, 57b.1–2, where it is called "the heart [mantra] for Vajrapāṇi to destroy all evils" [*vajrapāṇiḥ sarvā-pāpa-sphoṭanahṛdaya*]); (iv) by means of the *mudrā* for all activities and the wrathful mantra, "*vajrayakṣa hūṃ*," establishing the daggers marking the space, the surrounding fence, the lattices, the sealing of the boundaries, the five secret offerings, filling in the deities, protecting the implements, and so on.
52. Horiuchi, *Kongochokyo no Kenkyu*, vv. 202–206; *Sarvatathāgatatattvasaṃgraha*, 25a.7–26a.2. For an English translation of the relevant section, see Rolf W. Giebel, *Two Esoteric Sutras: The Adamantine Pinnacle Sutra, the Susiddhikara Sutra* (Berkeley, CA: Numata Center for Buddhist Translation and Research, 2001), 68–69.
53. Horiuchi, *Kongochokyo no Kenkyu*, v. 207; *Sarvatathāgatatattvasaṃgraha*, 26a.2–3.
54. *Kosalālaṁkāra*, vol. *yi*, 89a.7–89b.1. *nye bar mtshon pa'i don tsam du zad de / byin gyis brlab pa dang / dbang bskur ba dang/ bsrung ba dang / mchod pa dang / ting nge 'dzin yongs su bzung bas rdo rje sems dpar bdag nyid bsgom zhing dkyil 'khor gyi las bya'o / yang na mdor bsdus na badzra ban+d+ha traT ces bya la / badzra A be sha a: zhes bya ba 'dis ye shes dbab pa bskyed de / bdag nyid rdo rje sems dpa'i skur bsam mo.*
55. The instructions to follow, on the *pañcākārābhisaṃbodhikrama*, are based on the narrative portion of the *STTS*'s first chapter (consisting of the opening story of Sarvārthasiddhi and Vairocana's original emanation of the deities mandala), whereas the construction of the mandala, of which the *vajrāveśa* is a remnant, is based on the *karmarājāgrī-samādhi*, what I suggest might have been the tantra's "ritual core" (see n. 45 above). From this perspective, the redundancy seen in the *sādhanas* (and still preserved in the *Kriyāsaṃgraha*; see the summary in Skorupski, *Kriyāsaṃgraha*, 76–84) may be a reflection of the compositional strata of the tantra itself, with the *vajrāveśa mudrā* and mantra representing the vestigal remains of the earlier tradition. If this hypothesis is true, it might further suggest that the *karmarājāgrī-samādhi* is based on a hypothetical ritual manual that served as the ritual core of *STTS*. In other words, ritual manual preceded tantra. While significant, these ideas are difficult to prove, so they must for now remain restricted to these notes.
56. The same practice is described in the *Mahāvastu*, 2.214, translated in J. J. Jones, *The Mahāvastu*, 3 vols. (London: Pali Text Society, 1952), 2: 120. The name Sarvārthasiddhi is also used, though it is seen in other accounts of the Buddha's life story too.
57. For Śākyamitra's readings of the two moons, see *Kośalālaṁkara*, vol. *yi*, 20a.2–5 and 21b.7 (and again at 22a.2), respectively. Ānandagarbha prefers two full moon discs, stacked one atop the other, as in *Tattvālokakarī*, vol. *li*, 40a.4. As a result of our *sādhana*'s unusual take on the five stages, the mantra associated with each does not always match its result. Oddly, no mantras are mentioned, though the Dunhuang commentary has them in mind, as it provides the final one.

58. Pelliot tibétain 300, 9r.2–3. *de bzhin gshegs pa de dag thams chad gyi byin gyis rdo rje sems dpa' der zhugs nas / don thams cad grub pa byang cub sems dpa'i lusu gyur nas / bzhugso.*
59. Horiuchi, *Kongochokyo no Kenkyu*, vol. 1, v. 26: *atha yāvantaḥ sarv'ākāśa-dhātu-samavasaraṇāḥ sarva-tathāgata-kāya-vāk-citta-vajra-dhātavas, te sarve sarva-tathāgatādhiṣṭhānena tasmin sattva-vajre praviṣṭāḥ tataḥ sarva-tathāgataiḥ sa bhagavān Sarvārtha-siddhir mahā-bodhisattvo 'Vajra-dhātur Vajra-dhātur!! iti vajra-nāmābhiṣekeṇābhiṣiktaḥ. Sarvatathāgatatattvasaṃgraha*, 4r.7–4v.1: *de nas nam mkha'i dbyings thams cad du mnyam par 'jug pa'i de bzhin gshegs pa thams cad kyi sku dang gsung dang thugs rdo rje dbyings ji snyed pa de dag thams cad de bzhin gshegs pa thams cad kyi byin brlabs kyis sems dpa'i rdo rje der zhugs so / de nas de bzhin gshegs pa thams cad kyis bcom ldan 'das byang chub sems dpa' chen po don thams cad grub pa de la / rdo rje'i dbyings rdo rje'i dbyings zhes bya ba'i ming gis dbang bskur ro.*
60. Śākyamitra clarifies the situation when he says that stage 5's final form of the deity comes from the vajra of the previous stage: "He saw [himself] in the form of Vajrasattva who manifested out of the five-spoked vajra that was established from the subtle particles of the bodies of all the *tathāgatas*." *Kosalālaṁkāra*, vol. yi, 22a.6–7. *de bzhin gshegs pa thams cad kyi sku'i rdul phra rab las bsgrubs pa'i rdo rje rtse lnga pa las mngon par byung ba'i rdo rje sems dpa'i sku'i gzugs su thong ngo.*
61. *Kosalālaṁkāra*, vol. *yi*, 21b.6. *gang gi mthus she na de bzhin gshegs pa thams cad kyi byin gyi rlabs kyis.*
62. Horiuchi, *Kongochokyo no Kenkyu*, vol. 1, v. 29: *adhitiṣṭhata mām! bhagavantas tathāgatāḥ! imām abhisaṃbodhiṃ dṛdhī-kuruta ca. Sarvatathāgatatattvasaṃgraha*, 4b.4–5: *bcom ldan 'das de bzhin gshegs pa thams cad kyis bdag byin gyis rlobs la mngon par rdzogs par byang chub pa 'di brtan par mdzod cig.*
63. *Kosalālaṁkāra*, vol. *yi*, 23a.3. *zhugs zhes bya ba ni snying ga dang / smin mtshams dang lkog ma dang spyi bo rnams su zhugs pa ste / 'di'i byin gyis brlabs pa'o.* See also *Vajrodaya*, 16a.6–16b.3.
64. Pelliot tibétain 792, 1v.5–6. *thog mar bdagi rigs kyI phyag rgyas byang cub sems dpa' rnams kyI byind gyI rlabs bya'.*
65. See Pelliot tibétain 792, 2r.1. The *samayamudrās* for each of the four *pāramitās*, any of which appears capable of installing the four heads of the buddha families (as suggested by *Kosalālaṁkāra*, vol. *yi*, 21b.6), as well as for each of the sixteen bodhisattvas are provided by Horiuchi, *Kongochokyo no Kenkyu*, vv. 263ff., and *Sarvatathāgatatattvasaṃgraha*, 31a.7ff.
66. However, the *Vajrahūṃkara-sādhana*, which is focused on the vajra family, uses a different "vajra wrath" (*rdo rje khro bo*) *mudrā*; Pelliot tibétain 300, 9v.4.
67. *Kosalālaṁkāra*, vol. *yi*, 108a.4–6. *sems tsam du bzhag la sems tsam de yang zla ba'i dkyil 'khor lta bur bshad de / de brtan par bya ba'i phyir yang de ye shes kyi rdo rje rtse lnga pa gzhag pa 'di ni dam tshig yin te / theg pa chen po thams cad du sangs rgyas dang byang chub sems dpa' rnams kyi ye shes kyi skur bsgrubs pa yin no / gang gi phyir rdo rje bsdams pas ni zla ba'i dkyil 'khor ston pa yin la / so mo gnyis bsgreng bas ni rdo rjer bstan te.* Throughout our sources, the masculine and feminine forms of Sattvavajra/ī seem to be used indiscriminately. This may be related to the identity of, on the one hand, the *sattvavajra* in the narrative of the five stages of

manifest awakening, and on the other, the Sattvavajrī *pāramitā* goddess who performs the consecration in a ritual setting. In Amoghavajra's ritual manual for the worship of Uṣṇīṣavijayā (T. 972, 367a4), the same *mudrā* is used for a similar purpose, though there it is called the "*vajrapāramitā-mudrā*," which makes sense and likewise reflects the feminine gender of the *mudrā*.

68. IOL Tib J 447, r15.8–9. Apart from this helpful observation, however, the commentary is confused regarding the purpose of this moon disc. In the *Vajrahūṃkara-sādhana*, a further sun disc is created behind the moon disc; see Pelliot tibétain 300, 9v.3–4.

69. Horiuchi, *Kongochokyo no Kenkyu*, v. 256, and *Sarvatathāgatatattvasaṃgraha*, 30b.3. The *STTS* passage in question appears within a larger discussion of the *mahāmudrā*, i.e., transforming oneself into the deity.

70. *Kosalālaṁkāra*, vol. *yi*, 108a.2. According to Śākyamitra, the procedure around the mirror represents an alternative method for consecrating oneself with the *jñānasattva* (*Kosalālaṁkāra*, vol. *yi*, 108a.4ff.; his discussion of the procedure itself immediately precedes this statement [108a.1–3]; also relevant is 127b.4–5, where he again discusses the similarities of the two methods, in a context that fits more closely with our own, i.e., not that of the *mahāmudrā*). This *mahāmudrā* procedure too uses the *samayastvaṃ* mantra to produce the reflection of oneself in the moon disc.

71. *Sukusuma*, 114b.4: *rang snying dam tshig phyag rgya zhes te rang gi lha'i snying gar dam tshig gi phyag rgya ye shes sems dpa' gnas dang bcas pa'o*. The identity of the *samayamudrā* and the *jñānasattva* in early tantric sources is suggested in a brief note by Elizabeth English, *Vajrayoginī: Her Visualizations, Rituals, and Forms* (Boston: Wisdom, 2002), 470 n. 411, where she observes that the *Sarvadurgatipariśodhana* uses the term *samayamaṇḍala* in a sense that resembles that of the later *jñānasattva* (see Skorupski, *The Sarvadurgatipariśodhana Tantra*, 20).

72. Pelliot tibétain 656, ll. 17–18: *ye shes sems dpa' bdag la bcas pas dam tshig gyi phyag rgya zhes bya*.

73. *Kosalālaṁkāra*, vol. *yi*, 108a.6. *sems dpa' rdo rje ma'i phyag rgya dang / ye shes sems dpa' ni khyad par med do*.

74. *Tattvālokakarī*, vol. *li*, 152a.4. *de rnams dang lhan cig tu chu dang 'o ma ltar tha mi dad par bdag nyid bsgoms par bya'o*.

75. Bentor, "On the Symbolism of the Mirror," 64. On the role of mirrors in image consecration, see also Yael Bentor, *Consecration of Images and Stūpas in Indo-Tibetan Tantric Buddhism* (Leiden: E. J. Brill, 1996), and Koichi Shinohara, "The Esoteric Buddhist Ritual of Image Installation," in *Buddhist and Jaina Studies: Proceedings of the Conference in Lumbini*, ed. J. Soni, M. Pahlke, and C. Cüppers (Bhairahawa, Nepal: Lumbini International Research Institute, 2014), 289. Shinohara cites a tenth-century source translated by Dānapāla (T. 1418; *Yiqie rulai anxiang sanmei yiguijing*; 切如來安像三昧儀軌經) for a rite in which, having transferred the image into a mirror, one bathes the mirror image. Similar practices are observed by Bentor in numerous works.

76. *Bṛhatsaṃhitā* 4.2. *salilamaye śaśini raver dīdhitaye mūrcchitās tamo naiśam / kṣapayanti darpaṇodaranihitā iva mandirasyāntaḥ*. I thank Marko Geslani for

furnishing this verse, complete with his translation. Further evidence of the exchangability of moons and mirrors at Dunhuang appears in the interlinear notes to the *Guhyasamāja* at IOL Tib J 438, 15v.2: "In the center of the sky, visualize the minuscule likeness of a clear moon, unobscured and unobstructed. If one is unable [to do that], imagine it as a tiny mirror" (*nam ka'i dkyil du zla ba gsal ba sgrib pa'am thogs pa myed pa ltar cung zad dmyigs / myi nus na yang mye long chung ngu tsam du bsams*).

77. Pelliot tibétain 792, 1v.6–7.

78. IOL Tib J 447, r16.4–6. Note the residual problems around the two families that were added later, the *ratna* and the *karma*.

79. *Kosalālaṁkāra*, vol. *yi*, 23a.1–2. *de bzhin gshegs pa thams cad ces bya ba ni 'dir ye shes kyi sku'i ngo bo nyid mi bskyod pa la sogs pa'i de bzhin gshegs pa bzhi po rnams bzung ngo*.

80. That our *sādhana* has rewritten the five stages to edit out the doublings of both the moon disc and the vajra suggests other interests at work. It is tempting to suggest that our other *STTS*-based Dunhuang *sādhana*, the *Vajrahūṃkara-sādhana*, is an earlier work than the *Tattvasaṃgraha-sādhana*, precisely because it includes the mandala and sticks more closely to the *STTS*'s account of the five stages. But given that its mandala construction is highly abbreviated and its reading of the five stages flawed, in addition to its use of the *anuttaratantra* (chapter 23) and possibly of the later *Vajraśekhara-tantra*, I prefer to see it as a slightly later work by a more scholarly author more concerned with adhering to a fuller array of canonical sources.

81. *Sarvatathāgatatattvasaṃgraha*, 4b.5. *de nas de skad ces gsol pa dang / de bzhin gshegs pa thams cad de bzhin gshegs pa'i rdo rje dbyings kyi sems dpa'i rdo rje der zhugs so*.

82. *Tantrārthāvatāra*, 6a.3–4: *de bas na rgyud 'di nyid dang gzhan las kyang dam tshig gi phyag rgya sgrub pa na bsgrub par bya ba'i dam tshig gi phyag rgya bcings te snying ga'i phyogs su bzhag la rang gi snying gar sems rdo rjer bsam mo zhes bshad do*. For the *samayamudrā* that corresponds to each of the buddha families, see the *STTS* in Horiuchi, *Kongochokyo no Kenkyu*, vv. 263ff., or *Sarvatathāgata-tattvasaṃgraha*, 31a.6ff.

83. Explained by *Kosalālaṁkāra*, vol. *yi*, 128a.4–6.

84. The *Vajrahūṃkara-sādhana* lists four groups of four, with only the secret goddesses matching our own. The last group consists of the four gate guardians, which means that, in that *sādhana*, the practice of the four *mudrās* that is to come (stage 2 in my structural analysis) reduplicates the activities of these four deities and thus breaks the coherence of the structure. It seems this *sādhana* is thus more interested in constructing the mandala than having its every move correspond to a particular deity (which, as discussed below, is a central concern of our *sādhana*).

85. Dzong-ka-ba, *Yoga Tantra: Paths to Magical Feats* (Ithaca, NY: Snow Lion, 2005), 131.

86. The procedures here match quite closely to the tantra at Horiuchi, *Kongochokyo no Kenkyu*, v. 255; *Sarvatathāgatatattvasaṃgraha*, 30b.2.

87. IOL Tib J 447, r21.8–10. *lcags kyus/ beng dze [sic] zhes bdag gi khong du drang zhags pas / hung zhes bdag gi nang du gzhug lcags sgrog gis bang zhes bya ste / bdag dang*

lha dang myi bral bar bya ba'i phyir bcing / a bye sha'i bsnams pa'i phyag rgyas / ho zhes bya ste / bdag dang lha gnyis tha myi dad par bya ba'i phyir bsnam.

88. IOL Tib J 447, r22.1–4. The commentary adds that the *karmamudrā*, qua the activities of the buddha, is instantiated by the deity's postures and colors, but this too seems odd and is not confirmed by our other sources. It also says the *samayamudrā* is the implement held by the deity. Such a reading is also unusual, though not far off the widespread concept of the *samayamudrā* being the consecrating symbol (be it a vajra, a lotus, or whatever) that comes to rest at the heart.
89. *Kosalālaṁkāra*, vol. *yi*, 128b. 1–3. *de yang dbab pai snying po brjod la dbab pa byas nas / de'i 'og du sems dpa' chen po rje su dran pa'i snying po brjod par bya'o / de nas dgug pa dang gzhug pa dang bcing ba dang dbang du bya ba'i snying po brjod la yid kyis kyang bya ste / phyag rgya chen po dang rang gi dam tshig gi phyag rgya bzung nas / las kyi phyag rgya'i tshul du sngags pa'i rang kyi lus bsgyur zhing gzhag par bya'o / chos kyi phyag rgya yang zla ba'i dkyil 'khor la bzhag cing brjod par yang bya'o.* The relevant section of the *STTS* is at Horiuchi *Kongochokyo no Kenkyu*, vol. 1, vv. 299ff., and *Sarvatathāgatatattvasaṃgraha*, 34a.1ff. Still further confusion is added by our *sādhana* itself, which instructs the officiant to "perform the consecrations by means of the *karmamudrā* together with the *samayamudrā*" (IOL Tib J 551, 1r.3–4. *kar ma mu tra dang sa ma ya mu tra bcas pas byin gyis rlobs shig*). The inclusion of the *karmamudrā* here seems anomalous.
90. *Kosalālaṁkāra*, vol. *yi*, 128b.2–3. *rdo rje khu tshur bcing bar bya ste / sku gsung thugs kyi rdo rje rnams / bsdus pa.*
91. Śākyamitra definitely follows this order, with the protection first, followed by the 108 names, but it is possible our *sādhana* reverses this. It is a little unclear because the *sādhana* jumps around a little in this section. The *Vajrahūṃkara-sādhana* follows the same order as Śākyamitra, so I am assuming our *sādhana* really does too.
92. IOL Tib J 551, 1r.7. *de nas kar ma'I mu tra bcingste/ 'dzab baM bsgom ba bgyi shig.*
93. For a recent study of these materials, see Goodman, "The *Ritual Instructions for Altar Methods* (*Tanfa yize*)." I do not read Chinese, so my observations here are entirely derivative and dependent on Goodman's important research.
94. However, the manuscripts themselves appear to date to the tenth century. As Goodman, "The *Ritual Instructions for Altar Methods* (*Tanfa yize*)," discusses, the manuscripts also show some allegiance to early Chan lineages.
95. Goodman, "The *Ritual Instructions for Altar Methods* (*Tanfa yize*)," refers to the latter as "Recension B."
96. Goodman, "The *Ritual Instructions for Altar Methods* (*Tanfa yize*)," 15.
97. Goodman, "The *Ritual Instructions for Altar Methods* (*Tanfa yize*)," 30.
98. Goodman, "The *Ritual Instructions for Altar Methods* (*Tanfa yize*)," 47, citing Amoghavajra's *Jin'gangding yiqie rulai zhenshishe dasheng xianzheng dajiaowang jing* (Taishō 18.874).
99. *Tantrārthāvatāra*, 6a.1–3. *bdag nyid chen po rnams kyi thugs gsang ba ni dam tshig ces bya ba'i sgrar brjod de / rgyud nas bshad pa ni yang dag par 'thob pa 'am / rtogs par bya ba'i phyir ram/ mi 'da' ba'i don du dam tshig ces bya'o / gang gi phyir zhe na / de rang gi yul gyi de kho na nyid ni dam tshig gi phyag rgya ste / bdag nyid chen po rnams*

kyis mi 'da' ba'i ngo bo zhes sngar bshad pa yin no / de lta bas na lha'i thugs gsang ba'i mtshan ma ni dam tshig ces bshad pa'i don te.

100. Horiuchi, *Kongochokyo no Kenkyu*, vv. 218–222. *tato raktavastrottarīyo raktanaktakāvacchāditamukhaḥ sattvavajrimudrāṃ bandhayed anena hṛdayena / samayas tvam / tato madhyāṅgulidvayena mālāṃ granthya praveśayed anena hṛdayena / samaya hūṃ / tataḥ praveśyaivaṃ vadet / adya tvaṃ sarvatathāgatakulapraviṣṭaḥ. tad ahaṃ te vajrajñānam utpādayiṣyāmi, yena jñānena tvaṃ sarvatathāgatasiddhim api prāpsyasi. kim utānyāḥ siddhīḥ / na ca tvayādṛṣṭamahāmaṇḍalasya vaktavyaṃ, mā te samayo vyathed iti / tataḥ svayaṃ vajrācāryaḥ sattvavajrimudrām avamūrdhamukhīṃ baddhvā vajraśiṣyasya mūrdhni sthāpyaivaṃ vadet / ayaṃ te samayavajro mūrdhānaṃ sphālayed, yadi tvaṃ kasya cid brūyāt / tatas tathaiva samayamudrayodakaṃ śapathāhṛdayena sakṛt parijāpya tasmai śiṣyāya pāyayed iti / tatredaṃ śapathāhṛdayaṃ bhavati / vajrasattvaḥ svayaṃ te 'dya hṛdaye samavasthitaḥ / nirbhidya tatkṣaṇaṃ yāyād yadi brūyād imaṃ nayam / vajrodaka ṭhaḥ.*
101. Śākyamitra, vol. *yi*, 98b.2. *rdo rje ye shes ni rdo rje dbab pa ste.*
102. Śākyamitra, vol. *yi*, 99a.1. *ye shes dbab pa'i phyir sems dpa' rdo rje ma'i phyag rgya rdo rje slob ma'i snying gar bzhag la snying po brjod par bya'o.*
103. *Tattvālokakarī*, 151a.4. *rang gi lus la bye ma la bum pa'i chu rgyun blugs pa ltar sangs rgyas thams cad gzhug par bya'o.*
104. Christopher Daren Wallis, "To Enter, to Be Entered, to Merge: The Role of Religious Experience in the Traditions of Tantric Shaivism" (PhD diss., University of California, Berkeley, 2014), 1; on the term's appearance in the *Brahmayāmala*, see 158–61. On dating the same work to the late seventh century (or perhaps early eighth), I thank Shaman Hatley for sharing his views.
105. Alexis Sanderson, "The Śaiva Age: The Rise and Dominance of Śaivism during the Early Medieval Period," in *Genesis and Development of Tantrism*, ed. Shingo Einoo (Tokyo: Institute of Oriental Culture, University of Tokyo, 2009), 133–39, also observes that *āveśa*, despite being alien to antecedent Buddhism, is central to both initiatory and postinitiatory practice in the *STTS*. For more on *āveśa* in tantric religion, see Frederick M. Smith, *The Self Possessed: Deity and Spirit Possession in South Asian Literature and Civilization* (New York: Columbia University Press, 2006), 376–98.
106. Pelliot tibétain 792, 1v.7.
107. *Tattvālokakarī*, 150a.6–7. *'dis ni bcom ldan 'das dang lhan cig gcig tu gyur par lhag par mos par bsgrubs bas bsgom pa'i rab kyi mthar thug pa las byung ba phyag rgya chen po grub pa yin zhes bya ba 'di yang ston pa yin no.* Ānandagarbha is actually commenting on the mantra, *samayastvaṃ aham*, which occurs at the same point and plays the same role as our shorter *samayo'ham*. Perhaps the mantra was shortened to mirror more closely the opening mantra, *samayastvam*.
108. See Matthew Bryan Orsborn, "Chiasmus in the Early *Prajñāpāramitā*: Literary Parallelism Connecting Criticism and Hermeneutics in an Early *Mahāyāna Sūtra*" (PhD diss.,University of Hong Kong, 2012), and "Chiastic Structure of the Vessantara Jātaka: Textual Criticism and Interpretation through Inverted Parallelism," *Buddhist Studies Review* 32, no. 1 (2015): 143–59.
109. Mary Douglas, *Thinking in Circles: An Essay on Ring Compositions* (New Haven, CT: Yale University Press, 2007), 32.

110. Śākyamitra emphasizes the "intense devotion" (*lhag par mos pa*) that should be directed at both the image in the moon and the *mudrā* (*Kosalālaṁkāra*, vol. *yi*, 108a.3 and 6).
111. Pelliot tibétain 792, 1v.2 and IOL Tib J 551, 1v.3. The latter is seen throughout the *Bka' 'gyur* and *Bstan 'gyur*, sometimes with slight variations, but not in the *STTS* itself. It appears to be an example of the kind of verse that circulated widely through ritual writings and only occasionally made it into the canon.
112. *Dvitīkramamukhāgama*, 12b.3. *rje btsun man ngag chen po dang / sna* [*sic*] *nas rna bar 'pho byed.*

Appendix: *Tattvasaṃgraha-sādhanopāyika*

1. Title drawn from Pelliot tibétain 792, 1r.1. The same line provides the Tibetan title as the *De nyid 'dus pa'i bsgrub pa'i thabs*. IOL Tib J 417 provides the somewhat corrupted titles *Sādhupāyika* and *Bsgrub par bsdus pa*.
2. In what follows, boldface marks passages that are cited in the commentary.
3. IOL Tib J 447, r9.8, explains that this is a garland of jewels, and specifically of pearls. (Here I take *rin po che myi gu* as *sic* for *rin po che myu gu*, a translation of the Sanskrit, *ratnāṅkura*, i.e., pearl.) The commentary also says that, following one's prostration, the primary bodhisattva in the retinue accompanying each buddha approaches the practitioner and places another version of the implement already imagined on one's body at the same point, thereby consecrating it. Thenceforth, the commentary reads in each case, "the symbol will always reside there" (see, for example, IOL Tib J 447, r9.3 or r10.1).
4. At this point ends the missing folio from IOL Tib J 417.
5. I.e., the famous mantra, *oṃ svabhāvaśuddhāḥ sarvadharmāḥ svabhāvaśuddho'ham*. The *sādhana* here instructs the practitioner to recite the Tibetan translation of the mantra, rather than the Sanskrit mantra itself. The commentary explains, however, that one should recite first the Sanskrit mantra and then the translation, as is sometimes done today.
6. This is a meditation on emptiness, commented on by IOL Tib J 447, 12.1–7. Here the meditation is used for its purificatory powers and should not be confused with the meditation on emptiness that opens the *pañcākārābhisaṃbodhikrama* just below. The same mantra was still used for purificatory purposes at the beginning of the *Kriyāsaṃgraha*'s rendition of the three *samādhis* (see Toh. 2531, 265a.3; see also Tadesusz Skorupski, *Kriyāsaṃgraha* [Tring, UK: Institute of Buddhist Studies, 2002], 76). Pelliot tibétain 300 has in place of this mantra a series of meditations on conventional and ultimate bodhicitta (7r.3–7v.1). Pelliot tibétain 300 then opens its uniting with the deity section with another series of preliminary rites not present in our *sādhana*: (i) repairing one's vows (7v.2), (ii) entering the *maṇḍala* by means of the *vajra-cakra* mantra and *mudrā* (7v.3–4), (iii) expunging one's sins (7v.4-8r.1), and (iv) accomplishing all the activities for establishing the ritual space (8r.1–3).

7. Here the first extant folio from IOL Tib J 448 begins; see IOL Tib J 448, f. 6r: *bsnol ba ni/ rdo rje thal mor bka' stsal te* . . . (For other corresponding points, see IOL Tib J 417/1, 42r.5, and Pelliot tibétain 792, 1v.2.) IOL Tib J 448 was originally a concertina, the pages of which have been cut so that it appears as if it were a *poti*.
8. This begins the first of the "five stages of complete enlightenment" (*pañcākārābhisaṃbodhikrama*), whereby one generates oneself as the deity. It is a rather abbreviated account that may be supplemented by the commentary; see IOL Tib J 447, r13.8–15.4. The present account differs somewhat from that in the opening passage of the *STTS*, where the symbol appears in the third stage, then is stabilized in the fourth. Here, by contrast, the seed syllable appears in the third stage, then transforms into the symbol in the fourth. The account in Pelliot tibétain 300, 8v.3–9v.2, adheres more faithfully to the canonical conception (except of course for the fact that Pelliot tibétain 300 focuses on the deity Vajrahūṃkara of the vajra family). For a parallel point in Śākyamitra, see 126b.6, though there no mention is made of the five stages.
9. At this point, IOL Tib J 448, 6r.5, inserts the (somewhat corrupted) mantra, *snying po 'di yang brjod do / om tsad ta bi tang da ro mi*, which is missing from the two other extant versions of this passage. Moreover, the mantra, which is meant to correspond to the initial appearance of the moon disc, does not fit entirely well with the present meditation on a mind-only emptiness, the first stage in our *sādhana*. IOL Tib J 448 continues to insert the mantras for the remaining stages, as noted below. Regarding the deconstruction of the tiny particles into their six sides and the subsequent resting in mind only, see too *Kosalālaṁkāra*, *yi*, 19b.4–5.
10. *bsgos*; IOL Tib J 417, 42v.2, prefers *bskos*, while ITJ448, 6r.6, reads *bsgoms* (and IOL Tib J 447, r14.4, *bsgom*, which it glosses as *brgyan*), i.e., "the moon disc that has been cultivated through one's accumulations of merit." Here I follow what may be the *lectio difficilior*. Śākyamitra (*yi*, 20a.4) includes a similar description, using the verb *yongs su bsags pa*.
11. IOL Tib J 448, r14. 5–6: *snying po 'di yang brjod do/ om b+hi d+hi tsid ta ma pa da yI mi*.
12. IOL Tib J 447, r14.4–5, suggests this can be the syllables of one's mantra or just the seed syllable of one's *yidam*.
13. IOL Tib J 448, r14. 5–6: *snying po 'di yang brjod par bya'o / om ti Shwa badzra*.
14. *Yang dag par gshegs pa*, an early translation of *tathāgata*. Here the "particles" refer to the tiny *tathāgatas* at the end of each of the light rays that spread forth and retract to effect the transformation from syllable to symbol, on which see IOL Tib J 447, r14.7–8. Also, at this point IOL Tib J 448, r14.8, misses the following line (*de las kyang bdagi lha'I gzugs mngon bar 'grub par soMs shig*) and inserts instead the corresponding mantra, which is incomplete due to damage to the manuscript: *snying po 'di yang brjod do / om ya tha / bdag gi lha bar ma* . . . *ham*.
15. Compare Ānandagarbha's *Vajrodāya* (Toh. 2516, 16a.7) and Śākyamitra's *Kośalālaṃkāra*, vol. *yi*, 108a and again 127b.5). From this point IOL Tib J 448 has a folio missing, following f. 6r.
16. Śākyamitra (*Kosalālaṁkāra*, *yi*, 108a.7) prefers the mantra *samayastvam ahaṃ*, and writes that this means that both you are me and I am you.

17. IOL Tib J 447, r16.4–6, aligns the heart with the mind, the forehead with the body, the throat with the speech, and the crown of the head with the activities.
18. *Kosalālaṁkāra*, *yi*, 108a.7, prefers *samayastvaṃ aham*, while Ānandagarbha, *Tattvāloka*, 150a.5, recognizes either possibility.
19. Reading *glan ba* as *lhan pa*.
20. Pelliot tibétain 792.6 reads slightly anomalously: *sad twa ba dzra'i phyag rgya gny-isu bya*.
21. Likely refers to the preceding mantra, *Vajrasattva dṛśya hoḥ*.
22. IOL Tib J 447, r21.2–10, explains that the *krodhāṅkuśa-mudrā* summons the deity, who then manifests in front of oneself with the *vajrāveśa* and *dṛśya hoḥ* mantras, whereupon, after praising the deity by means of the 108 names, one draws the deity into oneself by means of the four syllables, "in order to make oneself and the deity inseparable" (*bdag dang lha gnyis tha myi dad par bya ba'i phyir*).
23. The first part of this sentence is corrupt. The only correct reading appears in IOL Tib J 551, 1r.3: *ba dzra spo Ta'i phyag rgya de nyid las lag pa gnyis kyi rgyab bsdoms la zhog shig*. The passage would seem to mean one should perform the *vajrāveśa mudrā* behind where the previous *mudrā* was bound.
24. IOL Tib J 447, 7.3–4 (while commenting on the *dharmamudrā* in another context) explains that this may be either the entire heart mantra or the single seed syllable. Alternatively, it adds, "one may cultivate many five-spoked vajras the size of tiny mustard seeds."
25. The commentary introduces the following two stages as follows: "When it says '*karmamudrā*,' it means the *mudrā* of the activities. One imagines [oneself in] the bodily postures and colors, however they may be. The existence of oneself like that purifies the activities. When it says '*samayamudrā*,' it means the seal of the sacrament (*dam tshig*). One imagines oneself holding the implements, whatever they may be." (IOL Tib J 447, r22.2–4: *kar ma mu tra zhes 'byung ba ni las gyi phyag rgya la bya ste / lha'i bzhugs stangs dang sku mdog ci 'dra bar bsam ste / bdag de ltar 'dug pa ni 'phrin las dag pa'o / sa ma ya mu tra zhes 'byung ba ni dam tshig gi phyag rgya la bya ste / bdag gi phyag mtshan gang yin pa de / thogs par bsam pa*.)
26. Pelliot tibétain 300, 4v.1: "in order to enact the ferocity" (*gnyan bar bya ba'i phyir*).
27. Could be about joining with the mind of the deity, i.e., the *samayamudrā*. Being a *sādhana* for the vajra family, Pelliot tibétain 300, 4v.1, adds here drawing Mahendra and his consort, Affliction Inciter, on the ground and then suppressing them (*nyon mongs 'doms ma dang dbang po chen po sa la bris te mnan na*).
28. Pelliot tibétain 300, 4v.5, adds the visualization of a tiny white vajra atop one's tongue while reciting the mantra. Note too IOL Tib J 447's commentary on how to perform the recitations, depending on which buddha family one wants to accomplish: "There are four ways to recite. One who has entered the *Vajradhātu* mandala recites mentally, while keeping the lips and teeth closed. One who has entered the mandala of *Trilokavijaya* keeps the lips and teeth closed and says the *hūṃ* while drawing the sound through the nose. One who has entered the *maṇḍala* of Jagadvinaya should recite with the breath on the top of the

tongue so that only oneself can hear [i.e., in a whisper]. One who has entered the *maṇḍala* for Sarvārthasiddhi should recite the words out loud" (IOL Tib J 447, r6.5–9).

29. Here a fifth *mudrā* is added for the fifth family that was not present in the original consecration by *nyāsa*. This suggests that the closing sequence was added later.
30. The tantra explains that here the practitioner enacts tying a garland around their head. "With one's two forefingers, encircle the garland and bind it." (*STTS*, 34b.4–5: *mdzub mo gnyis kyis phreng bar bskor zhing bcings.*)
31. The order of this mantra varies slightly from the canonical tantra; see *Sarvatathāgata-tattvasaṃgraha*, 34b.5.
32. This may be slightly corrupt, but in the *STTS* itself, one dons armor and a garland around one's head.
33. The Vajrahūmkara manual in this same manuscript ends with instructions to do as one pleases (*ci bder spyad do*); see IOL Tib J 417, 45r.5-45v.2. A "vajra dance" and "vajra song" are discussed at this point in the tantra itself, along with some final food offerings. Food offerings are also recommended by the colophon to IOL Tib J 447.
34. Colophon only in Pelliot tibétain 792, 3v.3–4: *ban de byang cub dbyangs kyi sku yon du bris te / sku tshe 'di la snyun myur du byang ba dang tse ring zhing sems chan gyi don bya ba dang ma 'ongs pa'I dus du myi dge ba thaMs chad ni bzhu bsal nas sku gsum lhun gyis grub par smon te/ dge ba'I bshes nyen du shog shig// / lan cig zhus /.*

4. Secretory Secrets

1. Bhadantācariya Buddhaghosa, *The Path of Purification* (*Visuddhimagga*), trans. Bhikkhu Ñāṇamoli (Kandy: Buddhist Publication Society, 2011), 184.
2. As translated by Patrick Olivelle in *The Early Upaniṣads: Annotated Text and Translations* (New York and Oxford: Oxford University Press, 1998), 155.
3. Sigmund Freud, *Beyond the Pleasure Principle* (New York: Norton, 1961), 11.
4. In Āyurvedic medical theory too, semen is considered "the highest essence of the body," the ultimate product of the body's digestive processes (Domink Wujastyk, *The Roots of Ayurveda* [London: Penguin, 1998], 5; see also 155 and 320). In the same passage, Wujastyk observes that "Āyurveda's picture of women's physiology includes no obvious equivalent to semen."
5. Ronald M. Davidson, *Indian Esoteric Buddhism: A Social History of the Tantric Movement* (New York: Columbia University Press, 2002), 198, referencing eighth-century tantras such as the *Guhyasamāja* and the *Sarvabuddhasamāyoga*, may be the first scholar to recognize this period of tantric ritual development: "The earliest siddha literature simply speaks of a sexual ritual that is sacramental rather than . . . the yogic associations of later *maṇḍalacakra* instructions that specify internal psychophysical centers, letters, and the manipulation of winds." Just one year later, however, noting the same centrality of sacramental fluids in Śaiva tantra, David Gordon White, *Kiss of the Yoginī: "Tantric Sex" in*

Its South Asian Contexts Chicago: University of Chicago Press, 2003), 76, writes: "In this and nearly every other early and authentic Kaula source, sexual intercourse is never portrayed as an end in itself, nor as a means to attaining the bliss of god-consciousness. Rather, it is simply a means to generating the clan nectar (*kulāmṛta*), the various mixtures of sexual fluids whose 'eucharistic' offering and consumption lay at the heart of Kaula practice . . . Already in the ninth- to tenth-century KJñN, such drinking was essential to Kaula practice." Still another year later, in Jacob P. Dalton, "The Development of Perfection: The Interiorization of Buddhist Ritual in the Eighth and Ninth Centuries," *Journal of Indian Philosophy* 32 (2004): 1–30, I further emphasized the significance of this "intermediate period" of ritual development. Though the overall arguments offered in that piece remain solid, it is so littered with errors that I am relieved to have the opportunity to clarify my earlier readings with the present chapter.

6. Some tantras such as the *Guhyasamāja* that are referred to as Mahāyoga tantras within the Dunhuang materials continued to be labeled Yoga tantras in some Indian circles, especially from the tenth century on, when they were juxtaposed to the Yoginī tantras that spread widely at that time. The classification of tantras is a complex topic. From the late eighth century on, all sorts of schemes proliferated in both India and Tibet, so the modern historian must use classificatory terms carefully, considering the context within which each functioned. For a diachronic study of some of these classificatory systems, see Jacob P. Dalton, "A Crisis of Doxography: How Tibetans Organized Tantra During the 8th–12th Centuries," *Journal of the International Association of Buddhist Studies* 28, no. 1 (2005): 115–81. There, I conclude that the well-known fourfold system of Kriyā, Caryā, Yoga, and Yoganiruttara "emerged in Tibet, probably during the twelfth century, just as the distinction between the old Rnying ma and the new Gsar ma schools was crystallizing" (161). I have since learned of at least one Indian source that may include such a scheme. The *Amṛtakaṇikoddyotanibandha*, a subcommentary on the *Mañjuśrīnāmasaṃgīti* by Vibhūticandra (twelfth /thirteenth century), appears to include the four classes where the printed edition reads *kriyācaryāyogata[ntra]niruttaratantrāḥ*. I thank Harunaga Isaacson (who recommends amending the line to read *kriyācaryāyogayoganiruttaratantrāḥ*) for bringing this reference to my attention. To this we can also add a reference to the four classes in Smṛtijñānakīrti's eleventh-century(?) *Vajravidāraṇa-nāmadhāraṇīvṛtti*, 226a.7. Given the existence of such passages, we must admit the possibility of occasional occurrences of the four classes in still other Indian writings of the *phyi dar* period. Nonetheless, the scheme remained relatively rare in India, just one among many, and its rise to prominence does appear to have been largely a Tibetan affair, driven by Tibetan concerns. In the same article (158–59), I emphasize the influence of the early Sa skya genre of *Rgyud sde spyi'i rnam bzhag* (*General Presentation of the Tantras*) in this rise, pointing to the scheme's appearance in the *Presentations* by both the first and second Sa skya patriarchs, Sa chen kun dga' snying po (1092–1158) and Bsod nams rtse mo (1142–1182). We may now push this back a bit further by noting the existence of a still earlier exemplar of the *Rgyud sde spyi'i rnam bzhag* genre attributed to 'Gos khug

pa lhas btsas (eleventh c.), now unfortunately lost. As observed in Dalton, "A Crisis of Doxography," 157–58, he may have been behind the (mis)translation of certain Indian fivefold systems to bring them into line with his fourfold scheme. That the four classes were important to his thinking is seen in his anti-Rnying ma polemical work, the *Sngags log sun 'byin* (see f. 19.6), which opens with a presentation of them. In short, 'Gos khug pa appears to have played an important role in making the fourfold scheme so central to the Sa skya school and thus to Tibetan Buddhism more generally.

7. See Rolf W. Giebel, "The Chin-Kang-Ting Ching Yu-Ch'ieh Shi-Pa-Hui Chih-Kuei: An Annotated Translation," *Journal of Naritasan Institute for Buddhist Studies* 18 (1995): 171–72. Giebel (172 n. 178) notes the parallels between Amoghavajra's description here and the *uttaratantra* of the *Trailokyavijaya-mahākalparājā*, 51b.4ff.
8. Horiuchi Hanjin, ed., *Kongochokyo no Kenkyu* (*Sarvatathāgata-tattvasaṃgraha-nāma-mahāyāna-sūtra*). Koyasan University: Mikkyo Bunka Kenkyujo, 1983), vol. 1, vv. 549–554. *tato rahasyapūjāmudrājñānaṃ śikṣayet / sarvakāyapariṣvaṅgasukhapūjā svayaṃbhuvā / niryātayaṃ bhavecchīghraṃ vajrasatvasamo hi saḥ / dṛḍhānurāgasa ṃyogakacagrahasukhāni tu / niryātayaṃstu buddhānāṃ vajraratnasamo bhavet / dṛ ḍhapratītisukhasakticumbitāgryasukhāni tu / niryātayaṃstu buddhānāṃ vajradharmasamo bhavet / dvayendriyasamāpattiyogasaukhyāni sarvataḥ / niryātayaṃstu pūjāyāṃ vajrakarmasamo bhaved*; see also *Sarvatathāgatatattvasaṃgraha*, 45a.4–6. Note the unusual line in the first chapter of the same tantra, about the "secret accomplishment" (*guhya-sādhana*): "Through the orifice (*bhaga*), one should enter the body a woman or a man. Having entered, imagine that one pervades their entire body" (v. 248: *bhagena praviśet kāyaṃ / striyāyāḥ puruṣasya vā / praviṣṭvā manasā sarvaṃ / tasya kāyaṃ samaṃ spared iti*; *Sarvatathāgatatattvasaṃgraha*, 29b.7).
9. See, for example, Horiuchi, *Kongochokyo no Kenkyu*, vv. 1918–1921 and 475–479. For translations of the former, see Do-Kyun Kwon, "*Sarva Tathāgata Tattva Saṃgraha, Compendium of All the Tathāgatas*: A Study of its Origin, Structure and Teachings" (PhD diss., School of Oriental and African Studies, University of London, 2002), 256, or David Gray, "Imprints of the 'Great Seal': On the Expanding Semantic Range of the Term of Mudrā in Eighth through Eleventh-Century Indian Buddhist Literature," *Journal of the International Association of Buddhist Studies* 34, nos. 1–2 (2011 [2012]): 466; for the latter, see Kwon, "*Sarva Tathāgata Tattva Saṃgraha*," 114.
10. Olivelle, *The Early Upaniṣads*, 155. On dating the *Bhṛadāraṇyaka*, see 12.
11. A reference to the seven kinds of sexual enjoyments prohibited by the Buddha in the *Saptamaithunasaṃyuktasūtra* (*'Khrig pa bdun dang ldan pa'i mdo*), in a passage cited in the *Sikṣāsamuccaya* (for an English translation, see Cecil Bendall, *Śikshā-samuccaya: A Compendium of Buddhist Doctrine compiled by Śāntideva Chiefly from Earlier Mahāyāna Sūtras* [London: John Murray, 1922], 81).
12. *Vajraśekhara*, 167b.7–168a.1: *'dod chags bde ba rjes dran nas / 'dod pa'i 'dod chags brtag mi bya / bud med khams ni bkug nas su / 'khrig pa bdun ni spang par bya / mtshan ma langs par rab gyur nas / dbang po nye bar zhi byas te / 'dod chags rjes dran gyur nas ni / sbyin sreg las ni yang dag brtsam*. I thank my student Paul Thomas for bringing these lines to my attention and for his observation that the passage is also cited

in Buddhagupta's *Tantrārthāvatāra*, 84a–b, a fact that suggests a *terminus ad quem* for at least these portions of the *Vajraśekhara* of around the mid-eighth century.

13. *Vajraśekhara*, 192a.2–4. *b+ha gar gur gum phyung nas ni / mtshan ma yang ni gzhug par bya / rdzas rnams bzang po thob par 'gyur / rnam pa bzhi yang 'grub par 'gyur / b+ha ga pad+ma zhes byar brjod / mtshan ma rdo rje zhes bshad do / rdzas ni pad+ma'i steng bzhag nas / rdo rje srub mas bsgrub par bya / shin tu chags pas 'dod chags can / des ni gsang ba rab bsgrub 'gyur.*

14. Dunhuang representations of Yoga tantra *sādhana* practice mostly lack any mention of such rites, but there is one manuscript that quotes the above-cited *STTS* passage on embracing, grasping the hair, kissing, and intercourse. IOL Tib J 576 is an incomplete concertina-style manuscript containing a series of short texts that, taken together, seem to comprise an initiation manual for the Vajradhatu mandala. If this is true, it may be the only initiation manual for the *STTS* system among the Tibetan Dunhuang documents. It appears to have been compiled in Tibet, possibly even at Dunhuang, and includes a variety of materials, not all of which are drawn from the *STTS*, its primary focus.

    The first folio or two are missing, so we join the proceedings as the ritual master is preparing himself for the performance. After some protective mantras, he arranges a nonstandard but elaborate mandala of deities upon his head, eyes, nose, ears, and tongue and on his fingers and toes. Each deity is accompanied by a female consort, each named in interlinear notes beneath their respective mantra, recited to place them at their proper bodily location. Thus prepared, the reader is then provided a series of unattributed quotations from different sources. The first five come from various chapters of the *Guhyasamāja-tantra*, passages offering praise to *bodhicitta*, the *dharmadhatu*, and so on, followed by a poetic homage to each of the chiefs of the five families. It would seem the ritual master would recite these lines to open the ritual proper.

    Next comes a brief passage on offering the *mudrāsamaya* (*phyag rgya dam tsig*); see IOL Tib J 576, r12.3–13.1. The same lines appear in the *Śrī-Paramādya*, though in a different order. In an order closer to the one here, they are also quoted in Buddhagupta's *Tantrārthāvatāra*. In both Indian works, the lines are recited to reinforce the importance of maintaining one's *samaya* vows (compare *Paramādya*, 229a.4–6, and *Tantrārthāvatāra*, 9a.7). That the *Tantrārthāvatāra* is our text's likely source is confirmed by the next four passages, each of which may be found at different points in Buddhagupta's work (compare *Tantrārthāvatāra*, 8a.1, 4b.6–7, and 81a.4–5, respectively). The first two offer brief observations on the royal nature of the *mudrā* (seal), while the third introduces the concept of the heart mantra (Skt. *hṛdaya*; Tib. *snying po*). The last passage is more or less the one cited above from the *STTS*, in which the reader is promised identity with the four chief bodhisattvas of the Vajradhātu mandala if he performs the four stages of sexual activity, of embracing, grasping the hair, kissing, and intercourse (IOL Tib J 576, r13.5–r14.5). The precise role of these passages remains unclear; they may simply represent some selections upon which the ritual master can draw during the initiation ceremony.

    The passages are followed by a lengthy list of the names and qualities of each deity in the mandala. Unfortunately, folios are missing from the end of the concertina, and the verso picks up in the midst of the actual initiations proper. While the secret sexual rites of the *STTS* do not play a central role in the proceedings, they may have been presented as a possible aspect of postinitiatory practice. The *Guhyasamāja*, a scripture that appeared among Amoghavajra's early list of Yoga tantras and later lists of Mahāyoga tantras, was drawn upon for its evocative language in order to set the scene for the larger *STTS*-based ceremony, further indication that the line separating Yoga and Mahāyoga was a porous one.

15. Tsuguhito Takeuchi, "Old Tibetan Buddhist Texts from the Post-Tibetan Imperial Period (Mid-9 c. to Late 10 c.)," in *Old Tibetan Studies*, ed. Cristina Scherrer-Schaub (Leiden: Brill, 2012), 208–9. In the same paper, Takeuchi explores the possible significance of these numbers more generally.
16. IOL Tib J 508, v9.3–11.2. *rigs lnga tshul gcig rang bzhin dbyer myed yang / btul pa'i dbang gyis rigs lnga so sor bstan / thams cad mkhyen pa'i sku ni mtha' dag myed / dbyer myed ye shes sku la phyag 'tshal lo / ye shes phung po mkha 'dra yang sku sku gsung thugs ni bdag nyld che / [spu] sprul pa kun gyis 'byung nas nas rdo rje sem pa gshegs su gsol.* This passage and others relating to Vajrasattva and the "single mode" (*tshul gcig*) have been analyzed by Sam van Schaik, "A Definition of Mahāyoga: Sources from the Dunhuang Manuscripts," in *Tantric Studies*, ed. Harunaga Isaacson (Hamburg: Center for Tantric Studies, 2008), 1: 51–54.
17. *Guhyasamāja*, 5. *atha khalv akṣobhyas tathāgato ratnaketus tthāgato 'mitāyus tathāgato 'moghasiddhis tathāgato vairocanas tathāgato bodhicittavajrasya tathāgatasya hṛdaye vijahāra.* Toh. 442, 91a.2–3. *de nas de bzhin gshegs pa my bskyod pa dang / de bzhin gshegs pa rin chen tog dang / de bzhin gshegs pa 'od dpag med dang / de bzhin gshegs pa don yod grub pa dang / de bzhin gshegs pa rnam par snang mdzad rnams de bzhin gshegs pa byang chub kyi sems rdo rje'i thugs la bzhugs so.*
18. IOL Tib J 481, 1v.5. *de nas rigs lnga'i sangs rgyas rdo rje sems dpa'i skur bzhugs so.* The existence of this note has already been highlighted by van Schaik, "A Definition of Mahāyoga," 52. As Kenneth W. Eastman, "The Dun-huang Tibetan Manuscript of the Guhyasmājatantra" (paper presented at the twenty-seventh convention of The Japanese Association for Tibetan Studies, Kyōto, Japan, November 17, 1979), 6, has observed, the interlinear notes in the Dunhuang *Guhyasamāja* are not specific to the manuscript, as the version preserved in today's *Rnying ma rgyud 'bum* (Gting skyes edition) interpolates one into the second verse. It is quite possible that the notes were made at the time of the tantra's translation, which might date them to the late eighth or early ninth century.
19. See Anthony Tribe, *Tantric Buddhist Practice in India: Vilāsavajra's Commentary on the Mañjuśrī-nāmasaṃgīti* (London and New York: Routledge, 2016), 68. It is also significant that Vilāsavajra identifies this *samaya* deity with *bodhicitta*. The idea that the sacramental drop of *bodhicitta* comes to rest at the practitioner's heart, like the *samayamudrā* discussed in chapter 3, is key to Mahāyoga practice as portrayed in the Dunhuang manuscripts.
20. The title of this text is somewhat complicated, as three variations are given in the first two lines, all embedded in larger sentences or interlinear commentary, making it difficult to discern what might be a title and what simply a

description of the work. Thus, it is referred to as a (1) *Sādhana for the Body, Speech, and Mind*; (2) *Precept for Supreme Goodness*; and in a note to this last, (3) *Method for the Cultivation of the Supreme Samantabhadra*. Given the presence of an interlinear note below title #1 that interprets it as an explanation of the work's threefold purpose (i.e., for accomplishing the body, speech, and mind of the Buddha) and the fact that #3 is an elaboration on #2, the second title may be the most likely proper title. For the author attribution, see IOL Tib J 331/1, 2r.5: *sIng ga la 'I slobs dpon 'jam dpal bshes gnyen gyIs mdzad pa*.

21. For a translation of this work, see Jacob P. Dalton, "Evoking the Divine Human: *An Appearance of Suchness: Ornament of the Sacred*," in *Living Treasure: Buddhist and Tibetan Studies in Honor of Janet Gyatso*, ed. Holly Gayley and Andrew Quintman (Boston: Wisdom, forthcoming).

22. The manuscript consists of nineteen folios in *poti* format and contains three separate texts. The first is the brief *Precept of Supreme Goodness*, the second is our more elaborate *sādhana*, and the third is a Vajrakīlaya *sādhana* (studied in Cathy Cantwell and R. Mayer, "Enduring Myths: Smrang, Rabs and Ritual in the Dunhuang Texts on Padmasambhava," *Revue d'Etudes Tibétaines* 15 [2008]: 68–135). It is likely that still more texts were included in the original collection but have since been lost, as the first item is marked with the Tibetan letter *kha* in the left margin of its first page, while the second item is similarly marked with a *cha*. Oddly, the third item lacks any such alphabetical marking. One further folio that may also have been part of the original collection is found at IOL Tib J 346; it is penned in the same hand, on the same size paper, and has holes in the same locations. Unfortunately, it bears no alphabetical marking in the left margin, though it is numbered as folio 7 (*bdun*).

23. Considerable material is added throughout, particularly to the descriptions of the mandala. For some reason Cathy Cantwell and Robert Mayer, *Early Tibetan Documents on Phur pa from Dunhuang* (Vienna: Verlag der Österreichischen Akademie der Wissenschaften, 2008), 71 n. 12, insist, contra my entry in Jacob Dalton and Sam van Schaik, *Tibetan Tantric Manuscripts from Dunhuang: A Descriptive Catalogue of the Stein Collection at the British Library* (Leiden: Brill, 2006), that "most of it [i.e., IOL Tib J 331/2] is present" in IOL Tib J 464, despite the fact that the two works differ considerably in length (twelve folio sides in IOL Tib J 331 vs. just over six somewhat smaller sides in IOL Tib J 464). Evidence of the later date of the text contained in IOL Tib J 331/2 includes the following: (1) in describing the proper location for the rite to be performed, IOL Tib J 331 interpolates lines that break the seven-syllable verse; (2) in describing the three *samādhis* for generating the visualization, IOL Tib J 331 changes the line breaks and inserts new syllables to further interrupt the versification; (3) at 2b.2, IOL Tib J 331/2 inserts a lengthy section about the mandala that is missing from IOL Tib J 464 (compare 3v.1), again breaking the versification and returning to the same verse only when it rejoins IOL Tib J 464 around IOL Tib J 331/2, 4v.1–2. Further examples could be offered. Evidence of the (re)interpretive agenda of the author of IOL Tib J 331/2 will be presented below.

24. *Guhyasamāja*, XII.3: *kāyavākcittavajreṣu mañjuvajraprabhāvanā / spharaṇaṃ kāyavākcitte mañjuvajrasamo bhavet*. Compare the equivalent lines in the

Dunhuang IOL Tib J manuscript of the Guhyasamāja at IOL Tib J 438, 31v.3 (*lus dang ngag sems rdo rje la / rdo rje 'jam pa rab tu bsgom / lus dang ngag sems las spros pas / rdo rje 'jam pa 'dra bar gyur*). The tantra itself refers to Mañjuvajra rather than Vajrasattva. The line, "how is [this] to be cultivated?" (IOL Tib J 331/2, 1r.2: *jI ltar bsgom zhe na*), breaks the *sādhana*'s versification, suggesting it is a later interpolation.

25. Such a reading is supported by the fact that the *mchan 'grel* to these lines in the Dunhuang copy of the *Guhyasamāja-tantra* sketch a brief *sādhana* for the accomplishment of the deity in question. Kenneth W. Eastman, "Mahāyoga Texts at Tun-Huang," *Institute of Buddhist Cultural Studies* 22 (Kyoto: Ryukoku University, 1983), 53, also notes the presence in IOL Tib J 331/1 of wrathful deities also seen in the *Guhyasamāja*, deities that are absent from IOL Tib J 464.
26. Three manuscripts bear consecutive site numbers: Ch. 73. III. 9, Ch. 73. III. 10, and Ch. 73. III. 10.a. Regarding paper size, IOL Tib J 552 measures 31.4 x 9.0 cm, IOL Tib J 553 measures 30.8 x 9.0 cm, and IOL Tib J 554 measures 31.0 x 9.4 cm. By the standards of Tibetan Dunhuang manuscripts, these are minor differences. They do show, however, that the pages for each manuscript were cut separately. As for the paper itself, no chain lines are visible, but the laid lines (i.e., the lines left in the paper from the sieve in the paper mold) are easily measured; all three manuscripts have six laid lines per centimeter, suggesting that they were made using the same kind of mold. IOL Tib J 552 and IOL Tib J 553 have vertical laid lines, running from the page's top to bottom rather than left to right, but IOL Tib J 554 has horizontal lines.
27. For a translation of this work, see appendix 3.
28. Neither the *Generation of Fortune Sādhana* (IOL Tib J 331/2) nor Mañjuśrīmitra's *Precept for Supreme Goodness* (IOL Tib J 331/1) includes a Sanskrit (*rgya gar skad du*) title, so their Indian origins are somewhat less secure. Particular causes for concern are certain elements that the two works share and therefore may reflect more local Tibetan interests. Both, for example, use the ཨ syllable in the all-illuminating *samādhi* (though in different ways) and "when one comes to know it is the time for the dismissal," a key line discussed below. These two elements may appear in both works because they were typical of early Mahāyoga practice in India, but the possibility remains that they reflect Tibetan interests, whether at Dunhuang or back in central Tibet.
29. The work bears a title and is more or less identical with the *De kho na nyid snang ba dam pa rgyan* preserved in the modern *Bstan 'gyur*; see, for example, Q. 4735. At least one version of the work, that in volume *nya* of a collection of rare texts from Klu mo a bse dgon in Nyag rong (BDRC: W3PD888), attributes it to the eighth-century master Buddhagupta (Sangs rgyas gsang ba).
30. The "four suchnesses," which I take to be identical with our *sādhana*'s "four principles," are discussed at length in chapter 5.
31. Pelliot tibétain 656, recto, ll. 25–26. *bsgom ba ni rnams ksuM rims kyis bskyed de bsgom ba'o.*
32. A search of the *bka' 'gyur* and *bstan 'gyur* reveals the three Mahāyoga *samādhis* in just two tantras and two commentaries. The two tantras both belong to the *Rnying ma rgyud 'bum*, while the two commentaries are (1) Mañjuśrīmitra's

Bodhicittabhāvanā (Tib. *Byang chub sems bsgom pa*; Toh. 2591, 4a.5) and his autocommentary, the *Bodhicittabhāvanādvādaśārthanirdeśa* (Toh. 2578, 56b.1–2), neither of which has a translator's colophon, though the former appears in the *Ldan dkar ma* catalogue (no. 610 in Marcelle Lalou, "Les textes bouddhiques au temps de Khri-sroṅ lde bcan," *Journal asiatique* 241 [1953]: 334); (2) Vajravarman's *Vajravidāraṇādhāraṇīvṛtti* (Toh. 2687, 214a.2), said to have been translated by Śraddhākaravarman and Rinchen Zangpo. On these connections, see Catherine Dalton, "Enacting Perfection: Buddhajñānapāda's Vision of a Tantric Buddhist World" (PhD diss., University of California, Berkeley, 2019), 24–25 n. 126. These three *samādhis* should not be confused with the far more widespread set of three *samādhis* that appear in the *STTS*, the *ādiyoga-samādhi*, the *maṇḍalarājāgrī-samādhi*, and the *karmarājāgrī-samādhi*. Finally, both Mañjuśrīmitra and Vajravarman are said to have hearkened from Śrī Laṅka (on the former, see IOL Tib J 331/1, 2r.5, and on the latter, see Tadeusz Skorupski, *The Sarvadurgatipariśodhana Tantra, Elimination of All Evil Destinies: Sanskrit and Tibetan Texts with Introduction, English Translation and Notes* [Delhi: Motilal Banarsidass, 1983], xxv), suggesting that the three *samādhis*' popularity within South Asia may have been partly regional.

33. More specifically, the three *samādhis* correspond to the Yogatantra five stages of manifest awakening, *pañcākārābhisaṃbodhikrama*. IOL Tib J 579, 1r, an initiation manual for the *Sarvadurgati* mandala, includes both the three *samādhis*, which are used to generate the palace, and the *pañcākārābhisaṃbodhi*, which are then used to generate oneself as the central deity. In later texts of the tenth and eleventh centuries, the two stages, and especially the perfection stage, become increasingly difficult to define, as the latter shifted constantly over time, serving as the category for whatever the latest or purportedly highest developments might be, sometimes with the result that practices previously considered part of the perfection stage were pushed down into the generation stage.

    One might be tempted to map the two stages onto the earlier ritual categories of propitiation (*sevā*) and accomplishment (*sādhana*), with the generation stage corresponding to propitiation and the perfection stage to accomplishment. While such a reading is supported by some early Mahāyoga authors (see, for example, Vaidyapāda's *Samyagvidyākara-nāma-uttaratantra-vyākhyāna*, in his commentary to verse 30 of the *Samājottara*; Toh. 1850, 184a.3–4), historically, as noted in chapters 2 and 3, earlier Yogatantra authors saw their *sādhanas* as effecting the accomplishment stage, with other preliminary rites (e.g., the early *vidyāvrata*) filling the role of propitiation. To read both propitiation and accomplishment, qua generation and perfection, into a single Mahāyoga *sādhana* thus does not make sense historically, though it may represent a legitimate hermeneutical move that reflects the gradual divorce of the two stages from their original ritual context.

34. That the transition is often unmarked has been noted by Elizabeth English, *Vajrayoginī: Her Visualizations, Rituals, and Forms* (Boston: Wisdom, 2002), 171–72, who then proceeds to summarize some of Isaacson's research on the wide variety of views on the perfection stage.

35. See, for example, IOL Tib J 594, 1v.1; IOL Tib J 647, 4v.4; and perhaps Pelliot tibétain 841, 4r.1–5. The issue of the Great Perfection at Dunhuang is returned to below. In Pelliot tibétain 656, recto, l. 26 and 29, the two stages are correlated with Mahāyoga and Anuyoga, respectively. As discussed in chapter 5, Pelliot tibétain 42, r81–82, explains that the rites preceding that point in the text were of the generation stage, probably implying that the subsequent ones are for the perfection stage.
36. On Buddhajñānapāda's dates, see chapter one of C. Dalton, "Enacting Perfection." Some scholars, e.g., English, *Vajrayoginī*, 25, have highlighted the *Samājottara*'s reference to the two stages, but as C. Dalton has also shown, that work may be slightly later than, or at least contemporaneous with, Buddhajñānapāda.
37. Here I follow the translation of the title by Catherine Dalton, who discusses her translation in chapter 2 of "Enacting Perfection." Internally, the *Dvitīyakrama* also includes several references to the two stages.
38. One apparently Buddhajñānapāda-authored nontantric commentary on the *Sañcayagāthā* does appear in the *Ldan dkar* catalogue of early ninth-century Tibetan translations; see text no. 518 in Lalou, "Les textes bouddhiques au temps de Khri-sroṅ lde bcan," 331; compare Toh. 3798, the translation of which is attributed to Vidyākarasiṁha and Dpal brtsegs, who are also said to have translated the *Sañcayagāthā* itself.
39. IOL Tib J 331/2 and the closely related IOL Tib J 554 add some elaborations. To begin, one recites the purificatory mantra that also opened the *Tattvasaṃgraha-sādhanoypāyikā* studied in chapter 3: *Oṃ svabhāvaśuddhāḥ sarvadharmāḥ svabhāvaśuddho[atmako]'ham.* Then, having cultivated the thusness *samādhi* as above, one imagines the glittering white ཨ at the center of space. Just as that syllable fades away, one recites "*raṃ*," whereby the fires of gnosis blaze up, incinerating all concepts, "like a feather entering a flame," adds IOL Tib J 554, whereupon, concludes IOL Tib J 331/2, "one intensively cultivates mind as if it were like the surface of the sky" (IOL Tib J 331/2, 2r.1: *nam ka 'I ngos ltar sems shIn du khug par bsgom mo*). For the corresponding point in IOL Tib J 554, see 1r.6–7. There is some confusion in these two other works regarding how to distinguish the three *samādhis*. IOL Tib J 554 inserts the breaks, but not without creating further problems. The entire sequence involving the white ཨ syllable represents the beginning of the causal *samādhi* (see IOL Tib J 554, 1r.5–1v.1). Such a reading is supported by similar descriptions of the causal *samādhi* in IOL Tib J 437, 6v–7r, and Pelliot tibétain 634, 2r.1, so perhaps the author of IOL Tib J 554 was influenced by local tradition. The trouble with applying this reading to our own *sādhana* is that it leaves out the all-illuminating *samādhi*, mentioned without any ritual form, and such is the awkward situation in IOL Tib J 331/2. IOL Tib J 554 solves this by inserting an additional line to represent the all-illuminating *samādhi*: "cultivate one's own mind as radiantly white like the sky at dawn" (1r.5–6: *bdag kyi sems nam nangs pa'i mkha' ltar dkard ya le bsgom mo*). For the purposes of the present *sādhana*, IOL Tib J 464, it seems best to identify the all-illuminating *samādhi* with the

appearance of the ཨ syllable, which is then replaced (perhaps as it fades away, as IOL Tib J 331/2 suggests) by the elemental syllables that inaugurate the causal *samādhi*. The fire element, symbolized by the syllable *raṃ*, is missing from IOL Tib J 464, and in this regard the additions of IOL Tib J 331/2 and IOL Tib J 554 are helpful. From here, the buildup of elements proceeds more or less as above, with each syllable producing an increasingly stable ground, from wind to water to earth and the palace.

40. IOL Tib J 552, 2r.3–6. *{de yang ci ltar bskyed na} phyi nang snang srid 'di dag thams cad sgyu ru ra 'i 'bras bu rlon pa lag thil du blangs pa lta 'u 'am / ston ka 'i mun nag thibs po langs nas nam nangs pa'i 'kha gsal bar mthong ba lta 'u 'am thing shing kyi pho ru snod dag pa'i nang du rdzas kyi dngos po ci bcug na yang / phyi nas ltas na ni nang du gsal / nang nas ltas na phyi ru gsal ba*. A more grammatically correct reading of the second image might take the subject of the verb "to arise" (*langs*) to be the same as the one who sees (*mthong ba*), but given the poetic semantics of the first and third images, I prefer to emphasize the sense of dawn's light seeming to come from within the sky itself.
41. IOL Tib J 437, 4v–5r, 1–6. *nam ka 'i ngos bzhin du snang snang bzhin du stong la stong bzhin du gsal / ye shes chu zla 'i drkyil 'khor dang 'dra bar / mkha gtIng dbus mtha myed par khyab pas / kun tu snang gyi ti nge 'dzIn zhes bya / bstong pa nyid kyi ti nge 'dzIn zhes kyang bya / thabs gyi bde sel zhes kyang bya / gzugs gi go byed zhes kyang bya / gzugs 'byung ba'I drgyu zhes kyang bya ste / nam ga bstong pi ngos blta bu 'am / mtsho tangs pi nang na nyi zla gza skar gi gzugs grnyan gsal bar snang yang / rang bzhin dang mtshan ma myed pa rgya long kha bsbub 'dra bu 'am / nam nangs pi mtsho 'dra bur bsnyin rje chen po 'i ngang las ma g.yos par bsgom mo.*
42. IOL Tib J 332/1, 8r.5–7. *de yang yab kyi rdo rje rtse lnga pa'i steng du / yi ge gcig bsgom / yum gi mkha' la pad ma 'dam brgyad kyi steng du / ma las nyi ma'i dkyil 'khor du bsams ste / 'dzA hUM pam hO zhes brjod pas / yab kyi phyag rgya lcags kyus bzungs / zhags pas bcings / lcags sgrog kyis bsdams.*
43. These same gatekeepers were used to summon and bind the deities in the *mahāmudrā* section of the *Tattvasaṃgraha-sādhanopāyikā* examined in chapter 3.
44. IOL Tib J 464, 4r.4–5. *bsrung ba 'i sbyor ba ci nus pas / grub pa 'i bdag nyid brtan bar bsrung*. IOL Tib J 331/2, 5r.1 makes some changes to the first line here: " By means of those ritual procedures that one knows for protecting, firmly protect the *siddhi* identity" (*bsrung ba 'I cho ga cI shes pas / grub pa bdag nyId brtan bar bsrung*). The *siddhi* identity appears to refer to the drop of *bodhicitta*, which, after being emitted and empowered by the buddhas of the mandala, is also referred to as the "great identity" (*bdag nyid chen po*).
45. The mantra itself is missing from IOL Tib J 464. It is unclear whether this is merely an oversight or reflective of a higher level of secrecy surrounding it. The mantra is provided by IOL Tib J 331/2. 5r.2. The same exhortation appears in the *Cāryamelāpakapradīpa*, where it is spoken "for mutual arousal;" see Christian Wedemeyer, *Āryadeva's* Lamp that Integrates the Practices (*Cāryamelapakapradīpa*): *The Gradual Path of Vajrayāna Buddhism* (New York: American Institute of Buddhist Studies, 2007), 299–301.
46. IOL Tib J 464, 4v.2–3. *bde ba chen po 'byord ba na / phyag rgya gsal bar bsgom ba dang / mchod pa dbul dang spruld pa spro.*

47. *Dvitīyakrama*, 6b.6. *'di ni rdzogs pa'i rim pa yin par bla ma mchog rnams kun gyis yang dag bshad.*
48. IOL Tib J 331/2, 5r.3–4. *bde ba chen po sbyor bas na / dkyil 'khor gsal bar dgod pa dang / mchod pa dbul dang sprul pa spro.*
49. IOL Tib J 332/1, 8v.4–6. *yuM gyi pad ma'i dkyil 'khor du / bde ba thugs kyI dkyil 'khor spro' / sangs rgyas sprin tshogs ma lus la / dgyes mnyam mchog gi sbyin bas thim / de las dkyil 'khor gsal bar bkod.* Compare *Guhyagarbha*, 122a.5–6.
50. IOL Tib J 332/1, 8v.1–2 has *shad ta pa*. For a canonical reference, see the *Sarvabu ddhasamāyogaḍākinījālasaṃvara*, 157a.1. *Nāṭyaśāstra* 28.95 includes a discussion of this melody. For a more recent Tibetan Buddhist take, see Jamgon Mipham, *Luminous Essence: A Guide to the Guhyagarbha Tantra*, trans. The Dharmachakra Translation Committee (Ithaca, NY: Snow Lion, 2009), 156–57: "With this approach, the tone is intense and forceful like thunder. The syllables are recited slightly fast and intensely, like water rushing off the face of the cliff." My thanks to Douglas Duckworth for bringing this reference to my attention. Dalton, "The Development of Perfection," 11, was *way* off in his interpretation of this term.
51. IOL Tib J 576, r8.1. *kye ma sangs rgyas thams cad kyI / byang cub sems nI rab byung ba / de bzhIn gshegs pa kun kyI gnas~~ng~~ / rab tu myI rtog gnas myed do.* Compare *Guhyasamāja*, 3v.2–3. The same lines open Pelliot tibétain 5, so it appears to have been commonly used.
52. *Guhyagarbha*, 122a.6. *bsgrub pa'i nyi zla'i dkyil 'khor de / dkyil 'khor rdo rje lce yis blang.* Here, however, I have corrected *nyi zla'i dkyil 'khor de* to *nyi zla'i snying po de*, which is seen in the Mtshams brag edition of the *Rnying ma rgyud 'bum* and numerous other sources. "Vajra tongue" refers to a visualization of one's tongue as a five-spoked vajra. IOL Tib J 332/1 inserts a lengthy description of the mandala that is generated within the drop of *bodhicitta*. Once the mandala has been consecrated with the *jñānasattva*, the entire visualization is dissolved, thus ending the first text, the *Cultivation Method That Is an Ornamental Sublime Appearance of Suchness* (referenced above in n. 29). Following a break (see 18v.5), a *gaṇacakra* manual begins.
53. Agehananda Bharati, *The Tantric Tradition* (London: Rider, 1975 [1965]), 265. Bharati goes on to explain this supposed difference by highlighting a further erroneous distinction between Hinduism and Buddhism according to which the former is focused on sacrificial offerings, while the latter "is purely esoteric" and "the notion of sacrificial oblation and libation means little if anything to him" (266).
54. White, *Kiss of the Yoginī*, 109. In a note, White cites the (probably tenth-century) *Hevajra Tantra* as an example of his "later conformist" sources that teach retention.
55. David Gray, *The Cakrasamvara Tantra (The Discourse of Śrī Heruka) (Śrīherukābhidhāna): A Study and Annotated Translation* (New York: The American Institute of Buddhist Studies, 2007), 122, has observed the presence of both practices within the *Cakrasamvara* too. He concludes, however, that "The *Cakrasamvara Tantra* appears to be a pivotal text that exhibits traces of both the older Hindu practice as well as the Buddhist transformation of it." Now we may suggest that no such pivot was necessary, as the supposedly Hindu-inspired sacramental use of the fluids

had long been a well-established part of Buddhist sexual yoga by the time of the *Cakrasaṃvara*'s composition in the early ninth century.

56. Compare IOL Tib J 464, 4r.2–3 (*gtsug du rin chen myu gu yang / cho ga bzhin du rab tu gzhag*) to IOL Tib J 331/2, 4v.4–5.
57. Compare IOL Tib J 464, 4r.5–5r.1 (*de nas pha rol phyin ma la / rjes su chags pas blta byas te / bskul tshig gus par gsung ba dang / bskul ba slar yang brjod par bya*) to IOL Tib J 331/2 (*bskul tshIg gus par gsung bar bsam*). Italics added.
58. Compare IOL Tib J 464, 4v.5 (*mchod pa dbul zhing grub pa blang*) to IOL Tib J 331/2, 5v.4–5 (*ban da dpal dang ldan la stsogs / dngos sam yang na bsams pa la / cho ga bzhIn du byIn brlabs te / rab du mchod cIng bsgrub pa blang*).
59. For just one example, see David L. Snellgrove, *Indo-Tibetan Buddhism*, 2 vols. (Boston: Shambhala, 1987), vol. 1, 181.
60. Isabella Onians, "Tantric Buddhist Apologetics or Antinomianism as a Norm" (PhD diss., Oxford University, 2003), 256.
61. *Bodhimārgapradīpapañjikā*, as translated by Onians, "Tantric Buddhist Apologetics," 269 (citing Harunaga Isaacson's reference).
62. Lding po pa, 24b.2–3. *bdag cag tsham* [(*sic*) for *tshom*] *bu brgya dang bcas pas 'dus pa chen po mdo yi lo sgrub bgyis / de'i lo rgyus guhya*. I am indebted to Jann Ronis for this reference.
63. Péter-Daniel Szántó, "The Case of the *Vajra*-Wielding Monk," *Acta Orientalia Academiae Scientiarum Hung* 63, no. 3 (2010): 294.
64. The triad of manuscripts, IOL Tib J 552, 553, and 554, as a group may provide a further example of the desexualization of an earlier *sādhana*. As mentioned above, all three may be elaborations on Mañjuśrīmitra's short work found at IOL Tib J 331/1, but all exclude that work's offering of the sacrament, the first two manuscripts replacing it with a simple emanation and regathering of "the light rays of *bodhicitta*" (IOL Tib J 552, 6r.1–3; IOL Tib J 553, 4r.2–3) and the last simply skipping the stage entirely (IOL Tib J 554, 3r.4).
65. An elaborate rite for preparing the fivefold ambrosia appears in IOL Tib J 437/1, translated by Jacob P. Dalton, "Mahāyoga Ritual Interests at Dunhuang: A Translation and Study of the Codex IOL Tib J 437/Pelliot tibétain 324," in *New Studies of the Old Tibetan Documents: Philology, History and Religion*, ed. Yoshiro Imaeda, Matthew Kapstein, and Tsuguhito Takeuchi (Tokyo: Research Institute for Languages and Cultures of Asia and Africa, 2011), 302. For an example of distributing the resulting ambrosia within a *gaṇacakra*, see Pelliot tibétain 321, 9v.3–10v.1.
66. Pelliot tibétain 841, 2v.2–4. *byang cub kyi sems babs na / a la la ho zhes brjod de / lha mo mnyes par bsam / rdo rje dang pad mo bar nas / lag pa g.yon gyi srIn lag gis / pad mo'I zil pa blangs nas / 'phags pa rnams la dbul / bdag dang gzungs mas mas* [*sic*] *kyang dam blang*. For additional examples of offering of the sacrament to both the buddhas and oneself, see Pelliot tibétain 332(e), 1v.1–4, and Pelliot tibétain 36, v1.4-v2.1.
67. *Guhyasamāja* VIII.25cd–26: *adhiṣṭhānapadaṃ dhyātvā tattvapūjāṃ prakalpayet / guhyaśukraṃ viśālākṣīṃ bhakṣayed dṛḍhabuddhimān*. For the equivalent Tibetan, see Toh. 442, 102b.5–6. Note that the Dunhuang version reads "the buddha" in place of "the reality" (*tattva*), which matches our manuals; see IOL Tib J 438,

21v.5–22r.1: *byIn kyIs brlabs kyI gnas bsams te / sangs rgya mchod pa rab du brtag / myIg bzangs brtan ba'I blo ldan bas / khu ba blangs nas bza bar bya.*

68. IOL Tib J 754/8, r24–r35. *dam tshig sems pa rnams kyis dam blang ba ni / ~~d~~pad ma ban da 'I nang nas mthe bo / dang srin lag kIs rhi dmar po gsum res kyis blangs ste / lce zla ba 'I dkyil 'khor du dmyigs pa 'i steng du bzhag cing myid pa nI / rhi dang po lce 'i steng du bzhag la aoM zhes brjod pas / rhi las aoM du gyur / aoM las rnam par snang mdzad kyI sku tshon gang par gyur te khong du gtang ba nI / bdagI lus skur byIn kyis brlabs pa 'o / rhi bar ma lce 'I steng du bzhag ste aM zhes brjod pas / rhi las aM du gyur / am las snang ba mtha' yas kyI sku tshon gang par gyur te / khong du gtang ~~ba~~ ba ni bdagi ngag gsung du byin kyIs brlabs pa 'o / rhi tha ma lce 'i steng du bzhag ste huM zhes brjod pas / rhi las hUM du gyur / hUM las rdo rje myi bskyod pa 'I sku tshon gang par gyur te / khong du gtang ba nI bdagI sems thugs su byin kyIs brlabs pa 'o / rhi gsum myid pa 'i 'og du / tish+tha ba dzra ho zhes brjod pa nI sku gsung thugs g.yung drung du brtan bar gyur cig ces bya ba 'I don no.* The syllable *rhi* transcribes the Sanskrit syllable *hrīḥ*, as suggested in a mantra found on Pelliot tibétain 321, 10a.5, where the Sanskrit *hṛdaya* is transcribed as "*rhi da ya.*"

69. Note that the same instruction appears in the Mañjuśrīmitra-attributed (IOL Tib J 331/1), though the wording is very slightly different. IOL Tib J 464, 4v.5–5r.1 and IOL Tib J 331/2, 6r.1 share the same wording (*gtong ba 'i dus ni shes pa na*), IOL Tib J 331/1, 2r.2 is slightly different (*gtang ba 'i dus tshod shes byas nas*).

70. In Dalton, "The Development of Perfection," 23 n. 64, I argue that Vaidyapāda, in his commentary to the *Dvitīyakrama*, rereads Buddhajñānapāda's description of the perfection stage sexual yoga as the third initiation. While the *Dvitīyakrama* does describe the second initiation (*Dvitīyakrama*, 5a.5–6) and probably the third initiations (5a.6–6a.2), I continue to believe Vaidyapāda's reading of the verses that immediately follow the latter (6a.2–6b.7) is anachronistic, particularly given the instruction to perform the yoga "in an isolated location" (*dben pa'i gnas su spyad*), which clearly places the practice outside of the initiatory setting. If such a reading is correct, it may be that the final line of the latter section describes a loss of the sense of time upon receiving the sacrament: "For eight hours, one day, one month, or one year, one aeon, or a thousand aeons, one will experience gnosis: the intelligent one takes up the semen nectar that rests in the lotus and drinks it" (*Dvitīyakrama*, 6b.7: *chu tshod brgyad dam nyin gcig dang ni zla ba gcig tu 'am / lo gcig bskal pa'am bskal pa stong du ye shes de myong bya / pad+ma la gnas bdud rtsi khu ba blo gros can gyis kha yis blangs nas btung bya'o*). It is also possible, however, that the reference to time refers to the experience of orgasm, when the *bodhicitta* is emitted but before it is consumed, and for this reason, this reference remains relegated to a note.

71. IOL Tib J 331/1, 2r.2. *'dzab bsgom de nas dngos grub blang / gtang ba 'I dus tshod shes byas nas / yum yang ye shes sems dpar bsdu.*

72. IOL Tib J 331/1, 2r.2. *bsnyen pa 'I grangs tshang 'am jI ltar dam bcas pa bzhIn du.*

73. IOL Tib J 321, 30r.5–30v.4. *khong du 'thungs na dngos 'grub mchog thob bo / . . . byang chub kyi sems te / rdo rje sems dpa' yin / des gzungs 'dzin las 'das nas / gnyis su myed pa mUM gi sa la snyoms par 'jug go / de 'i phyir rdo rje sems dpa' ni / rdo rje 'dzin kyi sa la gnas te / sa bcu gsum pa zhes kyang bya 'o / 'di ni dngos grub mchog yin te.* The

passage appears in chapter eight, in the context of a discussion of a group practice of sexual union (*tshom bu*) that culminates in a *gaṇacakra*-style feasting, singing, and dancing.

74. *Dvitīyakrama*, 6b.7–7a.1. *pad+ma la gnas bdud rtsi khu ba blo gros can gyis kha yis blangs nas btung bya'o / de 'dra'i dngos po thams cad kyi / mtha' yi de nyid zab gsal ba.*
75. IOL Tib J 437, 1v–2r, 2–4. *phyi 'i yul chos bya ba mo kun tu bzang mo mkha' lding dbus mtha myed pa la bya / nang gi yul rtogs pas tshus* [(*sic*) *tshur*] *bcad pa nI / yid yid* [*sic*] *byed kun tu bzang po la bya de yab* [(*sic*) *yang?*] */ yab yuM rnam gnyis dgongs pa byang chub kyi sems / dkyil 'khor ston te.*
76. IOL Tib J 437, 12v–13r. 7–13v–14r.2. *sku gsung thugs kyi byin rlabs bdud rtsi 'i mchog / rigs lnga yab yum thabs dang shes rab las / gnyis myed bde ba chen po 'i byang chub sems / gsang can zla gsang pad ma'i gzhal yas su / skye myed yid bzhin bdud rtsi 'i thig le 'phro / sngags kyi 'bras mchog phyag rgya 'i don nyid las / ra sa ya na rdo rje zil ngar chu / brjod myed kun bzangs dbyings su rab bkod cing / rdzogs cen bdag nyid chen po thugs kyi bcud / skye shi myed pa'i sman mchod dam pa 'di / thugs dam bskang ba'i dbyig du dbul lags na / rnal 'byor dbang phyug brgyan du bzhes su gsol.*
77. IOL Tib J 594, 1r.1. *rnal 'byor nang pa thabs kyi rgyud kyi theg pa la zhugs pa rnams kyi lta ba ni rnam pa gsum ste / bskyed pa'i tshul dang / rdzogs pa'i tshul dang / rdzogs pa chen po'i tshul lo.*
78. IOL Tib J 647, 4v.3–4. *brjod pa dang bral ba'i byang chub kyi sems / lhun kyis grub pas / bskyed rdzogs bya myi dgos par dkyil 'khor gdon pa.*
79. See *Man ngag lta ba'i phreng* ba, 152.2–5. *bskyed pa'i tshul ni / ting nge 'dzin rnam pa gsum rim gyis bskyed de dkyil 'khor rim gyis bkod cing bsgom pas 'grub pa'o / rdzogs pa'i tshul ni / don dam par skye 'gags med pa'i lha dang lha mo dang / rnam par mi rtog pa'i don dbu ma chos kyi dbyings las kyang ma g.yos la / kun rdzob tu 'phags pa'i gzugs kyi sku yang gsal bar bsgoms shing mnyam la ma 'dres par bsgom pas grub bo / rdzogs pa chen po'i tshul ni / 'jig rten dang 'jig rten las 'das pa'i chos thams cad dbyer med par sku gsung thugs kyi dkyil 'khor gyi rang bzhin ye nas yin par rtogs nas bsgom pa ste.*
80. PT841, 4r.1–5. *he ni 'bod pa dang po 'I sgra / 'khams suM thams cad sku gsung thugs kyi dkyIl 'khor 'chen por lhun kis grub pa ste / mkha'i dkyil na myi g.yo bar bzhugs so / 'khams suM thams cad ye shes kyi phyag rgya 'chen por lhun gis gnas par rig pas na / dgyes pa 'chen po 'o /! / ru ni dbyings su sdud pa'i don / ye shes kyi dkyil 'khor 'chen po nI yum gi ba ga' dang 'du 'bral myed par gnas pas / yuM chags pa'i dam tshig gis 'khams sum dbang du sdud pa'i phyIr / ru zhes gsung so / de yang ma lus pas thams cad kyi dbyings su sdud pa 'o / ! / ka ni byang cub sems chen pa'o / de lta bu yuM dang gnyis su myed par sbyor ba'i byang chub kyi sems / mkha' dang mnyam bar kun la gsal khyab ste / 'byung ba lnga dang / laM rgyud lnga'i sems can thams chad thugs rje 'i lba klong du shar te / kun tu bzang por snang ngo.*
81. PT322 emphasizes the term *rdzogs chen* (see B1r.1 and B1v.7.) and mentions the tantra by name (B1r.4).
82. The four passages are already identified in David Germano, "Architecture and Absence in the Secret Tantric History of the Great Perfection," *Journal of the International Association of Buddhist Studies* 17, no. 2 (1994): 214–15.
83. *Guhyagarbha*, 130a.3–4. *mnyam la mnyam par sbyor ba yis / mnyam pa'i dam tshig la gnas na / mnyam rdzogs chen po thob 'gyur bas / 'das na sangs rgyas ma yin no.* In

reading *yis* as *yi* in the first phrase, my translation follows the *Mtshams brag* edition of the *Rnying ma'i rgyud 'bum* (see 211.4–5), only because it makes a little more sense.

84. *Guhyagarbha*, 123b.4–5. *de nas de bzhin gshegs pa phyogs bcu dus bzhi'i de bzhin gshegs pa'i sku gsung thugs rdo rje'i dkyil 'khor thams cad gcig tu 'dus nas /_ /dgyes pa chen pos chos thams cad ye nas rdzogs pa chen por lhun gyis grub pa'i dam tshig shin tu gsang ba'i snying po sprin bkod pa'i ting nge 'dzin la snyoms par zhugs.*

85. *Guhyagarbha*, 124b.1–2. *snod ldan ngang tshul bzang la brtan / lus dang longs spyod gtong la sbyin / gzhan du nam yang sbyin mi bya*. The chapter's very last lines immediately following these describe the violent sufferings that will come to any unworthy recipients of the sacrament. This is a common theme in the early descriptions of the bestowal of the supreme sacrament; see, for example, PT321, 10a.

86. *Guhyagarbha*, 124b.5. *oM sku gsung thugs kyi rdzogs pa che / yon tan phrin las kun tu rdzogs / ye nas lhun rdzogs kun tu bzang / 'dus pa'i tshogs chen thig le che ho:.*

87. *Guhyagarbha*, 123b.7. *thugs kyi dkyil 'khor dkyil 'khor mchog / gsang ba'i thig le 'kyil 'khor dbyings.*

88. *Guhyagarbha*, 116a.1. *ye shes phyogs bzhi dbus brtags te / dkyil 'khor bsam yas lhun gyis grub / rdzogs chen rtogs pa'i rnal 'byor pas / kun 'byung dkyil 'khor chen po spyod.*

89. *Spar khab*, 80b.1–4. *dngos po gnyis kyis bsdus pa thams cad / ka nyid nas rang rig pa kho na'i phyir thams cad ma 'gags la / gzhan du ma skyes par bdag nyid du gsal bas / sku gsung thugs kho na las / gzhan du med pa ni rdzogs pa chen po'o / de la ltos pa'i kun brtags pa rnams kyis rgyu rkyen gyi rnam pa brjod kyang / de nyid rang byung gi ye shes nyid pas / rgyu rkyen med par rang snang ba las 'da' mi srid pa'i phyir / lhun gyis grub pa'i dam tshig ces bya'o.*

90. *Spar khab*, 84b.5–85a.2. *rol pa las / zla ba'i dkyil 'khor nor bur snang ba'i dus na / ye shes lnga'i dkyil 'khor du snang ba ni rang bzhin gyi 'od gsal bas / thabs nyid shes rab tu sbyor ba'o / de'i tshe nyi ma'i dkyil 'khor la thams cad kyi bcud 'dus pa'i phyir / ma lus pa'i rgyur gyur pas / thabs mkhas pas zin na phung po la sogs pa thams cad kyang dkyil 'khor tu lhun gyis grub par byin gyis rlob par byed pa'i mthu dang ldan pa / de ze 'bru'i rtser snang ba ni shes rab nyid thabs su sbyor ba'o / zla ba'i ro ma nyams shing dmigs pa mi 'gyur bas dus gcig tu bsres pas / mtha' gnyis las grol ba'i ro thob.*

91. In IOL Tib J 739/412, which was the focus of chapter 2, these were listed as the vase, garland, crown, wheel, "and so on." IOL Tib J 447, r2, in its commentary to the *Tattvasaṃgraha-sādhanopāyikā*, lists the five as (1) garland; (2) crown; (3) water; (4) one's deity, mantras, and *mudrās*; and (5) the vajra name. For a significantly more complex Yogatantra initiation manual involving at least ten empowerments, see IOL Tib J 576/4, v1–v16.

92. This was briefly noted already in Dalton, "The Development of Perfection," 16 n. 41.

93. *Guhyasamāja* VIII.19: *bhāvayeccāmaraṃ prājñaḥ kulānāṃ pūjahetunā / pañcakāmaguṇaiḥ svacchāṃ yādavīṃ ca samārabhet*. Toh. 442, 450b.3–4: *rigs rnams thams cad mchod pa'i phyir / shes rab can gyis gnas su bsgom / 'dod pa'i yon tan lnga rnams kyis / de la mchod pa rgya mtsho brtsam.*

94. *Pradīpodyotana*, p. 117: *kulānāṃ pañcakulānāmālayamādhyarabhụtaṃ prājño guhyābhiṣekajño yogī pūjāhetunā guhyābhiṣekārthaṃ bhāvayediti yāvat / evaṃ*

guruvyāpārānantaraṃ guhyābhiṣekakāmena śiṣyeṇa yadanuṣṭheyaṃ taddarśayannāha / pañcakāmaguṇairityādi. Toh. 1785, 61a.7: *rigs rnams te / rigs lnga rnams kyi gnas dang gzhir gyur par shes rab can te / gsang ba'i dbang bskur ba shes pa'i rnal 'byor pas mchod pa'i phyir te / gsang ba'i dbang bskur ba'i phyir bsgom par bya'o zhes bya ba'i bar du'o / de ltar bla ma'i bya ba bstan pa'i 'og tu gsang ba'i dbang bskur bar 'dod pa'i slob mas / gang zhi bya ba de bstan par bya ba'i phyir / 'dod pa'i yon tan zhes bya ba la sogs pa gsungs te*.

95. *Guhyasamāja*, VIII.26: *guhyaśukraṃ viśālākṣīṃ bhakṣayed dṛḍhabuddhimān*. Toh. 442, 102b.6: *mig yangs khu ba blangs nas ni / brtan pa'i blo dang ldan pas bza.'*
96. *Pradīpodyotana*, p. 119: *śukre gṛhyā viśālākṣyāmiti / samāpattipūjānantaraṃ viśālākyāḥ guruṇā dattamanena svakāyasthān sarvatathāgatān tarpayāmīti bhakṣayet abhyavahrediti*. Toh. 1785, 63a.1: *slob ma la bla mas byin pa 'dis rang gi lus la gnas pa'i de bzhin gshegs pa thams cad tshim par bya'o zhes bsams nas bza' bar bya*.
97. On dating the *Cakrasaṃvara*, see Gray, *The Cakrasamvara Tantra*, 6–8.
98. Following the translation of Gray, *The Cakrasamvara Tantra*, 174. For the Sanskrit, see 63: *tato hi pūjayen mudrām ācāryaḥ susamāhitaḥ / śiṣyāṇāṃ tu dvitīye ahani raktena trijaptena tilakaṃ tasya kārayet*.
99. For Gray's discussion of some early commentaries on this passage, see *The Cakrasamvara Tantra*, 11–112. I am less convinced that another passage from the same tantra's first chapter (discussed on 109–11) is about the secret initiation; rather, it appears to be about bestowing a sacrament in the context of a *gaṇacakra*.
100. C. Dalton, "Enacting Perfection," 379–80, and see her discussion of the verses on 254–56. In Buddhajñānapāda, however, the secret initiation's efficacy is already being downgraded to make room for the third, wisdom gnosis initiation.
101. IOL Tib J 331/1, 1r.2. *thigs pas dbang bskur*.
102. For further discussion of the evidence, see Jacob P. Dalton, "Bridging Yoga and Mahāyoga: Samaya in Early Tantric Buddhism," in *Buddhism in Central Asia II: Visual and Material Transfer, Practices and Rituals*, ed. Carmen Meinert and Henrik H. Sørensen (Leiden: Brill, 2022), 279–80.
103. This has been observed by Harunaga Isaacson, "Observations on the Development of the Ritual of Initiation (*abhiṣeka*) in the Higher Buddhist Tantric Systems," in *Hindu and Buddhist Initiations in India and Nepal*, ed. Astrid Zotter et al. (Wiesbaden: Harrassowitz Verlag, 2010), 264; and C. Dalton, "Enacting Perfection," 249–54. We might also add the above-cited reference from the *Precept for Supreme Goodness*, but also the comments from Nupchen Sangyé Yeshé's *Lamp for the Eye in Contemplation* (Gnubs chen saṅs rgyas ye śes, *Bsam gtan mig sgron* [Leh: S. W. Tashigangpa, 1974], 26.3: "Having found [the consort], one completes the stages of the outer rites, abiding in the generation stage. Then, one who has obtained the secret initiation inhabits the oral instructions of the upper {door}" (*rnyed nas phyi'i rim pa rdzogs / bskyed pa la gnas so / gsang ba'i dbang nod de gong gi {ste sgo'i /} gdams ngag la gnas so*; added {comments} appear in smaller hand).
104. *Dvitīyakrama*, 5a.6. *ltung bas snying gi padma zhugs*.
105. Some of these ideas have already been explored by Steven Neal Weinberger, "The Significance of Yoga Tantra and the *Compendium of Principles*

(*Tattvasaṃgraha Tantra*) within Tantric Buddhism in India and Tibet" (PhD diss., University of Virginia, 2003), 241–43, and Tribe, *Tantric Buddhist Practice in India*, 67. Mañjuśrīmitra seems an important figure in tracing these ritual developments.

106. IOL Tib J 553, 4r.4–4v.2. *rnal 'byord gi gzhung dang / mthun bar bsdu bar byas ste / da ci 'i 'od dang 'od du 'phros pa de dag thams cad kyang / yab yum gnyis thIm / yum yang yab la thim / yab kyang ye shes sems dpa' la thim / ye shes sems dpa' yang phyag mtshan rdo rje la thim / rdo rje yang chang zungs kyi hUM la thim / hUM zhab bskyed la thim / zhab skyed yang ha la thim / ha zla tshes la thim / zla tshes thig le la thim / thig le yang da ci 'i de bzhin nyid kyi ting nge 'dzin chos kyi dbyings stong pa' / bdag myed pa la thim bar bsgom*. Here I translate *da ci* more from context than any other knowledge of its meaning.

107. IOL Tib J 552, 6r.3–6v.1. *'gro ba sems can ma lus pa'i don yang der mdzad / nas / slar sang ha ra na hUM zhes brjod pas / gtso bo yab kyang yum la tim gis thim / yum yang yab la tim kyis thIm / yab kyang lha 'i ye shes mtshon pa la tim gis thim / ye shes mtshon gang pa de yang rdo rje nas tsam pa de la tim kyis thim / rdo rje nas tsam pa de yang hUM yungs 'bru tsam la tim gis thim / de nas hUM zhes hUM ring po cig brjod pas / hUM ni sems gi rta mang mgyogs dang 'dra ste / da ci gong du gsungs pa'i de bzhin nyid gi ting nge 'dzin chos kyi dbyings der tim gis thim mo*. Here I have taken *rta mang* as *rta [r]mang*, a compound meaning "horse." The other possibility would be to read this as a "herd of horses," though *rta khyu* is the more usual compound for that. I have taken some care to translate these lines with the verb at the end to better represent their evocative power; see below for an explanation of this verb-final aspect of the passage.

108. IOL Tib J 552, 2v.2 and 553, 1v.6.

Appendix: The *Generation of Fortune Sādhana*

1. This title may in part be a play on the closing prayer, written in the author's own voice, in which he explains that he composed the *sādhana* for those "lacking the fortune" i.e., to understand the tantra.
2. Given such a reading, the strange positioning of this *dang po* (in *dad pa dang po gtang bar 'os*) might be seen as possible evidence of the Sanskrit grammar in the original from which this *sādhana* was translated. IOL Tib J 331/2, 1r.4, prefers *dang por.*
3. Folio 1v is blank.
4. The manuscript is damaged at this point, so the verb is missing. I have inserted "emanate," but the true wording remains unsure to me. Curiously, both IOL Tib J 331/2 and IOL Tib J 554 skip over this line at the same point, suggesting that the ms. was already damaged at the time of their copying.
5. IOL Tib J 331/2, 1v.3, has instead "into the *dharmadhātu*" (*chos kyi dbyings su gyurd*), while IOL Tib J 554, 1r.4, matches the present reading (*chos nyid kyi rang bzhin tu 'gyurd*).

6. IOL Tib J 331/2, 2r.3, reads "*sa ma ya swaṃ bhruṃ*," while IOL Tib J 464, 2r.5, has "*sa ma ya stwom bruṃ*."
7. Folio 2v contains an outline of the proceedings; for discussion, see chapter 4.
8. Here *sattva* and *tathā* are reversed, compared to IOL Tib J 331. The present reading is probably better.
9. The actual words appear in IOL Tib J 331/2, 5r.2: *anurāgayāmi* ("I am impassioned").

5. Circles of Blazing Breaths

1. *Guhyasamājatantra* 18.113. *abhiṣekaṃ tridhā bhinnam asmiṃs tantre prakalpitam / kalaśābhiṣekaṃ prathamaṃ dvitīyaṃ guhyābhiṣekataḥ / prajñājñānaṃ tṛīyaṃ tu caturthaṃ tat punas tathā*. For the Tibetan verse, see *Samājottara*, 153a.4–5: *dbang bskur dbye ba rnam gsum du / | rgyud 'di la ni rab tu brtag / bum pa'i dbang bskur dang po ste / gnyis pa gsang ba'i dbang bskur ba / shes rab ye shes gsum pa ste / bzhi pa de yang de bzhin no*. The influence of this verse is evidenced by the fact that the description of the fourth initiation in the *Hevajra Tantra* repeats the same enigmatic phrase, that it is "likewise that again" (*Hevajra Tantra*, II, iii, 11). Although the verse represents the locus classicus for the four initiations as a set, and probably dates to around the mid-ninth century, Catherine Dalton, "Enacting Perfection: Buddhajñānapāda's Vision of a Tantric Buddhist World" (PhD diss., University of California, Berkeley, 2019), chapter 6, has shown that the *Samājottara* was likely predated by Buddhajñānapāda's *Dvitīyakrama*, which already references the fourth. Key too, as C. Dalton observes, are the only slightly later writings of Vaidyapāda, especially his *Yogasapta* and a mysterious, now-lost title that Vaidyapāda attributes to his teacher, Buddhajñānapāda, called the *Method of Engaging in the Fourth* (*Bzhi pa la 'jug pa'i thabs*).
2. Harunaga Isaacson, "Observations on the Development of the Ritual of Initiation (*abhiṣeka*) in the Higher Buddhist Tantric Systems," in *Hindu and Buddhist Initiations in India and Nepal*, ed. Astrid Zotter, et al. (Wiesbaden: Harrassowitz Verlag, 2010), 261–79, reviews the various Buddhist interpretations of the line, "likewise that again." On 269 n. 24, he quite rightly corrects my own suggestion (Jacob P. Dalton, "The Development of Perfection: The Interiorization of Buddhist Ritual in the Eighth and Ninth Centuries." *Journal of Indian Philosophy* 32 [2004]: 26) that the line might have referred to a further self-administering of the sacrament following the disciple's own performance of sexual union in the wisdom-gnosis initiation. On the same page, Isaacson writes: "That a separate Fourth empowerment was originally intended herewith [i.e., in the *Samājottara*] seems to me as to Sakurai . . . , extremely unlikely" (my addition). C. Dalton's subsequent work suggests that in fact the passage was intended as a reference to the fourth. Also of note here is Gnubs chen sangs rgyas ye shes's reference to the fourfold set in his *Mun pa'i go cha* commentary to the *Dgongs pa 'dus pa'i mdo* (see Jacob P. Dalton, *The Gathering of Intentions: A History of a Tibetan Tantra* [New York: Columbia University Press, 2016], 152), though there the fourth

initiation is called that of "great bliss"). As I have argued elsewhere, the *Mun pa'i go cha* likely dates to the mid-to-late ninth century, which fits well with our other evidence, and in the same work, Gnubs chen quotes from the *Samājottara* (see *Mun pa'i go cha*, vol. 50, 245–46).

3. Like the root *sādhana* of Pelliot tibétain 626 and 634, PC3835V describes an initial contemplation of the three syllables, *oṃ aṃ hūṃ*, for purificatory purposes, followed by a meditation on emptiness (roughly equivalent to our thusness *samādhi*), from which an A syllable emerges and transforms into sun and moon mandalas that serve as a base for the deity (like our all-illuminating and causal *samādhis*). Having generated oneself as Vajragarbha/Vajrasattva, one performs the recitation of a mantra that appears in the form of a rosary. Though the order of the syllables is scrambled, it is clear enough that the mantric syllables to be recited were once *oṃ āṃ hūṃ svāhā*, as in our *sādhana*. That sexual union is somehow involved is suggested by the gloss on the last two of these syllables (*svāhā*), which references a drop of water (or semen) rising through the jewel (or penis) to issue forth at the top. While the details of these ritual steps differ from our own *sādhana*, the overall pattern is similar. Given the differences, it is possible that PC3835V is only indirectly related to our Tibetan *sādhana*, though the other links between Chan and Mahāyoga seen in and around the two works support the possibility of a closer relationship. I thank Amanda Goodman for bringing this important item to my attention. For a summary of the manuscript, see Amanda K. Goodman, "The Vajragarbha Bodhisattva Three-Syllable Visualization: A Chinese Buddhist *Sādhana* Text from Tenth-Century Dunhuang," *BuddhistRoad Paper* 2, no. 7 (2022).
4. Under this title, the work is quoted at least three times by Nupchen Sangyé Yeshé in his *Bsam gtan mig sgron*; see 144.4 and 160.1. The *Brief Precept* and its commentary have been translated by Sam van Schaik, *Tibetan Zen: Discovering a Lost Tradition* (Boston and London: Snow Lion, 2015), 183–91.
5. On the two-way influences between the Tibetan manuscripts in this group, see Sam van Schaik and Jacob Dalton, "Where Chan and Tantra Meet: Buddhist Syncretism in Dunhuang," in *The Silk Road: Trade, Travel, War and Faith*, ed. Susan Whitfield (Chicago: Serindia, 2004), 63–71.
6. Compare, for example, PC2104V and PC3913 and Stein 2144 (Items 1–2).
7. For three additional manuscripts in the same hand, see van Schaik and Dalton, "Where Chan and Tantra Meet," 63–65. For an example of the same scribe's *dbu can* hand, see IOL Tib J 320, which opens with the same distinctive decorative marker. Still further examples might be listed; for now, it is worth mentioning only that IOL Tib J 689, which contains a copy of the Tibetan Chan *Brief Precept*, is probably also in the same hand.
8. For this line and the following one, the text switches to seven-syllable verse.
9. At this point, the verse switches to seven-syllable lines for the rest of the text.
10. Further parallel passages may yet be found as searchable Tibetan texts become more available and better organized. Also, one might be tempted to suggest that perhaps only the three last *samādhis* for the recitations (3r.1ff), which correspond to the verses in seven-syllable verse, were copied from elsewhere, but

such is not the case; the *Kun 'dus rig pa'i mdo* (Toh. 831, 105b.5–6) includes parallels for earlier lines in the second half on the recitations.

11. IOL Tib J 332/1, 2r.2–3. *e ma ngo mtshar rmad kyi chos / rdzogs pa'i sangs rgyas kun kyis* [*sic* for *kyi*] *gsang / skye ba myed las thams cad skye / skyes pa nyid na skyes pa myed.*
12. Particularly relevant for unpacking this verse is Philip Fisher's (*Wonder, the Rainbow, and the Aesthetics of Rare Experiences* [Cambridge, MA: Harvard University Press, 1998]) exploration of wonder in the aesthetics of rare experiences.
13. In later centuries, the philosophical view to be cultivated at the beginning of the generation stage became the subject of some debate; see Yael Bentor, "Meditation on Emptiness in the Context of Tantric Buddhism," *Journal of Buddhist Philosophy* 1 (2015): 136–55.
14. The Chan *Brief Precept* ends with a reference to the nonconceptual "gnosis of intrinsic awareness" (*rang rig ye shes*), a term that would become central to later Great Perfections writings. Already in Pelliot tibétain 699, 5r.2, the commentator to the *Brief Precept* turns to that nascent tradition (Atiyoga) to explain the phrase. That same commentary also uses the phrase *rig pa'i ye shes* on Pelliot tibétain 699, 2r.6, in a quotation from an unidentified source (*lung*).
15. See, for example, Or.8210/S.95, V.5, ll. 4–8; IOL Tib J 552, 1r.2–1v.1. The latter observes that the fivefold set may be referred to as either the five *mudrās* or the five methods for settling (*bzhag pa'i thabs lnga*).
16. Pelliot tibétain 699, 2r.2–3.
17. Bernard Faure, *The Will to Orthodoxy: A Critical Genealogy of Northern Chan Buddhism* (Stanford, CA: Stanford University Press, 1997), 61ff. On gazing at the mind in Tibetan Chan texts, see also Carmen Meinert, "The Conjunction of Chinese Chan and Tibetan rDzogs Chen Thought: Reflections on the Tibetan Dunhuang Manuscripts IOL Tib J 689-1 and PT 699," in *Contributions to the Cultural History of Early Tibet (extra Volume to Studies in Central and East Asian Religion)* (Leiden; Boston: Brill, 2007), 239–301.
18. Pelliot tibétain 699, 3r.1–2: *rang gi sems la bltas na / sems kyi ngo bo ci yang ma yin bas.*
19. That said, the *Guhyasamāja*'s sixth chapter, which describes the practice of a sexualized subtle vajra (Skt. *sūkṣmavajra*; Tib. *rdo rje phra mo*) not unrelated to our *sādhana*'s rite, opens with a similar observation of one's mind (*cittanidhyapti*), as well as of one's speech and body; see verses 4–6. There too, the resulting discovery of no essential nature (*svabhāva*) establishes the space within which (in verse 8) oneself is then generated as a buddha. Although this is probably not the source for our *sādhana*'s "gazing at the mind," similar meditations on the self are commonly used in *sādhanas* to enter the initial meditation on emptiness.
20. Bhadantācariya Buddhaghosa, *The Path of Purification* (*Visuddhimagga*), trans. Bhikkhu Ñāṇamoli (Kandy: Buddhist Publication Society, 2011), 270 and 274. Many other examples can be found in the surrounding pages. These are chosen for their relevance to the present *sādhana*.
21. Following Yanagida Seizan, McRae writes about the extensive use of metaphor in the writings of Northern School Chan. He too observes that other Buddhist texts use metaphor; "Hence, the mere use of metaphor, even its extensive use,

is not noteworthy. Rather, it is the way in which the device is used in Northern School texts that deserves our attention. . . . In a word, the Northern School used the device of metaphor to transform all of Buddhism into an allegory for the practice of contemplation of the mind" (John McRae, *The Northern School and the Formation of Early Ch'an Buddhism* [Honolulu: University of Hawaii Press, 1986], 198). "Contemplation of the mind" is McRae's equivalent for gazing at the mind.

22. Pelliot tibétain 626, 3v.1–2. *de la 'bru gzhom thabs la yang / chos can dang bsgrub par bya ba dang mthun ba'i dpe dang lung gi gtan tshigs so / kun 'dis 'gre 'o.*
23. Pelliot tibétain 634, 1v.2. *de gsuM 'dus pa la lung gi gtan tshigs.*
24. For more on these three tests and the use of scripture in Dharmakīrti more generally, see Tom J. F. Tillemans, *Scripture, Logic, Language: Essays on Dharmakīrti and His Tibetan Successors* (Boston: Wisdom, 1999), 27–51, especially 29–30.
25. Pelliot tibétain 626, 4r.1. *mun pa' dang 'dra ba'i zhi gnas kyi rlan du myi bying bar.*
26. Whereas the present *sādhana* has five syllables for the five great elements, the *Generation of Fortune* lists only four elements, with the initial element of space not included. The same variation between four and five elements is seen already in early Buddhist writings; see Alexander Wynne, *The Origin of Buddhist Meditation* (Abingdon and New York: Routledge, 2007), 31. In developing the stack of elemental discs here, our root *sādhana* is incorporating early Buddhist meditation practices that focus on the "consummations" (Skt. *kṛtsna*; Pali *kasiṇa*; Tib. *zad par*). Wynne (30–37) argues that the idea of meditating on a series of increasingly stable elemental discs marking stages of emanation out of nothingness (and back) likely originated in early Brahmanical circles. The discs also appear in the *Mahāvairocanābhisaṃbodhi*, where Buddhagupta comments on a (mistaken, he says) perception of their non-Buddhist origins (see *Mahāvairocanābhi saṃbodhi*, 141a.4–7, translated by Steven Hodge, *The Mahā-vairocana-abhisaṃbodhi Tantra, with Buddhaguhya's Commentary* [London: Routledge Curzon, 2003], 157–58), though the violent rites that immediately precede the discussion of the discs may have been the original cause for the concern (see Hodge, *The Mahā-vairocana-abhisaṃbodhi Tantra*, 153–56).
27. There is no mention of the two stages of generation and perfection in our *sādhana*, but Pelliot tibétain 42, r81–82, makes clear that a parallel moment in the proceedings there marks the end of the generation stage. We can probably assume that what follows in Pelliot tibétain 42 was understood as the perfection stage, and in those pages is a cycling of the breath similar to our own (and discussed below). For this reason, it seems safe to say that our four *samādhis* for recitation correspond to the perfection stage.
28. Translating these four lines presents some challenges. A direct translation of the Dunhuang Tibetan would be markedly different, in many ways more poetically evocative. But in the interest of attempting to understand tantric Buddhist writings in India, I have translated my own somewhat irregularly emended verse (reproduced here), reconstructed on the basis of versions found in two other Tibetan sources (see chart below). In doing so, I have also sought to reproduce a possible Indic original rather than an early Tibetan interpretation. This is particularly true in my translation of the first line's *srog chags brtsal ba'*, which I have emended to *srog dang brtsal ba'*, which probably translated the Sanskrit

prāṇāyāma (Tib. *srog rtsol*; "breath restriction"). The likely presence of this term is certainly relevant, as the vajra recitation practice that is closely related to our own (see below) is regularly cited as a prime example of *prāṇāyāma*. Tsongkhapa discusses the early Tibetan tendency to translate *prāṇāyāma* as twofold; see Gavin Kilty, trans., *Tsongkhapa's* A Lamp to Illuminate the Five Stages*: Teachings on the* Guhyasamāja Tantra (Boston: Wisdom, 2013), 269–70. Because doing so figures strongly in the verse's structure, I have translated the term as twofold, even though it may reflect a more Tibetan reading. For better or worse, I have also emended all of the line-final injunctions to "look" (*lta*) to "as if" (*ltar*), also on the basis of the other received versions of the verse.

29. For some examples from Dunhuang, see IOL Tib J 332/1 and Pelliot tibétain 321.
30. For a discussion of this term, see David Jackson, "Sa-skya Paṇḍita the 'Polemicist': Ancient Debates and Modern Interpretations," *Journal of the International Association of Buddhist Studies* 13, no. 2 (1990): 41–45.
31. "Of the body" is missing but clearly intended.
32. I.e., within the spherical handle of the vajra.
33. Pelliot tibétain 626, 5r.5–5v.2. *dran ba' rtsol ba zhes bya ba ni / spyir gtang ste / dran ba ni spyan rtsa rig rig 'dug pa' / srog ni dbugs kyib kyib 'dug pa' / rtsol ba' ni gsungs la khad pa' / / snyan ca zhes pa' ni / dran ba yid la gsal ba' ste / dbu'i thor tshugs dang zhabs kyi 'khor lo yan cad du rgyan chas kun sbrid be re re 'dug pa' / gzhi la rdo rje yig 'bru zhes bya ba ni thugs dran ba yid la gsal ba ste / bdag gi thugs ka zla ba'i dkyil 'khor ni lhan thabs ma yin la / rdo rje ni sbyar ma ma yin / mye long bzur pa' 'dra ba'i nang na gsal la / rdo rje bum pa'i dkyil ni yig 'bru bris par gyur pa' / shel dang ba'i nang na mtshan gnas pa' bzhin du phyi nas bltas na nang gsal ba 'o / / gug skyed zhes ba ni gsung dran ba yid la gsal ba' ste / yig 'bru rnams bi sar tsa na dang / bcas par gsal ba'o.*
34. Unfortunately, doing justice to these terms in translation is difficult. Such terms appear throughout Tibetan literature and folk songs. Beyond the repetition of syllables, the third example here, *sbrid be re re* (dazzling), exhibits a further trend whereby the first syllable, or some element of it, is repeated in what follows. Thus, the *br* in the initial syllable is echoed by the *be* and the *re re*.
35. Multiple drafts or attempts at local compositions are seen among the tantric manuals from Dunhuang, as noted in chapter 4 with reference to IOL Tib J 552, 553, and 554. The same may also be true of IOL Tib J 422 and 423, both discussions of a fire offering for pacification. Between Pelliot tibétain 626 and Pelliot tibétain 634, the latter seems the better polished of the two commentaries, perhaps indicating that it was composed second.
36. For more on Bde ba gsal mdzad, a supposed teacher of Gnubs chen sangs rgyas ye shes, and the contents of volumes 22–23 of this collection, see Jacob P. Dalton, "Lost and Found: A Fourteenth-Century Discussion of Then-Available Sources on gNubs chen sangs rgyas ye shes," *Bulletin of Tibetology (Special Issue, Nyingma Studies: Narrative and History)* 49, no. 1 (2013): 39–54.
37. *Phur pa'i 'dzab dgongs*, 230.1: *de'i don yid la bya ba'i phyir 'di skad do.*
38. Pelliot tibétain 626, 6r.1–2, makes clear the point about sympathetic resonance: "through one's recitation of the mantra, the syllables also recite, such that they are endowed with the sound of their own mantra" (*dril bu zhes pa ni / sgra bskor*

ba ste de 'i dus na bdag gis sngags brjod pas yI ge yang rang sngags kyi sgra dang bcas par brjod do).

39. Pelliot tibétain 626, 5v.7–6r.1. *'phreng ba zhes pa' ni yig 'bru las bsogs pa bdag gi rdo rje lam du phab ning kwa ra ra bskor ba 'o.* Here I read the syllable *ning* as *cing.* While not ideal, it brings the exclamatory phrase, *kwa ra ra*, more into line with the similar phrase (*dwa ra ra*) used in a similar context on line 3. It remains unclear just how to understand the metaphor of the sleeve opening here (and below in Pelliot tibétain 634). The phrasing seems to suggest that the circle is "the size of a sleeve opening" (*phu dung tsam*), but this seems small for a circle the moves between both sexual partners. For this reason, my translation focuses solely on the circle's general appearance and not its size.
40. Pelliot tibétain 626, 6r.2–3: *'od kyi zhes pa ni / 'od bskor ba' ste / gsang ba'i rdo rje lam du byung / yum gyi pad ma rnam par dag pa'i mkhar phab nas 'od phu dung tsam gyi nang na yig 'bru lnga 'i 'od zer tsha tsha 'dra ba dwa ra ra 'byung ngo.*
41. Pelliot tibétain 634, 3r.3.: *'od bskor ba dang sbyar te yi ge 'bru lnga dper na mgar ba'i sbud mye nang na tsha tsha 'phro ba dang 'dra bar 'od zer phu dung tsam sna lnga 'i nang tsha tsha dang 'dra bar yi 'bru lnga dang skad rang gis sgrogs nas rim par zlog go.* The final verb should probably be read as *zlos.*
42. Pelliot tibétain 634, 3r.3: *gsang ba'i rdzas hung badzra 'drig bya ba yin hung rkyang pa bya(?) yin te des myi phan de ltar rigs lnga 'i snying po bcu bar yang hung badzra 'drig kyang rgyan la bdag gi lte ba dbus kyi 'khor los mar btsir rdo rje lam du byung yum gi mkha' la [ph]abs sgal tshigs rta bskyon.* The extra [*ph*] inserted on the basis of Pelliot tibétain 626, 6r.2: *yum gyi pad ma rnam par dag pa'i mkhar phab nas.*"
43. While these two Dunhuang manuscripts cannot be taken as representative of all Indian tantric ritual development, they also suggest that that the concept of bodily *cakras* may have spread before that of the central channel.
44. As mentioned above (n. 3), PC3835V and several other Chinese manuscripts may also make oblique reference to the practice; see Goodman, "The Vajragarbha Bodhisattva Three-Syllable *Visualization.*"
45. Pelliot tibétain 42, r83.4–84.2: *de nas no pyi ka las 'byung ba bzhin / sngags kyi snying po 'phreng ba las / grangs brgya rtsa brgyad yan chad / bye ba la* [?one syllable damaged by tear?] *gi bar du bzlas pa yang / dbugs myed rab du phra ba'i ngag rab tu yongs su gsal ba ste / de bzhin grub pa bzlas pa ni ting nge 'dzin ye shes las 'byung ba'o / zhes 'byung ba bzhin bgyi 'o.* The relevance of the passage may also be suggested by the manuscript's use of what may be an alternative translation of the phrase that introduces our two commentaries' discussions of the first three lines of the first perfection-stage *samādhi* discussed above, i.e., "the mental illumination of the awareness" of body, speech, and mind (*rig pa yid la gsal ba*). In the parallel context, when describing the syllables upon a moon disc visualized at the practitioner's heart, Pelliot tibétain 42, r83.2, mentions "the mental illumination of awareness" (*rig pa'i blo la gsal*), which is a yoga of the body, speech, and mind.
46. IOL Tib J 464, 4r.1–4. *slar yang bsgyings pa nyid du brtan / gtsug du rin chen myu gu yang / cho ga bzhin du rab tu gzhag / AoM aM hUM sva hA / byin rlabs chen po 'i snying po lnga / gnas lnga dag du byin kyis brlab / bsrung ba 'i sbyor ba ꣸ ci nus pas / grub*

pa 'i bdag nyid brtan bar bsrung / de nyid rnam bzhi tshul gyis ni / bzlas brjod nyid kyang ci nus bya.

47. In a different context that comes prior to commencing sexual union, *Guhyasamāja* VIII.9 identifies these same five places as the top of the head, the throat, the heart, between the navel and the groin, and the "secret" place at the perineum. Candrakīrti's *Pradīpodyotana* (114–15) maps onto these locations the five syllables, *oṃ āḥ hūṃ svā hā.*
48. For a full translation of these notes, see chapter 4.
49. For an English translation of a relevant eighteenth-century presentation of Buddhagupta's commentary (Toh. 2670) on these four, see Jigme Lingpa, *Treasury of Precious Qualities: The Rain of Joy, Book Two*, trans. Padmakara Translation Group (Boston and London: Shambala, 2013), 100–2. According to Rongzom, the *Man ngag lta ba'i phreng ba* associates the *Dhyānotttarapaṭalakrama*'s four principles with Ubhayātantra (see Samten Karmay, *The Great Perfection* [Leiden: Brill, 1988], 155 n. 80). The reason for this shift from Kriyā to Ubhayā may be the *Dhyānottara*'s close association with the *Mahāvairocanābhisaṃbodhi*, the main Ubhayā tantra according to Buddhagupta (see Jacob P. Dalton, "A Crisis of Doxography: How Tibetans Organized Tantra During the 8th–12th Centuries," *Journal of the International Association of Buddhist Studies* 28, no. 1 [2005]: 123). *Hevajra*, I.27, includes another similar list: *ātmatattvaṃ mantratattvaṃ devatātattvaṃ jñānatattvaṃ*; see David Snellgrove, *The Hevajra Tantra: A Critical Study*, 2 vols. (London: Oxford University Press, 1959), 49, for the English translation.
50. There are parallels between our root *sādhana*'s lines, *dran ba srog chags brtsol ba' gsung gsung lta /* and *rnam gsum gcig tu yid la zhen sems pa'* (2v.2–3) and the *Dhyānottara*'s *yid la zhen par sems pa na / me yi nang nas zhi ba ste / tshig rnams dag ba yan lag ldan / srog dang rtsol ba'ang bkang pa'i bdag* (224b.1), but they are loose enough to be relegated to this note. Buddhagupta (*Dhyānottarapaṭalaṭīkā*, 13b.6–14b.7), in commenting on this same line in the *Meditation Supplement*, repeatedly references "mindfulness" (*dran pa*) in connection to the *srog dang rtsol ba*, which makes our *sādhana*'s addition of the third element of "mindfulness" a strange coincidence. Buddhagupta's commentary was known in early Tibet, as it appears in the Ldan kar catalogue (Marcelle Lalou, "Les textes bouddhiques"Les textes bouddhiques au temps de Khri-sroṅ lde bcan," *Journal asiatique* 241 [1953]: 326).
51. The passage continues immediately on (231.2–3) to reference the same firebrand image used in our own text: *phar spros pas ni thugs dam bskul / tshur 'dus pas ni tshogs chen rdzogs / mgal me klad la bskor bzhin / phar 'phros tshur 'dus rgyud mi chad.*
52. Though Pelliot tibétain 626, 5v.5–6, adds in passing that "one also cultivates it similarly on the tongue" (*gsung gi ni lce la yang de bzhin bsgom ba'o*).
53. Another question is the apparent disagreement between the two works over the number of syllables in the cycling garland. In commenting on the third *samādhi*, Pelliot tibétain 634 has five (*oṃ āṃ hūṃ svā hā*) resounding like the sound of a bell and appearing like a spinning firebrand. Also, in commenting on the third *samādhi*, Pelliot tibétain 626 describes a garland of only three syllables (*oṃ āṃ hūṃ*) that "descends down one's vajra path." We might be tempted

to resolve this difference by suggesting that five syllables circle at the heart but only three cycle between partners. But Pelliot tibétain 634 introduces its five syllables while commenting on the third *samādhi*, which is when the shift to the sexual cycling seems to begin. So we seem to be left with opposing opinions. Most likely, this reflects a change in thinking on the part of our single author, again suggesting two drafts, with Pelliot tibétain 626 written first.

54. IOL Tib J 438, 15v. 2–3. *nam ka'I dbyIngs kyI dbus gnas par / zla ba'I dkyIl 'khor bsgom bar bya / sangs rgyas gzugs nI rab bsgoms nas / phra mo'i sbyor ba kun tu brtsam / / sna'I rtse mor yungs kar bsam / 'gro dang myI 'gro yungs kar la / gsang ba'I sngags kyI brtags pa yI / ye shes mchog gi gnas bsgom mo.* Here I have translated the verse as preserved at Dunhuang. Compare (with some difference in verse 9) Toh. 442, 99a.2–3, and *Guhyasamāja* VI.8–9. *ākāśadhātumadhyasthaṃ bhāvayec candramaṇḍalam / buddhabimbaṃ vibhāvitā sūkṣmayogaṃ samārabhet / / nāsāgre sarṣapaṃ cintet sarṣape sacarācaram / bhāvayej jñānapadaṃ ramyaṃ rahasyaṃ jñānakalpitam.*
55. IOL Tib J 438, 15v.1–2. *bdagI lus nam ka bzhin bar dmyigs la nam ka'i dkyil du zla ba gsal ba sgrib pa'am thogs pa myed pa ltar cung zad dmyigs / myi nus na yang mye long chung ngu tsam du bsams la steng du bdag sdod pa de las lha'I skur bsgyur nas gnas te / zla ba dang bdagI lus bskyed pa'i yi ge sa bon ni yod kyang rung sems de ltar. / / de ltar phyag rgya chen por zhugs par byas la / snyIng kar yang yungs kar de gsal bar bsgoms nas khong nas rgyu ste snar rgyu ste snar byung nas sna'I rtse mor gnas par bsgoms te goms pa dang / yung kar gyI nang du snod dang bcud du bcas te kun la yang chud par bsgom.*
56. See, for example, Ratnākaraśānti's *Kusumañjali*, 261b.1: *sna rtse ste / ye shes rdo rje'i sngags kyi steng gi char gyur pas so . . .* The Dunhuang interlinear notes to chapter 3, on the *utpattikrama* subtle yoga, have the mustard seed-sized jewel move from one's heart up to the nose, though there the actual nose on one's face; see IOL Tib J 438, 10v.1.
57. IOL Tib J 438, 15v. 5. *de yang goms pa ring sbyor thabs 'dI'i gzungs 'dus 'phro mdzas pa la bya.*
58. Horiuchi Hanjin, ed., *Kongochokyo no Kenkyu* (*Sarvatathāgata-tattvasaṃgraha-nāma-mahāyāna-sūtra*) (Koyasan University: Mikkyo Bunka Kenkyujo, 1983), vol. 1, 262 (vv. 454ff.).
59. See, for example, Horiuchi, *Kongochokyo no Kenkyu*, 269, vv. 475–79, in the same third chapter, as well as 455–56, vv. 1110–1113. One Dunhuang manuscript offers a brief breathing practice, likely inspired by the *STTS*, wherein one's breath and a *hūṃ* syllable are emitted through the nostrils, purifying the universe. With the sound of an *oṃ* syllable, the breath regathers, filling the body's interior. This oscillation is repeated three times, after which a somewhat elaborate dissolution into emptiness is performed (IOL Tib J 447/3, r27.4–28.10). These instructions appear in the same manuscript that contains the commentary on the *STTS*-based *Tattvasaṃgraha-sādhanopāyikā* (see chapter 3).
60. On vajra recitation in Buddhajñānapāda's writings, see C. Dalton, "Enacting Perfection," 220–21 and 416–21. On the early Ārya school renditions, see Toru Tomabechi, "Étude du Pañcakrama: Introduction et traduction annotée," (PhD

diss., Université de Lausanne, 2006), 54–71 and 103–23; Christian Wedemeyer, *Āryadeva's* Lamp that Integrates the Practices (*Cāryamelapakapradīpa*): *The Gradual Path of Vajrayāna Buddhism* (New York: American Institute of Buddhist Studies, 2007), 88–95 and 175–205. In the former context, vajra recitation is the focus of the third *bindu* yoga of the perfection stage, though other forms of subtle yoga are the focus of the first two *bindus* as well. In the Ārya school sources, vajra recitation is generally associated with the stage of "speech isolation" (Skt. *vāgviveka*; Tib. *ngag rnam par dben pa*), the first of the five stages (*pañcakrama*) of the perfection stage.

61. The situation in the Ārya school grew increasingly complex, and by the time of Tsongkhapa (fourteenth century), vajra recitation proper had been separated from sexual union and referred only to the form of subtle yoga (or *prāṇāyāma*) performed at the tip of one's facial nose (as opposed to at one's heart or the tip of the penis); see, for example, Kilty, *Tsongkhapa's* A Lamp to Illuminate the Five Stages, 273–74. A further complication is whether vajra recitation, when performed in connection to sexual union, is to be performed only after the practitioner is no longer able to retain the *bodhicitta*, that is, after ejaculation. Buddhajñānapāda's third *bindu* yoga seems to occur just after emission, whereas the second *bindu* yoga involves a form of subtle yoga wherein the drop is held at the tip of the vajra during union. Similarly, Āryadeva's discussion of vajra recitation in his *Caryamelāpakapradīpa* begins with a quotation from the *Samājottara*, which says, "Emitting [it] at the lotus-nose-tip, [one] should imagine [it] in the form of a lump (*piṇḍa*)" (*Guhyasamājatantra*, XVII.147b: *niścārya piṇḍarūpena nāsikāgre tu kalpayet*; following the translation of Wedemeyer, *Āryadeva's* Lamp that Integrates the Practices, 177). If such a reading of "emission" (*niścārya*) is correct, even though both traditions couch their discussions of vajra recitation within a larger context of sexual yoga, the latter does not play much of a role.

62. See Hiromichi Hikita, "Consecration of Divine Images in a Temple," in *From Material to Deity: Indian Rituals of Consecration*, ed. Shingo Einoo and Jun Takashima (New Delhi: Manohar Publishers and Distributers, 2005), 184, and Dominic Goodall, *Bhaṭṭarāmakaṇṭhaviracitā kiraṇavṛttiḥ. Bhaṭṭa Rāmakaṇṭha's Commentary on the Kiraṇatantra. Vol. 1: chapters 1–6. Critical Edition and Annotated Translation*, Publications du département d'Indologie 86, no. 1 (Pondicherry: Institut français de Pondichéry/École française d'Extrême-Orient, 2015), 61.

63. See, for example, P. V. Kane, *History of Dharmaśāstra: Ancient and Mediaeval Religious and Civil Law*, Vols. I–V, 2nd ed. (Poona: Bhandarkar Oriental Research Institute, 1968–77 [1930–50]), II: 900; Gudrun Bühnemann, "The Ritual for Infusing Life (*prāṇapratiṣṭhā*) and the Goddess Prāṇaśakti," *Zeitschrift der Deutschen Morgenländischen Gesellschaft* 141, no. 2 (1991): 363. Further research on the origins of this practice would be required to say anything definitive. For a summary of a relatively early consecration ritual from the *Sātvata-saṃhitā* that includes vital breath consecration, see Hikita, "Consecration of Divine Images in a Temple," 168ff., especially 173, and for a list of other examples, see Frederick M. Smith, *The Self Possessed: Deity and Spirit Possession in South Asian Literature and Civilization* (New York: Columbia University Press, 2006), 411 n. 66.

64. Smith, *The Self Possessed*, 388–89, notes the presence of a related rite for "the restoration of life to a corpse" in the *Brahmāṇḍa Purāṇa*. On possessing others in the *Yogavāsiṣṭha*, see also 290–93. John R. Freeman, "Possession Rites and the Tantric Temple: A Case-Study from Northern Kerala," *Diskus* 2, no. 2 (1994), has also argued for links between the breath consecration of images and *teyyam* possession rites in contemporary Kerala. On the Buddhist side, we see breath cycling being used as a healing/reviving rite in both Buddhagupta's commentary on *Mahāvairocanābhisaṃbodhi* 6.57 (**Vairocanābhisambodhivikurvitādhiṣṭāna mahātantravṛtti*, 170b.1–6; translated in Hodge, *The Mahā-vairocana-abhisaṃbodhi Tantra*, 188) and the *Catuṣpīṭha* 1.2.64 (Péter-Daniel Szántó, "Selected Chapters from the Catuṣpīṭhatantra [1/2]: Introductory Study with the Annotated Translation of Selected Chapters," [Thesis, Balliol College, Oxford, 2012], 232). Snellgrove, *The Hevajra Tantra*, vol. I, 55 n. 1, also translates a similar ritual procedure from the *Yogaratnamālā* for summoning the goddess Khecarī into one's heart by using the breath.

65. *Dhyānottarapaṭalakrama*, 224.1–4. *lha yi sku yi gnas de la / dang po kho nar mchod nas ni / rnal 'byor gnas bcas shes rab can / bde gshegs mdun du bsams nas ni / phyi nas yan lag rnam grol ba'i / mi 'byed 'byed pa'i rnam par spangs / phra ma mi g.yo gsal ba ste / blo yi spyod pa mdun na gnas / bdag nyid 'di 'drar bzhag nas ni / sngags kyi rnam par shes pas bsgom / bsdams nas ting nges 'dzin la gnas / srog dang rtsol ba rab tu bsdams / sgra dang sems dang gzhi la gzhol / gsang sngags mi 'gyur gzhi la gnas / yan lag ma nyams gsang sngags bzlas / ngal na bdag la ngal so shig / mi 'gyur ba ni yi ger ldan / gzhi las gzhir 'gyur de bzhin te / rang sngags phyir ni gang brtags pa / yid kyi dag pa bsam par bya / slar sdud pa yis bkug nas ni / srog dang rtsol ba bsdams pa'i yid / gsang sngags rig pas sngags la sbyar / yid kyi bzlas brjod brtsam par bya.*

66. *Dhyānottarapaṭakaṭīkā*, 14b.3. *de bsdams pa yang skabs 'dir 'byung ba dang 'jug pa dgag pa'o.* Buddhagupta adds some interesting detail: "By means of one's winds being drawn upward, one retracts [like] the body of a tortoise and gathers in the manner of drinking water with one's tongue" (14b.4: *gyen du 'dren pa'i rlung gis / rus sbal gyi lus bskum pa dang / lce yis chu btung ba'i tshul du bsdus te*). We might take the latter act to be drinking through one's tongue as through a straw. Compare *Vāyu Purāṇā*, 11.26: "Just as water is taken up by applying force through a pipe or mechanical device, so also the Yogin should drink in the wind with effort" (following the translation of G. V. Tagare, *The Vāyu Purāṇa, Part I* [Delhi: Motilal Banarsidass, 1987], 95). Such manipulations of internal winds are significant for a history of such practices in early tantric Buddhism, but because they may reflect ritual influences that postdate the *Meditation Supplement* itself, I bracket them here. Here and elsewhere in his commentary, Buddhagupta also cites the **Vajroṣṇīṣa-tantra* (*Rdo rje gtsug tor gyi rgyud*), which appears to be relevant to the practices under discussion, but I have not yet been able to identify the corresponding work.

67. *Dhyānottarapaṭakaṭīkā*, 16b.5. *nga rgyal dang / dmigs pa gsum . . .* (the latter triad being elsewhere explained as corresponding to the body, speech, and mind).

68. *Dhyānottarapaṭakaṭīkā*, 17b.7–18a.2. *yang de nyid bye brag tu dbye ba'i phyir / gzhi las gzhir gyur zhes bya ba gsungs te / gzhi las zhes bya ba ni yang dag par rdzogs pa'i sangs rgyas kyi gzhi las so / gzhir gyur zhes bya ba ni rang gi lha'i sku bdag gi gzhir*

gyur pa ste / zla ba'i dkyil 'khor gyi rnam par gyur pa'i yid de / gsang sngags kyi yi ge dang bcas par bdag gi gzugs rang gi lhar gyur pa de'i snying gar blta zhing dbugs dbyung ba'i mtha'i bar du bzlas brjod bya'o / de las kyang de bzhin du yang dag par rdzogs par'i sangs rgyas kyi gzhi la blta'o / de las kyang yid kyi de slar bsdus te / snga ma bzhin rang gi lha'i sku'i gzhi la gnas par byas la bzlas brjod bya ste.

69. As already noted in chapter 2, Hodge dates the *Mahāvairocanābhisaṃbodhi* to "perhaps around 640 C.E., or a little earlier" (Hodge, *The Mahā-vairocana-abhisaṃbodhi Tantra*, 11 and 14–15). Cycling practices of this sort appear to have enjoyed some popularity during the seventh century. T. 1077, a ritual manual for worshipping the goddess Cundī, includes a similar practice, and the text is attributed to Divākara, who is said to have arrived in Changan in 660 C.E. and died in 688. I thank Koichi Shinohara for these clarifications. In East Asia, the circulation of mantra between practitioner and deity also forms part of the Shōnenju (formal recitation) section, which is the second of the "three mysteries," i.e., that of speech (see Robert H. Sharf, "Visualization and Mandala," in *Living Images: Japanese Buddhist Icons in Context*, ed. Robert H. Sharf and Elizabeth H. Sharf [Stanford, CA: Stanford University Press, 2001], 160).
70. For an English translation of the relevant verses, see Hodge, *The Mahā-vairocana-abhisaṃbodhi Tantra*, 164–65.
71. As translated by Hodge, *The Mahā-vairocana-abhisaṃbodhi Tantra*, 175. Buddhagupta provides further detail in his *Piṇḍārtha*; see Hodge, *The Mahā-vairocana-abhisaṃbodhi Tantra*, 520–25.
72. **Vairocanābhisambodhivikurvitādhiṣṭānamahātantravṛtti*, *de bzhin du rnam par snang mdzad mngon par rdzogs par byang chub pa rnam par sbrul ba byin gyis rlob pa'i rgyud 'di yang thabs dang shes rab gtso bor gyur pa rnal 'byor gyi rgyud yin mod kyi / bya ba la mos pa'i gdul bya'i 'gro ba rnams gzung ba'i phyir bya ba'i rgyud kyi rjes su mthun pa'i spyod pa dag kyang bstan pas bya ba'i rgyud dam / gnyis ka'i rgyud lta bur so sor brtags shing grags so.* For this reason I believe the class of Ubhayā tantras was originally rooted in the two alternative recitation methods offered by the *Mah āvairocanābhisaṃbodhi*.
73. For a later (fifteenth-century) example of cycling the breath between sexual partners, see Ngor chen Kun dga' bzang po's *Dpal kye rdo rje'i mngon par rtogs pa 'bring du bya ba yan lag drug pa'i mdzes rgyan*, 130.16–131.3: *bzlas pa'i rnal 'byor ni / dus rgyun du dkyil 'khor bsdus nas gtso bo yab yum gyi nga rgyal gyis byas kyang btub / snyen pa la sogs pa'i tshe skabs 'di kho nar bya ste / de yang yum gyi thugs ka'i oM las sngags kyi phreng ba byung zhal nas 'thon yab kyi zhal du zhugs sku'i dbyibs brgyud rdo rje'i lam nas byung ste yum gyi pad+mar zhugs / sku'i dbyibs brgyud de yum gyi zhal nas yab kyi zhal du zhugs te rgyun mi 'chad par 'khor ba las / las dang mthun pa'i 'od zer 'phros pas lha rnams dbang du 'dus par bsams la.* (My thanks to Kurt Keutzer for bringing this to my attention.) Other intriguing and possibly related examples of the cycling practice include the (second half of the eighth century) *Nām amantrārthāvalokinī*, where Vilāsavajra describes a similar rite for summoning the buddhas' gnosis into the syllables at one's heart; see Anthony Tribe, *Tantric Buddhist Practice in India: Vilāsavajra's Commentary on the Mañjuśrī-nāmasaṃgīti* (London and New York: Routledge, 2016), 137–38.

74. See his *Dvitīyakrama*, verse 115 and 122, translated by C. Dalton, "Enacting Perfection," on 390 and 392, respectively, though as observed (391 n. 245 and 248), the names of the channels are not yet those that would become the norm.
75. The Tibetan verb *brtag* is typically translated as something more like "analyze" or "determine." As noted in chapter 4, however, it is also used in Dunhuang manuscripts in the sense of "imagine" or "create," both of which are legitimate senses of the various Sanskrit words *brtag* translates, based on the Sanskrit root *kḷp*. Here, Nupchen seems to be using the term more in the sense of "create," but here and below I have opted for the somewhat loose translation "experience."
76. The PL480 edition (221.3) reads *dpra ba ka ru mtshon gang par gsal ba*, which appears to have been overcorrected as *he ru ka tshon gang bar gsal ba* in the *Bka' ma shin tu rgyas pa* edition. Transcribed Sanskrit terms are common throughout the *Bsam gtan mig sgron* and may have been used here in particular to obfuscate a portion of the text that is quite explicit about secret practices.
77. Here I take the three elements as what ceases, but their cessation may also imply death.
78. I remain unsure about this reconstruction of the Tibetan here: *na pa>sna ba*.
79. It is unclear, but these outer and inner stages *might* correspond to the vase and secret initiations. Note too the correspondence between the wisdom-gnosis initiation and the moon, which stands for means, perhaps because this initiation is associated with the practices of channels and winds, while the fourth initiation is associated with the sun and wisdom. That Nupchen's reference to the "great bliss" (*bde ba chen po*) is equivalent to the fourth initiation is suggested by his *Mun pa'i go cha*, vol. 50, 159.6–7; see Dalton, "How Dhāraṇīs WERE Proto-Tantric: Liturgies, Ritual Manuals, and the Origins of the Tantras," in *Tantric Traditions on the Move*, ed. David B. Gray and Ryan Overbey (New York: Oxford University Press, 2016), 152.
80. Here the sense in which Nupchen seems to be using the term *anuyoga* seems to be more in accord with the nine-vehicle system's use of it to denote tantric practice focusing on the perfection stage than with how the term is used by certain early *Guhyasamāja* exegetes. That he uses the Tibetan *rjes su 'jug pa'i rnal 'byor* as a translation of *anuyoga* may be seen in his *Mun pa'i go cha*, vol. 51, 427.4.
81. In the foregoing, Nupchen writes that, having received the four initiations, one should cultivate the realizations specific to each. Thus, the outer and inner stages (initiations?) correspond to the worldly and transcendent flavors, respectively, while the stirring and stabilization of bliss and the attainment of *anuyoga* corresponds to the wisdom-gnosis initiation, and the cultivation of gnosis without a support corresponds to the fourth initiation.
82. *Bsam gtan mig sgron*, 220.2–223.1. The page order is scrambled in the PL480 edition, so my translation and transcription follows the proper order as seen in the 133-vol. *Bka' ma shin tu rgyas pa* (2009), vol. 102, 213.5–216.2: *de la man ngag ni spyir gnyis te / rten can dang rten med do / de la rten med ni snyan khung brgyud pa'i man ngag de bzhin nyid bsgom pa bya bsam bslab pa bral bar ston pa ste / a ti yo ga la*

khyad du bzhugs so / rten can ni steng 'og gi gnyis te / steng gi sgo la brten pa ni / shi ra tsa kra bzhi gnas gzhi na gnas pa la / de spyir bsgom ste bsam pa'ang las kyi me rlung so so'i thabs mi mthun pa las bskul te / nam mkha'i ba bzhos la ye shes kyi bdud rtsi phab la bde ba brtag pa dang / de dag so sor rang re la rtsa dang thig le dang 'od la sogs pa / bsam pa'i gzhung mi mthun pa mang po dang / khyad par du 'du byed che 'am / yang na bskal pa can 'ga'i don du 'da' ka'i man ngag dang / nang gi gsang ba ye shes kyi sgrom bur nyon mongs pa can gyi yid nam mkha'i ri bong can du bsam pa dang / de'i thog tu kun gzhi spros pa bral ba dpra ba ka ru mtshon gang par gsal ba dang / de'i thog tu ye shes kyi ngo bor thugs kyi yi ge hUM dkar po skyes pa 'dra bar bsam pa dang / de gsum snga nas 'dris par byas pa nyid las mi dmigs par yang 'gyur la / gzhan 'gags pa'i dus su de gsum rlung dang re mos dang 'grogs te 'byung 'jug byas te / gcig la gcig bsdus la / mjug hUM la bsdud na ye shes kyi he ru ka mtshon gang bar bsams la / 'og min chen por bskul / tshon gang pa la bsdud na phyir byung nas chos so cog dang bdag ma dmigs pas / las ngan rgyun bcad do / sems 'byung sa ni na pa nas 'gro ba'i man ngag de dag la sogs pa dang / gzhan 'tshogs ma stong stong po'i nas 'byung ba'i man ngag la sogs pa'o / mdor steng 'og gi rlung 'jug gi phye ba'o / de dag la'ang 'jig rten dang / 'jig rten las 'das pa kun gyis ro yod pas / de dag brtags te mthar dbyung ngo / 'og gi sgo la rten pa ni / sngar bshad pa'i shes rab ma gzhung dang mthun pa dkar bas btsal te / bshad pa'i bla ma la mnyas phul nas / rim par rdzogs par bya ste phyi nang gi rdzogs pa dang / zla ba can la shes rab ye shes kyi dbang brtag / nyi ma can la bde ba chen po brtag go / de dag goms par byas te / 'jig rten pa'i ro dang / 'jig rten las 'das pa'i lam rim gyi ro brtag / de yang dang po shin tu bde ba'i ye shes g.yo ba dang / thob pa dang / 'jug brtan nas rjes su 'jug pa'i rnal 'byor thob bo / de nas rten dang bral yang mi nyams pas rten med pa'i / ye shes la 'dris goms su bya'o / de lta bu'i man ngag slob dpon bi ma la dang / 'bu ta kug ta dang / padmo'i gzhung la sogs pa bla ma'i zhal du rag lus so. I have not included the interlinear comments in my transcription and translation, as they are undated and add little. An abbreviated summary of the same basic practices, using some of the same wording seen toward the end of the passage translated here, also appears at *Bsam gtan mig sgron*, 25.5–26.6. Longchenpa appears to have drawn on these same lines on f. 26 in writing his *Guhyagarbha* work, *Dpal gsang ba'i snying po'i spyi don legs par bshad pa'i snang bas yid kyi mun pa thams cad sel ba*, v. 25, 155.

83. For an English translation of a sixteenth-century Kagyu discussion, see FabrizioTorricelli, "The Tibetan Text of the 'Karṇatantravajrapada,'" *East and West* 48, no. 3/4 (1998): 385–423, esp. 394 and 401. Sometimes consumption of the sacrament is replaced with drawing up the fluids to permeate the body (e.g., Jamgon Kongtrul, *The Treasury of Knowledge: Book Eight, Part Four: Esoteric Instructions*, trans. Sarah Harding [Ithaca, NY: Snow Lion, 2007], 72), mirroring the (re) interpretations of Vīravajra and Longchenpa discussed below.
84. The three levels of mind represented—the afflicted mind consciousness, the foundational consciousness, and awakened mind—are central to Nupchen's other writings; see David Higgins, *The Philosophical Foundations of Classical rDzogs chen in Tibet: Investigating the Distinction Between Dualistic Mind (sems) and Primordial Knowing (ye shes)* (Vienna: Arbeitskreis für Tibetische und Buddhistische Studien Universität Wien, 2013), 190–92, and Dalton, *The Gathering of Intentions*, 40–46.

85. It is possible that the offering of the sacrament is implied in the line, "Paying homage in a manner of realization." Pelliot tibétain 634, 3v.1–2, does say that with the fourth *samādhi*, "the propitiations are complete and the activities performed," which begs the question: which activities? If we take the last two lines as the final dissolution and the dedication of merit, the homage would seem the most likely candidate. Beyond this, however, there is no evidence of the sacramental moment in either of our commentaries.
86. David Gordon White, *Kiss of the Yoginī: "Tantric Sex" in Its South Asian Contexts* (Chicago: University of Chicago Press, 2003), 210.
87. White, *Kiss of the Yoginī*, 217.
88. The gap between the two forms of the perfection stage was so clear as to be summarized quite succinctly by the thirteenth-century Tibetan author Rok ban Shes rab 'od (1166–1244) in these terms: "Mother tantras chiefly focus on the channels (*rtsa*), while father tantras emphasize the winds or energies (*rlung*)" (José Cabezón, *The Buddha's Doctrine and the Nine Vehicles: Rog Bande Sherab's Lamp of the Teachings* [Oxford and New York: Oxford University Press, 2013], 129).
89. As translated by David Gray, *The Cakrasamvara Tantra (The Discourse of Śrī Heruka) (Śrīherukābhidhāna): A Study and Annotated Translation* (New York: The American Institute of Buddhist Studies, 2007), 121. Gray cites the passage in making precisely the same point that I make here.
90. As translated by Cabezon, *The Buddha's Doctrine and the Nine Vehicles*, 89.
91. *Guhyagarbha*, 122a.6. *bsgrub pa'i nyi zla'i dkyil 'khor de / dkyil 'khor rdo rje lce yis blang.* This same line was discussed in chapter 4, n. 52, where the first *dkyil 'khor* is read as *snying po.*
92. *Gsang snying 'grel pa phyogs bcu mun sel*, 396.2–3. *nyi ma dang zla ba'i snying po de rtsa 'khor lo bzhi'i dkyil 'khor du gsang ba rdo rje'i lce yis blangs ste / mas rim gyis dgang zhing lus kyi gnas thams cad du khyab par dgram zhing ye shes su la bzla'o / 'di la kha cig lhar gsal ba'i lce rdo rjer bsams pas blangs te khong du 'thung bar 'dod pa ni ma yin te / sbyor ba'i don ma go ba yin no.*

Appendix: *Samādhi Sādhana* with Commentary

1. Normally one would expect the gnosis of awareness to be the subject and the *dharmadhātu* to be the object. *Rig pa'i ye shes* appears in Pelliot tibétain 813, ka gnyis verso.1. The latter is a fragment of Pelliot tibétain 116. The term also ends the *Lung chung* (see IOL Tib J 1774, Pelliot tibétain 131, and IOL Tib J 689, as well as *Bsam gtan mig sgron* where it is quoted under the title *Lung chung*).
2. Added on the basis of Pelliot tibétain 626, 2v.7–3r.1.
3. Pelliot tibétain 626, 3r. 4–5, adds: "Realizing in that way is the gnosis of awareness, which is insight (*lhag mthong*), that is, the method for realization. The method for settling is to settle without abiding anywhere, that is, calm abiding (*zhi gnas*)."

4. Probably this was only meant to be applied to the buddhas' mind. Pelliot tibétain 626, 3r.5–6, explains that the three gates—signlessness, wishlessness, and emptiness—are aligned with the mind, speech, and body, respectively.
5. On *halāhala*, see Domink Wujastyk, *The Roots of Ayurveda* (London: Penguin, 1998), 188 n. 90.
6. Or one could read the final *sbyar* as commentarial, i.e., the method should be applied to . . .
7. Here it seems *btsas kyang* is mistakenly inserted, probably from below, where the same two syllables appear in their proper place.
8. *Ki* is a final emphatic stop, still used in Amdo skad.
9. *phas gzhan*, as in *phas rgol*.
10. I add this insertion on the idea that the medicine may have been applied by a compassionate buddha, but this may be a mistake in the text—this might be read *shes rab* instead of *thugs rje chen po*, since wisdom is supposed to be the topic.
11. I am not sure how to translate this odd ending, *sangs rgyas pa 'o na*.
12. Pelliot tibétain 626, 3v.5–6, explains this rather difficult line: "Like the analogy of drops that fall from earlier (*sna snga ba*) to later, initially one's mental concepts arise, and subsequently they arise continuously. They are realized as a nonconceptual unborn state, and later whatever arises is cultivated as a nonconceptual and unborn state. Like a gatekeeper, such a person is not interrupted by afflictions" (*dper na thigs pa' sna pa'i par phyi ma 'babs pa dang 'dra bar bdagi sems kyi rtog pa skad cig ma sna pa' 'byung ba' dang / phyi ma rgyun ma chad par 'byung ba de / rnam par myi rtog pa ma skyes pa'i ngang du rotgs pa' dang / phyi ma ci byung yang rnam par myi rtog cing ma skyes pa'i ngang du bsgom mo // de sgo srungs dang 'dra bar nyon mongs pas bar myi chod pa'o*). In other words, the rain, which begins falling slowly, drop by drop, and eventually falls continuously and all around, is how the arising of thoughts should feel, and one should look through them like a watchman who is not distracted by them.
13. Correcting *shes par bsgrub* to *ngo shes par bsgrub*.
14. Pelliot tibétain 626, 3v.6–7, adds: "In the analogy, when a thief is recognized, he runs away. Similarly, as soon as erroneous concepts arise, one should recognize them to be deluded and not follow the error" (*dper na rkun ma ngo shes nas 'bros pa dang 'dra bar // 'khrul rtog byung tsam na 'khrul pa' yin bar ngo shes par byas dang 'khrul pa'i rjes su myi 'brang ba 'o*).
15. Literally, "the stirring of illumination" (*gsal bar bskyod pa*), which is significant because Pelliot tibétain 626 plays on the two elements.
16. Pelliot tibétain 626, 4r.1, adds: "One does not sink into the wetness of *śamatha*, which is like darkness" (*mun pa' dang 'dra ba'i zhi gnas kyi rlan du myi bying bar*).
17. The ink is smudged in several places here. I read it as follows: *gsal zhing bskyod par bsgom mo*.
18. One syllable is missing from this line. Throughout this study, I have tried to translate the Sanskrit *abhiṣeka* (Tib. *dbang bskur*) as "initiation," but here "empowerment" seems more appropriate for the more abstract sense being employed.
19. The second syllable of *dran pa* is missing from Pelliot tibétain 634 but present in Pelliot tibétain 626.

20. The text actually seems to say that the vajra is "horizontal" (*'phred ka*). Perhaps mistakenly, I have followed the lead of other texts in translating its position as "vertical" (*thad ka*).
21. The editorial marks *ki* and *khi* seem to draw attention to the parallels between the first and second terms here, i.e., between the opposites, mindfulness and distraction and clarity and stupefication.
22. *kyi* corrected to *kyis* on the basis of Pelliot tibétain 626, 5v.6.

Bibliography

Dunhuang Manuscripts Cited

IOL Tib J 97, 116, 141, 311, 312, 320, 321, 322, 325, 331, 332, 337, 348, 351, 353, 363, 366, 368, 372, 384, 388, 394, 396, 397, 398, 399, 401, 417, 419, 420, 422, 423, 435, 438, 439, 447, 448, 454, 463, 464, 466, 470, 507, 519, 551, 552, 553, 554, 576, 583, 594, 612, 647, 656, 687, 688, 711, 712, 754, 790, 792, 841, 931, 1236

Or. 8210/S.95, S.421, S. 1000

Pelliot chinois (PC) 2104, 2630, 2964, 3594, 3835, 3865, 3913, 3937

Pelliot tibétain (PT) 5, 6, 22, 23, 24, 26, 36, 37, 42, 49, 54, 72, 73, 74, 78, 103, 116, 265, 270, 271, 283, 300, 322, 324, 336, 353, 368, 389, 535, 792, 841, 849, 996

Primary Sources

Āryaprajñāpāramitānayaśatapañcāśataka. Jñānamitra. Tōh. 2647, *rgyud*, vol. *ju*, 272b.7–294a.5.

Bka' ma rgyas pa. 58 vols.

Bṛhatsaṃhitā. *The Bṛhat Saṃhitā by Varāhamihira with the Commentary of Bhaṭṭotpala*, ed. Mahamahopadhyaya Sudharaka Dvivedi. Benares: E. J. Lazarus & Co., 1895, 1897.

Bsam gtan mig sgron. Gnubs chen saṅs rgyas ye śes. Leh: S. W. Tashigangpa, 1974.

Bstan 'gyur (sde dge). 213 vols. Ed. Shuchen Tsultrim Rinchen. Delhi: Delhi Karmapae Chodhey Gyalwae Sungrab Partun Khang, 1982–1985.

Candanāṅga-nāma-dhāraṇī (*'Phags pa tsan+da gyi yan lag ces bya ba'i gzungs*). Toh. 518, *rgyud*, vol. *na*, 37a.–39a.2. (Pagination differs from Ui.)

**Daśaśikṣāvidhi* (*Bslab pa bcu'i cho ga*). Toh. 4148, *'dul ba*, vol. *su*, 252b.6–2531.7.

Dba' bzhed. In *Bod kyi lo rgyus rnam thar phyogs bsgrigs* (31–60), 36: 1–62. Zi ling: mtsho sngon mi rigs dpa skrun khang, 2011.

Dgongs pa 'dus pa'i mdo. Full title: *De bzhin gshegs pa thams cad kyi thugs gsang ba'i ye shes don gyi snying po rdo rje bkod pa'i rgyud rnal 'byor grub pa'i lung kun 'dus rig pa'i mdo theg pa chen po mngon par rtogs pa chos kyi rnam grangs rnam par bkod pa zhes bya ba'i mdo*. Toh. 829, *rnying rgyud*, vol. *ka*, 86b.1–290a.7.

Dhyānottarapaṭalakrama. Toh. 888, *rgyud*, vol. *wa*, 223a.1–225b.7.

Dhyānottarapaṭalaṭīkā. Buddhagupta. Toh. 2670, *rgyud*, vol. *thu*, 1b.1–38a.3.

Dkar chag 'phang thang ma. Ed. Eishin Kawagoe. Sendai-shi: Tohoku Indo-Chibetto Kenkyukai, 2005.

Dpal gsang ba'i snying po'i spyi don legs par bshad pa'i snang bas yid kyi mun pa thams cad sel ba. In *Kun mkhyen klong chen rab 'byams kyi gsung 'bum*, 26 vols., 25: 52–183. Beijing: Krung go'i bod rig pa dpe skrun khang, 2009.

Dpal he ru ka snying rje rol pa'i rgyud gsang ba zab mo'i mchog. Toh. 840, *rnying rgyud*, vol. *ga*, 130a.1–202a.3.

Dpal kye rdo rje'i mngon par rtogs pa 'bring du bya ba yan lag drug pa'i mdzes rgyan. In *E waM bka' 'bum*, 20 vols., 14: 131–60. Beijing: Krung go'i bod rig pa dpe skrun khang, 2009–2010.

Dvitīyakramamukhāgama. Buddhajñānapāda. Full title: *Dvitīyakrama-tattvabhāvanā-mukhāgama*. Toh. 1853, *rgyud*, vol. *di*, 1a.1–17b.2.

Gnubs chen Sangs rgyas ye shes. *Sangs rgyas thams cad kyi dgongs pa 'dus pa mdo'i dka' 'grel mun pa'i go cha lde mig gsal byed rnal 'byor nyi ma*. In Bdud 'joms 'jigs bral ye shes rdo rje, ed., *Rnying ma bka' ma rgyas pa*, 56 vols., 50–51. Kalimpong, W.B.: Dubjang Lama, 1982.

Gsang snying 'grel pa phyogs bcu mun sel. Paro, Bhutan: Ngodrup, 1975.

Guhyagarbha Tantra. Full title: *Dpal gsang ba'i snying po de kho na nyid rnam par nges pa*. Toh. 832, *rnying rgyud*, vol. *kha*, 110b.1–132a.7.

Guhyasamājatantra. In Matsunaga, Yūkei, ed., *The Guhaysamāja Tantra: A New Critical Edition*. Osaka: Toho Shuppan, 1978. For the Tibetan, see Toh. 442, *rgyud 'bum*, vol. *ca*, 90a.1–148a.6.

Gu ru drag po ye shes rab 'bar gyi sgrub khog. Dge rtse Paṇḍita. In *Dge rtse ma hA paNDi ta'i gsung 'bum* (Chengdu: dmangs khrod dpe dkon sdud sgrig khang, 2001), vol. *ca*, f. 119.

Jayavatī-nāma-dhāraṇī. Toh. 568, *rgyud*, vol. *pha*, 191b.4–195a.5.

Jayavatī-nāma-mahāvidyārāja-dhāraṇī. Toh. 567, *rgyud*, vol. *pha*, 186a.3–191b.3.

Khro bo rdo rje rigs kyi bsgrub thabs. Attributed to Bde ba gsal mdzad. In *Snga 'gyur bka' ma shin tu rgyas* pa, vol. 22, f. 262a.3–285a.4 (pp. 523–69).

Kosalālaṁkāra-tattvasaṁgrahaṭīkā. Śākyamitra. Toh. 2503, *rgyud*, vols. *yi*, 1b.1–*ri*, 202a.5.

Kriyāsaṃgraha. (*Bya ba bsdus pa shes bya ba*.) Toh. 2531, *rgyud*, vol. *ku*, 227b.1–362a.7.

Kun du rig pa'i mdo. Full title: *De bzhin gshegs pa thams cad kyi thugs gsang ba'i ye shes don gyi snying po khro bo rdo rje'i rigs kun 'dus rig pa'i mdo rnal 'byor grub pa'i rgyud ces bya ba theg pa chen po'i mdo*. Toh. 831, *rñiṅ rgyud*, vol. *kha*, 1b.1–110a.7.

Kun mkhyen ngag gi dbang po'i rang rnam. Mkhan po ngag dga'. Hongkong: Tianma tushu youxian gongsi 天马图书有限公司, 2001.

Kusumañjaliguhyasamājanibandha. Ratnākaraśānti. Toh. 1851, *rgyud*, vol. *ti*, 202b.1–325a.7.

Lding po pa. *Dam pa bde gshegs kyi rnam thar bsdus pa grub mchog rjes dran*, ff. 1–30. N.p. TBRC RID: W26096.

Madhyamakahṛdayavṛtti-tarkajvāla. Bhavaviveka. Toh. 3856, *dbu ma*, vol. *tsha*, 40b.7–329b.4.

Mahāmāyātantraṃ: with the commentary Guṇavatīṭīkā by Ratnākaraśānti. Ed. Samdhong Rinpoche and Vajravallabha Dvivedi. Varanasi: Central Institute of Higher Tibetan Studies, 1992. (For Tibetan, see Toh. 425, *rgyud*, vol. *nga*, 167a.6–171a.1.)

Mahāmāyūrīvidyārājñī. Toh. 559, *rgyud*, vol. *pha*, 87b.1–117a.5.

Mahāpratisarāvidyārājñī-dhāraṇī. Toh. 561, *rgyud*, vol. *pha*, 117b.4–138b.5.

Mahāvairocanābhisaṁbodhi. Full title: *Mahāvairocanābhisaṁbodhivikurvitādhiṣṭhānava ipulyasūtrendrarāja-nāma-dharmaparyāya*. (*Rnam par snang mdzad chen po mngon par rdzogs par byang chub pa rnam par sprul pa byin gyis rlob pa shin tu rgyas pa mdo sde'i dbang po'i rgyal po zhes bya ba'i chos kyi rnam grangs*.) Toh. 494, *rgyud*, vol. *tha*, 151b.2–260a.7.

Man ngag lta ba'i phreng ba. In *Snga 'gyur bka' ma shin tu rgyas pa*, 133 vols., 73: 147–62. Chengdu: Si khron mi rigs dpe skrun khang, 2009.

Mañjuśrīmūlatantra (*'Phags pa 'jam dpal gyi rtsa ba'i rgyud*). Toh. 543, *rgyud*, vol. *na*, 105a.1–351a.6.

'Od gsal snying po. Mi pham rgya mtsho. Full title: *Gsang 'grel phyogs bcu'i mun sel gyi spyi don 'od gsal snying po*. Bylakuppe, Karnataka: Ngagyur Nyingma Institute, 2001.

Paramādya. Full title: *Śrī-Parmādyamantrakalpakhaṇḍa*. Toh. 488, *rgyud*, vol. *ta*, 173a.4–265b.7.

Phur pa'i 'dzab dgongs. In *Snga 'gyur bka' ma shin tu rgyas pa*, 133 vols., 11: 228.5–236.3. Chengdu: Si khron mi rigs dpe skrun khang, 2009.

Piṇḍārtha. Full title: *Vairocanābhisambodhitantrapiṇḍārtha*. *Rnam par snang mdzad mngon par dzogs par byang chug pa'i rgyud kyi bsdus pa'i don*. Buddhaguhya. Toh. 2662, *rgyud*, vol. *ñu*, 1b.1–65a.3.

Pradīpodyotana, chapter 8. *Dhīḥ: Journal of Rare Buddhist Texts* 50 (2010): 112–19.

Rgyal rabs zla rigs ma. Unpublished manuscript from western Tibet.

Rgyud gsum pa. Q. 471.

Rgyud rgyal gsang ba'i snying po'i 'grel pa. Rong zom chos bzang. In *Bka' ma rgyas pa*, 25: 5–435.

Rnam thar rgyas pa. Gu ge Paṇchen Grags pa rgyal mtshan dpal bzang po. *Lha bla ma ye shes 'od kyi rnams* [*sic*] *thar rgyas pa*. Unpublished 41-folio manuscript from 'Bras spungs monastery.

Samājottara. Full title: *Uttaratantra*. Toh. 443, *rgyud*, vol. *ca*, 148a.6–157b.7.

Samantamukha-praveśa. Full title: *Ārya-samantamukha-praveśaraśmi-vimaloṣṇīṣaprabhā-sasarvatathāgatahṛdaya-samayavilokate-nāma-dhāraṇī*. Toh. 599, *rgyud*, vol. *pha*, 250a.5–259b.9.

Sarvabuddhasamāyogaḍākinījālasaṃvara-nāma-uttaratantra. Toh. 366, *rgyud*, vol. *ka*, 151b–193a.

Sarvadurgatipariśodhana-tantra. Full title: *Sarvadurgatipariśodhana-tejorājasya Tathāgatasya Arhato Samyaksambuddhasya kalpa-nāma*. Toh. 483, vol. *ta*, 58b.1–96a.3.

Sarvatathāgatatattvasaṃgraha-nāma-mahāyānasūtra. (*De bzhin gshegs pa thams cad kyi de kho na nyid bsdus pa zhes bya ba theg pa chen po'i mdo*.) Toh. 479, *rgyud*, vol. *nya*, 1b.1–142a.7.

Sarvatathāgatoṣṇīṣavijaya-nāma-dhāraṇī-kalpa-sahita. Toh. 594, *rgyud*, vol. *pha*, 230a.1–237b.4.

Sba bzhed ces bya ba las sba gsal snang gi bzhed pa bzhugs. Sba Gsal snang. Ed. Mgon po rgyal mtshan. Beijing: Mi rigs dpe skrun khang, 1982.

Sgra sbyor bam po gnyis pa. In *Dkar chag 'phang thang ma / Sgra sbyor bam po gnyis pa*, ed. Rta mdo. Beijing: Mi rigs dpa skrun khang, 2003.

Snga 'gyur bka' ma shin tu rgyas pa. 133 vols. Chengdu: Si khron mi rigs dpe skrun khang, 2009.

Sngags log sun 'byin gyi skor bzhugs so. Chag Lo tsa ba dang 'Gos khug pa lhas rtsas sogs. Thimphu: Kunsang Tobgyel and Mani Dorji, 1979.

Spar khab. Attrributed to Vilāsavajra. Full title: *Gsang ba snying po'i 'grel pa spar khab sgeg pa'i rdo rjes mdzad pa*. Gangtok, Sikkim: Dodrup Sangyay Lama, 1976.

Subāhuparipṛcchā-nāma-tantra. Toh. 805, *rgyud*, vol. *wa*, 118a.1–140b.7.

Sukusuma. Vaidyapāda. Full title: *Sukusuma-nāma-dvitīyakramatattvabhāvanāmukhāgama-vṛtti*. (Tib. *Mdzes pa'i me tog ces bya ba rim pa gnyis pa'i de kho na nyid bsgom pa zhal gyi lung gi 'grel pa*.) Tōh. 1866, *rgyud*, vol. *di*, 87a.3–139b.3.

Susiddhikara. Full title: *Susiddhikaramahātantrasādhanopāyika-paṭala*. (*Legs par grub par byed pa'i rgyud chen po las sgrub pa'i thabs rim par phye ba*.) Toh. 807, *rgyud*, vol. *wa*, 168a.1–222b.7.

Tantrārthāvatāra. Buddhagupta. Full title: *Rgyud kyi don la 'jug pa*. Toh. 2501. *Rgyud*, vol. *'i*, 1b.1–91b.5.

Tattvālokakarī. Ānandagarbha. Full title: *De bzhin gshegs pa thams cad kyi de kho nan yid bsdus pa theg pa chen po mngon par rtogs pa zhes bya ba'i rgyud kyi bshad pa de kho nan yid snang bar byed pa zhes bya ba* [*Sarvatathāgatatattvasaṁgrahamahāyānābhisamaya-nāma-tantratattvālokakarī-nāma-vyākyā*]. Toh. 2510, *rgyud*, vol. *li*, 1b.1–352a.7.

Trailokyavijaya-mahākalparājā. Toh. 482, *rgyud*, vol. *ta*, 10a.1–58a.7.

Uṣṇīṣavijayā-dhāraṇī. Full title: *Ārya-Sarvadurgatipariśodhanī-uṣṇīṣavijayā-nāma-dhāraṇī*. (*'Phags pa ngan 'gro thams cad yongs su sbyong ba gtsug tor rnam par rgyal ba zhes bya ba'i gzungs*.) Toh. 597, *rgyud*, vol. *pha*, 243b.1–248a.3.

Vairocanābhisambodhi-vikurvitādhiṣṭāna-mahātantravṛtti. (*Rnam par snang mdzad mngon par byang chub pa'i rgyud chen po'i 'grel bshad*.) Buddhagupta. Toh. 2663, vol. *nyu*, 65a.3–vol. *tu*, 116a.7.

Vajraḍāka-nāma-mahātantra (*Rgyud kyi rgyal po chen po dpal rdo rje mkha' 'gro*). Toh. 370, *rgyud*, vol. *kha*, 1b.1–125a.7.

Vajrapāṇyabhiṣeka-mahātantra (*'Phags pa lag na rdo rje dbang bskur ba'i rgyud chen po*). Toh. 496, *rgyud*, vol. da, 1b.1–156.7.

Vajraśekhara-mahāguhyayogatantra. (*Gsang ba rnal 'byor chen po'i rgyud rdo rje rtse mo*.) Toh. 480, *rgyud*, vol. *nya*, 142b.1–274a.5.

Vajravidāraṇa-nāma-dhāraṇīvṛtti. Ascribed to Smṛtijñānakīrti. Toh. 2684, *rgyud*, vol. *thu*, 226a.3–233b.2.

Vajravidāraṇa-nāma-dhāraṇīvyākhyāna-vajrāloka. (*Rdo rje rnam par 'joms pa zhes bya ba'i gzungs kyi rnam par bshad pa rdo rje sgron ma*.) Ascribed to Padmasambhava. Toh. 2679. Bka' 'gyur, rgyud 'bum, vol. *thu*: 161b.6–176a.6.

Vajrodaya. Full title: *Vajradhātumahāmaṇḍalavidhisarvavajrodaya-nāma*. Ānandagarbha. Toh. 2516, *rgyud*, vol. *ku*, 1b.1–50a.4.

Zangs gling ma. Nyang nyi ma 'od zer gyis gter nas bton. Full title: *Slob dpon padma'i rnam thar zangs gling ma bzhugs*. Chengdu: Si khron mi rigs dpe skrun khang, 1989.

Secondary Sources

Aalto, Pentti. "Prolegmena to an Edition of the Pañcarakṣā." *Studia Orientalia* 19 (1954): 5–48.

——. *Qutut-tu Pañcarakṣā Kemekü Tabun Sakiyan Neretü Yeke Kölgen Sudur*. Wiesbadan: Otto Harrassowitz, 1961.

Abé, Ryiūchi. *The Weaving of Mantra: Kūkai and the Construction of Esoteric Buddhist Discourse*. New York: Columbia University Press, 1999.

Ahn, Gregor. "Das Sutra der 'Acht Erscheinungen:' Bemerkungen zu den tibetischen Versionen." In*Religionbegenung und Kulturaustausch in Asien: Studien zum Gedenken an Hans-Joachim Klimkeit*, ed. W. Gantke, K. Hoheisel, and W. Klein, 63–71. Wiesbaden: Harrassowitz, 2002.

Appleton, Naomi. *Jātaka Stories in Theravāda Buddhism*. Surrey, England: Ashgate, 2010.

Arci, Andrea. "Between Impetus, Fear and Disgust: 'Desire for Emancipation' (Saṃvega) from Early Buddhism to Pātañjala Yoga and Śaiva Siddhānta." In *Emotions in Indian Thought-Systems*, ed. P. Bilimoria and A. Wenta, 199–227. Delhi: Routledge, 2015.

Aśvaghosa. *Handsome Nanda*. Trans. Linda Covil. New York: New York University Press, 2007.

Bendall, Cecil. *Śikshā-samuccaya: A Compendium of Buddhist Doctrine compiled by Śāntideva Chiefly from Earlier Mahāyāna Sūtras*. London: John Murray, 1922.

Bentor, Yael. "On the Symbolism of the Mirror in Indo-Tibetan Consecration Rituals." *Journal of Indian Philosophy* 23 (1995): 57–71.

——. *Consecration of Images and Stūpas in Indo-Tibetan Tantric Buddhism*. Leiden: E. J. Brill, 1996.

——. "Meditation on Emptiness in the Context of Tantric Buddhism." *Journal of Buddhist Philosophy* 1 (2015): 136–55.

——. "Women on the Way to Enlightenment." In *From Bhakti to Bon. Festschrift for Per Kvaerne*, ed. H. Havnevik and C. Ramble, 89–96. Oslo: Novus Press, 2015.

Bharati, Agehananda. *The Tantric Tradition*. London: Rider , 1975 [1965].

Bialek, Joanna. *Compounds and Compounding in Old Tibetan.Vol. 2: A Corpus Based Approach*. Marburg: Indica et Tibetica Verlag, 2018.

Bodhi, Bhikkhu. *The Connected Discourses of the Buddha: A Translation of the Saṃyuta Nikāya*. Boston: Wisdom, 2000.

Brons, Lajos L. "Facing Death from a Safe Distance: Saṃvega and Moral Psychology." *Journal of Buddhist Ethics* 23 (2016): 83–128.

Buddhaghosa, Bhadantācariya. *The Path of Purification* (*Visuddhimagga*). Trans. Bhikkhu Ñāṇamoli. Kandy: Buddhist Publication Society, 2011.

Bühnemann, Gudrun. "The Ritual for Infusing Life (*prāṇapratiṣṭhā*) and the Goddess Prāṇaśakti." *Zeitschrift der Deutschen Morgenländischen Gesellschaft* 141/2 (1991): 353–65.

Cabezón, José Ignacio. *The Buddha's Doctrine and the Nine Vehicles: Rog Bande Sherab's Lamp of the Teachings*. Oxford and New York: Oxford University Press, 2013.

Cantwell, Cathy, and Robert Mayer, R. *Early Tibetan Documents on Phur pa from Dunhuang*. Vienna: Verlag der Österreichischen Akademie der Wissenschaften, 2008.

——. "Enduring Myths: Smrang, Rabs and Ritual in the Dunhuang Texts on Padmasambhava." *Revue d'Etudes Tibétaines* 15 (2008): 289–312.

Chattopadhyaya, Brajadulal. *The Making of Early Medieval India*. Delhi: Oxford University Press, 1994.

Chen, Jinhua. "*Śarīra* and Scepter: Empress Wu's Political Use of Buddhist Relics," *Journal of the International Association of Buddhist Studies* 25, nos. 1–2 (2002): 33–150.

Chou, Yi-liang. "Tantrism in China." *Harvard Journal of Asiatic Studies* 8 (1945): 241–332.

Collins, Steven. "On the Very Idea of the Pali Canon." *Journal of the Pali Text Society* 15 (1990): 89–126.

Conze, Edward, trans. *The Perfection of Wisdom in Eight Thousand Lines and Its Verse Summary*. Bolinas, CA: Four Seasons Foundation, 1973.

Coomaraswamy, Ananda K. "*Samvega*: Aesthetic Shock." In *The Essential Ananda K. Coomaraswamy*, 193–99. Bloomington, IN: World Wisdom, 2004 [1943].

Copp, Paul. "Manuscript Culture as Ritual Culture in Late Medieval Dunhuang: Buddhist Seals and Their Manuals." *Cahiers d'Extrême-Asie* 20 (2011): 193–226.

——. *The Body Incantatory: Spells and the Ritual Imagination in Medieval Chinese Buddhism*. New York: Columbia University Press, 2014.

——. "Writing Buddhist Liturgies in Dunhuang: Hints of Ritualist Craft." In *Language and Religion*, ed. Robert A. Yelle, Courtney Handman, and Christoph I. Lehrich, 68–86. Berlin: De Gruyter, 2019.

Crosby, Kate and Andrew Skilton, trans. *Śāntideva: The Bodhicaryāvatāra*. Oxford: Oxford University Press, 1995.

Dalton, Catherine. "Enacting Perfection: Buddhajñānapāda's Vision of a Tantric Buddhist World." PhD diss., University of California, Berkeley, 2019.

Dalton, Jacob P. "The Development of Perfection: The Interiorization of Buddhist Ritual in the Eighth and Ninth Centuries." *Journal of Indian Philosophy* 32 (2004): 1–30.

——. "A Crisis of Doxography: How Tibetans Organized Tantra During the 8th–12th Centuries." *Journal of the International Association of Buddhist Studies* 28, no. 1 (2005): 115–81.

——. "Mahāyoga Ritual Interests at Dunhuang: A Translation and Study of the Codex IOL Tib J 437/Pelliot tibétain 324." In *New Studies of the Old Tibetan Documents: Philology, History and Religion*, ed. Yoshiro Imaeda, Matthew Kapstein, and Tsuguhito Takeuchi, 293–313. Tokyo: Research Institute for Languages and Cultures of Asia and Africa, 2011.

——. *Taming of the Demons: Violence and Liberation in Tibetan Buddhism*. New Haven, CT: Yale University Press, 2011.

———. "Lost and Found: A Fourteenth-Century Discussion of Then-Available Sources on gNubs chen sangs rgyas ye shes." In *Bulletin of Tibetology (Special Issue, Nyingma Studies: Narrative and History)* 49, no. 1 (2013): 39–54.

———. "Preliminary Remarks on a Newly Discovered Biography of Gnubs chen sangs rgyas ye shes." In *Himalayan Passages: Tibetan and Newar Studies in Honor of Hubert Decleer*, ed. Benjamin E. Bogin and Andrew Quintman, 145–62. Somerville, MA: Wisdom, 2014.

———. "Power and Compassion: Negotiating Religion and State in Tenth-Century Tibet." In *The Illuminating Mirror, Tibetan Studies in Honour of Per K. Sørensen*, ed. Olaf Czaja and Guntram Hazod, 101–18. Wiesbaden: Dr. Ludwig Reichert Verlag, 2015.

———. *The Gathering of Intentions: A History of a Tibetan Tantra*. New York: Columbia University Press, 2016.

———. "How Dhāraṇīs WERE Proto-Tantric: Liturgies, Ritual Manuals, and the Origins of the Tantras." In *Tantric Traditions on the Move*, ed. David B. Gray and Ryan Overbey, 199–229. New York: Oxford University Press, 2016.

———. "On the Significance of the *Ārya-tattvasaṃgraha-sādhanopāyikā* and Its Commentary." In *Chinese and Tibetan Esoteric Buddhism*, ed. Yael Bentor and Meir Shahar, 321–27. Leiden: Brill, 2017.

———. "Bridging Yoga and Mahāyoga: Samaya in Early Tantric Buddhism." In *Buddhism in Central Asia II: Visual and Material Transfer, Practices and Rituals*, ed. Carmen Meinert and Henrik H. Sørensen, 272–89. Leiden: Brill, 2022.

———. "Evoking the Divine Human: *An Appearance of Suchness: Ornament of the Sacred*." In *Living Treasure: Buddhist and Tibetan Studies in Honor of Janet Gyatso*, ed. Holly Gayley and Andrew Quintman. Boston: Wisdom, forthcoming.

Dalton, Jacob and Sam van Schaik. *Tibetan Tantric Manuscripts from Dunhuang: A Descriptive Catalogue of the Stein Collection at the British Library*. Leiden: Brill, 2006.

Dalton, Jacob, Tom Davis, and Sam van Schaik. "Beyond Anonymity: Paleographic Analyses of the Dunhuang Manuscripts." *Journal of the International Association of Tibetan Studies* 3 (2007): 1–23.

Davidson, Ronald M. *Indian Esoteric Buddhism: A Social History of the Tantric Movement*. New York: Columbia University Press, 2002.

———. "The Problem of Secrecy in Indian Tantric Buddhism." In *The Culture of Secrecy in Japanese Religion*, ed. Bernhard Scheid and Mark Teeuwen, 60–77. Oxon and New York: Routledge, 2006.

———. "Sources and Inspirations." In *Esoteric Buddhism and the Tantras in East Asia: A Handbook for Scholars*, ed. Charles Orzech, 19–24. Leiden: Brill, 2011.

———. "Some Observations on an Uṣṇīṣa Abhiṣeka Rite in Atikūṭa's *Dhāraṇīsaṃgraha*." In *Transformation and Transfer of Tantra/Tantrism in Asia and Beyond*, ed. István Keul, 77–97. Berlin: Walter de Gruyter, 2012.

Davis, Richard. *Ritual in an Oscillating Universe: Worshiping Śiva in Medieval India*. Princeton, NJ: Princeton University Press, 1991.

Decaroli, Robert. *Haunting the Buddha: Indian Religions and the Formation of Buddhism*. New York: Oxford University Press, 2004.

de Certeau, Michel. *Heterologies: Discourse on the Other*. Minneapolis: University of Minnesota Press, 1985.

de Jong, J. W. "Review of Yoshiro Imaeda, *Histoire du cycle de la naissance et de la mort*." *Indo-Iranian Journal* 25 (1983): 222–24.

——. "Recent Japanese Studies on the Lalitavistara." *Indologica Taurinensia* 23, no. 4 (1997–1998): 247–55.

Deleanu, Florin. *The Chapter on the Mundane Path (Laukikamārga) in the Śrāvakabhūmi: A Trilingual Edition (Sanskrit, Tibetan, Chinese), Annotated Translation and Introductory Study*. 2 vols. Tokyo: International Institute for Buddhist Studies, 2006.

Doney, Lewis. "Imperial Gods: A Ninth-Century *Tridaṇḍaka* Prayer (*rGyud chags gsum*)." *Central Asiatic Journal (Special Issue: Old Tibet and Its Neighbors)* 61, no. 1 (2018): 71–101.

Dotson, Brandon. "Complementarity and Opposition in Early Tibetan Ritual." *Journal of the American Oriental Society* 128 (2008): 41–67.

——. "The Remains of the Dharma: Editing, Rejecting, and Replacing the Buddha's Words in Royally Sponsored Sutras from Dunhuang, 820s to 840s," *Journal of the International Association of Buddhist Studies* 36/37: 5–68.

——. "The Dead and Their Stories: Preliminary Remarks on the Place of Narrative in Tibetan Religion." In *Zentral-Asiatische Studien*, ed. Peter Schwieger et al., 45: 77–112. Andiast: International Institute for Tibetan and Buddhist Studies, 2016.

——. "Misspelling 'Buddha': The Officially Commissioned Tibetan *Aparimiāyur-nāma mahāyāna-sūtras* from Dunhuang and the Study of Old Tibetan Orthography." *Bulletin of the School of Oriental and African Studies* 79, no. 1 (2013–14 [2015]): 129–51.

Dotson, Brandon and Agnieszka Helman-Ważny. *Codicology, Paleography, and Orthography of Early Tibetan Documents*. Vienna: Wiener studien zur tibetologie und buddhismuskunde, 2016.

Douglas, Mary. *Thinking in Circles: An Essay on Ring Compositions*. New Haven, CT: Yale University Press2007.

Drège, Jean-Pierre. "Les cahiers des manuscrits de Touen-houang." In *Contributions aux études sur Touen-houang*, ed. Michel Soymié, 17–28. Genève: Droz, 1979.

Dudjom Rinpoche. *The Nyingma School of Tibetan Buddhism*. 2 vols. Trans. Gyurme Dorje. Boston: Wisdom, 1991.

Dzong-ka-ba. *Yoga Tantra: Paths to Magical Feats*. Trans. Jeffrey Hopkins. Ithaca, NY: Snow Lion, 2005.

Eastman, Kenneth W. "The Dun-huang Tibetan Manuscript of the Guhyasmājatantra." Paper presented at the twenty-seventh convention of The Japanese Association for Tibetan Studies, Kyoto, Japan, November 17, 1979.

——. "The Eighteen Tantras of the Vajraśekhara/Māyājāla." Unpublished paper presented at the 26th International Conference of Orientalists, Tokyo, Japan, May 8, 1981. Summary: *Transactions of the International Conference of Orientalists in Japan* XXVI (1981): 95–96.

——. "Mahāyoga Texts at Tun-Huang." *Institute of Buddhist Cultural Studies* 22 (1983): 42–60.

Eimer, Helmut. *Der Tantra-Katalog des Bu ston im Verglieich mit der Abteilung Tantra des tibetischen Kanjur*. Bonn: Indica et Tibetica Verlag, 1989.

Einoo, Shingo. "The Formation of the Pūjā Ceremony." *Studien zur Indologie und Iranistik (Festschrift für Paul Thieme)* 20 (1996): 73–87.

——. “The Formation of Hindu Ritual.” In *From Material to Deity: Indian Rituals of Consecration*, ed. Shingo Einoo and Jun Takasima, 7–49. New Delhi: Manohar, 2005.

Einoo, Shingo and Jun Takasima, eds. *From Material to Deity: Indian Rituals of Consecration*. New Delhi: Manohar, 2005.

Eltschinger, Vincent. “Pure Land Sūtras.” In *Brill's Encyclopedia of Buddhism*, ed. Jonathan A. Silk, 1: 210–30. Leiden: Koninklijke Brill NV, 2015.

English, Elizabeth. *Vajrayoginī: Her Visualizations, Rituals, and Forms*. Boston: Wisdom, 2002.

Faure, Bernard. *The Will to Orthodoxy: A Critical Genealogy of Northern Chan Buddhism*. Stanford, CA: Stanford University Press, 1997.

Fisher, Philip. *Wonder, the Rainbow, and the Aesthetics of Rare Experiences*. Cambridge, MA: Harvard University Press, 1998.

Flood, Gavin. *An Introduction to Hinduism*. Cambridge: Cambridge University Press, 1996.

Fraser, Sarah. *Performing the Visual: The Practice of Buddhist Wall Painting in China and Central Asia, 618–960*. Stanford, CA: Stanford University Press, 2004.

Freeman, John R. “Possession Rites and the Tantric Temple: A Case-Study from Northern Kerala.” *Diskus* 2, no. 2 (1994). https://urldefense.proofpoint.com/v2/url?u=http-3A__jbasr.com_basr_diskus_diskus1-2D6_FREEMAN.TXT&d=DwMFaQ&c=009klHSCxuh5AI1vNQzSO0KGjl4nbi2Q0M1QLJX9BeE&r=Xs_kWMu4D1LNt1XpkRe-Pd6P_fVZS5k0QjvwoGiIFAg&m=eF7XTFhSdCpTFJe71ygO5gVyy1jzCfnrZw2kXwuQ4vGu7hX6PUYiaHdo1iAIrNj7&s=SKQXaZnchErzHWLalMF6oRFvSvlt9xrSWa6kG9kl38Y&e=

Freud, Sigmund. *Beyond the Pleasure Principle*. New York: Norton, 1961.

Galambos, Imre. *Dunhuang Manuscript Culture*. Berlin/Boston: Walter de Gruyter GmbH, 2020.

Germano, David. “Architecture and Absence in the Secret Tantric History of the Great Perfection.” *Journal of the International Association of Buddhist Studies* 17, no. 2 (1994): 203–335.

Giebel, Rolf W. “The Chin-Kang-Ting Ching Yu-Ch'ieh Shi-Pa-Hui Chih-Kuei: An Annotated Translation,” *Journal of Naritasan Institute for Buddhist Studies* 18 (1995): 107–201.

——. *Two Esoteric Sutras: The Adamantine Pinnacle Sutra, the Susiddhikara Sutra*. Berkeley, CA: Numata Center for Buddhist Translation and Research, 2001.

Gimello, Robert. “Manifest Mysteries: The Nature of the Exoteric/Esoteric Distinction in Later Chinese Buddhism.” Paper presented at the American Academy of Religion conference, Washington, D.C., November 21, 2006.

Gombrich, Richard. “The Monk in the Pāli Vinaya: Priest or Wedding Guest?” *Journal of the Pali Text Society* 21 (1995): 193–97.

Gomez, Luis O. “The Direct and Gradual Approaches of Zen Master Mahayana: Fragments of the Teachings of Mo-ho-yen.” In *Studies in Ch'an and Hua-yen*, ed. Robert Gimello and Peter Gregory, 69–167. Honolulu: University of Hawaii Press, 1983.

Goodall, Dominic. *Bhaṭṭarāmakaṇṭhaviracitā kiraṇavṛttiḥ. Bhaṭṭa Rāmakaṇṭha's Commentary on the Kiraṇatantra. Vol. 1: chapters 1–6. Critical Edition and Annotated Translation*. Publications du département d'Indologie 86.1. Pondicherry: Institut français de Pondichéry/École française d'Extrême-Orient, 1998.

Goodall, Dominic, ed., in collaboration with Alexis Sanderson and Harunaga Isaacson. *The Niśvāsatattvasaṃhitā: The Earliest Surviving Śaiva Tantra*, vol. 1: *A Critical and Annotated Translation of the Mūlasūtra, Uttarasūtra and Nayasūtra*. Pondichéry: Institut Français de Pondichéry; Paris: École française d'Extrême-Orient; Hamburg: Asien-Afrika-Institut, Universität Hamburg, 2015.

Goodman, Amanda K. "The *Ritual Instructions for Altar Methods* (*Tanfa yize*): Prolegomenon to the Study of a Chinese Esoteric Buddhist Ritual Compendium from Late-Medieval Dunhuang." PhD diss., University of California, Berkeley, 2013.

——. "The Vajragarbha Bodhisattva Three-Syllable Visualization: A Chinese Buddhist *Sādhana* Text from Tenth-Century Dunhuang." *BuddhistRoad Paper* 2, no. 7 (2022).

Granoff, Phyllis. "A Portable Buddhist Shrine from Central Asia." *Archives of Asian Art* 22 (1968/1969): 80–95.

——. "Reading Between the Lines: Colliding Attitudes Towards Image Worship in Indian Religious Texts." In *Rites hindous, transferts et transformations*, ed. Gérard Colas et Gilles Tarabout, 389–421. Paris: Écoles des hautes études en sciences sociales, 2006.

Gray, David. *The Cakrasamvara Tantra (The Discourse of Śrī Heruka) (Śrīherukābhidhāna): A Study and Annotated Translation*. New York: The American Institute of Buddhist Studies, 2007.

——. "Imprints of the 'Great Seal': On the Expanding Semantic Range of the Term of Mudrā in Eighth Through Eleventh-Century Indian Buddhist Literature." *Journal of the International Association of Buddhist Studies* 34, nos. 1–2 (2011 [2012]): 421–81.

Greene, Eric M. *Chan Before Chan: Meditation, Repentance, and Visionary Experience in Chinese Buddhism*. Honolulu: University of Hawai'i Press, 2021.

Griffiths, Arlo. "Written Traces of the Buddhist Past: *Mantras* and *Dhāraṇīs* in Indonesian Inscriptions." *Bulletin of the School of Oriental and African Studies* 77, no. 1: 137–94.

Halkias, Georgios T. "Tibetan Buddhism Registered: Imperial Archives from the Palace-Temple of 'Phang-thang." *The Eastern Buddhist*, 36, nos. 1 & 2 (2004): 46–105.

Harrison, Paul. "Preliminary Notes on a *gZungs 'dus* Manuscript from Tabo." In *Suhllekhā: Festgabe für Helmut Eimer*, ed. M. Hahn, J.-U. Hartmann and R. Steiner, 49–68. Wisttal-Odendorf: Indica et Tibetica Verlag, 1996.

——. "Mediums and Messages: Reflections on the Production of Mahāyāna Sūtras." *The Eastern Buddhist* 35, no. 2 (2003): 115–51.

Hartzell, James F. "Tantric Yoga: A Study of the Vedic Precursors, Historical Evolution, Literatures, Cultures, Doctrines, and Practices of the Eleventh-Century Kasmīri Saivite and Buddhist Unexcelled Tantric Yogas." PhD diss., Columbia University, 1997.

Hatley, Shaman. "Converting the Ḍākinī: Goddess Cults and Tantras of the Yoginīs Between Buddhism and Śaivism." In *Tantric Traditions in Transmission and Translation*, ed. David B. Gray and Ryan Richard Overbey, 37–86. Oxford: Oxford University Press, 2016.

Heesterman, J. C. *he Inner Conflict of Tradition: Essays in Indian Ritual, Kingship, and Society*. Chicago: University of Chicago Press, 1985.

Heim, Maria. "The Aesthetics of Excess." *Journal of the American Academy of Religion* 71, no. 3 (2003): 531–54.

Heller, Amy. Early Ninth-Century Images of Vairochana from Eastern Tibet." *Orientations* 25, no. 6 (1994): 74–79.

——. "Ninth-Century Buddhist Images Carved at lDan Ma Brag to Commemorate Tibeto-Chinese Negotiations." In *Tibetan Studies: Proceedings of the 6th International Seminar of the International Association for Tibetan Studies*, ed. Per Kværne, 1: 335–49; appendix to 1: 12–19. Oslo: Institute for Comparative Research in Human Culture, 1994.

——. "Buddhist Images and Rock Inscriptions from Eastern Tibet." In *Tibetan Studies: Proceedings of the Seventh Seminar of the International Association for Tibetan Studies*, ed. H. Krasser, M. T. Much, E. Steinkellner, and H. Tauscher, 1: 385–403. Vienna: Austrian Academy of Science, 1997.

——. Eighth- and Ninth-CenturyTemples and Rock Carvings of Eastern Tibet." In *Tibetan Art: Towards a Definition of Style*, ed. J. C. Singer and P. Denwood, 86–103. London: Laurence King, 1997.

Hidas, Gergely. "*Mahāpratisarā-mahāvidyārājñī*, the Great Amulet, Great Queen of Spells: Introduction, Critical Editions and Annotated Translation." PhD thesis, Oxford University, 2008.

Higgins, David. *The Philosophical Foundations of Classical rDzogs chen in Tibet: Investigating the Distinction Between Dualistic Mind (sems) and Primordial Knowing (ye shes)*. Vienna: Arbeitskreis für Tibetische und Buddhistische Studien Universität Wien, 2013.

Hikita, Hiromichi. "Consecration of Divine Images in a Temple." In *From Material to Deity: Indian Rituals of Consecration*, ed. Shingo Einoo and Jun Takashima, 143–97. New Delhi: Manohar, 2005.

Hodge, Stephen. "Considerations on the Dating and Geographical Origins of the *Mahāvairocanābhisambodhi-sūtra*." In *The Buddhist Forum*, ed. Tadeusz Skorupski and Ulrich Pagel, 3: 57–83. London: School of Oriental and African Studies, 2005.

——. *The Mahā-vairocana-abhisaṃbodhi Tantra, with Buddhaguhya's Commentary*. London: Routledge Curzon, 2003.

Horiuchi Hanjin, ed. *Kongochokyo no Kenkyu* (*Sarvatathāgata-tattvasaṃgraha-nāma-mahāyāna-sūtra*). Koyasan University: Mikkyo Bunka Kenkyujo, 1983.

Imaeda, Yoshirō. "The *History of the Cycle of Birth and Death*: A Tibetan Narrative from Dunhuang." In *Contributions to the Cultural History of Early Tibet*, ed. Matthew Kapstein and Brandon Dotson, 105–82. Leiden: Brill, 2007.

Isaacson, Harunaga. "Observations on the Development of the Ritual of Initiation (*abhiṣeka*) in the Higher Buddhist Tantric Systems." In *Hindu and Buddhist Initiations in India and Nepal*, ed. Astrid Zotter, et al., 261–79. Wiesbaden: Harrassowitz Verlag, 2010.

Iwao, Kazushi. The Purpose of Sūtra Copying in Dunhuang Under the Tibetan Rule." In *Dunhuang Studies: Prospects and Problems for the Coming Second Century of Research*, ed. Irina Popova and Liu Yi, pp. 102–5. St. Petersburg: Slavia, 2012.

Jackson, David. "Sa-skya Paṇḍita the 'Polemicist': Ancient Debates and Modern Interpretations." *Journal of the International Association of Buddhist Studies* 13, no. 2 (1990): 17–116.

Jones, J. J. *The Mahāvastu.* 3 vols. London: Pali Text Society, 1952.

Kane, P. V. *History of Dharmaśāstra: Ancient and Mediaeval Religious and Civil Law,* Vol. I–V. 2nd ed. Poona: Bhandarkar Oriental Research Institute, 1968–77 [1930–50].

Kano, Kazuo. "Sarvatathāgatatattvasaṃgraha." In *Brill's Encyclopedia of Buddhism,* ed. Jonathan A. Silk, 373–81. Leiden: Brill, 2015.

——. "Vairocanābhisaṃbodhi." In *Brill's Encyclopedia of Buddhism,* ed. Jonathan A. Silk, 382–89. Leiden: Brill, 2015.

Kapstein, Matthew. *The Tibetan Assimilation of Buddhism.* Oxford: Oxford University Press, 2000.

——. "New Light on an Old Friend: PT 849 Reconsidered." In *Tibetan Buddhist Literature and Praxis,* Proceedings of the Tenth Seminar of the IATS 2003, ed. R. Davidson & C. Wedermeyer, 4: 9–30. Leiden: Brill, 2006.

Karmay, Samten. "King Tsa/Dza and Vajrayāna." *Mélanges chinois et bouddhiques* 20 (1981): 192–211.

——. *The Great Perfection.* Leiden: Brill, 1988.

——. *he Arrow and the Spindle.* Kathmandu: Mandala Book Point, 1998.

Kieshnick, John. *The Eminent Monk: Buddhist Ideals in Medieval Chinese Hagiography.* Honolulu: University of Hawai'i Press, 1997.

Kilty, Gavin, trans. *Tsongkhapa's* A Lamp to Illuminate the Five Stages*: Teachings on the* Guhyasamāja Tantra. Boston: Wisdom, 2013.

Kongtrul, Jamgön. *The Treasury of Knowledge: Book Eight, Part Four: Esoteric Instructions.* Trans. Sarah Harding. Ithaca, NY: Snow Lion, 2007.

Kwon, Do-Kyun. "*Sarva Tathāgata Tattva Saṃgraha, Compendium of All the Tathāgatas: A Study of its Origin, Structure and Teachings.*" PhD diss., School of Oriental and African Studies, University of London, 2002.

Lahiri, Latika. *Chinese Monks in India.* Delhi: Motilal Banarsidass, 1986.

Lalou, Marcelle. "Notes à propos d'une amulette de Touen-houang: les litanies de Tārā et la Sitātapatrādhāraṇī." In *Mélanges chinois et bouddhiques,* 4 : 134–49. Brussels: Imprimerie Sainte Catherine, S. A., 1936

——. *Inventaire de Manuscrits tibétains de Touen-houang.* 3 vols. Paris: Libraire d'Amérique et d'Orient, 1939–1961.

——. *Rituel bon-po des funérailles royales (fonds Pelliot tibétain 1042).* Paris: Société Asiatique, 1953.

——. "Les textes bouddhiques au temps de Khri-sroṅ lde bcan." *Journal asiatique* 241 (1953): 313–53.

——. "Les manuscrits tibétains des grandes *Prajñāpāramitā* trouvés à Touen-houang." In *Silver Jubilee Volume of the Zinbun-Kagaku-Kenkyusho Kyoto University,* 257–61. Kyoto: Zinbun kagaku kenkyusho, 1954.

——. "Les plus anciens rouleaux tibétains trouvés à Touen-houang." *Rocznik Orientalistyczny* 21 (1957): 149–52.

——. "Manuscrits tibétains de la *Śatasāhasrikā-prajñāpāramitā* cachés à Touen-houang." *Journal Asiatique* 252 (1964): 479–86.

Lévi, Sylvain. "Sur la récitation primitive des texts bouddhiques." *Journal Asiatique* 11, no. 6 (1915): 401–47.

Li Zhengyu 李正宇. "Shazhou Zhenyuan sinian xianfan kao" 沙州貞元四年陷蕃考 [A Study of the Fall of Shazhou to Tufan in Zhenyuan 4]. *Duhuang yanjiu* 敦煌研究 [Dunhuang Research] 104, no. 4 (2007): 98–103.

Lin, Li-Kouang. "Punyodaya (Na-T'i), un propageteur du tantrisme en Chine et au Cambodge à l'époque de Hiuan-tsang." *Journal Asiatique* 227 (1935): 83–100.

Lingpa, Jigme. *Treasury of Precious Qualities: The Rain of Joy*. Book Two. Trans. the Padmakara Translation Group. Boston and London: Shambala, 2013.

Lopez, Donald S., Jr. *Elaborations on Emptiness: Uses of the Heart Sūtra*. Princeton, NJ: Princeton University Press, 1996.

Luczanits, Christian. "Ritual, Instruction and Experiment: Esoteric Drawings from Dunhuang." In *The Art of Central Asia and the Indian Subcontinent in Cross Culture Perspective*, ed. Anupa Pande and Mandira Sharma, 140–49; 11 figs. New Delhi: National Museum Institute-Aryan Books International, 2009.

Martin, Dan. "Review of *Facets of Tibetan Religious Tradition and Contacts with Neighbouring Cultural Areas, Orientalia Venetiana Series no. 12*. by Alfredo Cadonna, Ester Bianchi, Leo S. Olschki." *The Tibet Journal* 29, no. 1 (2004): 91–95.

Matsunaga, Yukei. A History of Tantric Buddhism with Reference to Chinese Translations." In *Buddhist Thought and Asian Civilization*, ed. Leslie S. Kawamura and Keith Scott, 167–91. Emeryville, MA: Dharma Publishing, 1977.

McBride, Richard D. "Is There Really 'Esoteric' Buddhism?" *Journal of the International Association of Buddhist Studies* 27, no. 2 (2004): 329–56.

——. "Dhāranī and Spells in Medieval Sinitic Buddhism." *Journal of the International Association of Buddhist Studies* 28, no. 1 (2005): 85–114.

McRae, John R. *The Northern School and the Formation of Early Ch'an Buddhism*. Honolulu: University of Hawaii Press, 1986.

——. "Daoxuan's Vision of Jetavana: The Ordination Platform Movement in Medieval Chinese Buddhism." In *Going Forth: Visions of Buddhist Vinaya*, ed. William M. Bodiford, 68–100. Honolulu: University of Hawai'i Press.

Meinert, Carmen. "The Conjunction of Chinese Chan and Tibetan rDzogs Chen Thought: Reflections on the Tibetan Dunhuang Manuscripts IOL Tib J 689–1 and PT 699." In *Contributions to the Cultural History of Early Tibet (extra Volume to Studies in Central and East Asian Religion)*, 239–301. Leiden/Boston: Brill, 2007.

Meisezahl, R. O. The *Amoghapāśahṛdaya-dhāraṇī*: The Early Sanskrit Manuscript of the Reiunji, Critically Edited and Translated." *Monumenta Nipponica* 17 (1962): 265–328.

Mipham, Jamgon. *Luminous Essence: A Guide to the Guhyagarbha Tantra*. Trans. the Dharmachakra Translation Committee. Ithaca, NY: Snow Lion, 2009.

Mollier, Christine. *Buddhism and Taoism Face to Face: Scripture, Ritual, and Iconographic Exchange in Medieval China*. Honolulu: University of Hawai'i Press, 2008.

Nariman, J. K. *Literary History of Sanskrit Buddhism [From Winternitz, Sylvain Levi, Huber]*. Delhi: Motilal Banarsidass, 1992 [1919].

Nattier, Jan. *A Few Good Men: The Bodhisattva Path According to The Inquiry of Ugra (Ugraparipṛcchā)*. Honolulu: University of Hawai'i Press, 2003.

Olivelle, Patrick. *The Early Upaniṣads: Annotated Text and Translations*. New York and Oxford: Oxford University Press, 1998.

Onians, Isabella. "Tantric Buddhist Apologetics or Antinomianism as a Norm." PhD diss., Oxford University, 2003.

Orsborn, Matthew Bryan. "Chiasmus in the Early *Prajñāpāramitā*: Literary Parallelism Connecting Criticism and Hermeneutics in an Early *Mahāyāna Sūtra*." PhD diss., University of Hong Kong, 2012.

——. "Chiastic Structure of the Vessantara Jātaka: Textual Criticism and Interpretation Through Inverted Parallelism." *Buddhist Studies Review* 32, no. 1 (2015): 143–59.

Orzech, Charles D. "The 'Great Teaching of Yoga,' the Chinese Appropriation of the Tantras, and the Question of Esoteric Buddhism." *Journal of Chinese Religions* 34 (2006): 29–78.

Overbey, Ryan. "Vicissitudes of Text and Rite in the *Great Peahen Queen of Spells*." In *Tantric Traditions in Transmission and Translation*, ed. David B. Gray and Ryan R. Overbey, 257–83. New York: Oxford University Press, 2016.

Pal, Pratapaditya. "A Note on the Mandala of the Eight Bodhisattvas." *Archives of Asian Art* 26 (1972/1973): 71–73.

Patton, Laurie L. "Poetry, Ritual, and Associational Thought in Early India and Elsewhere." In *Figuring Religions: Comparing Ideas, Images, and Activities*, ed. Shubha Pathak. Albany: State University of New York Press, 2013, 179–98.

Pollock, Sheldon, trans. and ed.*A Rasa Reader: Classical Indian Aesthetics*. New York: Columbia University Press, 2016.

Radich, Michael. *How Ajātaśatru Was Reformed: The Domestication of "Ajase" and Stories in Buddhist History*. Tokyo: The International Institute for Buddhist Studies of the International College for Postgraduate Buddhist Studies, 2011.

Rotman, Andy. *Thus Have I Seen: Visualizing Faith in Early Indian Buddhism*. Oxford: Oxford University Press, 2008.

Rta mdo, ed. *Dkar chag 'phang than ma. Sgra sbyor bam po gnyis pa*. Beijing: Mi rigs dpe skrung khang, 2003.

Ruegg, David Seyfort. "Sur les Rapports entre le Bouddhisme et le 'substrat religieux' indien et tibétain." *Journal Asiatique* 252 (1964): 77–95.

——. "Review of David Snellgrove, *Indo-Tibetan Buddhism: Indian Buddhists and Their Tibetan Successors*." *Journal of the Royal Asiatic Society* 1 (1989): 173.

——. *The Symbiosis of Buddhism with Brahminism/Hinduism in South Asia and of Buddhism with 'Local Cults' in Tibet and the Himalayan Region*. Vienna: Verlag der Österrischeischen Akademie der Wissenschaften, 2008.

Sanderson, Alexis. "Vajrayāna: Origin and Function" In *Buddhism Into Year 2000*, ed. Dhammakaya Foundation,. 87–102. Bangkok and Los Angeles: Dhammakaya Foundation, 1994.

——. "The Lākulas: New Evidence of a System Intermediate Between Pāñcārthika Pāsupatism and Āgamic Śaivism." *The Indian Philosophical Annual* 24 (2006): 143–217.

——. "The Śaiva Age: The Rise and Dominance of Śaivism during the Early Medieval Period." In *Genesis and Development of Tantrism*, ed. Shingo Einoo, 41–350. Tokyo: Institute of Oriental Culture, University of Tokyo, 2009.

Scherrer-Schaub, Christina. "Some Dhāraṇī Written on Paper Functioning as Dharmakāya Relics: A Tentative Approach to PT 350." In *Tibetan Studies:*

Proceedings of the 6th Seminar of the International Association for Tibetan Studies, 2: 711–27. Oslo: Insitute for Comparative Research in Human Culture, 1994.
Schmidt, Nicholas. "The Jewel's Radiance: A Translation of '*Ratnabhāsvara,' an Extensive Commentary on the *Vajravidāraṇa-nāma-dhāraṇī*." MA thesis, Centre for Buddhist Studies at Rangjung Yeshe Institute, Kathmandu University, 2018.
Schopen, Gregory. "The *Bodhigarbhālaṅkāralakṣa* and *Vimaloṣṇīṣa Dhāraṇīs* in Indian Inscriptions." *Wiener Zeitschrift für die Kunde Südasiens* 29 (1985): 119–49.
——. *Bones, Stones, and Buddhist Monks*. Honolulu: University of Hawai'i Press, 1997.
——. On the Absence of Urtexts and Otiose Ācāryas: Buildings, Books, and Lay Buddhist Ritual at Gilgit." In *Écrire et transmettre en Inde classique*, ed. Gérard Colas and Gerdi Gerschiheimer, 189–219. Paris: École française d'Extrême-Orient, 2009.
——. "On Incompetent Monks and Able Urbane Nuns in a Buddhist Monastic Code." *Journal of Indian Philosophy* 38, no. 2 (2010): 133–62.
Sharf, Robert H. "Visualization and Mandala." In *Living Images: Japanese Buddhist Icons in Context*, ed. Robert H. Sharf and Elizabeth H. Sharf, 151–97. Stanford, CA: Stanford University Press, 2001.
——. *Coming to Terms with Chinese Buddhism*. Honolulu: University of Hawai'i Press, 2002.
——. "Buddhist Veda and the Rise of Chan." In *Chinese and Tibetan Esoteric Buddhism*, ed. Yael Bentor and Meir Shahar, 85–120. Leiden: Brill, 2017.
Sharma, Ram Sharan. "Early Medieval Indian Society: A Study in Feudalisation." *Indian Historical Review* 1, no. 1 (1974): 1–9.
——. *Urban Decay in India (c. 300–c. 1000)*. New Delhi: Munishiram Manoharlal, 1987.
——. *Early Medieval Indian Society: A Study in Feudalisation*. Calcutta: Orient Longman Limited, 2001.
Shinohara, Koichi. "The All-Gathering Maṇḍala Initiation Ceremony in Atikūṭa's Collected Dhāraṇī Scriptures: Reconstructing the Evolution of Esoteric Buddhist Ritual." *Journal Asiatique* 298, no. 2 (2010): 389–420.
——. "The Esoteric Buddhist Ritual of Image Installation." In *Buddhist and Jaina Studies: Proceedings of the Conference in Lumbini*, ed. J. Soni, M. Pahlke, and C. Cüppers, 265–98. Bhairahawa, Nepal: Lumbini International Research Institute, 2014.
——. *Spells, Images, and Mandalas: Tracing the Evolution of Esoteric Buddhist Rituals*. New York: Columbia University Press, 2014.
——. "The Ritual of the Buddhoṣṇīṣa Vijaya Dhāraṇī Maṇḍala." *Hualin International Journal of Buddhist Studies* 1, no. 2 (2018): 143–82.
Shulman, David. *More Than Real: A History of the Imagination in South India*. Cambridge, MA: Harvard University Press, 2012.
Silk, Jonathan A. *Managing Monks: Administrators and Administrative Roles in Indian Buddhist Monasticism*. Oxford and New York: Oxford University Press, 2008
——. "Chinese Sūtras in Tibetan Translation: A Preliminary Survey." *Annual Report of The International Research Institute for Advanced Buddhology at Soka University* 22 (2019): 227–46.
Skilling, Peter. "The Rakṣā Literature of the Śrāvakayāna." *Journal of the Pali Text Society* 16 (1992): 109–82.
——. *Mahāsūtras*. 2 vols. Oxford: Pali Text Society, 1994–1997.

——. *Buddhism and Buddhist Literature of South-East Asia: Selected Papers*. Ed. Claudio Cicuzza. Bangkok: Fragile Palm Leaves Foundation, 2009.

Skorupski, Tadeusz. *The Sarvadurgatipariśodhana Tantra, Elimination of All Evil Destinies: Sanskrit and Tibetan Texts with Introduction, English Translation and Notes*. Delhi: Motilal Banarsidass, 1983.

——. *Kriyāsaṃgraha*. Tring, UK: Institute of Buddhist Studies, 2002.

Smith, Frederick M. *The Self Possessed: Deity and Spirit Possession in South Asian Literature and Civilization*. New York: Columbia University Press, 2006.

Snellgrove, David L. *The Hevajra Tantra: A Critical Study*. 2 vols. London: Oxford University Press, 1959.

——. *Indo-Tibetan Buddhism*. 2 vol. Boston: Shambhala, 1987.

Sogyal Rinpoche. *The Tibetan Book of Living and Dying*. San Francisco: Harper, 1992.

Stein, Aurel. 1921. *Serindia*. 5 vols. Oxford: Clarendon Press.

Stein, Rolf A. "Un document ancien relatif aux rites funéraires des Bon-po tibétains," *Journal asiatique* 258 (1970): 155–85.

——. "Du récit au rituel dans les manuscrits Tibétains de Touen-houang." In *Études Tibétaines dédiées à la mémoire de Marcelle Lalou*, 479–547. Paris: Adrien Maisonneuve, 1971.

——. *Tibetan Civilization*. Stanford, CA: Stanford University Press, 1972.

Stevenson, Daniel B. "The T'ien-t'ai Four Forms of Samādhi and Late North-South Dynasties, Sui, and Early T'ang Buddhist Devotionalism." PhD diss., Columbia University, 1987.

Strickmann, Michel. "The *Consecration Sūtra:* A Buddhist Book of Spells." In *Chinese Buddhist Apocrypha*, ed. Robert E. Buswell, 75–118. Honolulu: University of Hawaii Press, 1990.

——. *Mantras et mandarins: Le bouddhisme tantrique en Chine*. Paris: Gallimard, 1996.

——. *Chinese Magical Medicine*. Stanford, CA: Stanford University Press, 2002.

Szántó, Péter-Daniel. "The Case of the *Vajra*-Wielding Monk." *Acta Orientalia Academiae Scientiarum Hung* 63, no. 3 (2010): 289–99.

——. "Selected Chapters from the *Catuṣpīṭhatantra* (1/2): Introductory Study with the Annotated Translation of Selected Chapters." MA thesis, Balliol College, Oxford, 2012.

Tagare, G. V. *The Vāyu Purāṇa, Part I*. Delhi: Motilal Banarsidass, 1987.

Takahashi, Kammie Morrison. "Lamps for the Mind: Illumination and Innovation in dPal dbyangs's *Mahāyoga*." PhD diss., University of Virginia, 2009.

Takakusu, J. *A Record of the Buddhist Religion as Practiced in India and the Malay Archipelago*. Oxford: Clarendon Press, 1896.

Takeuchi, Tsuguhito. "Old Tibetan Buddhist Texts from the Post-Tibetan Imperial Period (Mid–9 c. to Late 10 c.)." In *Old Tibetan Studies*, ed. Cristina Scherrer-Schaub, 205–14. Leiden: Brill, 2012.

Tanaka, Kimiaki. "*Navarasa* Theory in the *Sarvabuddhasamāyogaḍākinījālasaṃvaratantra* Reconsidered." *Tōhō* 10 (1994): 323–31.

——. *Tonkō: Mikkyō to Bijutsu (Essays on Tantric Buddhism in Dunhuang: Its Art and Texts)*. Kyoto: Hōzōkan, 2000.

——. *Indoniokeru mandara no seiritsu to hatten*, 58–66. Tokyo: Shunjusha, 2010.

——. *An Illustrated History of the Maṇḍala: From Its Genesis to the Kālacakatantra*. Somerville, MA: Wisdom, 2018.

Thomas, Frederick William. *Tibetan Literary Texts and Documents Concerning Chinese Turkestan*. London: Royal Asiatic Society, 1951.

Thomas, F. W. and L. Giles. "A Tibeto-Chinese Word-and-Phrase Book." *Bulletin of the School of Oriental and African Studies* XII, no. 3 (1948): 753–69.

Tillemans, Tom J. F. *Scripture, Logic, Language: Essays on Dharmakīrti and His Tibetan Successors*. Boston: Wisdom, 1999.

Tomabechi, Toru. "Étude du Pañcakrama: Introduction et traduction annotée. " PhD diss., Université de Lausanne, 2006.

Torricelli, Fabrizio. "The Tibetan Text of the 'Karṇatantravajrapada.'" *East and West* 48, no. 3/4 (1998): 385–423.

Törzsök, Judit. "Theatre, Acting and the Image of the Actor in Abhinavagupta's Tantric Sources." In *Around Abhinavagupta: Aspects of the Intellectual History of Kashmir from the Ninth to the Eleventh Century*, ed. Eli Franco and Isabelle Ratié, 451–93. Berlin: LIT Verlag, 2016.

Tribe, Anthony. *Tantric Buddhist Practice in India: Vilāsavajra's Commentary on the Mañjuśrī-nāmasaṃgīti*. London and New York: Routledge, 2016.

Tucci, Giuseppe. *Minor Buddhist Texts: Part II*. Rome: Istituto italiano per il Medio ed Estremo Oriente, 1958.

Ui, Hakuju, et al., eds. *A Complete Catalogue of the Tibetan Buddhist Canons (Bkaḥ-ḥgyur and Bstan-ḥgyur)*. Sendai: Tōhoku Imperial University, 1934.

Urban, Hugh B. "The Extreme Orient: The Construction of 'Tantrism' as a Category in the Orientalist Imagination." *Religion* 29 (1999): 123–46.

van Schaik, Sam. "A Definition of Mahāyoga: Sources from the Dunhuang Manuscripts." In *Tantric Studies*, ed. Harunaga Isaacson, 1: 45–88. Hamburg: Center for Tantric Studies, 2008.

——. "The Sweet Sage and *The Four Yogas*: A Lost Mahāyoga Treatise from Dunhuang." *Journal of the International Association of Tibetan Studies* 4 (2008): 1–67.

——. "Dating Early Tibetan Manuscripts: A Paleographical Method." In *Scribes, Texts and Rituals in Early Tibet and Dunhuang*, ed. Brandon Dotson, Kazushi Iwao, and Tsuguhito Takeuchi, 119–35. Weisbaden: Reichert Verlag, 2013.

——. *Tibetan Zen: Discovering a Lost Tradition*. Boston and London: Snow Lion, 2015.

——. "The Uses of Implements Are Different: Reflections on the Functions of Tibetan Manuscripts." In *Tibetan Manuscript and Xylograph Traditions: The Written Word and Its Media Within the Tibetan Cultural Sphere*, ed. Orna Almogi, 221–42. Hamburg: Department of Indian and Tibetan Studies, Universität Hamburg, 2016.

——. *Buddhist Magic: Divination, Healing, and Enchantment Through the Ages*. Boulder: Shambala, 2020.

van Schaik, Sam and Jacob P. Dalton. "Where Chan and Tantra Meet: Buddhist Syncretism in Dunhuang." In *The Silk Road: Trade, Travel, War and Faith*, ed. Susan Whitfield, 63–71. Chicago: Serindia, 2004.

van Schaik, Sam and Lewis Doney. "The Prayer, the Priest and the Tsenpo: An Early Buddhist Narrative from Dunhuang." *Journal of the International Association of Buddhist Studies* 30, nos. 1–2 (2007), 175–217.

Waley, Arthur. *A Catalogue of Paintings Recovered from Tun-Huang*. London: British Museum, 1931.

Wallis, Christopher Daren. "To Enter, to Be Entered, to Merge: The Role of Religious Experience in the Traditions of Tantric Shaivism." PhD diss., University of California, Berkeley, 2014.

Wangdu, Pasang and Hildegard Diemberger. *dBa' bzhed: The Royal Narrative Concerning the Bringing of the Buddha's Doctrine to Tibet*. Wien: Verlag der Osterreichischen Akademie der Wissenschaften, 2000.

Warren, H. C. *Buddhism in Translation*. Cambridge, MA: Harvard University Press, 1896.

Wedemeyer, Christian. *Āryadeva's* Lamp that Integrates the Practices (*Cāryamelapakapradīpa*): *The Gradual Path of Vajrayāna Buddhism*. New York: American Institute of Buddhist Studies, 2007.

——. *Making Sense of Tantric Buddhism: History, Semiology, and Transgression in the Indian Traditions*. New York: Columbia University Press, 2013.

Weinberger, Steven Neal. "The Significance of Yoga Tantra and the *Compendium of Principles* (*Tattvasaṃgraha Tantra*) within Tantric Buddhism in India and Tibet." PhD diss., University of Virginia, 2003.

White, David Gordon. *Kiss of the Yoginī: "Tantric Sex" in Its South Asian Contexts*. Chicago: University of Chicago Press, 2003.

Whitfield, Roderick. *The Art of Central Asia: The Stein Collection in the British Museum*. 3 vols. Tokyo: Kodansha International, 1982–1985.

Whitfield, Susan. *The Silk Road: Trade, Travel, War, and Faith*. Chicago: Serindia, 2004.

Wujastyk, Domink. *The Roots of Ayurveda*. London: Penguin, 1998.

Wynne, Alexander. *The Origin of Buddhist Meditation*. Abingdon and New York: Routledge, 2007.

Yamabe, Nobuyoshi. "The Significance of the '*Yogalehrbuch*' for the Investigation into the Origin of Chinese Meditation Texts." *Buddhist Culture* 9 (1999): 1–75.

Zacchetti, Stefano. "Prajñāpāramitā Sūtras." In *Brill's Encyclopedia of Buddhism*, ed. Jonathan A. Silk, 1: 171–209. Leiden: Koninklijke Brill NV, 2013.

Zwalf, Wladimir, ed. *Buddhism, Art and Faith*. London: British Museum Publications Limited, 1985.

Index

āgama, 1, 185, 245 n. 63
Amoghapāśahṛdaya-dhāraṇī, 38–39, 43
Amoghapāśakalparāja, 103, 262 n. 13
Amoghavajra, 25, 40, 44, 59–60, 103, 121, 138, 141, 239 n. 35, 263 n. 22, 281 n. 14
An Appearance of Suchness: Ornament of the Sacred (*De kho na nyid snang ba dam pa rgyan*), 142–43, 148–50, 221
Ānandagarbha, 105, 116, 123, 125, 264 n. 31, 266 n. 40, 268 n. 57, 275 n. 15, 276 n. 18
antecedent tale (*rmang*, *rabs*, or *lo rgyus*), 62–63, 252 n. 43
Anuyoga, 157–58, 204, 285 n. 35, 305 n. 80
Aparamitāyur-nāma-mahāyāna-sūtra, 31
arhat, 79, 95, 114
Ārya school, 8, 161, 197, 199, 202, 222, 301 n. 60, 302 n. 61
Aśoka, 37
Atikūṭa, 75–76, 226 n. 10, 241 n. 43, 244 n. 60, 256 n. 78, 261 n. 11, 262 n. 13
Atiśa, 152
Atiyoga, 157–58, 203–4, 296 n. 14
Avalokiteśvara, 10, 38, 43, 103, 226 n. 10, 249 n. 17, 250 n. 23, 262 n. 13
āveśa ("possession"), 23–24, 109–11, 115, 118–20, 123–24, 128, 220–21, 267 n. 46, 268 n. 55, 273 n. 105

Bde ba gsal mdzad, 191, 298 n. 36
Bhaiṣajyaguru, 42
Bharati, Aghehananda, 150, 287 n. 53
bodhicitta, 58, 67, 84–85, 94, 113, 136–37, 141, 149–73, 194–95, 197, 201, 222, 254 n. 60, 274 n. 6, 280 n. 14, 281 n. 19, 286 n. 44, 287 n. 52, 288 n. 64, 289 n. 70, 302 n. 61
Bodhicittabhāvanā, 160, 284 n. 32
Bodhicittavajra, 141
Bon, 69, 248 n. 12
Bṛhadāraṇyaka Upaniṣad, 135, 138
Bṛhatsaṃhitā, 116, 199
buddha family (*buddhakula*), 103, 106, 109, 114, 116, 118, 148, 266 n. 39, 271 n. 82, 276 n. 28
Buddhaghoṣa, 135, 184
Buddhagupta (a.k.a. Buddhaguhya), 47, 63, 74, 76, 100, 107, 117, 122, 201, 205, 221, 227 n. 11, 265 n. 32, 280 nn. 12,14, 283 n. 29, 297 n. 26, 300 nn. 49,50, 303 nn. 64,66

Buddhajñānapāda, 128, 145–46, 149, 155, 162, 199, 202, 285 nn. 36,38, 289 n. 70, 292 n. 100, 294 n. 1, 301 n. 60, 302 n. 61

cakra, 173–74, 194, 197, 203–6, 222, 277 n. 5, 299 n. 43
Cakrasaṃvara, 8, 162, 206, 287 n. 55, 292 n. 97
Candanāṅga-dhāraṇī, 75, 257 nn. 82,83
Candrakīrti, 161–62, 300
Caryāmelāpakapradīpa, 199, 286 n. 45, 302 n. 61
Chan, 16, 173, 175–76, 182–84, 191, 232 n. 50, 256 n. 74, 272 n. 94, 295 nn. 3,7, 296 nn. 14,21
channels (Skt. *nāḍī*; Tib. *rtsa*), 151, 173–74, 194, 202–7, 221–22, 299 n. 43, 305 nn.74,79, 307 n. 88
chiasmus, 126–27
Compendium of All Knowledge (*Kun 'dus rig pa'i mdo*), 191–92
Consecration Sutra (*Guanding jing*), 45, 242 n. 53, 243 n. 55
Cuckoo of Awareness (*Rig pa'i khu byug*), 156, 160
Cundī, 40, 304 n. 69

Dajiyishenzhoujing (*Dhāraṇī for Great Benefit*), 45, 243 n. 54
Dampa Deshek, Katok, 152
Davidson, Ronald, 6–7, 23, 47–48, 56, 61, 227 n. 15, 243 n. 53, 244 nn. 60,62, 261 n. 9, 277 n. 5
de Certeau, Michel, 6, 25–26
demon(s), 12, 35, 50, 59, 85, 89–90, 92, 106, 234 n. 4, 238 n. 26, 255 n. 73, 264 n. 28
dhāraṇīsaṃgraha, 16, 29, 33–34, 38, 66, 75–76, 237 n. 20, 244 n. 60, 256 n. 78, 261 n. 11, 262 n. 13
dharmakāya, 85, 93–94
Dharmakīrti, 101, 185, 297 n. 24
Dignāga, 6
Divākara, 40, 239 n. 35, 304 n. 69
Dotson, Brandon, 62–63, 245 n. 2, 252 n. 43
Douglas, Mary, 126
Dvitīyakrama-tattvabhāvanā-mukhāgama, 145, 149, 155, 162, 285 n. 37, 289 n. 70, 294 n. 1

Eight Illuminations Sutra (Tib. *Snang brgyad mdo*; Ch. *Ba yang jing*), 31

Facheng (a.k.a. 'Go Chos grub), 9
five stages of manifest awakening (*pañcākārābhisaṃbodhikrama*), 110–14, 117, 124, 182, 253 n. 57, 268 n. 55, 274 n. 6, 275 n. 8, 284 n. 33
Freud, Sigmund, 136–37
foundation (Skt. *ālaya*; Tib. *gzhi*), 203
foundational consciousness (Skt. *ālayavijñāna*; Tib. *kun gzhi*), 112, 215, 306
Fushi Meng Huaiyu (副使孟壞玉), 11, 231 n. 45

gaṇacakra ("tantric feast"), 11–12, 16, 23, 153, 155, 174, 206, 230 n. 38, 287 n. 52, 288 n. 65, 290 n. 73, 292 n. 99
Gaṇḍavyūhasūtra, 55
gazing at the mind (Ch. *kanxin*, 看心; Tib. *sems la bltas ba*), 177, 183–84, 209, 296 n. 19, 297 n. 21
generation stage (Skt. *utpattikrama*; Tib. *bskyed rim*), 17, 143, 145, 156, 158, 160, 167, 179–80, 182, 187, 197, 231 n. 42, 263 n. 23, 284 n. 33, 285 nn. 35,36,37
Great Perfection (*Rdzogs chen*), 145, 155–60, 164, 182, 232 n. 50
Guhyagarbha, 25, 137, 142–43, 148–50, 158–59, 206–7, 221, 306 n. 82
Guhyasamāja, 8, 137, 141–43, 145, 150, 153, 161–62, 174, 197–99, 222, 225 n. 4, 271 n. 76, 277 n. 5, 278 n. 6, 280 n. 14, 281 nn. 14,18, 282 n. 24, 283 n. 25, 287 n. 51, 294 n. 1, 296 n. 19, 298 n. 28, 300 n. 47, 302 n. 61, 305 n. 80
Gupta dynasty, 6, 30, 48, 245 n. 66

Harṣa Śīlāditya, 37
Heller, Amy, 69

Heshang Moheyan, 9
Hevajra, 8, 205–6, 287 n. 54, 294 n. 1, 300 n. 49, 303 n. 64
Hopkins, Jeffrey, 118

Imaeda, Yoshirō, 55, 58, 247 nn. 11,12, 249 n. 19
"inner heat" (Skt. *caṇḍālī*; Tib. *gtum mo*), 203–5
Invitation to the Great Gods and Nāgas (*Lha klu chen po rnams spyan drang ba*, or: *Rgyud gsum pa*), 34–35, 37–38, 44, 66, 238 n. 26

Jayavatī-nāma-dhāraṇī, 31, 42, 241 n. 44
Jñānapāda school, 8, 197, 199, 202, 222
jñānasattva, 109, 115–16, 119–25, 143–44, 154, 163, 164, 166, 221, 270 nn. 70,71, 287 n. 52

Kaniṣka, King, 37
Kapstein, Matthew, 69, 228 n. 21, 255 nn. 68,70
Khedrup Delek Pelzang (Mkhas grub dge legs dpal bzang), 118–19
Khotan, 11, 229 n. 34
Kīlaya, 97, 191–92, 196, 282 n. 22
Kriyāsaṃgraha, 263 n. 22, 268 n. 55, 274 n. 6
Kriyātantra, 47–48, 106, 118, 137, 196, 200, 202, 220, 227 n. 11, 237 n. 20, 264 n. 30, 278 n. 6, 300 n. 49
Kucha/Kuchean, 11, 229 n. 31

Lasso of Means (*Thabs kyi zhags pa*), 11, 155
Lha yul du lam bstan pa, 55, 69, 247 n. 12
Longchen Rapjam (Klong chen Rab 'byams), 206–7, 306 n. 82

Mahāmāyūrī/Mahāmāyūrīvidyārājñī, 37, 40, 46, 236 n. 16, 229 n. 34, 243 n. 55
mahāmudrā, 107, 118–20, 123, 125, 132, 157, 198, 215, 266 n. 40, 270 nn. 69,70, 286 n. 43
Mahāpratisarāvidyārājñī, 31, 38, 40, 66, 74, 236 n. 16, 240 n. 36, 257 nn. 82, 83
Mahāśītavana-sūtra, 39–40, 236 n. 16
(Mahā)vairocana, 50, 60–61, 63, 69–70, 72, 76, 106, 112, 114, 131, 141, 153, 250 n. 23, 264 n. 27, 268 n. 55
Mahāvairocanābhisaṃbodhi, 42, 47, 50, 60, 63, 76, 103, 106–7, 202, 220, 222, 227 n. 11, 256 n. 78, 257 n. 80, 258 nn. 88,90, 261 n. 7, 264 n. 27, 265 n. 35, 297 n. 26, 300 n. 49, 303 n. 64, 304 n. 69
(Mahā)vajradhara, 24, 95, 141, 142
Maheśvara, 50
Māmakī, 37
Mañjuśrīmitra, 142–43, 154, 160, 163, 283 n. 28, 284 n. 32, 288 n. 64, 289 n. 68, 293 n. 105
Mañjuśrīnāmasaṃgīti, 141, 225 n. 4, 278 n. 6
Matsunaga, Yukei, 30
Meditation Supplement in Progressive Stages (*Dhyānottarapaṭalakrama*), 196, 200, 202, 300 nn. 49,50, 303 n. 66
Meru, Mount, 50, 89, 146, 170, 187
moods, nine (*navarasa*). *See rasa*
Moses, 126
myth, 1, 3, 4–5, 35, 50–51, 62–65, 68, 77–78, 103, 137, 226 n. 10, 238 n. 25, 259 n. 2

Nam ka'i snying po, 237 n. 18
Niśvāsatattvasaṃhitā, 199, 227 n. 13, 245 n. 63
Nupchen Sangyé Yeshe (Gnubs chen Sangs rgyas ye shes), 203–5, 292 n. 103, 295 n. 4, 305 nn. 75,79,80,81, 306 n. 84
nyāsa, 44, 116, 149, 195, 264 n. 31, 277 n. 29
Nyen Pelyang (Gnyan Dpal dbyangs), 9, 229 n. 24

Oḍḍiyāna, 107
Old Tibetan Annals, 18

Padmasambhava, 44, 155, 156, 158, 204–5, 242 n. 49, 255 n. 70
pañcākārābhisaṃbodhikrama. *See* five stages of manifest awakening
Pañcakrama, 302
pañcāmṛta ("fivefold ambrosia"), 12, 17, 153, 288 n. 65
Pañcarakṣā, 33, 236 n. 16, 236 n. 20
Pangtangma, 9, 41
pāramitā goddesses, 109, 151, 171, 262 n. 13, 267 n. 43, 269 n. 65, 270 n. 67
perfection stage (Skt. *utpannakrama*; Tib. *rdzogs rim*), 145, 149, 156–57, 160–61, 163, 174, 179, 182, 187–88, 191, 193, 194, 197, 199, 203, 205–7, 221–22, 284 n. 34, 285 n. 35, 289 n. 70, 297 n. 27, 299 n. 45, 302 n. 60, 305 n. 80, 307 n. 88
Pith Instructional Garland of Views (*Man ngag lta ba'i phreng ba*), 156–58
poṣadha, 12
possession. *See* *āveśa*
Pradīpodyotana, 161–62, 300 n. 47
Prajñāpāramitā, 9, 232 n. 46
prāṇāyāma (Tib. *srog rtsol*; "breath restriction"), 178, 188, 190, 200–1, 214, 298 n. 28, 302 n. 28
Precept for Supreme Goodness (*Bzang po mchog gi lung*), 142–43, 148, 154, 162, 164, 282 nn. 20,22, 283 n. 28, 292 n. 103
Pugyel dynasty, 8–10
Pūjāmegha-dhāraṇī, 37

rasa ("mood"), 23–25, 189, 233 n. 52
Rok Bande Sherap ö (Rog ban de Shes rab 'od), 206, 307 n. 88

Śaiva/Śaivism, 1, 5, 6, 124, 205–6, 227 n. 15, 232 n. 51, 245 n. 63, 277 n. 5
Śakra, 52–54, 79–80, 82
Śākyamitra, 105, 107–20, 123, 252 n. 50, 263 n. 24, 264 n. 30, 265 n. 38, 266 nn. 40,41, 267 nn. 41,44,46, 268 n. 57, 269 n. 60, 270 n. 70, 272 n. 91, 274 n. 110, 275 nn. 8,10,16
Śākyamuni, 1, 24, 44, 50, 55, 61, 68, 79, 81, 85, 98, 112, 225 n. 1, 247 n. 12, 256 n. 76. *See also* Sarvārthasiddhi
samādhis, three (of the generation stage), 143–48, 156, 167–69, 177, 179–82, 186–87, 213, 263 n. 23, 282 n. 23, 283 n. 32, 284 nn. 32,33, 285 n. 39, 295 n. 3
Samājottara-tantra, 174–75, 284 n. 33, 285 n. 36, 294 n. 2, 302 n. 61
Samantabhadra, 87, 113, 155, 157–59, 163–64, 250 n. 23
Samantabhadrī, 155–56
Samantamukha-praveśa-dhāraṇī (= Vimaloṣṇīṣa), 41, 53, 240 n. 38, 246 n. 7
samayamudrā, 107, 115, 117–24, 133, 144, 154, 163, 220–21, 269 n. 65, 270 n. 71, 271 n. 82, 272 nn. 88,89, 276 nn. 25,27, 281 n. 19
Sanderson, Alexis, 6, 23, 225 n. 6, 227 n. 15, 273 n. 105
*Sanghabhara, 40, 46, 244 n. 55
Sarvārthasiddhi, 112–14, 163, 267 n. 43, 268 nn. 55,56, 277 n. 28. *See also* Śākyamuni
**Sarvaprajñā-dhāraṇī*, 41, 240 n. 38, 246 n. 7
Sarvatathāgata-tattvasaṃgraha (*STTS*), 44, 60, 73, 102–18, 121–24, 127, 138–39, 150, 163, 198–99, 220–21, 227 n. 11, 228 n. 18, 250 n. 25, 252 n. 50, 253 n. 57, 261 nn. 7,10, 263 n. 24, 265 n. 38, 266 n. 40, 267 nn. 43,46, 268 nn. 51,55, 269 n. 65, 270 n. 69, 271 nn. 80, 82,86, 273 n. 105, 274 n. 111, 275 n. 8, 277 nn. 30,31, 279 n. 8, 280 n. 14, 284 n. 32, 301 n. 59
Sarvavid-Vairocana. *See* (Mahā) vairocana
Sattvavajrī, 114–17, 122–26, 130, 134, 270 n. 67
seven-limbed worship (*saptapūjā*, or: *anuttarapūjā*), 37–38, 45–46
seven mothers (Skt. *saptamātaraḥ*), 34, 251 n. 35

Shinohara, Koichi, 76, 226 n. 10, 238 n. 25, 241 n. 42, 258 n. 88, 261 n. 11, 262 n. 13, 270 n. 75
siddhi, 35, 62, 66, 82–83, 86, 88, 91–92, 94, 118, 149, 152, 154, 171, 195, 252 n. 50, 258 n. 83, 266 n. 40, 286 n. 44
Siṅghala, 210
Small Hidden Seed (*Sbas pa'i rgum chung*), 156
Snellgrove, David, 152
Spar khab, 159
Stein, Sir Aurel, 140
Story of the Cycle of Birth and Death (*Skye shi'i lo rgyus*), 55, 58, 69, 247 nn. 11,12, 249 n. 19
Strickmann, Michel, 29, 45, 234 n. 4
Śubhākarasiṃha, 60–61, 227 n. 11, 250 n. 30
subtle vajra (Skt. *sūkṣmavajra*; Tib. *rdo rje phra mo*), 198–99, 296 n. 19
Sudhana, 55
Supratiṣṭhita, 52
Susiddhikara, 47, 220, 244 n. 59

Takeuchi, Tsuguhito, 140, 246 n. 2, 281 n. 15
Tanfa yize (壇法儀則; *Ritual Instructions for Altar Methods*), 121, 263 n. 25
tantric feast. *See gaṇacakra*
Testament of Wa (*Dba' bzhed*), 69–70, 255 n. 68
Tibetan Chronicle, 18
Trailokyavijaya, 37, 107, 138
Trāyastriṃśa (heaven), 52, 79, 82
tridaṇḍaka (*rgyud chags gsum pa*), 35–38, 44, 66, 239 n. 31
Tri Songdetsen, 37, 69
Tsongkhapa, 118, 298 n. 28, 302 n. 61

Ubhayātantra, 196, 202, 300 n. 49, 304 n. 72
uṣṇīṣa buddhas, eight, 60–61, 69–70, 160, 250 n. 29, 254 n. 60
Uṣṇīṣasitātapatra/*Uṣṇīṣasitātapa tre-aparājitā-nāma-dhāraṇī*, 32, 44, 60, 86, 91, 255 n. 73
Uṣṇīṣavijayā(-dhāraṇī), 31, 35, 51–61, 65, 68, 70, 77, 90, 241 n. 43, 246 n. 4, 247 nn. 11,12, 248 n. 17, 250 nn. 22,29, 270 n. 67
Uyghur, 11, 31, 229 n. 30

Vajradhara. *See* (Mahā)vajradhara
vajra recitation (Skt. *vajrajāpa*; Tib. *rdo rje'i bzlas pa*), 199, 202, 222, 298 n. 28, 301 n. 60, 302 n. 61
Vairocana. *See* (Mahā)vairocana
Vajrabodhi, 40, 103, 121, 239 n. 35
vajrācārya, 12, 50, 123, 144, 153, 169, 230 n. 35
Vajradhātu, 101, 106, 112–17, 119, 121, 138, 256 n. 76, 262 n. 13, 276 n. 28, 280 n. 14
Vajrahūṃkara, 104–8, 110, 112–13, 264 n. 28, 265 nn. 31,32, 266 n. 41, 266 n. 46, 269 n. 66, 270 n. 68, 271 nn. 80,84, 272 n. 91, 275 n. 8, 277 n. 33
Vajrapāṇi, 44, 85, 90, 103, 250 n. 23, 268 n. 51
Vajrasattva, 9, 11, 24, 76, 106, 109–11, 113, 119, 123, 129, 133–34, 138, 141, 143–44, 148, 151, 155, 169–70, 172, 194, 264 n. 31, 269 n. 60, 281 n. 16, 283 n. 24, 295 n. 3
Vajraśekhara-tantra, 105, 138–39, 227 n. 10, 248 n. 15, 253 n. 57, 263 n. 21, 264 n. 28, 271 n. 80, 280 n. 12
Vajravidāraṇa, 44, 242 n. 49, 247 n. 8, 278 n. 6, 284 n. 32
Vajroṣṇīṣa (sometimes **Vajraśekhara*), 59–60, 103, 138, 248 n. 15, 253 n. 57, 303 n. 66
Vidyādharapiṭaka, 5, 103, 215, 226 n. 10, 235 n. 6, 244 n. 59
vidyāvrata, 107, 265 nn. 32,35, 284 n. 33
Vilāsavajra, 141, 159, 281 n. 19, 304 n. 73
*Vimalamaṇigarbha (Nor bu'i snying po dri ma med pa), 53, 68
Vimalamaṇiprabha, 52–55, 64, 255 n. 70
Vimalamitra, 204–5

Vimalaprabha, 50–51, 61–64, 77, 79–80, 82, 84
Vimaloṣṇīṣa-dhāraṇī. *See Samantamukha*
Vīravajra, 206, 206 n. 83
Visuddhimagga, 135

White, David G., 150, 205–6, 226 n. 6, 277 n. 5, 287 n. 54
Wuxing (630–674), 5, 257 n. 80

Yamāntaka, 37
Yeshe Ö, King Lha Lama, 10
Yidam ("daily commitment" or "tutelary deity"), 11, 33, 237 n. 18, 265 n. 32, 275 n. 12
Yixing (684–727), 5, 36–37, 60, 76, 103, 258 n. 88, 264 n. 27
yoginī (goddess), 5, 205–6
Yoginī tantra, 8, 265 n. 31, 278 n. 6

GPSR Authorized Representative: Easy Access System Europe, Mustamäe tee 50, 10621 Tallinn, Estonia, gpsr.requests@easproject.com

www.ingramcontent.com/pod-product-compliance
Lightning Source LLC
Chambersburg PA
CBHW031232290426
44109CB00012B/259
* 9 7 8 0 2 3 1 2 0 5 8 3 2 *